EASTERN CHEROKEE BY BLOOD
1906-1910
Volume I Applications 1 - 3000

From the U.S. Court of Claims 1906-1910
Cherokee-Related Records of
Special Commissioner Guion Miller

Transcribed by
Jeff Bowen

NATIVE STUDY
Gallipolis, Ohio
USA

Originally published:
Baltimore, Maryland
2005

Santa Maria, California
2020

Reprinted by:

Native Study LLC
Gallipolis, Ohio
www.nativestudy.com

Library of Congress Control Number: 2022905475

ISBN: 978-1-64968-144-7

Front cover, picture of Welch Family from
Eastern Cherokee, Qualla Boundary, NC
L-R: George French (Maude's nephew), William Henry Welch,
Maude French Welch and Edith Evelyn Welch (Will & Maude's daughter).
Picture donated by Joyce Welch Tranter, Eastern Cherokee.

Made in the United States of America.

Other Books and Series by Jeff Bowen

Compilation of History of the Cherokee Indians and Early History of the Cherokees by Emmet Starr with Combined Full Name Index
(Hardbound & Softbound)

1901-1907 Native American Census Seneca, Eastern Shawnee, Miami, Modoc, Ottawa, Peoria, Quapaw, and Wyandotte Indians (Under Seneca School, Indian Territory)

1932 Census of The Standing Rock Sioux Reservation with Births And Deaths 1924-1932

Census of The Blackfeet, Montana, 1897- 1901 Expanded Edition

Eastern Cherokee by Blood, 1906-1910, Volumes I **thru** ***XIII***

Choctaw of Mississippi Indian Census 1929-1932 with Births and Deaths 1924-1931 Volume I
Choctaw of Mississippi Indian Census 1933, 1934 & 1937, Supplemental Rolls to 1934 & 1935 with Births and Deaths 1932-1938, and Marriages 1936-1938 Volume II

Eastern Cherokee Census Cherokee, North Carolina 1930-1939 Census 1930-1931 with Births And Deaths 1924-1931 Taken By Agent L. W. Page Volume I
Eastern Cherokee Census Cherokee, North Carolina 1930-1939 Census 1932-1933 with Births And Deaths 1930-1932 Taken By Agent R. L. Spalsbury Volume II
Eastern Cherokee Census Cherokee, North Carolina 1930-1939 Census 1934-1937 with Births and Deaths 1925-1938 and Marriages 1936 & 1938 Taken by Agents R. L. Spalsbury And Harold W. Foght Volume III

Seminole of Florida Indian Census, 1930-1940 with Birth and Death Records, 1930-1938

Texas Cherokees 1820-1839 A Document For Litigation 1921

Starr Roll 1894 (Cherokee Payment Rolls) Districts: Canadian, Cooweescoowee, and Delaware Volume One
Starr Roll 1894 (Cherokee Payment Rolls) Districts: Flint, Going Snake, and Illinois Volume Two
Starr Roll 1894 (Cherokee Payment Rolls) Districts: Saline, Sequoyah, and Tahlequah; Including Orphan Roll Volume Three

Cherokee Intruder Cases Dockets of Hearings 1901-1909 Volumes I & II

Indian Wills, 1911-1921 Records of the Bureau of Indian Affairs Books One **thru** ***Seven***

Other Books and Series by Jeff Bowen

Native American Wills & Probate Records 1911-1921

Turtle Mountain Reservation Chippewa Indians 1932 Census with Births & Deaths, 1924-1932

Chickasaw By Blood Enrollment Cards 1898-1914 Volume I thru *V*

Cherokee Descendants East An Index to the Guion Miller Applications Volume I
Cherokee Descendants West An Index to the Guion Miller Applications Volume II (A-M)
Cherokee Descendants West An Index to the Guion Miller Applications Volume III (N-Z)

Applications for Enrollment of Seminole Newborn Freedmen, Act of 1905

Eastern Cherokee Census, Cherokee, North Carolina, 1915-1922, Taken by Agent James E. Henderson
Volume I (1915-1916)
Volume II (1917-1918)
Volume III (1919-1920)
Volume IV (1921-1922)

Complete Delaware Roll of 1898

Eastern Cherokee Census, Cherokee, North Carolina, 1923-1929, Taken by Agent James E. Henderson
Volume I (1923-1924)
Volume II (1925-1926)
Volume III (1927-1929)

Applications for Enrollment of Seminole Newborn Act of 1905 Volumes I & II

North Carolina Eastern Cherokee Indian Census 1898-1899, 1904, 1906, 1909-1912, 1914 Revised and Expanded Edition

1932 Hopi and Navajo Native American Census with Birth & Death Rolls (1925-1931) Volume 1 - Hopi
1932 Hopi and Navajo Native American Census with Birth & Death Rolls (1930-1932) Volume 2 - Navajo

Western Navajo Reservation Navajo, Hopi and Paiute 1933 Census with Birth & Death Rolls 1925-1933

Cherokee Citizenship Commission Dockets 1880-1884 and 1887-1889
Volumes I thru *V*

Applications for Enrollment of Chickasaw Newborn Act of 1905
Volumes I thru *VII*

Other Books and Series by Jeff Bowen

Cherokee Intermarried White 1906 Volume I thru *X*

Applications for Enrollment of Creek Newborn Act of 1905
Volumes I thru *XIV*

Applications for Enrollment of Choctaw Newborn Act of 1905 Volumes I thru *XX*

Choctaw By Blood Enrollment Cards 1898-1914 Volumes I thru *XX*

Oglala Sioux Indians Pine Ridge Reservation 1932 Census Book I
Oglala Sioux Indians Pine Ridge Reservation Birth and Death Rolls 1924-1932
Book II

Census of the Sioux and Cheyenne Indians of Pine Ridge Agency
1896 - 1897 Book I
Census of the Sioux and Cheyenne Indians of Pine Ridge Agency
1898 - 1899 Book II

Northern Cheyenne Tongue River, Montana 1904 - 1932 Census
1904-1916 Volume I
Northern Cheyenne Tongue River, Montana 1904 - 1932 Census
1917-1926 Volume II

Identified Mississippi Choctaw Enrollment Cards 1902-1909 Volumes I, II & III

Sac & Fox - Shawnee Estates 1885-1910 (Under Sac & Fox Agency)
Volumes I-VIII
Sac & Fox - Shawnee Estates 1920-1924 (Under The Sac & Fox Agency,
Oklahoma) & Wills 1889-1924 Volume IX
Sac & Fox - Shawnee Deaths, Cemetery, Births, & Marriage Cards (Under The Sac
& Fox Agency, Oklahoma) 1853-1933 Volume X
Sac & Fox - Shawnee Marriages, Divorces, Estates Log Books Volumes 1 & 2, Log
Book Births & Deaths (Under Sac & Fox Agency, Oklahoma)1846-1924 Volume XI
Sac & Fox - Shawnee Guardianships Part 1 (Under Sac & Fox Agency, Oklahoma)
1892-1909 Volume XII
Sac & Fox - Shawnee Guardianships, Part 2 (Under The Sac & Fox Agency,
Oklahoma) 1902-1910 Volume XIII
Sac & Fox - Shawnee Guardianships, Part 3 (Under The Sac & Fox Agency,
Oklahoma) 1906-1914 Volume XIV

This series is dedicated to the Cherokee people and their descendants.

INTRODUCTION

On the 12 rolls of this microfilm publication are reproduced the report and related records of Special Commissioner Guion Miller. In 1906 Mr. Miller was appointed by the U.S. Court of Claims to determine who was eligible for funds under the treaties of 1835-36 and 1845 between the United States and the Eastern Cherokee. Mr. Miller submitted his report and roll on May 28, 1909, and submitted a supplementary report and roll on January 5, 1910.

An act of Congress approved July 1, 1902 (32 Stat. 726), gave the Court of Claims jurisdiction over any claim arising under treaty stipulations that the Cherokee tribe, or any band thereof, might have against the United States and over any claims that the United States might have against any Cherokee tribe or band. Suit for such a claim was to be instituted within 2 years after the act was approved. As a result, three suits were brought before the court concerning grievances arising out of the treaties. These suits were (1) The Cherokee Nation v. The United States, General-Jurisdiction Case No. 23199; (2) The Eastern and Emigrant Cherokees v. The United States, General-Jurisdiction Case No. 23212; and (3) The Eastern Cherokees v. The United States, General-Jurisdiction Case No. 23214.

On May 18, 1905, the court decided in favor of the Eastern Cherokees and instructed the Secretary of the Interior to ascertain and identify the persons entitled to participate in the distribution of more than $1 million appropriated by Congress on June 30, 1906, for use in payment of the claims. The task of compiling a roll of eligible persons was begun by Guion Miller, then special agent of the Interior Department. In a decree of April 29, 1907, the court vacated that part of its earlier decision that gave the Secretary of the Interior responsibility for determining the eligibility of claimants and appointed Mr. Miller as a special commissioner of the Court of Claims.

The decree also provided that the fund was to be distributed to all Eastern and Western Cherokee Indians who were alive on May 28, 1906, who could establish the fact that at the time of the treaties they were members of the Eastern Cherokee Tribe of Indians or were descendants of such persons, and that they had not been affiliated with any tribe of Indians other than the Eastern Cherokees or the Cherokee Nation. The decree further provided that claimants should already have applications on file with the Commissioner of Indian Affairs, or should file such applications with the special commissioner of the Court of Claims on or before August 31, 1907. According to the decree, applications for minors and persons of unsound mind were to be filed by their parents or persons having their care and custody, and applications for persons who had died after May 28, 1906, were to be filed by their children or legal representatives.

In his report of May 28, 1909, Guion Miller stated that 45,847 separate applications had been filed, representing a total of about 90,000 individual claimants, of which 30,254 were enrolled as entitled to share in the fund—3,203 residing east and 27,051 residing west of the Mississippi River. On June 10, 1909, the court confirmed and approved the roll of Eastern Cherokees who were entitled to share in the distribution of the fund as submitted by the special commissioner of the Court of Claims with his report of May 28, 1909, except "so much as shall be expected [excepted] to on or before August 30, 1909." After the exceptions had been filed and investigated, Mr. Miller submitted a supplemental report and roll to the court on January 5, 1910. In this report he stated that about 11,750 exceptions had been made; that names of 610 persons, of which 238 resided east and 372 resided west of the Mississippi, had been added to the roll; and that names of 44 persons, 5 residing east and 39 residing west of the river, had been stricken from the roll because clerical errors in enrollment had been discovered. Thus the final figure on the total number of persons entitled to share in the fund was 30,820, of which 3,436 persons resided east and 27,384 resided west of the Mississippi River. On March 15, 1910, the court finally decreed that the rolls be approved and that, after certain deductions for expenditures, payments were to be made equally among the Eastern Cherokees who were enrolled. The court also authorized the Secretary of the Treasury to issue a warrant in favor of each person.

In certifying the eligibility of the Cherokees, Mr. Miller used earlier census lists and rolls that had been made of the Cherokees by Hester, Chapman, Drennen, and others between 1835 and 1884. Copies of some of these rolls and the indexes to them are filed with the Guion Miller records and are filmed as a part of this publication. Other enrollment records used by Mr. Miller are among the classified files of the Bureau and are designated as "33931-11-053 Cherokee Nation."

The records reproduced in this microcopy are in the National Archives and are part of Record Group 75, Records of the Bureau of Indian Affairs, with the exception of the Supplemental Roll of Eastern Cherokee, January 5, 1910, and Supplement to the Siler Roll, Act of Congress, July 31, 1854, which are part of Record Group 123; Records of the United States Court of Claims. A Census Roll, 1835, of the Cherokee Indians East of the Mississippi and Index to the Roll, which have been reproduced on Microcopy T-496, are also part of Record Group 75. Other records relating to the enrollment, including applications submitted by claimants, are in Record Group 123.

Volume I

Applications 1 - 3000

IN THE COURT OF CLAIMS.

THE EASTERN CHEROKEES,	)	
	)	
vs.	)	No. 23214.
	)	
THE UNITED STATES.	)	

Report of Guion Miller, Special Commissioner.

In the matter of the enrollment of the Eastern Cherokees for participation in the fund arising from the judgment of the Court of Claims of May 28, 1906, and under the supplemental order of April 29, 1907, I have the honor to report that 45,857 separate applications have been filed, which represent a total of about 90,000 individuals claimants. Of these I have enrolled *30,254* as entitled to share in the fund, *3,203* of these residing east of the Mississippi river, and *27,051* residing west of the Mississippi. This roll I have made in two parts, as above indicated, so far as the alphabetical arrangement is concerned. The action taken upon each of these applications is set forth below.

In this report, references are made to the Eastern Cherokee roll of 1835 and to the rolls of 1851 made by Agent Alfred Chapman in the east, and by Agent John Drennen in the west. In the 1835 roll only the heads of families are designated, with the number of individuals in each family, without naming these individuals specifically. The Chapman roll is very complete and is arranged by number, each individual being named, and his age and relationship to other members of the family being distinctly set forth. References to this roll are therefore made by number. The Drennen roll is much less complete. It is divided into nine parts, representing eight districts as follows: Canadian, Delaware, Flint, Going Snake, Illinois, Saline, Skin Bayou and Tahlequah, together with a division known as the Disputed roll. In these rolls the family groups are indicated, but the relationship between the various members of the group is not stated, nor are the ages given. In my report references are made to these rolls by abbreviations, such as Del. for Delaware; G.S. for Going Snake, etc.

In 1851 an enrollment was made in the west of the Cherokees known as Old Settlers. Frequent references are made to this roll in the report, where it is usually indicated by the abbreviations of O.S.

In addition to these regular rolls, under the Act of Congress of 1854, a small additional roll was made by the Secretary of the Interior, of individual Eastern Cherokees residing in the east, whose names were inadvertently omitted from the Chapman roll of 1851, or more strictly speaking, from the Siler roll of 1851, upon which the Chapman pay roll was based. References in my report are made to this roll under the title of "Act of Congress roll", or abbreviated, A. of C. roll.

Also, in 1884 under the Act of Congress of 1882, a complete roll of the Eastern Cherokees residing east of the Mississippi river was made by Agent Joseph G. Hester, and frequent references in my report are made to this roll by way of confirmation.

Where the claimant has shown an ancestor enrolled upon either the Drennen or Chapman Rolls, or the Roll of 1835, his case has been marked for admission, unless he has become disqualified through affiliation with some other tribe. In a few cases where claimants have been unable to state the name of an ancestor found upon one of said rolls, testimony has been taken which has established the fact that such claimants are Eastern Cherokees by blood and their claims have been admitted. These cases are mostly among the full-blood Cherokees where the name under which their ancestor was enrolled in 1851 has been changed or forgotten by the present generation. In most of these instances, the claimants are now enrolled and allotted as Cherokees, and the fact of their Cherokee descent is in no way open to question, the only possible doubt being as to whether they might be included among the Old Settlers. In these cases, however, the names of the ancestors given have not been found upon the roll of the Old Settlers made in 1851, so the testimony of witnesses is accepted as establishing the fact of Eastern Cherokee descent.

In considering these applications they were first, as far as possible, arranged in family groups, and in the report the action taken is set forth at length in connection with the application in the group having the lowest number, and the action taken as to the other applications is indicated by reference to the number of the head of the group. In this way the action taken on each application is specifically indicated. There were quite a number of duplicate applications filed, which are shown in the report.

In 1835 the Eastern Cherokee domain comprised all or part of the following counties in the states of Georgia, Alabama, Tennessee and North Carolina:

Georgia,---Bartow, Catoosa, Chattooga, Cherokee, Cobb, Dade, Dawson, Fannin, Floyd, Forsyth, Gilmer, Gordon, Haralson, Lumpkin, Milton, Murray, Paulding, Pickens, Polk, Town, Union, Walker and Whitfield, counties.

Alabama,---Blount, Calhoun, Cherokee, Cleburne, De Kalb, Etowah, Jackson and Marshall counties.

Tennessee,--Blount, Bradley, Hamilton, James, Marion, Meigs, Monroe and Polk counties.

North Carolina,--Cherokee, Clay, Graham, Macon and Swain counties.

In course of the investigation a large amount of testimony has been taken, either by me or my assistants. A copy of this testimony is filed, herewith, and references are made in my report to the same.

More than 4500 witnesses have been examined, in nineteen different states. This testimony is divided into four parts. One consisting of general testimony in regard to a large number of cases, which is described as "Miscellaneous Testimony", and includes 4417 pages. The second relates exclusively to the claim of the "Sizemore family", and consists of 75 pages. The third is testimony taken in reference to the claims of certain Creek Indians, or persons located in southern Alabama and northwestern Florida, who, if Indians at all, are probably of Creek origin, and the testimony has been designated as "Creek Testimony", and consists of 12 pages. The Fourth relates to the claims of the "Poindexter family", and consists of 29 pages.

The report as to each application follows:--

[NOTE: Pages iv through x are copied exactly as stated on the *microfilm.]

*Microfilm Roll M685; Rolls 1-5, CHEROKEE (EASTERN), ENROLLMENT BY GUION MILLER, 1906-1910; May 28, 1909: Vols. 1-10.

The transcriber felt that a full Introduction wasn't necessary because all information in the front matter of each volume is self-explanatory. This series is republished by Native Study LLC (*nativestudy.com*) with Joyce Welch Tranter and family, past and present, in our hearts.

Jeff Bowen
Gallipolis, OH
NativeStudy.com

Eastern Cherokee By Blood 1906-1910: Applications 1-3000

App: 1 Isom Durham White, Joplin, Mo., 314 Main St.

Rejected. Applicant was not enrolled in 1851. He was born in Washington Co., Mo. In 1841 and his parents were born in Allen Co., Ky., which is more than 100 miles from the Eastern Cherokee domain in 1835. His parents and grandparents were not enrolled in 1835 or 1851. In reply to letter, applicant states: "I cannot furnish living witnesses as to my descent from the Cherokee tribe".

App: 2 John Hilderbrand, Bartlesville, Okla.

Admitted. Applicant and his father and mother, David and Elizabeth Hilderbrand, were enrolled by Drennen in 1851 in Group 136 Tahlequah.

App: 3 Nancy Bradford, Kansas City, Mo.

Rejected. Applicant was born in Kentucky in 1805. Her mother was a slave and she was a slave and was not enrolled as an Eastern Cherokee in 1835 or 1851. That applicant was a slave is stated by her attorney, G.G. Wright, in letter dated Nov. 19, 1907.

App: 4 Wm. J.K. Lawson and 6 children , Bigfall, Tenn.

Rejected. Nephew of #66 and claims through same source.

App: 5 William Waters, deceased Madison, Ga.
By Maria Waters, wife,

Rejected. Claimant died Nov. 6, 1906. He was a colored man but it is said was not a slave. He was born in 1826. He was not enrolled in 1851 and cannot name his parents or grandparents. There is nothing in the case to justify his enrollment.

App: 6 Wiley Taylor, Andrews, N.C.

Admitted. Son of David Taylor and Mary or Polly Taylor nee Bigby. Applicant enrolled in Flint #662, also Hester #1458. David Taylor, applicant's father, enrolled on 1835 roll, page 23, and by Chapman #1251. Mother, Mary or Polly Taylor, enrolled by Chapman #1243. Applicant was in the west in 1851. (See letter herein marked "Exhibit A").

App: 7 Richard Burgess and 4 children, Andrews, N.C.

Rejected. It does not appear that any ancestor was a party to the treaties of 1835-6 or 1846, nor does it appear that any ancestor was ever enrolled. Shows no real connection with the Eastern Cherokees. (Miscel. Test. Page 1555).

App: 8 Mary L. Byrd and 3 children, Mena, Ark.

Rejected. It does not appear that ancestors were ever enrolled or were parties to the treaties of 1835-6 and 1846. Applicant shows no real connection with Eastern Cherokees. (Miscel. Test. Page 2086).

App: 9 Joe L. Ward and 1 child, Maysville, Ark.

Admitted. Applicant and applicant's mother were enrolled by Drennen, Del. 50.

App: 10 Jennie Downing, Peggs, Okla.

Admitted. Applicant and her mother, Arle Clinging, appear on the Drennen roll, Sal. 178, and her maternal grandparents, Arch and Jennie Roe, appear on the same roll, Flint 21.

App: 11 Leni[sic] Leoti Logan and 1 child, Pryor Creek, Okla

Admitted. Applicant's mother, Frances H. Warwick, was enrolled by Chapman #1790. Applicant's grandmother, Elizabeth Scudder, was enrolled by Chapman #1785.

App: 12 James A. Coleman and 1 child, Ft. Gibson, Okla.
Admitted. Applicant is on the Chapman roll #2129. Applicant's mother and brother enrolled by Chapman, #2126 and #2128.
App: 13 Nannie Coleman, Ft. Gibson, Okla.
Admitted. Applicant's father enrolled as T.M. Walker, Tah. 321. Applicant's mother is enrolled as Elizabeth Walker, Tah. 321. Applicant enrolled Tah. 321.
App: 14 Nancy M.J. Hibbs and 4 children, Muskogee, Okla.
Admitted. Applicant's father and grandfather enrolled by Drennen, S.B. 128. (Miscel. Test. Page 3149).
App: 15 Mrs. Sally Mack and 7 children, Tellico Plains, Tenn.
Rejected. It does not appear that any ancestor was a party to the treaties of 1835-6 or 1846, nor does it appear that any ancestor was enrolled. Shows no real connection with the Eastern Cherokees. (Miscel. Test. P. 632).
App: 16 Mary White, Stilwell, Okla.
Rejected. Applicant claims through John Tidwell. The names of John Tidwell and those of his family do not appear on either the roll of 1835, Chapman roll of 1851, or Hester roll of 1882. Siler enrolled John Tidwell and his family, but their names were subsequently stricken off the roll, because their names or the name of the head of the family did not appear on the roll of 1835. This family, after their names were stricken off the roll, was again considered for enrollment by the Secretary of the Interior and again rejected, for they were not placed on the Act of Congress roll of 1858. In consideration of the premises, therefore, the applicants claiming through John Tidwell and his descendants are rejected.
App: 17 Charles L. Morris and 6 children, Baptist, Okla.
Admitted. Applicant and his mother on the Chapman roll, Nos. 2018 and 2023, respectively.
App:18 Gideon Morgan and 1 child, Pryor Creek, Okla.
Admitted. Applicant and his father, Geo. W. Morgan, and grandfather, Gideon Morgan, enrolled by Chapman, Nos. 1548, 1546 and 1549.
App: 19 August H. Tankersley and 4 children, Pryor Creek, Okla.
Admitted. Applicant claims through his mother, whose maiden name was Sarah Mahala Satterfield or Sarah Narcissa or Mary Satterfield. Her mother's maiden name was Lucy Ward, who was a half-blood Cherokee Indian. In this report the applicant's mother will be referred to as Mary Moss. She had, a full brother by the name of Edly Satterfield. After applicant was born his father and mother separated and his mother married a man by the name of Moss. Mary Moss was enrolled by Chapman in 1851-#2037. She was enrolled by Hester #2521. Edly Satterfield, uncle of applicant, was enrolled by Chapman in 1851 #2048. John Satterfield, the grandfather of applicant, was enrolled by Chapman in 1851 #2069. John Satterfield's first wife's name was Lucy Ward. She was a half-blood Cherokee. After she died he married a woman by the name of Adelphia Ann Trammel who was a full white woman. Chapman shows that in 1851 Mary Moss was 26 years old and her brother, Edly Satterfield was 22. Then they were both living in 1835. John Satterfield was enrolled in 1835 (see page 45, 1835 roll) at the head of a family of 2, 1 half-blood Indian and 1 white person associated by marriage. The half-blood was a male and under 18 years of age. This must have been Edly Satterfield, as it could not have been John Satterfield, for Chapman shows him to have been 56 years old in 1851. Then he was 40 years old in 1835 and the white person

referred to on the 35 roll must have been John Satterfield himself. After his first wife died and he married Adelphia Ann Trammel he had a son born in 1843*(or 1842)* by the name of William Henry Satterfield, who from the deductions heretofore made must have been a full-blooded white person. The said William Henry Satterfield has filed an application #17521. He was not enrolled in 1851, although his half-brother and sister were. He not being a Cherokee by blood and not being enrolled in 1851, his claim is rejected. All the other applicants in this group being Cherokees by blood and claiming through ancestors enrolled by Chapman in 1851 are admitted. (Miscel. Test. P. 3558).

App: 20 Berenice M. Wade, Ft. Gibson , Okla
Admitted. Sister of #12 and claims through the same source.

App: 21 Saphronia G. Finger and 3 children, Louisville, Tenn.
Admitted. Applicant's father and grandmother enrolled by Chapman in 1851 #1219 and #1222.

App: 22 Charles Buffington and 1 child, Chelsea, Okla
Admitted. Applicant's father enrolled by Drennen in 1851, Del 576.

App: 23 No application was given this number. It was omitted by mistake.

App: 24 Loza Goble and 3 children, Boaz, Ala.
Admitted. Applicant's mother, Rebecca Goble, was enrolled by Chapman #1915 and her grandmother, Nancy Goble, was enrolled by Chapman #1913.

App: 25 Addie Matthews and 4 children, Claremore, Okla
Admitted. Niece of #6. Applicant's father enrolled by Chapman #1250.

App: 26 John M. Taylor, Jr. and 5 children, Claremore, Okla.
Admitted. Brother of #25 and claims through same source.

App: 27 Jack Falling, Claremore, Okla.
Admitted. Applicant's father, Tsoo-wa-loo-ke was enrolled in 1851 by Drennen, Sal. 125. Grandfather, Samuel Fallen, enrolled in 1851 by Drennen, Sal. 128 (Miscel. Test. P. 2421).

App: 28 Flora J. Harris, Long View, Texas.
Admitted. Applicant's grandmother, Nancy Bushyhead, was enrolled by Drennen, Tah. 132.

App: 29 Emily C. Howell, Marietta, Ga.
Admitted. Applicant enrolled by Hester #2316 and by Chapman #2119. Her mother, Williamina Cleland, enrolled by Chapman #2118. Her grandfather, Geo. W. Waters, enrolled by Chapman #1936.

App: 30 Wm. T. Taylor and 4 children, Claremore, Okla.
Admitted. Brother of #25 and claims through the same source.

App: 31 John D. Matuey, Mena, Ark.
Rejected. The ancestors of applicant are not on any rolls of the Eastern Cherokees. It does not appear that they were parties to the treaties of 1835-6 and 1846.

App: 32 Hicks Carter and 1 child, Blue Ridge, Ga.
Rejected. It does not appear that any ancestor was a party to the treaties of 1835-6 or 1846, nor does it appear that any ancestor was ever enrolled. (Miscel. Test. P. 1447).

App: 33 Jane Carter, Blue Ridge, Ga.
Rejected. Sister of #32 and claims through the same source.

App: 34 Eliza Catherine Miller and 2 children (E. St. Louis, Mo.
(1306 N.11th. St.

Rejected. It does not appear that ancestors were ever enrolled or were parties to the treaties of 1835-6 and 1846. Applicant shows no real connection with Eastern Cherokees. (Miscel. Test. Pages 2087 and 2483).

App: 35 Elijah Eanes, Day, Mo.

Rejected. Applicants herein claim to be descendants of the Alexander Brown whose name appears on the roll of 1835, enrolled at Oostennolles River, Ga. The Alexander Brown on the roll was enrolled with two others, making a family of three, 2 males under 18 and 1male over 18, being Alexander Brown himself, all half-breeds. No reservees or descendants of reservees. The substance of the evidences in the case contained in affidavits and testimony, is given below: Nancy M. Seadley, Appl. 39591, Miscel. Test. P' 2232, states she claims through her father, John Brown, son of Isom. Alexander Brown and her father was born in Virginia in 1814. Isom Alexander Brown was probably the son of Alexander Brown, the original ancestor. She states that her grandfather Brown lived with the Cherokees in Virginia, and that her father lived with the Cherokees in Virginia. Michael A. Fender, Appl. 3242, Miscel. Test. P. 2016, states that he was born in Monroe Co., Tenn. In 1829; that he claims through his mother, Dicie Boyd nee Brown, and that his mother was born in Virginia; that his mother got her Indian blood from her father, Alexander Brown; does not know where the latter was born; that he died in 1838 in Polk Co., Mo; that he had been two years in Missouri before his death; that his grandfather, Alexander Brown, was living during the fall and winter of 1835 in Illinois near St. Louis, Mo.; that the wife of Alexander Brown was a white woman; that neither he nor any of his ancestors have received any money or land, and were never enrolled, with the exception of Alexander Brown, who he states was enrolled in Tennessee in 1835 in Monroe Co. That neither he nor his mother ever lived with the Cherokees as a member of the tribe, and he does not know of his grandfather ever living with the Cherokee Indians as a member of the tribe; that his grandfather lived as a white settler in Missouri, among white people; does not know how much Indian blood his grandfather had; that in 1851 he and his mother were living in Polk Co., Mo. In 1835 they were living in Illinois and came from Tennessee with his grandfather Alexander Brown. Samuel Z.G. Anglen, Appl. 2658, Miscel. Test. P. 2017, states that he was born in Polk Co., Mo. In 1850, and that his mother was born in the same place in 1832; that his mother got her Indian blood through her father, Thomas Brown, who was a son of Alexander Brown; claims that Alexander Brown lived with the Cherokees as a member of the tribe in Tennessee; does not know whether his grandfather, Thomas Brown, ever lived with the Cherokees as a member of the tribe or not; states that neither he nor his mother nor his grandfather, Thomas Brown, were ever enrolled or ever received any money or land from the Government on account of Indian blood; claims that his great grandfather, Alexander Brown, was enrolled; does not know on what roll. That his great grandfather, Alexander Brown, was a half blood Cherokee. James Harralson, age 80, states in an affidavit of July 30, 1906, that he was acquainted with Alexander Brown; that he came from McMinn or Monroe Co., Tenn. And settled in Polk Co., Mo. In or about the year 1836 or 1837; that when he first knew Alexander Brown he lived in Tennessee; that he heard, he came from Georgia to Tennessee. He states that he has "a very clear and distinct recollection of hearing the said Alexander Brown say that he was registered or that his name was on the roll of Cherokee Indians prior to his leaving Tennessee, and I have heard him tell this both before he left Tennessee and after he came to Missouri". That Alexander Brown was a half-blood Cherokee Indian. He states that Alexander

Brown had the following children: Thomas, Isom, John, Jack, Sarah (Hambleton), Dicie, Elizabeth (Ruth), Susan (Proctor), Annie (Pace) and Violet (Ruth). Russell Stokes, age 86, in his affidavit of July 31, 1906, states that he was acquainted with Alexander Brown after he came to Polk Co., Mo., which was about the year 1835 or 1836; that Alexander Brown told him that he was half Cherokee and that he came to Missouri from Tennessee. He further states that "he told me that he had his papers showing his Indian rights, and that his name was on the roll of Cherokee Indians; that the said Alexander Brown has always claimed to be a half-blood Cherokee Indian, and he has children claiming to be part Indian and were recognized and reputed to be such by all who knew them". This affiant[sic] and others state that Alexander Brown was a tall man, broad shouldered, rather slim, with dark hair and eyes and dark complexion. Michael Fender in his affidavit of Aug. 6, 1906, states that he is 77 years old; that he was well acquainted with Alexander Brown, who was his grandfather; that he came from McMinn Co., Tenn. And that he lived about four or five miles from his father's residence in Tenn. And that he can remember his being in his father's house several times. That when Alexander Brown left Tennessee and came to Missouri "there were about 6 families came together, including my father's family and Alexander Brown's family, said families were all related to each other. We left Tenn. In fall of 1833 and came to a place in Illinois 15 or 18 miles east of St. Louis, and stopped there over the winter, and in the spring coming on to what is now known as Brighton, Polk Co., Mo., arriving there May 10, 1836; I was with them during their journey from Tenn." That Alexander Brown was a half-breed Cherokee; that he was enrolled as a Cherokee Indian on the roll of 1835; that he died in 1838. From the foregoing, it appears that it is unknown when Alexander Brown was born that there is contradiction in the evidence as to where he was living in 1835, the weight of it being to the effect, however, that he was in Illinois or Missouri at that time. There is some also to the effect that he was in Tennessee. The weight of the evidence is that Alexander Brown lived in Tennessee prior to moving west – only one person, James Harralson in his affidavit stating that he "heard he (Alexander Brown) came from Ga. To Tenn." The Alexander Brown on the 1835 roll was enrolled in Georgia. He was enrolled with two males under 18 years of age. Alexander Brown, ancestor of applicants herein, had several children, at least 6, and most of them must have been over 18 years of age in 1835. Michael Fender testified that he was born in Monroe Co., Tenn. in 1829, and that his mother, Dicie Boyd, who was a daughter of Alexander Brown, was born in Virginia. The name of Boyd or Fender does not appear on the roll of 1835. If Dicie Boyd was a daughter of the Alexander Brown on the 1835 roll, why was she not enrolled at that time? If she was not enrolled because she had gone west prior to 1835, she could not be considered as a member of the Eastern Cherokee tribe at the time or her descendants be beneficiaries under the decree of the Court of Claims herein. Nancy M. Seadley states that her father who was a grandson of Alexander Brown was born in Virginia in 1814, and that her father and grandfather lived with the Cherokees in Virginia. It would thus appear that applicant's ancestor, Alexander Brown, originally came from Virginia and lived with some Indians there – not the Cherokees, as they, as well known never lived in Virginia. If applicant's ancestor Alexander Brown, had left Tenn. prior to 1835, to which effect is the weight of evidence, he could not have been enrolled in Tenn. or Georgia in 1835, and the Alexander Brown on the 1835 roll could not be applicant's ancestor. The statements of Affiants[sic] to the effect that Alexander Brown told them that he was enrolled with the Cherokee Indians prior to his leaving Tenn. should be discounted when considering the age of affiants[sic] at that time. Such statements would have hardly made such an impression upon a child. In consideration of the premises, the applications of all persons claiming through Alexander Brown and his children, Thomas, Dicie, Isom, Zach, Sarah, Susan, Annie and Violet, are hereby rejected. (See Miscel. Test. Pages 2016, 2017 and 2232). *3091 & 2407 (Hand written).

App: 36 Robert E. Tompkins and 7 children, Rock Hill, S.C. 371 E. Main St.

Rejected. Claims through Hannah C. Ross, who is on the Old Settler roll, page 114, Group 2.

App: 37 Mary Davis Howell, Marietta, Ga., 312 Kennesaw Ave.

Admitted. Enrolled by Hester #2327 as daughter of Emily C. Howell, 2nd wife of Archibald Howell. Emily C. Howell, who was enrolled by Chapman #2119 as daughter of Williamina C. Cleland, Chapman #2118. The latter was the daughter of Geo. W. Waters, Chapman #1936.

App: 38 Nancy Blevins, Vinita Okla.

Admitted. Applicant claims through her mother who was enrolled by Drennen, Dis. 26, under the name of Creasy Humphreys.

App: 39 Mary Vick and 4 children, Quarles, Ga.

Admitted. First cousin of #24. Daughter of #3022. Grand-daughter of #1521.

App: 40 James D. Quarles and 3 children, Quarles, Ga.

Admitted. First cousin of #24 and claims through same source. Son of #3022; grandson of #1521.

App: 41 Dora Vick and 2 children, Quarles, Ga.

Admitted. First cousin of #24. Claims through same source. Daughter of #3022. Grand-daughter of #1521.

App: 42 Eleanora Pankey and 2 children, Quarles, Ga.

Admitted. First cousin of #24. Daughter of #3022; grand-daughter of #1521.

App: 43 Arvaline Davis, Blue Ridge, Ga.

Rejected. It does not appear that any ancestor was a party to the treaties of 1835-6 or 1846, nor does it appear that any ancestor was ever enrolled. Shows no real connection with the Eastern Cherokees. (Miscel. Test. P. 1439).

App: 44 Emma Welch and 5 children, Blue Ridge, Ga.

Rejected. It does not appear that any ancestor was a party to the treaties of 1835-6 or 1846. Nor does it appear that any ancestor was ever enrolled. Shows no real connection with the Eastern Cherokees. (Miscel. Test. P. 1423).

App: 45 James A. Blackburn and 3 children, Moneta, Cal.

Rejected. These applicants allege that they are descendants of the Dave Weaver who was enrolled in 1835. They claim through Elizabeth Weaver, daughter of Dave, who married John Eddings, and who had the following children: Frances Blackburn nee Eddings, Ivan Eddings, Richard D. Eddings and Jesse Eddings. The applicants herein are descendants of these children. There is a conflict of evidence as to where Elizabeth Eddings was residing in 1835. There is some evidence to the effect that she died in that year. Levi R. Eddings, Elizabeth's grandson (Appl. #2370), states that she died in Marion Co., Ill. In 1835 (see Exhibit 2). Andrew E. Blackburn (Appl. #6007). another grandson, states that she died in Mo. in 1841 (see Exhibit 4). Josiah Eddings (Appl. #1671), also a grandson of Elizabeth, states that his grand mother was living in Tenn. in

1835 (see Exhibit 6). There is a "Dav" Weaver on the roll of 1835, Cherokee Co., Ga. Page 38, enrolled with 6 others, making a family of 7, all full-bloods, and it is stated on that roll that there were in that family, 4 males under 18 years of age, 2 over 18, and 1 female under 16. Elizabeth Eddings, as shown by applications and other evidence, was a grandmother in 1835, having several grandchildren who were born in about 1830 and one in 1828, who was a brother of Levi R. Eddings (Appl. #2370) and the son of Ivan Eddings. There is no evidence in this case as to whether Dave Weaver had any other children than Elizabeth Eddings, and there is no evidence tending to prove that the Dave Weaver on the roll of 1835 is the ancestor of applicants herein, except their statements to that effect. Elizabeth Eddings or her husband should have been on the roll of 1835 under the name of Eddings, if she were living in the Cherokee domain or were recognized as a member of the tribe at that time. Most of her children were also heads of families in 1835, and should also have been enrolled at that time under their own names. Neither the names of any of the ancestors nor the names of any of the applicants herein, with the exception of that of Dave Weaver, appear on the rolls of 1835, 1851 or 1882. The necessary supposition is, therefore, that if Elizabeth Eddings was an Eastern Cherokee and was ever a recognized member of the tribe, she had left the tribe prior to 1835, and since that time neither she nor any of her descendants have been connected with or recognized as members of the tribe. If she and her children had not left the Cherokee tribe but had been recognized members thereof, they would certainly have been enrolled on some of the Eastern Cherokee rolls. As above shown, the Dave Weaver on the roll of 1835 was enrolled with a family of 6, 4 being males under 18 years of age and 1 female under 16. Elizabeth Eddings, who as claimed by applicants herein, was the daughter of Dave Weaver, and was as above shown, a grandmother in 1835 and had a grandchild 7 years old at that time, so that it is extremely improbable that Dave Weaver would have had several children under 18 years of age and one who was a grandmother at the same time. Even conceding that applicants herein are the descendants of the Dave Weaver whose name appears on the roll of 1835, they would not be entitled, as Elizabeth Eddings and her children as above shown, were old enough to have been enrolled on the 1835 roll in their own names as heads of families, and if Elizabeth had left the tribe they would be classed as Old Settlers, if Cherokees at all, and applicants herein would not be entitled on that ground. In consideration of the premises, therefore, the applications of all persons claiming through Dave Weaver and his daughter, Elizabeth, are hereby rejected.

App: 46 Jennie Colbert, Blue Ridge, Ga.

Rejected. Claimant was born in about 1872 or 1873. She claims Indian Blood through both parents. She claims Jack Thompson as her father but admits that she is an illegitimate child and there is nothing to show that Jack Thompson was really her father or even recognized her as his child. Then too the Jack Thompson on the rolls was enrolled in the west in 1851 and claimant states he died out there, so that it is not probable that the Jack Thompson enrolled is the one claimed as the father of applicant. Claimant is not enrolled by Hester, nor do the names of any of her mother's people appear on any Cherokee roll. Claimant seems to know very little about her ancestors, and on correspondence has been unable to furnish any satisfactory proof. Claimant was notified to appear at Blue Ridge, Ga. in June 1908 and produce additional evidence, but failed to appear.

App: 47 James S. Stapler and 2 children, Tahlequah, Okla.
Admitted. Claimant was born in 1856 and claims his Indian blood through his mother. Mother and her parents enrolled in 1851 by Drennen, Sal. 530.

App: 48 Ross Cheney and 7 children, Muskogee, Okla.
Rejected. The names of the ancestors of applicant are not on any Eastern Cherokee rolls. It does not appear that they were parties to the treaties of 1835-6 and 1846.

App: 49 David A. Russell and 4 children, Muskogee, Okla.
Rejected. Brother of #113 and claims through the same source.

App: 50 Thomas J. Moore, Verdigris, Okla.
Admitted. Applicant's grandmother. Martha Lea, and great grandfather, Walter Lea, were enrolled by Drennen in 1851, S.B. 197. His great grandfather, Walter Lea, also enrolled in 1835 with the Eastern Cherokees.

App: 51 Elizabeth Emily Stone, South West City, Mo.
Admitted. Claimant probably enrolled by Chapman in 1851 #2052 as Rebecca McAllister. Mother enrolled by Chapman #2049. Maternal grandparents, Chapman #2053 and #2054.

App: 52 Charlotte Townsend and 2 children, Pryor Creek, Okla.
Admitted. Claimant's father and 1 brother and sister enrolled by Drennen in 1851, G.S. 407. Paternal grandfather enrolled in 1835, Page 5.

App: 53 Phenias B. Tompkins, Buffalo, N.Y., 64 Putnam St.
Rejected. Brother of #36 and claims through the same source.

App: 54 Carolina R. T. Butler and 1 child, Athens, Ga.
Rejected. Sister of #36 and claims through the same source.

App: 55 Mark L. Paden and 1 child, Centralia, Okla.
Admitted. Applicant's father and grandparents were enrolled by Chapman, Nos. 1733, 1734 and 1736.

App: 56 Annie Boynton Brown and 3 children, Kansas City, Mo., 3230 E. H. St.
Rejected. Applicant claims through her mother, Laura Narcissa Rider or Boynton. Her father has no Indian Blood. (See letter "A"). Applicant was born in 1857 but her mother was living in Flint District, Okla. in 1851 and is on the Old Settler roll, Fl. 118. Emma J. Starr, Appl. #5582, is a first cousin on her father's side of this applicant. #5582 says her father was an Old Settler. (See Old Settler roll, Flint District #99).

App: 57 Missouri C. Lambert and 4 children, Seymour, Texas R #1, Box 16.
Rejected. Claimant was born in 1867 and claims her Indian blood through her father who was born in 1823 in Cherokee Co., Ga. and always lived in Ga. and Ala. (See Miscel. Test. P. 3247 – 8). He does not appear on any roll nor does his mother nor any of his or her family. Claimant makes no claim that either she or any of her ancestors were ever enrolled. It would seem if claimant's father or his mother had any Indian blood it was not recognized by the Cherokees and that they derived it from some other tribe or had severed their connection with the Cherokees prior to 1835.

App: 58 Jeremiah L. Pilgrim and 3 children, Atlanta, Ga.
Rejected. This claim is founded on John Williams whose Indian name is said to have been Lum Thum. The name "John Williams" appears on the roll of 1835 and also on the roll of 1851. There is no attempt made to relate applicant to the John Williams who is on the roll of 1851 and who is not the party by that name who is on the roll of 1835. The John Williams on the roll of 1851 is still alive and has an application on file here and is in no way related to the applicant. Applicant, however, claims through the John Williams who is on the roll of 1835. There are two persons by that name on the roll of 1835 but it does not appear satisfactorily that applicant is related to either of them. No subsequent ancestor was ever enrolled nor does it appear that any other ancestor ever lived with the Cherokee tribe. Testimony shows that the witnesses know practically nothing about the matter and that all or most of the applicants obtained their information from L.J. Ledbetter of Texas, who when called to testify, could throw practically no light on his family history. It therefore does not appear that any ancestor was ever enrolled or that any any[sic] ancestor was party to the treaties of 1835-6 and 1846. Shows no real connection with the Eastern Cherokees. (Mis. Test. P 1962, 920 and 2001).
App: 59 Lewis J. Williams and 2 children, Ball Ground, Ga.
Rejected. First cousin once removed of #58 and claims through same source.
App: 60 Lou D. Gilstrap and 8 children, Ball Ground, Ga.
Rejected. Cousin of #58 and claims through the same source.
App: 61 Rhoda M. Merritt and 8 children, Cumming, Ga.
Rejected. Sister of #58 and claims through the same source.
App: 62 Rufus M. Choate and 1 child, Pryor Creek, Okla.
Admitted. Applicant's father enrolled by Drennen in 1851, Dis. 74.
App: 63 John B. Choate and 2 children, Pryor Creek, Okla.
Admitted. Brother of #62 and claims through the same source.
App: 64 Jesse B. Burgess, Claremore, Okla
Rejected. Applicant and his parents were Old Settlers.
App: 65 John B. Stapler and 2 children, Tahlequah, Okla.
Admitted. Brother of #47 and claims through same source.
App: 66 Robbin Lawson, Hancock, Tenn.
Rejected. It does not appear that any ancestor was a party to the treaties of 1835-6 or 1846. Nor does it appear that any ancestor was ever enrolled. Shows no real connection with the Eastern Cherokees. (Miscel. Test. P. 1791).
App: 67 Elisha R. Lawson and 1 child, Bigfall, Tenn.
Rejected. Grand-nephew of #66 and claims through the same source.
App: 68 John T. Lawson, Bigfall, Tenn.
Rejected Grand-nephew of #66 and claims through the same source.
App: 69 Drewrey Lawson, Bigfall, Tenn.
Rejected. Grand-nephew of #66 and claims through the same source.
App: 70 Alvin T. Lawson and 1 child, Bigfall, Tenn.
Rejected. Grand-nephew of #66 and claims through the same source.
App: 71 Daniel R. Coodey, Jr. and 3 children Porum, Okla.
Admitted. Applicant's father, Lewis Coodey, and his grandmother, Sarah Coodey, were enrolled by Drennen, Can. #4.

App: 72 Lurena Rivet, Owasso, Okla.
Admitted. Applicant enrolled by Chapman #1305. Applicant's father, Joseph Henson, enrolled by Chapman #1302. Brother, Leonidas, George and sister, Martha, enrolled by Chapman #1303, 1306 and 1304, respectively. (Miscel. Test. P. 2669).
App: 73 Mattie Clifton, minor, Owasso, Okla.
By Geo. Clifton, Gdn.
Admitted. Great-niece of #72. Applicant's grandfather, Leonidas Henson, enrolled by Chapman #1303.
App: 74 Daniel M. Hause, Claremore, Okla.
Admitted. Applicant's mother enrolled by Drennen in 1851, Tah. 224.
App: 75 George E. Foreman and 6 children, Foyil, Okla.
Rejected. Applicant and children are enrolled by Dawes Commission as Creeks and must be rejected for affiliation with that tribe. D.C. No. 9712, Creeks by Blood.
App: 76 Ellen L.R.T. Connors, Lancaster, S.C.
Rejected. Applicant is a sister of #36 and claims through same source.
App: 77 Barbra A. Presley, Ladonia, Texas.
Rejected. It does not appear that ancestors were ever enrolled or were parties to the treaties of 1835-6 and 1846. Applicant shows no real connection with Eastern Cherokees. (Mis. Test. P. 2222).
App: 78 John Blossom and 4 children, Locust Grove, Okla.
Admitted . Applicant's mother, Lila Vann Blossom, Appl. #79, Grandparents, Saturday and Sallie Vann, enrolled by Drennen, Sal. 196.
App: 79 Lila Blossom and 1 child, Locust Grove, Okla.
Admitted. Applicant and her parents, Saturday and Sallie Vann, enrolled by Drennen, Sal. 196.
App: 80 Lucy Grass, Locust Grove, Okla.
Admitted. Applicant enrolled by Drennen, Sal. 328, and applicant's parents enrolled as Tu-ser-ne and Susannah.
App: 81 Rider Grass, Locust Grove, Okla.
Admitted. Applicant enrolled by Drennen in 1851, Sal. 244.
App: 82 Betsey Littledave and 4 children, Locust Grove, Okla.
Admitted. Applicant's father and grandfather enrolled by Drennen in 1851, Sal. 349. (See Miscel. Test. P. 3754).
App. 83 Maggie M. Dunham and 3 children, Locust Grove, Okla.
Admitted. Applicant's grandfather, Daniel Vann, enrolled by Drennen, Sal. 207.
App: 84 Alsie Blackfox, Dragger, Okla.
Admitted. Applicant enrolled by Drennen in 1851, Sal. 320.
App: 85 Enola Blackfox, Dragger, Okla.
Admitted. Applicant enrolled by Drennen in 1851, Del. 290.
App: 86 Rachel Walker, Locust Grove, Okla.
Admitted. Sister of #85. Enrolled by Drennen, Del. 290 as A-chin-ee.
App: 87 Betsey Potts, Locust Grove, Okla.
Admitted. Applicant enrolled by Drennen in 1851, Sal. 213.
App: 88 Jennie Cochran and 2 children, Locust Grove, Okla.
Admitted. Applicant's parents enrolled by Drennen in 1851, Sal. 166.

App: 89 Woluke Pigeon and 1 child, Locust Grove, Okla.
Admitted. Applicant's father and grandmother enrolled by Drennen in 1851, Sal. 329, Claimant himself and mother probably Fl. 13. (Miscel. Test. P. 3778).

App: 90 Alice Ross Howard, Ft. Gibson, Okla.
Admitted. Applicant's father, Robert D. Ross, was enrolled by Drennen, Sal. 460.

App: 91 John Sanders and 1 child, Claremore, Okla.
Admitted. Applicant born after 1851. Father, Aleck Sanders, enrolled in 1851, G.S. 522. (Miscel. Test. P. 4118).

App: 92 Belle Ross, Ft. Gibson, Okla.
Admitted. Sister of #90 and claims through same source.

App: 93 Fannie R. Kneeland, and 4 children Ft. Gibson, Okla.
Admitted. Sister of #90 and claims through the same source.

App: 94 John Woodard, McLain, Okla.
Admitted. Applicant claims through his mother, Martha Woodard, Appl. #269. Martha Woodard claims through her grandparents, Mose and Caty Harris, Drennen Roll, Can. 82, and father, Kla-na-noo, Drennen roll, Sal. 527. Also there appears on the roll of 1835, the grandfather of Martha Woodard, Robert Barry, P. 39, also grandfather, Parch Corn, P. 13. The father of applicant, enrolled by Drennen as George Woodward, together with his father, Thomas Woodward, Del. 402.

App: 95 Walter McSpadden and 1 child, Maryville, Tenn. R.F.D. 5.
Admitted. Nephew of #18 and Claims throught same source.

App: 96 Cynthia Dickson and 7 children, Ochelata, Okla.
Admitted. Claims through her mother, Dianna Carter, and her grandmother, Jane Carter, both enrolled by Drennen, Tah. 289.

App: 97 Serena C. McSpadden and 7 children, Chelsea, Okla.
Admitted. Sister of #96.

App: 98 John B. Davis and 5 children, Claremore, Okla.
Admitted. Applicant is entitled through his grandmother, Rachel Davis nee Martin, who married Daniel Davis, applicant's grandfather. Daniel Davis was recognized as the head of a Cherokee family and was enrolled in 1835, P. 45, and also by Chapman #2024, with applicant's brothers and sisters. Martin Davis and Lorenzo D. Davis, sons of Daniel, uncles of applicant, and through whom a number of applicants herein claim, were enrolled by Chapman, #2034 and #2072, respectively.

App: 99 Mary Ross Jones and 6 children, Chelsea, Okla.
Admitted. Claims through her father, Oliver Ross, and her grandfather, Andrew Ross, both enrolled by Drennen, Sal. 448 and 447, respectively.

App: 100 Minnie Walden and 3 children, Pryor Creek, Okla.
Admitted. Sister of #99.

App: 101 Andrew L. Payne, Foyil, Okla.
Admitted. Applicant claims through mother probably born after 1851. Grandfather, Benjamin Wisner, enrolled by Drennen in 1851, Sal. 396. Great grandfather, Laugh at Mush, also enrolled by Drennen in 1851, Del. 189. (Miscel. Test. P. 4128).

App: 102 Walter D. Nave, Claremore, Okla.
Admitted. Claims Cherokee descent through his father, Daniel R. Nave, and his mother, Jennie Nave, enrolled by Drennen, S.B. 253. See app. #10676.
App:103 Edward D. Hicks and 5 children, Tahlequah, Okla.
Admitted. First cousin of #47 and claims through same source.
App: 104 Heb. A. Hughes, Andrews, N.C.
Rejected. It does not appear that any ancestor was ever enrolled or that any ancestor was party to the treaties of 1835-6 and 1846. Shows no real connection with the Eastern Cherokees.
App: 105 John C. Hughes and 4 children, Aquone, N.C.
Rejected. Claims through same source as #104.
App: 106 Mary E. Holland, Foyil, Okla.
Admitted. Applicant was enrolled by Chapman #2133, and her father enrolled by Chapman #1390.
App: 107 Wm. M. Chambers, Claremore, Okla.
Admitted. Applicant's father, Henry Chambers, was enrolled by Drennen, Tah. 228, and his grandmother, Alsey Chambers, was enrolled Tah. 240, also Joseph Chambers, Tah. 241.
App: 108 Bernard L. Coon, Claremore, Okla.
Rejected. Applicant fails to establish his claim. There is not sufficient information in his application to connect him with rolls of 1835 or 1851, and no replies have been received to letters sent him. Two separate notices were sent him to appear for personal examination at Claremore, Okla., but he did not appear either time. Inquiry at Claremore failed to elicit information.
App: 109 James Neal, Sr. McClain, Okla.
Admitted. Applicant enrolled by Chapman #1706.
App: 110 Nancy J. Candler and 5 children, Candler, N.C.
Rejected. Sister of #113 and claims through the same source.
App: 111 Edgebert Holloway, Candler, N.C.
Rejected. Son of #113 and claims through the same source.
App: 112 Armstrong Holloway and 4 children, Asheville, N.C.
Rejected. Duplicate of #26199.
(**Note:** The applicant number, (Re Appli. No. 119). Was on the film between applications 112 and 113.)
App: RE Appli. No. 119.

Extract from report of George Manypenny.
Commissioner of Indian Affairs to the Secretary of
the Interior: January 14, 1857.

I have the honor to submit x x x x x
Elijah Murphy male 19

This is a son, illegitimate, of Polly Murphy a white woman by a white man. Her history is this:-

She had Wm. R. Matoy by a white man, and he and his family were improperly paid under Siler's Roll by the name of William Murphy. She then had three sons, Arch, John and Joe by a negro. Then another son named James by a white man. She then co-habited with Whiplash, an Indian, and had three sons by him, David, Jess and Martin, these with their mother were paid under Siler's Roll, but David now comes forward claiming for five children, the oldest of whom is 14 years of age, when he himself is not more than 25. The solution of which apparent impossibility is, that he took up with a white woman who had several bastards. He may be the father of some of the youngest, but has not married the mother. Elijah was begotten by a white man after she was left by Whiplash, and any claim upon his part could only be derived from the cohabitation by the mother with Whiplash prior to 1836.

App: 113 Julia A. Holloway and 4 children, Candler, N.C.
Rejected. It does not appear that any ancestor was party to the treaties of 1835-6 or 1846, nor does it appear that any ancestor was ever enrolled. Shows no real connection with the Eastern Cherokees. (Miscel. Test. P. 1699).

App: 114 Mary An[sic] Perkins, Ft. Gibson, Okla.
Admitted. Applicant's mother enrolled by Chapman #1717. Applicant herself probably enrolled by Chapman #1720 as Martha A. West.

App: 115 Alpha Burgess, Andrews, N.C.
Rejected. It does not appear that any ancestor was ever enrolled or that any ancestor was party to the treaties of 1835-6 and 1846. Shows no connection with the Eastern Cherokees.

App: 116 James Taylor, Pryor Creek, Okla.
Admitted. Applicant brother of #6. Applicant enrolled by Chapman #1250.

App: 117 Mary A. Thompson and 3 children, Blue Ridge, Ga.
Rejected. It does not appear that any ancestor was a party to the treaties of 1835-6 or 1846, nor does it appear that any ancestor was ever enrolled. Shows no real connection with the Eastern Cherokees. (Miscel. Test. P. 1436).

App: 118 William Powell, Blue Ridge, Ga.
Admitted. Applicant's father, Marcus Powell, enrolled by Chapman #1203.

App: 119 James Murphy, Andrews, N.C.
Rejected. Grandson of Polly Murphy and rejected for the reasons set out in the report on Polly Murphy and her descendants.
(**Note:** Last of statement handwritten. *By Court of Indian Affairs Janury*[sic] *14, 1857. See half sheet attached.)*

App: 120 Elbert Ramsey Blue Ridge, Ga.
Rejected. Shows no connection with Eastern Cherokees. No ancestor enrolled. No ancestor appears to have been party to the treaties of 1835-6 and 1846.Applicant's father was a slave. See Letter.

App: 121 Margaret M. Higgins and 1 child, Shady, Ark.
Rejected. Claims through Alex Brown. See #35.

App: 122 Dicey A. Bryant, Carthage, Mo.
Rejected. Claims through Alex Brown. See #35 Duplicate #25317.

App: 123 Crofford V. Collake, Mt. Vernon, Tenn.
Admitted. Applicant was enrolled by Chapman #1556. His father and mother enrolled by Chapman #1552 and #1553.

App: 124 Sarah E. Antoine, Ft. Gibson, Okla.
Admitted. Sister of #114 and claims through the same source.

App: 125 Jessie L. Brown, Asheville, N.C.
Rejected. Niece of #113 and claims through the same source.

App: 126 Anna R. Cothran and 3 children, Topton, N.C.
Rejected. It does not appear that ancestors were ever enrolled or were parties to the treaties of 1835-6 and 1846. They show no real connection with the Eastern Cherokees. (Mis. Test. P. 1550).

App: 127 Alice R. Cothren and 3 children, Topton, N.C.
Rejected. Sister of #126 and claims through same source.

App: 128 Stephen C. Rowland and 2 children, Hayesville, N.C.
Rejected. Brother of #126 and claims through the same source.

App: 129 Martha Garrish, Topton, N.C.
Rejected. Mother of #126 and claims through the same source.

App: 130 Sallie Bright, Westville, Okla.
Admitted. Applicant was enrolled as Sally Ann Morten in 1851, Dis. 90 by Drennen. Mother, Rebecca Morten and brothers and sisters of applicant enrolled Dis. 90. (Miscel. Test. P. 2943).

App: 131 Barsha Bright, Westville, Okla.
Admitted. Sister of #130 and claims through same source.

App: 132 Sidney Elizabeth *Wil~~leie~~* Westville, Okla.
(Handwritten above name kie)
Admitted. Applicant was enrolled by Chapman #1779.

App: 133 Margaret A. Lindsey and 2 children, Westville, Okla.
Admitted. Daughter of #132. Applicant enrolled by Chapman #1780.

App: 134 Watson Spade and 2 children, Proctor, Okla.
Admitted. Claimant was born in 1869. His mother and her parents enrolled by Drennen in 1851, G.S. 668. Claimant enrolled by Dawes Commission #28564 as full-blood.

App: 135 Johnson Spade, Proctor, Okla.
Admitted. Applicant enrolled by Indian name, Chu-suh-wah-lah, in 1851 by Drennen, G.S. 533. Also his parents. (Miscel. Test. P. 3392)

App: 136 Sarah L. Price and 2 children, Evansville, Ark.
2 Admitted. 1 Rejected. This claim is rejected as to Sarah L. Price who claims for her husband who died in 1898. It is admitted as to the 2 grandchildren who claim through their grandfather, Samuel J. Price. He was living in 1851 but not enrolled. His grandfather, Samuel Keys, *Sr.,(Handwritten)* enrolled by Chapman #1684. His uncles and aunt enrolled as Samuel Keys, Jr., by Chapman #1680. Richard Keys, Chapman #1684. James M. Keys, Chapman #1690. Eveline McCoy, Chapman #1692. Samuel J. Price was admitted as a citizen of the Cherokee Nation. (Miscel. Test. P. 4024 and 3346).

App: 137 Versa Noy Tidwell, Stilwell, Okla.
Rejected. Claims through John Tidwell. See #16

App: 138 Laura A. Henry, Claremore, Okla.
Admitted. Parents of claimant and her brothers enrolled by Drennen in 1851, G.S. 37.

App: 139 Nancy J. Smith, Claremore, Okla.
Admitted. Claimant and her mother and brother enrolled by Drennen in 1851, Tah. 229 (NOTE: Or could be 239). Claimant's father was an Old Settler. See her application under head of "remarks".

App: 140 Rachel D. Green and 1 child, Claremore, Okla.
Admitted. Daughter of #138 and claims through the same source.
App: 141 Mary V. Barton and 1 child, Chelsea, Okla.
Admitted. Applicant's mother, Sarah Walker, and uncle Ebenezer, enrolled in 1851 by Drennen, Tah. 260. Grandmother, Nancy, died before 1851, but brother, Jesse, who died before 1851, left many children enrolled by Drennen in 1851, G.S. 227. Great uncle to applicant, Charles Bushyhead, enrolled in 1851 by Drennen, I11. 289. Another great uncle enrolled in 1851 by Drennen, Tah. 133. (Miscel. Test. P. 4104).
App: 142 Martha Matney and 1 child, Pryor Creek, Okla.
Admitted. Sister to #72. Applicant enrolled by Chapman #1304.
App: 143 Sally Ann Livingston and 3 children, Choteau, Okla.
Admitted. Claimant and her mother enrolled by Drennen in 1851, Del. 138. Claimant's half-sister enrolled by Drennen, Del. 967.
App: 144 Richard Neal and 1 child, McLain, Okla.
By Bessie L. Neal.
Admitted. Nephew of #109 and claims through the same source.
App: 145 Josuha Ross, Muskogee, Okla.
Admitted. Claimant enrolled by Drennen in 1851, Tah. 236. His mother enrolled in 1851 by Drennen, Sal. 445. His father enrolled in 1835, Page 12.
App: 146 William Dixon, Gideon, Okla.
By Isaac Dixon, Gdn. And brother (#147)
Admitted. Applicant claims through mother, Mary Still, whose mother, Katy Still, enrolled by Drennen in 1851, Dis. 87. Mary Still was not born in 1851. (See app. #23735). (Miscel. Test. P. 3379 and 2339).
App: 147 Isaac Dixon, Claremore, Okla.
Admitted. Brother and guardian of #146.
App: 148 Louisa McKellar and 3 children, Sparks, Okla.
Rejected. The names of the ancestors of the applicants do not appear upon any of the Eastern Cherokee rolls. It is not shown that the applicant's ancestors were parties to the treaties of 1835-6 and 1846.
App: 149 Drayton C. Hall and 4 children, Knoxville, Tenn.,
604 W. Baxter Ave.
Rejected. Applicant claims through mother and grandfather, Kizerah and Jerry Shelton, neither of which are enrolled. Parents of applicant were born in Gwinnett Co., Ga. which is not within the Cherokee domain. It appears that the ancestors were not parties to the treaties of 1835-6 and 1846. Information in application insufficient.
App: 150 William Cochran and 3 children, Hulbert, Okla.
Admitted. Claims through father, Price Cochran, enrolled as Too-ger-wal-le Gilmer, by Drennen in 1851, Sal. 276, along with mother, Ail-le Gilmer, and brothers and sisters. Applicant's mother enrolled in 1851 by Drennen, Tah. 125. (Mis. Test. P. 3251).
App: 151 Price Cochran, Hulbert, Okla.
Admitted. Applicant enrolled as Too-ger-wa-le Gilmer in 1851 by Drennen, Sal. 276, also his mother, Ail-le Gilmer and brothers and sisters Oo-nor-le, A-tor-he, Polly, An-ne and Wut-te. (Miscel. Test. P. 3251).

App: 152 Walker Cochran, Hulbert, Okla.
Admitted. Applicant enrolled in 1851 by Drennen, Sal. 276, as A-tor-he. Brother of Price Cochran (#151) and claims through same source.

App: 153 Richard W. Adams, Gillsville, Ga.
Rejected. There are a great many applicants who base their claims solely upon the Indian blood derived from one Annie or Nancy Blythe, and these claims are given color by the fact that there is a Nancy Blythe on Page 28 of the Eastern Cherokee census roll of 1835. On this roll Nancy Blythe appears as residing on Shooting Creek, N.C., and one minor child, female, over 16 years of age, is enrolled with her. These claims are given further color by the fact that James Blythe and Betsey Welch, two of the children of Nancy Blythe, were enrolled with the Eastern Cherokees in 1851. The facts as set forth in the various applications and as developed by the testimony (see Miscel. Test. P. 1633 to 1644) are inconsistent with the idea that Nancy Blythe, wife of Johnathan Blythe, was the Nancy Blythe whose name appears on the Eastern Cherokee roll of 1835. The testimony of James Lewis McDonald (Miscel. Test. P. 1639-1640) who is 87 years of age, and a grandson of Nancy Blythe, shows conclusively that Nancy Blythe must have been an old woman in 1835. He says: "In 1835 she was living with Johnathan Blythe, her husband. No one else was living in the house with them at that time as far as I recollect. At that time all her children were married or had left. She had no grandchildren living in the house with her. I never heard of Nancy Blythe, my grandmother, drawing any money as an Indian. I never heard her say she was enrolled as an Indian. I never heard her say that her mother was an Indian. I will not state that I heard her say to what tribe of Indians she belonged. The first I heard of her being enrolled was 6 or 8 or 10 years ago. Jim Taylor told me then. He was acting for Belva Lockwood. In 1835 it was well known where my mother lived. She was well known in this country at that time. I never heard of her getting any money as an Indian. The reason my mother was not enrolled in 1835 was because they held their heads up and were sort of biggish and did not have sense enough. I can give no reason why my mother's brothers and sisters were not enrolled in 1835. My mother's brothers and sisters were all of age at that time and living in this locality. In 1851 I was living on Hanging Dog. I do not remember anything about a payment in 1851. Did hear that the Cherokees were drawing some money then. I did not apply because I did not have sense enough. We have always had the privileges of white people but recognized as having Indian blood. I do not claim Indian blood through any source other than Annie Blythe". It appears that Nancy Blythe had 7 adult children living in 1835 and no minor children. None of her children were enrolled in 1835. The testimony fails to disclose just where this Nancy Blythe was living in 1835, although it very clearly establishes the fact that she and several of her children were born in S.C., and Edmond A. Dewese (Miscel. Test. P. 1633) a white man 87 years old testifying on behalf of the claimants, states that he first knew Annie Blythe in Macon Co., N.C. in 1836 or 1837, and that she was living somewhere near Franklin on the Tennessee River. Other witnesses testified that she was living in 1835 and 1836 in Macon or Jackson Counties, but it does not appear anywhere that this Nancy Blythe ever lived at Shooting Creek, at which point the Nancy Blythe enrolled in 1835 was living. This testimony further discloses the fact that James Blythe and Betsey Welch, the two children of Nancy Blythe who enrolled in 1851, had married Eastern Cherokee Indians prior to the treaty of 1835. Joseph G. Hester, Special Agent, who made a roll of Eastern Cherokees in 1884, enrolled this James Blythe as No. 1177,

and under the names of ancestors on previous rolls, wrote: "white", and under "Remarks" added: "White on Mullay roll – adopted before Treaty". Agent Hester also enrolled Betsy or Elizabeth Welch as No. 1421. Likewise inserting in a column of names of ancestors on previous rolls: "White" and adding under "Remarks", "Married to a Cherokee before Treaty". These circumstances would seem to be conclusive and the testimony of Martha Ann Meroney (Miscel. Test. P. 1641), 73 years of age, an intelligent and apparently thoroughly honest witness, seems to completely destroy all claims on behalf of these applicants. She testifies that she is the granddaughter of this Nancy Blythe in question, she being a daughter of Elizabeth or Betsy Welch above referred to. She testifies: "I know James L. McDonald. His mother was Sally Blythe who married a McDonald. I never talked with Sallie McDonald about her having Indian blood and never heard of it until this affair came up. I knew her intimately. She was my mother's sister. Annie Blythe was my grandmother. I have heard my mother and some of the citizens say Annie Blythe was Annie Barnes. She was born in England, I have heard my mother say. She came to S.C. with her father and mother, and Annie Barnes married Johnathan Blythe in S.C. and then moved to N.C., about Jackson Co., or up that way. I never heard how old Nancy Blythe was at the time of her death. I have heard my mother say that she did not have any Indian in her. I knew James Blythe and Betsy Welch. Betsy Welch was my mother. She married a man who was called a Cherokee Indian. She married John Welch before the emigration. James Blythe married Sallie Downing, a full blood Cherokee Indian. The marriage took place prior to 1835". This testimony fully accounts for the fact that none of the children of Nancy Blythe were enrolled with the Eastern Cherokees in 1835, and for the further fact that none of her children or grandchildren, except James Blythe and Betsy Welch, were enrolled in 1851. The testimony is conclusive that Nancy Blythe, the ancestor of these claimants, was a white woman, and as they make no claim through any other source, their applications must all be rejected. At the personal request of Mrs. Belva A. Lockwood, attorney for most of these claimants, John H. Sutherland, a white man 71 years of age was examined. (See Miscel. Test. P. 1635). He testifies as follows: "I was born in Spartanburg Co., S.C. and lived there until 1859, and then moved to Madison Co., N.C. I know James L. McDonald, and I have known him since coming to this county. I did not know him or any of his family prior to that time. All I know about Annie or Nancy Blythe's Indian blood is what I heard my mother tell a neighbor woman one day. My mother's name was Martha Sutherland. My mother said that when she was first married there came to their home near Greenville, S.C., a very fine looking Cherokee Indian – the finest she had ever seen – and they had a lady there by the name of Annie Barnes who was a quadroon or half-breed Cherokee Indian, and the prettiest woman she ever saw. That big Indian fell in love with Annie Blythe and there was a man there by the name of Johnathan Blythe, who was a little man but a swift runner, and this Annie Blythe was an interpreter. The Chief of the Indians was a man by the name of Oo-sta-alle, and Annie Barnes acted as his interpreter, and he adopted Annie Barnes. A big Indian wanted to marry Annie Barnes, as did Johnathan Blythe, and the Indian wanted to fight for her but the Chief said it would not be fair, but that if he could outrun Johnathan Blythe, he could have her, and they had a race and Johnathan beat and so married Annie Barnes. This happened after my mother was married. My mother died in 1880 and she was then about 80 years of age. My mother said that this Chief Oo-sta-alle was a Cherokee Indian. My mother said that the Indians left Greenville after Annie Barnes' marriage and moved to Toxoway and then to the Little Tenn. River". This pretty little romance, is, of course, not testimony but if it is true it is perfectly evident that the Annie Barnes who was there married to Johnathan Blythe, could not have been the ancestor of these claimants, as their ancestor was certainly a grandmother at the time of the alleged contest for the hand of the said Annie Barnes.

App: 154 Adolphus Adams and 3 children, Gillsville, Ga.
Rejected. This applicant claims through Annie Blythe. See full report in #153.

App: 155 Maria Crane, Baltimore, Md. 222 W. Madison St.
Admitted. Sister of #74.

App: 156 Malissia J. Matheson and 3 children, Maysville, Ga.
Rejected. This applicant claims through Annie Blythe. See full report in #153.

App: 157 Alex S. Hampton and 6 children, Maysville, Ga.
Rejected. This applicant claims through Annie Blythe. See full report in #153.

App: 158 Sarah Watson, Urbana, Ill.
Rejected. It does not appear that ancestors were ever enrolled, or were parties to the treaties of 1835-6 and 1846. Applicant shows no real connection with the Eastern Cherokees. (Miscel. Test. P. 2656).

App: 159 Pickens E. Willis, Dawsonville, Ga.
Admitted. Applicant enrolled by the Act of Congress. Brother, Priestly Willis, enrolled by Chapman #2005. Applicant's father dead in 1851. Mother enrolled by Chapman #2009 as Mary Burnhill. See "Remarks" in application.

App: 160 Lucinda Vaught and 3 children, Webbers Falls, Okla.
Admitted. Applicant's mother, Mary Simmons, was enrolled in 1851 by Drennen, F1. 95. Brothers, George and Thomas, also enrolled, F1. 95. Grandfather, Moses Otterlifter, and his children, Betsy, David, Rachel and others enrolled in 1851 by Drennen, F1. 61.

App: 161 Florence D. Weaver and 4 children, Briartown, Okla.
Admitted. Applicant claims through mother, Rebecca McClure, enrolled in 1851 by Chapman #1969, and her children, Susan, William and John enrolled by Chapman in 1851 #1970, 1971 and 1972, respectively. Two uncles of applicant, Bryson and Pinkney Howell, enrolled by Chapman in 1851, #1968 and #2066, respectively.

App: 162 Mary J. Norman and 3 children, Porum, Okla.
Admitted. Sister of #161 and claims through the same source. (Applicant died about Oct. 1907. See letter with application).

App: 163 Rufus Miller, Centralia, Okla.
Admitted. Rufus and several brothers and sisters are enrolled with their parents, Alfred and Nancy Miller, in 1851 by Drennen, G.S. 398.

App: 164 Samuel Candy, Claremore, Okla.
Rejected. A Samuel Candy appears on the Old Settler roll, Tah. 126, and in application, applicant states his parents, Thomas and Susan Candy, were Old Settlers. These names appear on the O..S. roll, Tah. 126.

App: 165 Catherine H. King, Maple, Okla.
Admitted. Applicant claims through mother, Catherine Autrey, enrolled in 1851 by Chapman #1802. Brothers and sisters of applicant enrolled by Chapman in 1851, Columbus #1807, Edward #1806, Elizabeth #1805, Martha #1804, Mary A. #1803.

App: 166 Catherine H. King, Maple, Okla.
Duplicate of #165.

App: 166 1/2 Jackson J. King and 1 child, Maple, Okla.
Admitted. Son of #165 and claims through the same source.
App: 167 Nancy Walden and 4 children, Childers, Okla.
Admitted. Applicant claims through Judge or John Butler enrolled in 1851 by Drennen G.S. 699. Half-uncles, John and Joseph enrolled by Drennen, G.S. 703. Aunt Ann enrolled, G.S. 166. See statement with testimony. (Miscel. Test. P. 4109 and 4110).
App: 168 Katie Snell, South West City, Mo.
Admitted. Claimant under the name of Caty, step-father Moses, mother, Uh-sa-kee, and half-brothers and sisters enrolled by Drennen in 1851, Tah. 126. (Miscel. Test. P. 4285).
App: 169 Allen Latta, Ada, Okla.
Rejected. Enrolled as a Chickasaw Indian. Chickasaw by Marriage. (Miscel. Test. P. 2164).
App: 170 Reddy A. Reese, Manard, Okla.
Admitted. Applicant claims through mother, Widow Reese, and is enrolled as Roderick with her and several brothers and sisters by Drennen in 1851, Tah. 251.
App: 171 Berly E. Geny and 1 child, Hutchinson, Kans., 228 E. Sherman St.
Admitted. Applicant claims through mother who was not living in 1851. Mother's father, Oscar Rogers, enrolled by Drennen in 1851, Del. 925. His children, John, Catherine, Josef-Ann are also enrolled by Drennen in 1851, Del. 925. Great grandfather, Joseph Rogers, enrolled in 1835.
App:172 Luke Sapsucker and 3 children, Zena, Okla.
Admitted. Applicant enrolled in 1851 by Drennen, Del. 245, with his brother, Levi, and parents - Chu-aah-chuck-er. Many of the brothers and sisters of applicant enrolled by Drennen, Del. 257.
App: 173 Edward McDonald and 3 children, Okra, Okla.
Rejected. Applicant born in 1840 but does not appear on the 1851 roll. He was born in Marion Co., Tenn. outside of the Cherokee domain. Grandparents and uncles on the roll of 1835 and some of them on the 1851 roll, but the mother does not appear. She should have been enrolled on the 1835 roll as to age, but was probably with the Choctaw tribe, having married a Choctaw. Applicant not enrolled by the Dawes Commission.
App: 174 Mary Squirrel, Locust Grove, Okla.
Admitted. Applicant claims through father, Johnson, enrolled in 1851 by Drennen, G.S. 66, with his mother, Nancy, brother, Sal-lah-tee-skee, and sister Lucy, father Kah-tah-la-nah. (Miscel. Test. P. 3847).
App: 175 Betsey Swimmer and 3 children, Rose, Okla.
Admitted. Claims through self enrolled as Betsey Sunday, father, William Sunday, mother Caty Sunday, brother James Sunday, sister Nelly Sunday, enrolled by Drennen in 1851, Sal. 80.
App: 176 Lucy Proctor, Rose, Okla.
Admitted. Applicant was enrolled by Drennen in 1851, F1. 87, under the name of Lucy. She was enrolled with her husband, Ta-Kah-no-see.
App:177 Winnie Sixkiller, Stilwell, Okla.
Admitted. Applicant together with parents enrolled by Drennen in 1851, G.S. 177.

App: 178 Johnson Downing, Peggs, Okla.
Admitted. Applicant enrolled in 1851 by Drennen, Tah. 558, under the name of Johnson Downing. His father, Daniel Downing, was enrolled in the same group, also mother and sisters.

App: 179 Nancy Pegg and 1 child, Locust Grove, Okla.
Admitted. Father and father's parents enrolled in 1851 by Drennen, Sal. 320, under the names of Ar-ta-yor and Jesse Deer-skin and Tse-york-er. (Miscel. Test. P. 3878 and 5776.)

App: 180 Ida Rowe, Locust Grove, Okla.
Admitted. Applicant's grandfather enrolled by Drennen in 1851, G.S. 89.

App: 181 Katie Littlebird, Locust Grove, Okla.
Admitted. Daughter of #87. Claims through the same source. Claimant enrolled by Drennen in 1851 as Caty Mouse. Sal. 213.

App: 182 Patsy Johnson, Locust Grove, Okla.
Admitted. Applicant enrolled in 1851 by Drennen, Tah. 345 under the name of Patsy. She was enrolled with her sister, Lucretia Tadpole. (Applicant died July 12, 1907).

App: 183 Lewis W. Ross, Locust Grove, Okla.
Admitted. Father of applicant enrolled in 1851 by Drennen, Sal. 450, under the name of Joseph Ross. His mother was enrolled under the name of Ruthy Drew, with her mother, Martha Riley, Sal. 450. Nephew of #145.

App: 184 Runaway Bridge, Locust Grove, Okla.
Admitted. Father of applicant was enrolled by Drennen in 1851, Sal. 349 under the name of Nar-hoo-lar. Grandfather on father's side enrolled in same group under the name of Setting on the Bridge. Cousin of #82.

App: 185 Luney McClain and 4 children, Locust Grove, Okla.
Admitted. Father of applicant was enrolled in 1851 by Drennen, Ill. 260 under the name of Lewis McClean. (Miscel. Test. P. 3780).

App: 186 Dick Rowe, Locust Grove, Okla.
Admitted. Son of James Rowe, App. #195, who was enrolled by Drennen in 1851, F1. 22.

App: 187 James Parris, Rose, Okla
Admitted. Applicant and his mother enrolled in 1851 by Drennen, G.S. 253 under the names of James and Anna Parris. Father of claimant appears to be an Old Settler. (See O.S. Roll).

App: 188 Stephen Foreman, Locust Grove, Okla.
Admitted. Father of applicant was enrolled by Drennen in 1851, G.S. 326 under the name of Edward Foreman. Applicant's parents were separated and it is probable that he (applicant's father) had married again. Paternal grandparents enrolled in 1851 by Drennen, G.S. 329. Maternal grandparents enrolled in 1851 by Drennen, F1. 85.

App: 189 Mary Downing and 1 child, Locust Grove, Okla.
Admitted. Applicant and her parents were enrolled in 1851 by Drennen, Sal. 212, under the names of Kar-ter-ka-we, David Kar-ter-wal-le and Tar-ne.

App: 190 Napoleon B. Rowe, Locust Grove, Okla.
Rejected. Applicant and his parents were enrolled on the Old Settler roll, Page 40.

App: 191 David Downing and 2 children, Locust Grove, Okla.
Admitted. Applicant's mother enrolled in 1851 by Drennen, Sal. 280.

App: 192 Thomas Pegg and 1 child, Locust Grove, Okla.
Admitted. Nephew of #89. Claims through the same source.

App: 193 Blue Murphy, Locust Grove, Okla.
Admitted. Applicant's grandparents enrolled in 1851 by Drennnen, F1. 22 and 528. (Miscel. Test. P. 3782).

App: 194 Thomas F. Conseen, Locust Grove, Okla.
Admitted. Applicant is entitled through mother and father. Mother was not born in 1851, grandfather, Joseph L. Martin, enrolled in 1851 by Drennen, Sal. 468. Applicant's father enrolled on Old Settler roll F1. 22 as Car-tas-kee. Maternal grandmother enrolled on Old Settler roll under maiden name, Sal. #93.

App: 195 James Rowe, Locust Grove, Okla.
Admitted. Applicant enrolled by Drennen in 1851, F1. 22. His mother enrolled in the same group. His grandparents, Arch and Jennie Rowe, enrolled in 1851 by Drennen, F1. 21.

App: 196 Rebecca Blackbird, Locust Grove, Okla.
Rejected. It appears from the testimony in #185 and from the application filed by applicant, that she is an Old Settler.

App: 197 Dave Hitchcock, Murphy, N.C.
Rejected. Applicant and ancestors were slaves. (See application and letter).

App: 198 John Hitchcock, Murphy, N.C.
Rejected. Son of #197 and claims through same source.

App: 199 Hill Stansill and 3 children, Baron, Okla.
Admitted. Applicant's grandmother enrolled in 1851 by Drennen, S.B. 117. (Miscel. Test. P. 3348).

App: 200 Lucy Ellen Johnson, Oklahoma City, Okla.
311 N. Walker St.
Rejected. Sister of #262 and claims through the same source.

App: 201 Susie J. Martin and 7 children, Leach, Okla.
Admitted. Applicant's mother, Sarah Ann Clark, and her grandmother, Ann Clark, enrolled in 1851 by Drennen, Del. 864.

App: 202 Rachel Tootle and 2 children, Marble City, Okla.
Admitted. Applicant's parents, Dick and Wutty Chu-ke-la-te, enrolled in 1851 by Drennen, F1. 321.

App: 203 Thomas Sanders and 5 children, Stilwell, Okla.
Admitted. Applicant's mother enrolled by Drennen in 1851, S.B. 178.

App: 204 Riley Ragsdale, Baron, Okla.
Admitted. Applicant's father enrolled in 1851 by Drennen, F1. 401.

App: 205 Annie Leach, Leach, Okla.
Admitted. Applicant and his[sic] parents enrolled in 1851 by Chapman, Nos. 1920, 1916 and 1917. Applicant's father, although enrolled by Chapman, was a white man. Applicant gets her Cherokee blood from her mother. (See Siler and Sweatland rolls).

App: 206 Fannie Tipton, Leach, Okla.
Admitted. Sister of #205 and claims through the same source. Applicant herself enrolled by Chapman in 1851, #1926.

App: 207 Emily Bennett, Muskogee, Okla.
Admitted. Applicant enrolled by Drennen in 1851, Sal. 458.
App: 208 Mary E. Cobb and 5 children, Muskogee, Okla.
Admitted. Applicant's father enrolled in 1851 by Drennen, Del. 867.
App: 209 Mary P. Lyman, Talala, Okla.
Admitted. Applicant enrolled by Drennen in 1851, Ill. 6. Mother, Elisa Patrick (Hilderbrand) enrolled in 1851, Ill. 6 by Drennen.
App: 210 Whit Burrows and 3 children, Talala, Okla.
Admitted. Applicant's mother and grandmother enrolled by Chapman in 1851, #1866 and 1867. Great grandfather enrolled in 1835, Charles Harris.
App: 211 William Lewis Raper, Choteau, Okla.
Admitted. Claims through grandfather enrolled as Lewis Raper; great grandfather, Jesse Raper; great grandmother, Mary Raper; great uncle, Martin Raper; great aunt Martha Raper; great uncle Gabriel Raper; great uncle Powell Raper; great uncle Lonzo Raper, great aunt Rachel Raper. All were enrolled by Chapman in 1851, Nos. 1422 to #1430 inclusive.
App: 212 John A. Raper, Choteau, Okla.
Admitted. Great uncle of #227. Applicant enrolled by Chapman in 1851, #1408.
App: 213 Jesse Busheyhead[sic] and 7 children, South West City, Mo.
Admitted. Claims through father enrolled as Bird Bushyhead, mother enrolled as Ti-yane. Both enrolled by Drennen in 1851, Sal 559.
App: 214 Lydia Roberts, Oologah, Okla.
Admitted. Claims through father, Ah-quan-Kee, and through mother Che-nah-yee, both enrolled in 1851 by Drennen, G.S. 208. (Miscel. Test. P. 2441).
App: 215 Susannah Edmonds and 3 children, South West City, Mo.
Rejected. Applicant's parents were enrolled as Old Settlers in 1851, as Joseph and Sabra England. Susana England, William, Cornelius and Sabra England, See Old Settler Roll, Del. 30.
App: 216 Margrett Hanan and 10 children, Talala, Okla.
Admitted. Applicant's mother enrolled in 1851 by Drennen, Ill. 1. Applicant's grandmother enrolled at the head of same group.
App: 217 Amanda C. Summers, Talala, Okla.
Admitted. First cousin of # 98 and claims through the same source.
App: 218 Lena Stallsworth and 1 child, Talala, Okla.
Admitted. Claims through father enrolled as John L. Adair. Aunt enrolled as Ann A. Adair. Aunt enrolled as Elizabeth O. Adair. All were enrolled by Drennen in 1851, Fl. 243.
App: 219 John Haney and 3 children, Duvall, N.C.
Rejected. It does not appear that any ancestor was a party to the treaties of 1835-6 and 1846, nor does it appear that any ancestor was ever enrolled. Shows no real connection with the Eastern Cherokees. (Miscel. Test. 1368 and 1369).
App: 220 Evelyn Victoria Green, (Note: *Hand Written*) *Denver, Colo. c/o Cherokee Com. Co.* ~~Koles, Okla.~~
Admitted. Claims through grandmother enrolled as Catharine Rogers by Drennen in 1851, Del. 925. Cousin once removed of #171.

App: 221 Charles M. Kell, Vallejo, Cal., 329 Capitol St.
Rejected. The name of the applicant and that of the mother on the Old Settler roll. Names of ancestors not on Eastern Cherokee rolls.

App: 222 James L. McDonald, Grandview, N.C.
Rejected. Applicant claims through Annie Blythe. See full report in #153.

App: 223 Sarah McKinzie and 1 child, Ardmore, Okla.
Rejected. It does not appear that applicant or the ancestors through whom he[sic] claims were enrolled with the Eastern Cherokees. It is not shown that ancestors were parties to the treaties of 1835-6 and 1846.

App: 224 Enoch Six, South West City, Mo.
Admitted Applicant's father enrolled as Ah-te-tle-daw-he by Drennen in 1851, Del. 806. Paternal grandparents enrolled in same group. (Miscel. Test. P. 4286, 4303 and 3668).

App: 225 Susie Jordan and 6 children, Kansas Okla.
Admitted. Claims through mother enrolled as Lucy Crittenden. Grandfather enrolled as Harry Crittenden. Grandmother enrolled as Suky Crittenden. Aunts and uncles enrolled as Charles, John, George, Rebecca, Mary, Sarah and Charlotte Crittenden. All enrolled by Drennen in 1851, G.S. 316.

App: 226 Joshua Sixkiller and 3 children, Brushy, Okla.
Admitted. Claims through mother enrolled as Martha Hood. Grandfather enrolled as David Hood. Uncles and aunts enrolled as William, Catherine, Caroline, Sarah, Henry and Minerva Hood. All enrolled in 1851 by Drennen, S.B. 130.

App: 227 Charles Raper and 2 children, Oolagah, Okla.
Admitted. Claims through father enrolled as Charles Raper. Aunts enrolled as Ailsey, Vianna, Josephine and Julian Raper. All enrolled in 1851 by Chapman, Nos. 1417 to 1421 inclusive.

App: 228 George Ketcher and 5 children, Baptist, Okla.
Admitted. Applicant's father, Richard Tecahneyeske, (App. 3812) enrolled as Richard (last name in group) by Drennen in 1851, G.S. 496, enrolled with uncle and his family. (See Test. P. 3552). Applicant's mother enrolled as Martha Whiting in 1851 by Drennen, Tah. 605. (See Test. P. 3131 and original Tah. roll). Applicant's paternal grandmother enrolled as Susan Walkingstick in 1851 by Drennen, G.S. 502. Applicant's paternal grandfather probably enrolled in 1851 by Drennen, Tah. 137. (Miscel. Test. P. 3131 – 3552)

App: 229 Harvey D. Garrison, Oklahoma City, Okla.
Rejected. Nephew of #375. Son of #233. Claims through same source.

App: 230 Hurbert Garrison, Oklahoma City, Okla.
Rejected. By G.W. Garrison, father. Nephew of #375; son of #233. Claims through same source.

App: 231 Sula Garrison, Oklahoma City, Okla.
Rejected. Niece of #375; daughter of #233. Claims through the same source.

App: 232 Elmo Garrison, Oklahoma City, Okla.
Rejected. By G.W. Garrison, father. Nephew of #375; son of #233 and claims through same source.

App: 233 George W. Garrison, deceased, Oklahoma City, Okla.
Rejected. Brother of #375 and claims through same source.

App: 234 Pauline Garrison, Oklahoma City, Okla.
Rejected. Niece of #375; daughter of #233. Claims through same source.
App: 235 Allie L.G. Overholser, Oklahoma City, Okla.
Rejected. Niece of #375; daughter of #233. Claims through same source.
App: 236 Malvern L. Garrison, Oklahoma City, Okla.
Rejected. By G.W. Garrison, father Nephew of #375; son of #233. Claims through same source.
App: 237 Thomas M. Raper and 6 children, Murphy, N.C.
Admitted. Uncle of #211 and claims through the same source.
App: 238 Alford Haney, Lookout, N.C.
Rejected. Brother of #219 and claims through the same source.
App: 239 William R. Mulkey, Ramona, Okla.
Admitted. Applicant enrolled in 1851 by Drennen, Tah. 238. Brother of #277.
App: 240 Anna Alberty and 3 children, Pryor Creek, Okla.
Admitted. Applicant claims through parents enrolled as E.B. Towers and Charlotte Towers. Brothers enrolled as M.E. Towers, I.C. Towers, William J. and Elizabeth Towers. All enrolled in 1851 by Drennen, G.S. 56.
App: 241 Cora A. Rogers, Ft. Gibson, Okla.
Admitted. First cousin of #47 and claims through same source.
App: 242 Angeline Carpenter and 4 children, Talala, Okla.
Admitted. Claims through mother enrolled as Mary Fields, Jr. Uncles enrolled as George and Ezekiel Fields. All enrolled in 1851 by Drennen, Del. 135.
App: 243 Rosettie Deshane and 3 children, Catale, Okla.
Admitted. Sister of #242 and claims through the same source.
App: 244 Mary Dick, Catale, Okla.
Admitted. Mother of #242. Enrolled as Mary Fields, Jr., Del. 135.
App: 245 Ruth J. Hawkins and 3 children, White Oak, Okla.
Admitted. Sister of #242 and claims through the same source.
App: 246 George Dick, Catale, Okla.
Admitted. Brother of #242 and claims through the same source.
App: 247 Washington Dick and 6 children, Catale, Okla.
Admitted. Brother of #242 and claims through the same source.
App: 248 Johnathan R. Payne and 2 children, Claremore, Okla.
Admitted. Claims through mother enrolled as Caroline Foster. Grandfather enrolled as John Foster. Grandmother enrolled as Nancy Foster. Uncles and aunts enrolled as Benjamin Foster, Mary, Samuel and Margaret Foster. All enrolled in 1851 by Drennen, G.S. 243.
App: 249 John Sturdivant, Cherokee City, Ark.
Admitted. Claims through self enrolled as John Sturdivant. Mother enrolled as Avry Sturdivant. Brothers and sisters enrolled as Butler, Robert, Martha and Sabra Sturdivant. All enrolled by Drennen in 1851, G.S. 315.
App: 250 Sarah Elizabeth Sturdivant, Cherokee City, Ark.
Admitted. Claims through self enrolled as Elizabeth McLaughlin. Father enrolled as Andrew McLaughlin; step-mother enrolled as Elizabeth McLaughlin. Brothers and sisters enrolled as George, William, Anne, James, Andrew, Mary and Joshua McLaughlin. All were enrolled by Drennen in 1851 in Delware[sic] District #857.

App: 251 Thos. T. Rogers and 1 child. Cowskin, Mo.
Admitted. Applicant and mother enrolled in 1851 by Drennen, Can. 54. Applicant's father, Robert Rogers, was enrolled by Chapman in 1851 #1827. Applicant's parents separated, the wife going to Oklahoma.

App: 252 Jane Snail Bushyhead, South West City, Mo.
Admitted. Applicant's father, John Snail, and his mother, Akey, enrolled in 1851 by Drennen, Del. 128. (Miscel. Test. P. 2978 – 2981).

App: 253 Lucy L. Keys, Vinita, Okla.
Admitted. Applicant enrolled in 1851 by Drennen, Dis. 40, and her mother, Lydia Hoyt, enrolled in 1851 by Drennen, Dis. 38.

App: 254 Cleranda Downing Martin and 4 children, Texanna, Okla.
Admitted. Applicant's parents, Benjamin and Peggy Downing, enrolled in 1851 by Drennen, Tah. 539.

App: 255 Henry Hall, Oolagah, Okla.
Rejected. It does not appear that ancestors were ever enrolled or were parties to the treaties of 1835-6 and 1846. Applicant claims through his mother, Margaret Caulk, who was the daughter of Elebian Caulk and Rhoda Caulk. Rhoda Caulk was the daughter of John and Edith Schrimsher. Applicant does not claim through his father's side for the reason that they were white people. His grandmother, Rhoda Caulk, had the following brothers and sisters: Isaac, Martin, Lee Schrimsher, and Margaret Rogers nee Schrimsher. Applicant's grandmother was not enrolled in 1835 or 1851. Neither were any of her brothers and sisters enrolled, except Martin Schrimsher, who was enrolled in 1835 at the head of a family of 5, consisting of 1 male under 18 years of age, 1 male over 18, 2 females under 16 and 1 female over 16 years of age. In the family there were 3 quadroons, one half-blood and one white person associated by marriage. From investigation, it would appear that the white person was Martin Schrimsher. He was not living in 1851 and therefore was not enrolled at that time, but he had a brother by the name of Isaac Schrimsher, who was living in 1851, who had a family at the time. All the members of Isaac Schrimsher's family were enrolled in 1851 with the exception of himself. (See Del. 966). None of the other brothers and sisters of Rhoda Caulk, except as above named, were ever enrolled. Referring to Application #2977, the applicant who was the daughter of Isaac Schrimsher, and a niece of Rhoda Caulk, Martin Schrimsher, Lee Schrimsher and Margaret Rogers, in her application under "Remarks", states that her father's people were white. Therefore, from the fact that Rhoda Caulk and all her brothers and sisters with the exception of Martin Schrimsher were living in 1851 and were not enrolled at that time or at any other time, from the fact that Isaac Schrimsher was expressly left off of the roll of 1851, and from the fact that applicant #2977 expressly states that her father's people were white, we are forced to the conclusion that they were white people, and that the said Martin Schrimsher was enrolled in 1835 because of the fact that he had married a Cherokee woman and was an adopted white man. Applicants are enrolled by the Dawes Commission, however. in Miscel. Test. P. 2594, witness, in part of the lines 7 and 8, state that he was enrolled on the doubtful list. The fact that Martin Schrimsher was on the 1835 roll may account for the applicants being enrolled by the Dawes Commission. In view of the premises, this group of cases is rejected.

App 256 Sarah Mayfield, Oolagah, Okla.
Admitted. Applicant and her mother, Sally Foreman, were enrolled in 1851 by Drennen, G.S. 242.

App: 257 Sarah A. Ditmore, Ranger, N.C.
Rejected. This applicant claims through Annie Blythe. See full report in #153.
App: 258 Ulysses F. Ditmore and 2 children, Ranger, N.C.
Rejected. This applicant claims through Annie Blythe. See full report in #153.
App: 259 Ples Henry Ditmore and 5 children, Ranger, N.C.
Rejected. This applicant claims through Annie Blythe. See full report in #153.
App: 260 Charles L. Ditmore, Ranger, N.C.
Rejected. This applicant claims through Annie Blythe. See full report in #153.
App: 261 John Duck and 1 child, Claremore, Okla.
Admitted. Applicant claims through Sally Duck who was enrolled by Drennen in 1851, Fl. 282.
App: 262 Nellie Shorter, Shawnee, Okla. 326 N. Penn. Ave.,
Rejected. It does not appear that ancestors were ever enrolled or were parties to the treaties of 1835-6 and 1846. Applicant shows no real connection with the Eastern Cherokees. (Miscel. Test. P. 2703).
App: 263 Leverda A. Tatum and 3 children, Cornelia, Ga.
Rejected. Applicant claims through Annie Blythe. See full report in #153.
App: 264 Susie Partain, Rush Springs, Okla.
Admitted. Niece of #187. Applicant's mother enrolled as Letha Parris in 1851 by Drennen, G.S. 253.
App: 265 James K. Landrum and 3 children, Echo, Okla.
Admitted. Applicant's father, Hiram Landrum, and his grandfather, Charles Landrum, enrolled in 1851 by Drennen, Del. 43.
App: 266 Sarah A. Brown and 4 children, Narcissa, Okla.
Admitted. Niece of #390. Applicant's mother enrolled by Drennen in 1851, Del. 142.
App:267 George T. Candy, Rose, Okla.
Admitted. Applicant's grandparents, Jack and Darkey Candy, enrolled in 1851 by Drennen, Ill 181, and his father, Chu-law-qua enrolled in same group.
App: 268 John R. Hurst and 2 children, Chetopa, Kans.
Admitted. Applicant's mother and grandfather enrolled in 1851 by Drennen, Del. 943.
App: 269 Martha Woodard and 1 child, McLain, Okla.
Admitted. Mother of #94 and claims through the same source.
App: 270 Charlotte Scott, Nowata, Okla.
Admitted. Niece of #187. Applicant's mother enrolled in 1851 by Drennen, G.S. 253.
App: 271 Mary E. Balentine and 2 children, Vinita, Okla.
Admitted. Daughter of #253 and claims through same source.
App: 272 Lenorie E. Haddock, Moneta, Cal.
Rejected. Claims through Elizabeth Eddings, daughter of Dave Weaver. See report in #45.
App: 273 Daniel M. Williams and 3 children, Isabella, Tenn.
Admitted. Applicant's grandparents, Edmund and Jane Fallen, enrolled on Act of Congress roll.

App: 274 James D.M. Williams and 2 children, Isabella Tenn.
Admitted. Brother of #273 and claims through same source.

App: 275 Judge Jones, Grove, Okla.
Admitted. Applicant's parents, Jesse and Sale Jones enrolled in 1851 by Drennen, Del. 237.

App: 276 Tobitha Anderson, Gdn. for 3 children, Shooting Creek, N.C.
Rejected. There are a large number of applicants claiming as descendants of Martin Maney and Keziah Vann Maney. This family has been the subject of dispute among the Cherokees a number of times, and from the various reports on file in the Indian office, it appears that Martin Maney was an Irishman and died about 1832 or 1833; that he served in the Revolutionary War and in the Expedition of Col. Rutherford against the Cherokees. His wife was named Keziah and was said to have been the daughter of one Agnes Weatherford, a white woman, and the claim was made that John Vann, a part Cherokee, was her father. From the same source it appears that prior to the treaties of 1817 and 1819, Martin Maney and his wife were not living with the Cherokee Indians, but that soon after those treaties, at the suggestion of one Nehemiah Blackstock, who is reported to have been a man of fine character and great integrity, who says that he jestingly remarked to Martin Maney that he ought to make a claim to an allotment with the Cherokees. Martin Maney and his family made an effort to secure the allotment under the treaty of 1819. While he appears to have occupied the land there was a controversy as to his right to do so, and he and his family were not returned as entitled to allotments, as reported by the Secretary of War to Congress on Jan. 23, 1823. It does not appear that the Maney family were enrolled with the Eastern Cherokees in 1835, and in 1851 it appears from the records that their names were considered but their rights to enrollment were denied. Shortly after this, about 1856, under the provisions of the Act of March 3, 1855, 10th Statute at large, Page 700, a second investigation was made into the claims of those who had been omitted by Siler and Chapman in the enrollment of 1851, and the right of the Maneys was again considered and denied. Later the subject was the matter of a special report by Charles E. Mix, Acting Commissioner of Indian Affairs, to Hon. Jake Thompson, Secretary of the Interior, and the Acting Commissioner under date of Jan. 16, 1858, reviewed the entire matter, but the Maneys were not given any rights and the former action of the Secretary in rejecting their claim appears to have remained unchanged. In view of this repeated investigation on the part of the Indian Office and the Secretary of the Interior, which investigations began so many years ago, it does not appear proper to reconsider the question as to whether Keziah Maney, the daughter of Alice Weatherford, was in fact the daughter of John Vann. It certainly does not appear that this family were recognized members of the Eastern Cherokee tribe at the time of the treaty of 1835-6; nor does it appear that they ever lived with the tribe as members of the tribe. These claims are therefore rejected.

App: 277 Lewis A. Mulkey, Fawn, Okla.
Admitted. Applicant was enrolled in 1851 by Drennen, Tah. 238.

App: 278 Elizabeth Mehlin, Alluwee, Okla.
Admitted. Applicant's parents, Jackson and Ailsey R. Gourd, enrolled in 1851 by Drennen, Tah. 478.

App: 279 Agga Phariss, Choteau, Okla.
Admitted. Applicant enrolled in 1851 by Drennen, Sal. 390. Applicant's mother, Peggy Nellums, enrolled in 1851 by Drennen, Dis. 34.

App: 280 Mary A. Arterberry and 3 children, Choteau, Okla.
Admitted. Applicant's mother, Jinny, and her grandfather, Bullfrog, enrolled in 1851 by Drennen, Fl. 609.
App: 281 Josephine B. Johnson and 2 children, Nowata, Okla.
Admitted. Applicant's mother, Polly Fivekiller, was enrolled by Drennen in 1851, Fl. 127.
App: 282 Nicholas B. McNair and 5 children, Pryor Creek, Okla.
Admitted. Applicant's parents, Nicholas B. and Mary McNair, enrolled in 1851 by Drennen, Sal. 476.
App: 283 Elizabeth Ledford and 5 children, Shooting Creek, N.C.
Rejected. Applicant claims through Keziah Vann. See full report in #276.
App: 284 Robert L. Anderson and 5 children, Shooting Creek, N.C.
Rejected. Applicant claims through Keziah Vann. See full report in #276.
App: 285 Lucius L. Owenby, Barefoot, Ga.
Rejected. Applicant claims through Keziah Vann. See full report in #276.
App: 286 Rilative Ledford, Shooting Creek, N.C.
Rejected. Applicant claims through Keziah Vann. See full report in #276.
App: 287 Albert Maney and 6 children, Shooting Creek, N.C.
Rejected. Applicant claims through Keziah Vann. See full report in #276.
App: 288 Docia Anderson, Shooting Creek, N.C.
Rejected. Applicant claims through Keziah Vann. See full report in #276.
App: 289 Liddy L. Watkins and 2 children, Shooting Creek, N.C.
Rejected. Applicant claims through Keziah Vann. See full report in #276.
App: 290 Bettie S. Maney, Tree, Ga.
Rejected. Applicant claims through Kezian Vann. See full report in #276.
App: 291 Robert L. Anderson for 5 children, Shooting Creek, N.C.
Rejected. Applicants claim through Kezian Vann. See full report in #276. (Note:[sic], Repeat of #284).
App: 292 Linkeson Anderson and 1 child, Shooting Creek, N.C.
Rejected. Applicant claims through Keziah Vann. See full report in #276.
App: 293 Samantha Ledford and 4 children, Shooting Creek, N.C.
Rejected Applicant claims through Keziah Vann. See full report in #276.
App: 294 Lillie L. Arrowood, Barefoot, Ga.
Rejected. Applicant claims through Keziah Vann. See full report in #276.
App: 295 William Anderson and 3 children, Shooting Creek, N.C.
Rejected. Applicant claims through Keziah Vann. See full report in #276.
App: 296 Iler Hogsed and 3 children, Shooting Creek, N.C.
Rejected. Applicant claims through Keziah Vann. See full report in #276.
App: 297 Clingman Maney, Tree, Ga.
Reject. Applicant claims through Keziah Vann. See full report in #276.
App: 298 Sallie Ledford and 3 children, Shooting Creek, N.C.
Rejected. Applicant claims through Keziah Vann. See full report in #276.
App: 299 James Maney and 8 children, Shooting Creek, N.C.
Rejected. Applicant claims through Keziah Vann. See full report in #276.
App: 300 Lenola V. Davenport and 8 children, Shooting Creek, N.C.
Rejected. Applicant claims through Keziah Vann. See full report in #276.

App: 301 Nancy E. Owenby, Barefoot, Ga.
Rejected. Applicant claims through Keziah Vann. See full report in #276.
App: 302 Kizziar Marsengill and 3 children, Tree, Ga.
Rejected. Applicant claims through Keziah Vann. See full report in #276.
App: 303 Jennie A. Davenport, Shooting Creek, N.C.
Rejected. Applicant claims through Keziah Vann. See full report in #276.
App: 304 Wm. Anderson, Jr. and 6 children, Shooting Creek, N.C.
Rejected. Applicant claims through Keziah Vann. See full report in #276.
App: 305 Patience L. Anderson, Shooting Creek, N.C.
Rejected. Applicant claims through Keziah Vann. See full report in #276.
App: 306 B.L. Anderson Shooting Creek, N.C.
Rejected. Applicant claims through Keziah Vann. See full report in #276.
App: 307 Henry Van Maney and 2 children, Tree, Ga.
Rejected. Applicant claims through Keziah Vann. See full report in #276.
App: 308 Harvey Davenport, Shooting Creek, N.C.
Rejected. Applicant claims through Keziah Vann. See full report in #276.
App: 309 Sarah M. Owenby, Barefoot, Ga.
Rejected. Applicant claims through Keziah Vann. See full report in #276.
App: 310 Ranie A. Ledford, Shooting Creek, N.C.
Rejected. Applicant claims through Keziah Vann. See full report in #276.
App: 311 Sallie Moss, Shooting Creek, N.C.
Rejected. Applicant claims through Keziah Vann. See full report in #276.
App: 312 Mary E. A. James, Fairland, Okla.
Admitted. Applicant's father enrolled by Drennen in 1851, Del. 957.
App: 313 Sylvania B. Hudson and 1 child, Fairland, Okla.
Admitted. Brother of #312 and claims through the same source.
App: 314 John R. Allison and 6 children, Talala, Okla.
Admitted. Applicant's mother enrolled as Mary E. Alison[sic] in 1851 by Drennen, Del. 875.
App: 315 Sarah Jane Reece and 4 children, Spring Place, Ga. R.F.D. 3
Rejected. Applicant claims through father, Anderson Green Franklin, who was born in S.C. in 1823, and Gardner Green, applicant's great great grandfather. Applicant's father is living and has filed Application #1774. Neither applicant nor his father nor grandfather nor great grandmother were ever enrolled, although they were living nearby or within the Cherokee country, and if recognized Eastern Cherokees since 1800 or prior thereto, some of them would certainly have been enrolled. They do not establish fact of descent from the Gardner Green on the 1835 roll, and even if they did, would not be entitled as there are two generations who should have been enrolled in 1835 as they were old enough and were heads of families at that time. (See application #1774). (Note: Handwritten to the side. *See report on #5145*).
App: 316 Jesse Locust and 5 children, Porum, Okla.
Admitted. Applicant's father, Joe Locust, enrolled in 1851 by Chapman #939. (Miscel. Test. P. 3204).
App: 317 William J. Eldridge and 2 children, Oolagah, Okla.
Admitted. Applicant's father, Jefferson Eldridge, enrolled in 1851 by Drennen,

G.S. 191. Applicant's grandmother, Alsie Eldridge, probably enrolled in 1851 by Drennen, G.S. 188 as Alsie Murphy. (See App. #12506).

App: 318 Sarah Cunigan and 1 child, Grove, Okla.
Admitted. Applicant's father, Jack Ballard, enrolled in 1851 by Drennen, Dis. 12. Applicant's grandfather, Arch Ballard, enrolled in 1851 by Drennen, Dis. 11.

App: 319 Vaden Wicked, Bartlesville, Okla.
Admitted. Applicant's father, John N. Wicked (Wicket) enrolled in 1851 by Chapman, #1986, also grandfather, John Wicket enrolled in 1851 by Chapman #1985.

App: 320 Lelia M. Carey, Nowata, Okla.
Admitted. Applicant's grandfather enrolled in 1851 by Drennen, Walker Carey, Tah. 346.

App: 321 Flora Carey, et al, Nowata, Okla.
By Emma M. Carey, Gdn.
Admitted. Brothers and sisters of #320 and claim through same source.

App: 322 Margaret E. Toombs and 1 child, Muskogee, Okla.
Rejected. Ancestors not enrolled. Were not parties to the treaties of 1835-6 and 1846. Does not establish genuine connection with the Cherokee tribe. Applicant received certain Old Settler money in 1901 from the estate of his[sic] deceased uncle, James Smith, but she does not appear to be entitled through either side. (Miscel. Test. P. 3126).

App: 323 Bettie Rodgers, Nowata, Okla.
Admitted. Applicant's maternal grandparents enrolled in 1851 by Drennen as Johnson Robbins, G.S. 684 and Sarah Hummingbird, G.S. 517.

App: 324 John Lowry and 2 children, Nowata, Okla.
Admitted. Applicant enrolled as John Fourkiller in 1851 by Drennen, G.S. 476. His mother enrolled as Lucy Fourkiller in same group. Maternal grandfather enrolled in 1851 by Drennen at the head of group, G.S. 475. Applicant's father enrolled as William Lowry in 1851 by Drennen, F1. 83.

App: 325 Spencer Shelton, Nowata, Okla.
Admitted. Applicant enrolled with his mother in 1851 by Drennen, F1. 538.

App: 326 William C. Betterton, Grove, Okla.
Admitted. Applicant claims through father, George Thomas Henson, enrolled in 1851 by Chapman, #1313. (Miscel. Test. P. 2669).

App: 327 William Star, deceased, Grove, Okla.
By Sarah Starr[sic], widow,
Admitted. Claims for husband who died Aug. 15, 1906. Husband's father enrolled as George. Mother enrolled as Ool-soar-ste in 1851 by Drennen, Del. 317.

App: 328 James R. Gourd, Alluwee, Okla.
Admitted. Applicant's mother enrolled in 1851 by Drennen, as Letha Parris, G.S. 253.

App: 329 Salley England, Dodge, Okla.
Admitted. Applicant enrolled as Sah-linda Scraper in 1851 by Drennen, Del. 337.

App: 330 Paulina Williams and 1 child, Dodge, Okla.
Admitted. Applicant's mother enrolled in 1851 by Drennen, S.B. 40.

App: 331 Louisa Privat, Grove, Okla.
Admitted. Applicant was enrolled in 1851 by Drennen, under her maiden name, Louisa Baley, Del. 401. (Miscel. Test. P. 2724).
App: 332 Susan Dougherty, Cumming, Ga.
Admitted. Sister of #352 and claims through same source.
App: 333 James R. Ruskins, Marble, N.C.
Rejected. First cousin of #119 and claims through the same source. (Miscel. Test. P. 1562).
App: 334 Pleasant Holland and 1 child, Centralia, Okla.
Admitted. Claimant and mother enrolled in 1851 by Chapman, #1996 and #1995 respectively.
App: 335 Jackson Raper and 3 children, Farner, Tenn.
Admitted. Claimant born in 1869 and enrolled by Hester #1540. Father enrolled in 1851 by Chapman #1431.
App: 336 Allice Shadwick and 6 children, Farner, Tenn.
Admitted. Sister of #335 and claims through the same source.
App: 337 Elizabeth Oldfield, Maysville, Ark.
Admitted. Claimant and parents enrolled in 1851 by Drennen, Del 586.
App: 338 Helen E. Pierce and 2 children, Nowata, Okla.
Admitted. Applicant's mother born after 1851. Grandmother, Elvira Price and her daughters, Mary and Susan, enrolled in 1851 by Drennen, Tah. 287. (Miscel. Test. P. 4131).
App: 339 Phesant Tanner and 2 children, Maysville, Ark.
Admitted. Applicant enrolled under the name of Tlun-de-stah in 1851 by Drennen, Del. 802. Claimant's father, Se-quo-ye and mother, Lucy, enrolled in same group. (Miscel. Test. P. 2974).
App: 340 Annie Oldfield and 2 children, Maysville, Ark.
Admitted. Claimant's parents and brothers and sister enrolled in 1851 by Drennen, Del. 512.
App: 341 James D. Duncan and 5 children, Blunt, Okla.
Admitted. Applicant's father and paternal grandfather enrolled in 1851 by Chapman #1792 to #1801 inclusive. Grandfather enrolled in 1835 on Page 38.
App: 342 Jesse Locust Porum, Okla.
Duplicate of #316.
App: 343 Oscar Cannon and 4 children, Ballard, Okla.
Admitted. Applicant's mother and maternal grandparents enrolled in 1851 by Chapman, Nos. 2013 and 1997 to 2001 inclusive.
App: 344 Ben Oldfield, Maysville, Ark.
Admitted. Applicant's father and paternal grandmother enrolled in 1851 by Drennen, Del. 588. Mother and maternal grandparents enrolled in 1851 by Drennen, Del. 586.
App: 345 Rider Rattler and 4 children, Porum, Okla.
Admitted. Applicant's grandfather, Choo-no-whin-kih, enrolled in 1851 by Chapman #898, also his grandmother, Ool-skar-stih, enrolled in 1851 by Chapman #576. (Miscel. Test. P. 2585).
App: 346 Martha C. Cloud, McKey, Okla.
Admitted. Sister of #106 and claims through the same source.

App: 347 James L. Moss, Mossville, Ark.
Rejected. It does not appear that ancestors were ever enrolled or were parties to the treaties of 1835-6 and 1846. Applicant shows no real connection with the Eastern Cherokees. (Miscel. Test. P 2546).
App: 348 John C. Cannon and 5 children, Siloam Springs, Ark.
Admitted. Brother of #343. Claims through same source.
App: 349 Edwin R. Cannon and 3 children, Ballard, Okla.
Admitted. Brother of #343 and claims through the same source.
App: 350 Wilson L. Cannon and 6 children, Siloam Springs, Ark.
Admitted. Brother of #343 and claims through the same source.
App: 351 William R. Quarles, Baptist, Okla.
Rejected. Applicant only claims share of his former wife who died in 1875.
App: 352 Frances E. Morris, Ballard, Okla.
Admitted. Applicant and her sisters and paternal grandmother enrolled in 1851 by Chapman, Nos. 2014 to 2017 inclusive and #2010.
App: 353 Jane Langley, Ballard, Okla.
Rejected. Applicant was not enrolled in 1851 has no ancestral Cherokee blood and only claims through her deceased husband, Lock Langley. (Miscel. Test. P. 4061).
App: 354 Marion Duncan and 1 child, Sallisaw, Okla.
Admitted. Uncle of #341 and is enrolled in 1851 by Chapman #1801.
App: 355 Joe Fox Raven, South West City, Mo.
Admitted. Applicant is admitted through his father, Caw-luh-nah, enrolled in 1851 by Drennen, Tah. 360. (Miscel. Test. P. 2664 & 2665 A)
App: 356 William Pendleton Adair, Adair, Okla.
Admitted. Applicant's father enrolled in 1851 by Chapman #1960.
App: 357 Martha Duncan, Blunt, Okla.
Admitted. Aunt of #341 and is enrolled in 1851, Chapman #1795.
App: 358 Katie Cheater or Ca-hu-cah and deceased husband, Grove, Okla.
Admitted. Applicant and her parents enrolled by Drennen in 1851, Del. 220. Husband who died on July 17, 1906 enrolled by Drennen in 1851, Del. 320.
App: 359 Thomas Rabbit, South West City, Mo.
Admitted. Brother of #358 and claims through the same source.
App: 360 William A. Day and 6 children, Big Cabin, Okla.
Admitted. Applicant's mother and grandmother enrolled in 1851 by Chapman, Nos. 1594 and 1596.
App: 361 David L. Whitaker, Andrews, N.C.
Admitted. Applicant enrolled by Chapman in 1851 #1233.
App: 362 George Whitmire, Hayden, Okla.
Admitted. Brother of #323 and claims through same source.
App: 363 George W. Walker, Welch, Okla.
Admitted. Applicant and mother enrolled in 1851 by Drennen, Tah. 465.
App: 364 David Chu-a-lu-kee and 2 children, Eucha, Okla.
Admitted. Applicant's father, Chu-wa-lu-ke and mother Na-ke, enrolled in 1851 by Drennen, Del. 261. Applicant also enrolled in same group. (Miscel. Test. P. 2727).
App: 365 Susan Soldier, Eucha, Okla.
Admitted. Niece of #364 and claims through the same source.

App: 366 Moses Ridge, Chloeta, Okla.
Admitted. Claimant and parents enrolled in 1851 by Drennen, Del. 205. (Note: Middle number is blurred, could also be a 6 or an 8)
App: 367 William Hooper, Warner, Okla.
Rejected. Ancestors of applicant are not enrolled on any roll of the Eastern Cherokees. Applicant was not enrolled by the Dawes Commission. Mother of applicant was born in 1820 in Plymouth Co., N.C. 200 miles from the Cherokee domain in 1835, therefore the ancestors of applicant could not have been parties to the treaties of 1835-6 and 1846. Affidavits in #31804 show applicant to be of Choctaw blood.
App: 368 Carlie[sic] Galcatcher, Eucha, Okla.
Admitted. Applicants parents enrolled in 1851 by Drennen, Del. 570 and 643.
App: 369 Runaway Beaver and 2 children, Eucha, Okla.
Admitted. Nephew of #364 and claims through the same source.
App: 370 Sam Boney and 1 child, Cove, Okla.
Admitted. Applicant's paternal grandfather and uncles and aunts enrolled in 1851 by Drennen, Del. 714.
App: 371 James B. Hampton and 6 children, Buford, Ga.
Rejected. Applicant claims through Annie Blythe. See full report in #153.
App: 372 Wm. J. McDonald and 4 children, Athens, Tenn.
Rejected. Applicant claims through Annie Blythe. See full report in #153.
App: 373 John L. Raven, South West City, Mo.
Admitted. Brother of #355 and claims through same source.
App: 374 Bettie Cecelia Ayres, Oktaha, Okla.
Rejected. Applicant nor ancestors through whom she claims were ever enrolled. It does not appear that they were living within the limits of the Cherokee Domain in 1835-6 and 1846 as recognized members of the tribe. It does appear that they left the tribe before that time. (Miscel. Test. P. 2579).
App: 375 Emma Howard, Excelsior, Ark.
Rejected. Applicant claims her Indian blood through her mother who was married and had children in 1844. Claimant's mother and none of her ancestors appear on any Indian roll, except she claims that Ned Christy, who is on the roll of 1835, was a brother of her maternal grandmother. However, the grandmother's maiden name was Rountree and evidently she was no more than a half sister of Ned Christy and that on the side which was not Indian. Applicant states her mother was born in Tuscaloosa Co., Ala. which is over a hundred miles removed from any Cherokee domain as it was constituted in 1835. The family, therefore, if they ever lived with the Cherokees, must have left them long prior to 1835.
App: 376 Dick Pann, Hulbert, Okla.
Admitted. Claimant himself and father enrolled in 1851 by Drennen, Tah. 434.
App: 377 Roy N. Skinner, Talala, Okla.
Admitted. Claimant's maternal grandfather and great grandfather enrolled in 1851 by Drennen, Del. 866.
App: 378 Leander or Lean Vann Chu-a-lu-kee, Eucha, Okla.
Admitted. Applicant's parents enrolled in 1851 by Drennen, Del. 207.
App: 379 Houston Downing, South West City, Mo.
Admitted. Applicant's father, Noo-nah-dah-hoo-yah, is enrolled by Drennen in 1851, Del. 980.

App: 380 Lucinda Sul-sah and 1 child, South West City, Mo.
Admitted. Applicant's mother and sister enrolled in 1851 by Drennen, Sal. 134. Applicant's father enrolled in 1851, Sal. 160.

App: 381 Nathan Raper and 4 children, Eucha, Tenn, R.F.D. 2
Admitted. Brother of #227 and claims through same source.

App: 382 Sallie Thornton, Vian, Okla.
Admitted. Claimant's father and mother enrolled in 1851 by Drennen, Ill. 180 and S.B. 183.

App: 383 William W. Bean, Kilgore, Texas.
By John E. Bean, Gdn.
Admitted. Applicant's mother enrolled in 1851 by Drennen, Del. 1048. His father on the Old Settler Roll, F1. 63.

App: 384 Henrietta Bean, Kilgore, Texas.
Admitted. Applicant, mother and maternal grandparents enrolled in 1851 by Drennen, G.S. 719.

App: 385 James P. Evans, Claremore, Okla.
Admitted. Applicant's grandmother enrolled in 1851 by Drennen, G.S. 410.

App: 386 Francis E. Russell, Ballard, Okla.
Admitted. First cousin of #352 and claims through same source.

App: 387 Mary E. Sloan, Baptist, Okla.
Admitted. Sister of #17 and claims through the same source.

App: 388 Silas R. Morris, Baptist, Okla.
Admitted. Brother of #17 and claims through the same source.

App: 389 William Metcalf, Flag Pond, Tenn.
Rejected. Applicant claims through Keziah Vann. See full report in #276.

App: 390 Thomas J. McGhee and 1 child, Afton, Okla.
Admitted. Applicant enrolled in 1851 by Drennen, Del. 142 under the name of Jefferson H. McGee. Mother and brothers in same group.

App: 391 Henry B. Martin and 7 children, Aquone, N.C.
Rejected. Cousin of #126 and claims through same source.

App: 392 Richmond V. Martin and 4 children, Lookout, N.C.
Rejected. Cousin of #126 and claims through the same source.

App: 393 James P. Pace and 4 children, Marble, N.C.
Rejected. Uncle of #126 and claims through same source.

App: 394 Lester A. Pace and 1 child, Tomotla, N.C.
Rejected. Cousin of #126 and claims through same source.

App: 395 Loney F. Pace, Tomotla, N.C.
Rejected. Cousin of #126 and claims through same source.

App: 396 Alexander Pace and 4 children, Tomotla, N.C.
Rejected. Uncle of #126 and claims through same source.

App: 397 Malissie H. Coffee and 2 children, Marble, N.C.
Rejected. Cousin of #126 and claims through same source.

App: 398 Mary C. Trull and 4 children, Marble, N.C.
Rejected. Cousin of #126 and claims through same source.

App: 399 Josephine Wilson and 3 children, Marble, N.C.
Rejected. Aunt of #126 and claims through the same source.

App: 400 Augustus L. Rogers and 3 children, Duluth, Ga.
Admitted. Applicant enrolled in 1851 by Chapman #1856. Also his father #1848.
App: 401 Margaret Brackett, Vinita, Okla.
Admitted. Claimant enrolled in 1851 by Drennen, Ill. 282. (See letter in application #401).
App: 402 John Lewis Miller and 1 child, Wimer, Okla.
Admitted. Applicant's father and grandfather enrolled in 1851 by Drennen, F1. 120.
App: 403 Eliza J. Rose, Lenapah, Okla.
Admitted. Sister of #323 and claims through same source.
App: 404 Lucy I. Edwards and 1 child, Oglesby, Okla.
Admitted. Niece of #109 and claims through the same source.
App: 405 George W. Hampton and 4 children, Sallisaw, Okla.
Admitted. Applicant's mother, Delilah Hampton, enrolled in 1851 by Drennen, Dis. 76.
App: 406 Mary J. Cloud, Lenapah, Okla.
Admitted. Applicant's mother enrolled in 1851 by Drennen as Jane Horn, Tah. 55. Applicant's grandfather on 1835 roll, P. 23.
App: 407 George Sanders, Locust Grove, Okla.
Admitted. Applicant's mother, Qual-le-you-kee, and applicant himself enrolled in 1851 by Drennen, F1. 310. Applicant's father, Che-wee enrolled in 1851 by Drennen, Tah. 322. (Miscel. Test. P 3790)
App: 408 Fisher Vann, Locust Grove, Okla.
Admitted. Applicant's mother enrolled by Drennen in 1851, Sal. 152. (Miscel. Test. P. 3845).
App: 409 Walter Squirrel, Locust Grove, Okla.
Admitted. Applicant's father, mother and applicant himself enrolled in 1851 by Drennen, Sal. 409. (Miscel. Test. P. 3187).
App: 410 John Coats and 1 child, Choteau, Okla.
Admitted. Brother of #280 and claims through the same source.
App: 411 Samuel Adair and 5 children, Lenapah, Okla.
Admitted. Applicant's grandfather, Andrew Adair, enrolled in 1835 and in 1851 by Drennen, F1. 244. Applicant's father also enrolled by Drennen, F1. 244. (Miscel. Test. P. 2303).
App: 412 Sabrina Scott and 1 child, Maysville, Ark.
Admitted. Applicant;s[sic] mother and maternal grandfather enrolled in 1851 by Drennen, Dis. 15. (Miscel. Test. P. 2093 and 4290).
App: 413 Harvey M. Beck, Independence, Kans.
Admitted. Applicant's paternal grandmother and great grandfather enrolled in 1851 by Drennen, G.S. 419. See application #4042 of Mary Paden, great aunt of applicant. (Miscel. Test. P. 2132 & 2280).
App: 414 Wm. D. McGuire, Crescent, Okla.
Rejected. Applicant claims through Alexander Brown. See full report in #35. Duplicate of #22915.

App: 415 Elizabeth Ramsey and 2 children, Swain, Ark.
Rejected. Applicant nor ancestors ever enrolled. Does not establish fact of descent from a person who was a party to the treaty of 1835-6 and 1846. Applicant's ancestor through whom she claims left the Cherokees in about 1825 and lived with white people ever afterward.

App: 416 Mareyan Ramsey and 4 children, Swain, Ark.
Rejected. Claims through same source as #415.

App: 417 Geo. Washington Plummer, Saratoga, Wyo.
Rejected. Applicant is one of the Sizemore claimants. These applicants claim through Ned (or Edward), John (or Doctor Johnny Gourd), Joseph Sizemore and William Sizemore, and for convenience, they are designated the Sizemore claims. These applications number about 2000, representing approximately 5000 individuals. The claimants reside chiefly in northwestern North Carolina, northeastern Tennessee, southwestern Virginia, and southern West Virginia, and northwestern and western Alabama. The statements in the applications and affidavits filed in support of the same and in the testimony taken are not entirely consistent but substantially the same claim is made for all these individuals. More than 80 witnesses were examined in the field and their testimony will be found in Sizemore testimony, Pages 1 to 75. It does not appear that any one of the claimants or any one of the ancestors of any of the claimants was ever enrolled with the Eastern Cherokees, nor does it appear that any of these claimants or their immediate ancestors ever lived as Indians with the Cherokee Nation or with the Eastern Cherokees. None of them appears to have been living within the Cherokee Domain at the date of the treaty of 1835-6, but, on the contrary, most of these claimants or their immediate ancestors were living from 150 to 300 miles from the Cherokee Domain at that time. From the applications, affidavits and testimony, it appears that Ned Sizemore, John Sizemore, and Joseph Sizemore were brothers, but the exact date or place of birth could not be definitely determined. It is probable, however, that they were born somewhere between 1740 and 1760. Some accounts fix the place of birth as Halifax Co., Va., while others say it was Halifax Co., N.C., while still another account states that Ned Sizemore "was duly enrolled upon the rolls of the Cherokee Nation, taken and made in the year 1748, in the Catawba Reservation", and William H. Blevins, a prominent man among the claimants and one who has been largely instrumental in prosecuting this claim, testified (Sizemore Testimony P. 56): "I remember one Elisha Blevins who said that old Ned Sizemore came from the Catawba River, or the Catawba Reservation, as he called it. Elisha Blevins has been dead some time. Wesley Blevins also testified in 1896 to the same effect". This would seem to indicate that Ned Sizemore came from South Carolina, but, in any event, none of the accounts places their origin within the territory of the Cherokee Indians. The claimants who were examined as witnesses were nearly all well advanced in years and testified almost without exception that they and their parents were generally recognized as white people, that neither they nor their parents had ever received any money from the Government as Indians and had never been enrolled as such. Many of them stated that until this enrollment had been agitated they had never heard to what tribe of Indians they belonged but only that they had Indian blood. Henry A. Holland testified at Pilot Mountain, North Carolina (Sizemore Testimony P. 1) that he was 63 years of age, and that he knew John Sizemore (or Doctor Gourd) and Joseph Sizemore; that he never heard either of them state where they were born, and that: "I never heard either of them say that they were Indians. I heard that they were kin to them. I never

heard either of them say that they were kin to the Indians. I don't remember hearing it said to what Indians they were kin. There were no bands of Indians living in Stokes County in my life time, as Indians. I never heard them spoken of as Cherokees. I am not a claimant myself; I was asked to come here by Mr. Whittaker, as agent for Mrs. Belva A. Lockwood". Morgan D. Sizemore testified at Pilot Mountain, N.C. (Sizemore Test. P. 2), that he is 46 years of age, and that: "So far as I can say, I have no Indian blood. I do not know whether there is any tradition in my family that we have Indian blood. I have never heard my father, Atha Sizemore, say that he was of Indian blood". Benjamin F. King testified at Pilot Mountain, N.C. (Sizemore Test. P. 3) that he is 53 years of age and that: "I claim Indian blood from having heard my mother say that I am kin to the Indians. I remember my grandmother quite well. I do not remember ever hearing her say anything about the Indians. Neither my mother nor my grandmother ever lived with the Indians. My mother never said to what tribe of Indians she belonged – simply said she was kin to the Indians. I never heard her mention the Cherokees. Neither my mother nor my grandmother were ever enrolled with the Indians. I have never been enrolled". Tandy Bennett testified at Pilot Mountain, N.C. (Sizemore Test. Pages 4 and 5) that he is 67 years of age and has Indian blood in his veins through his mother who was a Sizemore; that his mother died in 1898 at the age of 82; that she was born in Halifax Co., Va.; that she got her Indian blood through her father, Joseph Sizemore who died in Halifax Co., Va.; that his understanding was that he was born there and that he (Joseph Sizemore) "was born here when the war broke out; he must have come to Stokes County about 1821 or 1822, but doctor Johnny Gourd came out here several years before he did. Dr. Johnny Gourd died and was buried in Stokes Co., I have seen him thousands of times and he was a very old man. I could not say that I have heard him say that he was Indian. He resembled an Indian right smart; I don't recollect his saying that he was an Indian. I remember Joseph Sizemore. I don't remember hearing him say he was an Indian. I was in the twenties when he died. I saw him frequently in my life-time and have talked some to him. He was pretty dark-skinned but he passed as a white man. I never heard of Joseph Sizemore or Dr. Gourd receiving any money from the Government as Indians nor my mother, Rebecca Bennett; if she had gotten it I would have known it. My mother lived in Stokes Co., N.C. in 1851. I never heard her say anything about any enrollment of Indians by the Government. I have heard Dr. Gourd called an old Indian doctor. I never was enrolled for any benefits as an Indian. I have heard of there being Indians ever since I can recollect. I know they have been called Cherokees. When people would get mad they would call them Cherokee Indians. They would not take it very well. I have been called a Cherokee Indian but of course I did not like it. I have always lived as a white man and have tried to fill a white man's place. There are none of our family who claim Indian blood other than through Joseph Sizemore". James H. Sizemore testified at East Bend, N.C. (Sizemore Test. P. 7 and 8), that he is 67 years of age and was born and raised in Yadkin Co., N.C.; that he has never lived with the Indians and never received any money from the government on account of his Indian blood; that his father was Isom Sizemore who was born in Halifax Co., Va. – that his father never received any money from the government on account of his Indian blood, and that: "I never heard him say to what tribe of Indians he belonged. In 1851 he lived in Stokes County and lived there in 1835 also. Dr. Johnny Gourd had fair skin and dark eyes and light hair. I remember him. He lived with my father right smart while before he died. I have heard my grandfather say that he was an Indian, but I don't recollect him telling of what Indian he was, but he said he was from Cherokee. My father voted and was mustered. My great grandfather lived in Virginia but was born and married in Cherokee, and then he moved to Virginia when my grandfather was a small boy. My grandfather, John, told me this. I have heard it said that my great grandfather, John Sizemore, was a captain in the Revolutionary War, fighting with the Colonies". John E. Stallings testified at Yadkinville, N.C. (Sizemore Test. P. 13) that he was 55 years of age and that: "I have always been a voter and my grandfather, Isom Sizemore, was a voter. I have always been considered a white man in this community". Leah M. Harris also testified at Yadkinville, N.C. (Sizemore Test. P. 14) that she is 69 years of age and that her father was Isom Sizemore, and that he died 23 years ago at the age of 92, and that he was born in Va. And that she knew Dr. Johnny Sizemore, and that: "He was born in Cherokee; I don't recollect in which Cherokee he was born; he just said he was born in Cherokee. I have always passed as a white woman and my father as a white man. I have heard Dr. John Sizemore say that he was an Indian. He said that he belonged to the white complexion Indians. I never heard him say any other tribe of Indians than that. I never paid much attention to him. He was a good looking old man and was light complexioned. I made him a suit of clothes, got him a new hat, and he shaved up and looked like another man. I have heard my father say he was kin to the Indians. I never heard him say to what tribe of Indians he was kin. When grandfather came to our house he wore his hair down on his shoulders, his beard down on his chest, and wore a little old green cap." John Henry Sizemore testified at Wilkesboro, N.C. (Sizemore Test. P. 16) that he is 61 years of age and had heard his father speak of having Indian blood; that: "He said his father was kin to the Indians. He did not say to what tribe of Indians. We always passed in the community as white people". James Woody, 84 years of age who is not a claimant but was produced as a witness on behalf of these claimants, in speaking of Ned Sizemore (Sizemore Test. P. 20) states that he had seen old Ned Sizemore. "I do not know what descent he originated from, but he was represented to be somewhat Indian". He also states that he knew Owen Sizemore and that: "I did not hear it talked when I first knew them what they were or what they originated from. Ned Sizemore was here in this country when I was a boy. Owen Sizemore was regarded as a white man but he had a little grain of Indian in him. Before this present money question came up, I never heard that the Sizemores were Cherokee Indians. They used to meet on the hills and muster. I do not know whether Ned Sizemore mustered or not, but the younger men did". Catharine Petty, 64 years of age (Sizemore Test. P. 21) testified that she was born and always lived in Ashe Co., N.C., and claims Cherokee blood through her father, David Osborn; that her father was 92 or 93 years of ageat the time of his death, which took place in 1902, and that: "I have heard my father say that he was kin to the Indians. He never said what kin we were. He never received any money from the Government on account of his Indian blood that I know of. I never knew of my father visiting the Indians. He was recognized as a white man in the community in which he lived. My father always voted". Jesse D. Osborn, a brother of Catharine Petty, testified (Sizemore Test. P. 22) that his grandfather, Jesse Osborn, lived and died in Ashe Co., N.C., and that: "I have been a voter all my life: I have never heard that the Indians visited my father or grandfather or that they ever visted[sic] the Indians". Frances M. Woody, 82 years of age and brother of James Woody referred to above, testified (Sizemore Test. P. 26) that he knew old Ned Sizemore when affiant[sic] was 17 or 18 years of age, and that Ned Sizemore was then about 60 or 70 years of age, and claimed to be a full-blood Cherokee Indian. He testified that: "I have heard old Ned say that he was an Indian many a time. He used to brag of being a Cherokee Indian. He never spoke of having received any money from the government on account of his Indian blood that I ever heard. He went backwards and forwards to Cherokee to visit the tribe many a time. He died in Allegheny Co., to the best of my recollect - that he was probably in the fifties". If the Ned Sizemore referred to was the one referred to as the ancestor of so many of these claimants, he certainly must have been more than 60 or 70 years of age when this affiant[sic] was 16 years old, and if he lived in the fifties, he must have been considerably over a hundred years of age at the time of his death. This witness testified: "Ned Sizemore's beard was not gray when I first saw him. I never knew any Indians living in this country except the Sizemores". This is the most direct testimony connecting the Sizemores with the Cherokee people and is not consistent with the testimony of his brother, James Woody, above referred to, nor with the testimony of other witnesses and claimants that Ned Sizemore came from Halifax Co. or from the Catawba Reservation. Eli J. Phipps testified at Jefferson, N.C. (Sizemore Test. P. 30) and that he is 64 years of age and lived in Ashe Co. all his life, and that: "I have always been a recognized white man in the community and have always voted. I have always been taught that I am a descendant of an Eastern Cherokee Indian". Nancy E. Porter testified at Jefferson, N.C. (Sizemore Test. P. 31) that she was born in Grayson Co., Va. And that: "I have always been taught that I have Indian blood by my father and mother and have also heard other say the same thing. I do not remember what kind of Indian they said I was descended from. My father lived with white people all of his life. I did not know of any Indians living in Grayson Co., with the exception of my father and his connections". John A. Peak testified at Grassy Creek, N.C. (Sizemore Test. P. 32) that he is 61 years of age and that: "I claim my Indian blood through my mother and the Sizemores only. My mother and her ancestors were recognized as white people but it was claimed through the country that we had Indian blood". Claban H. Pennington testified at Grassy Creek, N.C. (Sizemore Test. P. 36) that he is 77 years of age and claims his Indian blood from the Sizemore race; that "Old Ned Sizemore lived on a creek called Blackwater that ran into the Clinch River right at where he lived in Lee County, Va. Old man Owen lived up on Clinch River on the Virginia side. I suppose they were recognized white people, for there was nothing said about Indian or Negro in those days. I do not recollect hearing anything mentioned about their being Indians – I cannot remember. I did not apply because I thought I was Indian, for I did not know, but I am kin to the Sizemores". Owen Blevins testified at Grassy Creek, N.C. (Sizemore Test. P. 37) that he is 62 years of age and claims Indian blood through his father. "I heard that Sizemore was a full blood Cherokee. I have been taught that all my life. My father was a recognized white man in the community in which he lived. My father's Indian blood came through his mother, Lydia Blevins, who was a daughter of Owen Sizemore". George Blevins testified at Grassy Creek, N.C. (Sizemore Testimony P. 39) that he was born and raised in Ashe Co. and in[sic] 79 years of age, and that: "I have been a voter and was always recognized as a white man with the exception of the Indian blood in[sic] I never received any money from the Government on account of my Indian blood nor did my father. I claim Indian blood through my father's side only. He claimed to be of Cherokee Indian blood". John Baldwin also testified at Grassy Creek, N.C. (Sizemore Test. P. 40) that he is 70 years of age and was born in Ashe Co., N.C. and that: "I have always been taught that I had Cherokee Indian ancestors. My father lived in Grayson Co, Va. He was a very old man when he died". His father died in 1898. He claimed through his father's mother,

Catherine Hart. He further testified that his grandmother, Catherine Hart, lived in Ashe Co., and that: "My grandmother, father and I were considered white people, but when people got mad with us they would throw up the Indian". In this connection, it may be well to note that the Cherokee Nation surrendered all claim to the territory that now constitutes Ashe Co., N.C. by the Treaty of 1777, and no portion of Ashe County is within a hundred miles of what constituted the Cherokee domain in 1835-6. Mary A. Sullivan testified at Weasels, N.C. (Sizemore Test. P. 44) that she claims through her mother, Louisa Baldwin who is 77 years of age, who was born and raised in Grayson Co., Va. And that her mother's Indian blood came through her father, William Baldwin, who was also born in Grayson Co., Va. This is likewise in territory which was surrendered by the Cherokees as early as 1768 and is still further removed from the Cherokee domain in 1835-6. Matilda Davis testified at Weasels, N.C. (Sizemore Test. P. 47) that she is 68 years of age, was born in Ashe Co., N.C. and that: "I do not know what kind of Indians the Sizemores were throught[sic] to be. My Indian blood comes through my mother who was a Blevins. I have heard my mother say that her grandfather was a full blood Indian. His name was Neddie Sizemore. I reckon she was born in Ashe Co. and lived there most of her life". David Tucker who lives near Weasels, N.C. and who is not a claimant, testified (Sizemore Test. P. 48) that he is 87 years of age and moved to Ashe Co. when he was ten years old; that he had seen Ned Sizemore many times, that he was an old man and claimed to be Cherokee; that his acquaintance with him terminated when affiant[sic] was about grown; that he believed he went west; that the people in neighborhood recognized Ned Sizemore as an Indian, and that: "I have heard it said he took part in the war[sic] of 1812, but I do not know. Old Ned Sizemore was a preacher. I have heard him preach. He talked English very well. He did not show any signs of white blood. I have heard all through life that Old Ned ought to have a claim, although the Sizemores I have known have not talked a great deal about their Indian blood until the time of the land matters in the Indian Territory". Byron Sturgill testified at Weasels, N.C. (Sizemore Test. P. 49) that he is 62 years of age and claims his Indian blood through his mother only; that she has been dead about thirty years, and that- "She never spoke to me about her Indian blood. Cicero Price, up in the mountains, told me about my Indian blood since this Cherokee judgment. Before that, I had not heard that I was related to the Cherokees". William H. Blevins, 67 years of age, testified at Marion, Va. (Sizemore Test. P. 56) that he was born in Ashe Co., N.C. and claims through his father who lived and died in Ashe Co., N.C. That he never received any money from the Government on account of his Indian blood; and that; "I have heard my father say that old Ned Sizemore lived in what is now Allegheny Co., N.C., but was then Ashe Co. I have heard that old man Ned Sizemore's father was John Sizemore and he lived in Stokes Co., N.C. and had a son, Dr. Johnny Gourd Sizemore who was a brother of Old Ned. I remember one Elisha Blevins, who said that Old Ned Sizemore came from the Catawba River or Catawba Reservation, as he called it. Elisha Blevins has been dead some time. Wesley Blevins also testified in 1896 to the same effect. I never heard that any of the Sizemores ever received any money from the Government on account of their Indian blood. If they did, I think I should hace known it – that since I was old enough to recollect. I was not enrolled on the census of Eastern Cherokee Indians in 1885 and never heard of it before. I was not enrolled in 1851 by the Government. I did not receive any of the money paid in 1851 and none of the Sizemore family did that I know of. I have heard my father and his brothers talk something about the enrollment of 1851. They were afraid of the enrollment, were afraid they would be carried to the Territory and scattered on that account. I do not think my father was enrolled in 1835 or any of the Sizemores that I know anything of. They were afraid of enrollment. My father, Armstrong Blevins, I do not think was a party to the treaty of 1836 and 1846. Elisha Blevins who gave testimony in 1888 and 1896 before me, was not a party to the treaty of 1835 and 1836, and di[sic] not claim to be an Indian at all. I suppose Wells Blevins was living in 1835 and 1836. He lived in Ashe Co., N.C. I do not know that he was a party to the Treaty of 1835-6. I do not know that any of the descendants of the Sizemores, or Old Ned himself, ever lived with the Cherokee Indians". While it seems certain that there has been a tradition in this family that they had a certain degree of Indian blood, the testimony is entirely too indefinite to establish a connection with the Eastern Cherokee Indians at the time of the Treaty of 1835. The locality where these claimants and their ancestors are shown to have been living from a period considerably prior to 1800 up to the present time, is a territory that, during this time, has not been frequented by Cherokee Indians. It is a region much more likely to have been occupied by Indians from Va. or by the Catawba Indians who ranged from South Carolina up through North Carolina into Va. It is also significant that the name of Sizemore does not appear upon any of the Cherokee rolls. For the foregoing reasons, all of these Sizemore claims have been rejected.

App: 418 Rachel Thompson, Eucha, Okla.
Admitted. Applicant enrolled in 1851 by Drennen, Del. 728.

App: 419 Jennie Starr, Eucha, Okla.
Admitted. Applicant's parents enrolled in 1851 by Drennen, Del. 890. (Miscel. Test. P. 3405 and 3180).

App: 420 James Tanner and 5 children, Eucha, Okla.
Admitted. Applicant's father and grandfather enrolled in 1851 by Drennen, Del. 885.

App: 421 Jennie Oldfield and 3 children, Eucha, Okla.
Admitted. Sister of #420 and claims through the same source.

App: 422 Custis Harnage, Talala, Okla.
Admitted. Applicant's mother, Emily Harnage, enrolled in 1851 by Drennen, G.S. 428.

App: 423 John M. Tucker, Cherry Log, Ga.
Admitted. Applicant enrolled in 1851 by Chapman #1895. Also enrolled by Hester #1923. (Miscel. Test. P. 1401).

App: 424 William P. Tucker, Cherry Log, Ga.
Admitted. Son of #423 and claims though same source. Applicant enrolled by Hester #1829.

App: 425 Laura J. Cornett and 4 children, Cherry Log, Ga.
Admitted. Daughter of #423 and claims through same source. Applicant enrolled by Hester #1926.

App: 426 Martha A Carter and 2 children, Cherry Log, Ga.
Admitted. Daughter of #423 and claims through same source.

App: 427 Mary P. Tucker and 1 child, Cherry Log, Ga.
Admitted. Daughter of #423 and claims through same source. Applicant enrolled by Hester #1927.

App: 428 John W. Tucker and 4 children, Blue Ridge, Ga.
Admitted. Son of #423 and claims through same source. Applicant enrolled by Hester #1925.
App: 429 Elizabeth Downing and 7 children, South West City, Mo.
Admitted. Applicant's mother enrolled as Na-ke by Drennen in 1851, Del. 318. (Miscel. Test. P. 2983).
App: 430 John Starr and 2 children, Grove, Okla.
Admitted. Brother of #429 and claims through same source.
App: 431 Tom Scraper, South West City, Mo.
Admitted. Half brother of #429 and claims through same source.
App: 432 Nellie Suwagee and 1 child, South West City, Mo.
Admitted. Half sister of #429 and claims through same source.
App: 433 Henry Scraper and 1 child, South West City, Mo.
Admitted. Brother of #429 and claims through same source.
App: 434 Lourinda H. Pettit, Pawhuska, Okla.
Admitted. Sister of #405. Applicant enrolled by Drennen in 1851, Dis. 76.
App: 435 John W. Williamson, Decatur, Ill., 739 S. Colfax.
Rejected. Ancestors not enrolled. "Slave". (Miscel. Test. P 2655). (*Handwritten: See also #1383).*
App: 436 Mary E. Earnest and 1 child, Decatur, Ill.
Rejected. Sister of #435 and claims through same source.
App: 437 Margaret E. Steward and 2 children, Decatur, Ill. 437 N. Union St.
Rejected. Sister of #435 and claims through same source.
App: 438 Mattie A. Neal and 3 children, Minneapolis, Minn.
Rejected. Sister of #435 and claims through same source.
App: 439 Marcus L. Martin, Topton, N.C.
Rejected. Cousin of #126 and claims through same source.
App: 440 Nathaniel R. Martin, Topton, N.C.
Rejected. Cousin of #126 and claims through the same source.
App: 441 Louis Henry Wolfe and 6 children, Louisville, Tenn.
Admitted. Brother of #21 and claims through same source.
App: 442 Alfred Richardson, Nashville, N.C.
Rejected. It does not appear that any ancestor was ever enrolled or that any ancestor was party to the treaties of 1835-6 and 1846. Ancestors did not live in the Cherokee country, not within 250 miles of the Cherokee domain. Shows no connection with the Eastern Cherokees.
App: 443 Nellie Proctor and 3 children, Spavinaw, Okla.
Admitted. Applicant's parents were not living in 1851 but his[sic] grandmother enrolled as Sally in 1851 by Drennen, G.S. 572. (See Miscel. Test. 4257).
App: 444 Teach Blackbear, Eucha, Okla.
Admitted. Brother of #10211 and claims through same source.
App: 445 Alex Proctor and 1 child, Spavinaw, Okla.
Admitted. Applicant's parents enrolled by Drennen in 1851, Del 15).

App: 446 Betsy Buck, Spavinaw, Okla.
Admitted. Applicant claims through her father, Squot-ta-le-chee, enrolled in 1851 by Drennen, Del. 278. (Miscel. Test. P. 3156).
App: 447 John L. Springston and 1 child, Vian, Okla.
Admitted. Applicant enrolled in 1851 by Drennen, Del. 748.
App: 448 John L. Springston
Duplicate of #447.
App: 449 John L. Springston,
Duplicate of #447.
App: 450 John L. Springston,
Duplicate of #447.
App: 451 Sallie Sugar, Spavinaw, Okla.
Admitted. Applicant enrolled by Drennen in 1851, Sal. 253.
App: 452 Tooyennie Grass and 1 child, Dragger, Okla.
Admitted. Applicant's parents enrolled by Drennen in 1851, Sal. 321. (See Miscel. Test. P. 3857).
App: 453 Sarah Proctor and 2 children, Spavinaw, Okla.
Admitted. Niece of #452 and claims through same source.
App: 454 James S. Perdue and 1 child, Eucha, Okla.
Admitted. Applicant's father enrolled in 1851 by Drennen, Dis. 57.
App: 455 Ezekiel Cline and 6 children, Ruby, Okla.
Admitted. Applicant's mother enrolled in 1851 by Drennen, G.S. 711.
App: 456 Nellie Landrum, Vinita, Okla.
Admitted. Applicant enrolled in 1851 by Drennen, F1. 72.
App: 457 Bird Mockson, Spavinaw, Okla.
Admitted. Applicant's mother under the name of Jane and maternal grandmother and step-grandfather enrolled in 1851 by Drennen, Del. 746. (Miscel. Test. P. 4332).
App: 458 Lola Proctor and 7 children, Spavinaw, Okla.
Admitted. Applicant's parents enrolled by Drennen in 1851, Sal. 248, under names Ne-kar-we and Warl-se. (Miscel. Test. P. 3632).
App: 459 Steve Buck, Spavinaw, Okla.
Admitted. Claims through grandparents, Buck and Caty, enrolled in 1851 by Drennen, Del. 463. Applicant also enrolled same group.
App: 460 Betsy Backwater, Spavinaw, Okla.
Admitted. Applicant and her parents enrolled in 1851 by Drennen, Sal. 253.
App: 461 Ancy Lacy, Spavinaw, Okla.
Admitted. Daughter of #87 and claims through same source.
App: 462 Sarah Hair, Spavinaw, Okla.
Admitted. Applicant enrolled in 1851 by Drennen, with her mother, Sal. 562. Her father and brothers enrolled, Sal. 216.
App: 463 Jennie Buck, Spavinaw, Okla.
Admitted. Sister of #462 and claims through same source.
App: 464 Daniel Backbone, Choteau, Okla.
Admitted. Applicant's parents enrolled in 1851 by Drennen, Tah. 107. (Miscel. Test. P. 4275).

App: 465 James Brown and 2 children, Chocotah, Okla.
Admitted. Applicant's mother enrolled in 1851 by Drennen, Fl. 84. Applicant died May 5, 1907.
App: 466 Walter R. Beck et al, Independence, Kans.
Admitted. Brothers and sister of #413 and claim through same source. (This application by Mary J. Beck, parent and gdn).
App: 467 Gertrude B. Woods and 1 child, Table Mound, Okla.
Admitted. Sister of #413 and claims through same source.
App: 468 Nellie Buck, and 5 children, Spavinaw, Okla.
Admitted. Applicant's father enrolled in 1851 by Drennen, Sal. 226.
App: 469 Toowaite Proctor, Spavinaw, Okla.
Admitted. Applicant's parents enrolled in 1851 by Drennen, Del. 683.
App: 470 May Simon and 1 child, Spavinaw, Okla.
Admitted. Niece of #452 and claims through same source.
App: 471 David Simon and 2 children, Eucha, Okla.
Admitted. Nephew of #452 and claims through same source.
App: 472 Ollie Walker, et al, Coffeyville, Kans.
By Geo. L. Walker, Gdn.
Admitted. Applicants' mother and grandmother enrolled in 1851 by Drennen, Del. 918.
App: 473 James O. Smith and 4 children, Coffeyville, Kans.
Admitted. Brother of #472 and claims through same source.
App: 474 Archibald Reeves Holmes, Knoxville, Tenn.
Rejected. Applicant claims through Sizemores. See full report in #417.
App: 475 Orley Edward Plummer, Grant, Va.
Rejected. Applicant claims through Sizemores. See full report in #417.
App: 476 Thelmus Gentry Plummer, Grant, Va.
Rejected. Applicant claims through Sizemores. See full report in #417.
App: 477 Silas William Henry, Springville, Ala.
Rejected. Applicant fails to show any genuine connection with the Eastern Cherokees. No ancestor ever enrolled. No ancestor a party to the treaties of 1835-6 and 1846.
App: 478 Eliza Jane Stephens, Springville, Ala.
Rejected. Applicant fails to show any genuine relation to the Eastern Cherokees. No ancestors ever enrolled and no ancestor party to the treaties of 1835-6 and 1846.
App: 479 Wm. R. and Susan M. Dubois, Grove, Okla.
By Jacob Dubois,
Admitted. Applicants' grandmother and great grandparents enrolled in 1851 by Drennen, Tah. 257, Fl. 62.
App: 480 Charley Dirteater, Moodys, Okla.
Admitted. Applicant's grandfather enrolled in 1851 by Drennen, Tah. 382.
App: 481 Sarah Snail, South West City, Mo.
Admitted. Niece of #252 and claims through same source.
App: 482 Agnes Roberts and 3 children, South West City, Mo.
Admitted. Niece of #252 and claims through same source.

App: 483 Jennie Jones and 1 child, South West City, Mo.
Admitted. Niece of #252 and claims through same source.
App: 484 Nannie A. Keen, Coffeyville, Kans.
Admitted. Applicant's ancestors enrolled in 1851 by Drennen, 920.
App: 485 Ophelia Thelma Plummer, Grant, Va.
Rejected. Applicant claims through Sizemores. See full report in #417.
App: 486 Mrs. Lou Dora Taliferro, Haley, Tenn.
Rejected. Applicant claims through Sizemores. See full report in #417.
App: 487 Mary Etta Holmes, Knoxville, Tenn. 640 Asylum St.,
Rejected. Applicant claims through Sizemores. See full report in #417.
App: 488 Fannie G. Gilbert, Haley, Tenn.
Rejected. Applicant claims through the Sizemores. See full report in #417.
App: 489 Elizabeth Hurley, Silas Creek, N.C.
Rejected. Applicant claims through Sizemores. See full report in #417.
App: 490 Charles Luther Plummer, Denver, Colo., 3316 Witter St.
Rejected. Applicant claims through the Sizemores. See full report in #417.
App: 491 Robert E. Lee Plummer, Grant, Va.
Rejected. Applicant claims through the Sizemores. See full report in #417.
App: 492 Daisy Bell Eller, Crumpler, N.C.
Rejected. Applicant claims through the Sizemores. See full report in #417.
App: 493 Frances Ella Plummer, Haley, Tenn.
Rejected. Applicant claims through the Sizemores. See full report in #417.
App: 494 William P. Honney and 1 child, Callas, Mo.
Rejected. It does not appear that any ancestor was ever enrolled or that any ancestor was party to the treaties of 1835-6 and 1846. Shows no real connection with the Eastern Cherokees.
App: 495 Allen M. Jetter, Wallville, Okla.
Rejected. Ancestors not on rolls. Were not parties to the treaties of 1835-6 and 1846. Does not establish genuine connection with the Cherokee tribe. (Miscel. Test. P. 3123).
App: 496 Edmond D. Carey and 1 child, Grove, Okla.
Admitted. Applicant enrolled as Edward Carey in 1851 by Drennen, Del. 413. (Miscel. Test. P. 2723).
App: 497 Lydda A. Carey and 1 child, Grove, Okla.
Admitted. Applicant's parents enrolled by Drennen in 1851, Del. 409.
App: 498 Julia Barnett, Leach, Okla.
Admitted. Niece of #205 and claims through the same source.
App: 499 Caroline Martin and 4 children, Leach, Okla.
Admitted. Niece of #205 and claims through the same source.
App: 500 Wm. P. Hyde, and 4 children, Whittier, N.C.
Rejected. There are a large number of applications from persons claiming their Cherokee descent only through one Betsey Walker, alleged to have been a full blood Cherokee Indian and to have been allotted under the Treaties of 1817 and 1819 with the Cherokee Indians, and also said to be a sister of one Richard Walker, who was also allotted under the above Treaties. It is also alleged that Betsey Walker, the ancestor of

these claimants, was enrolled in 1835. Color is given to these claims by the fact that there was a Betsey Walker enrolled in 1835, and by the further fact that the name of Richard Walker does appear as an allottee under the Treaties of 1817 and 1819. No one of these claimants was enrolled in 1851 with the Eastern Cherokees, and no ancestor was enrolled at that time nor in 1835, unless the Betsey Walker referred to above was the ancestor of these claimants. A close examination of the roll of 1835, however, not only throws doubt upon the claim that the Betsey Walker there named was the ancestor of these claimants, but also makes it appear very doubtful whether the Betsey Walker there enrolled was in herself a Cherokee Indian. The name appears with the following entries: under "Heads of Families, Indians, Half-breeds, Quadroons and Whites", the name "Betsey Walker" is entered; under the head of "Residence, State and County and Water-course", is entered "McMinn City, Tennessee, Mouse Creek"; under head of "Males over eighteen years, one"; no entry under "Females"; "Total Cherokees, one"; then follow entries as to "Slaves, Farms, Crops, etc.", until the entry under "Half-breeds, one", and under "Weavers, Spinsters and Reservees, one each". If these entries are correct, it is obvious that the beneficial party enrolled was a male over 18 years of age and under 21, and Betsey Walker was only named as the head of the family because of some relationship or guardianship over this minor. It further appears that the party thus enrolled was a half-breed and not a full-blood Cherokee as claimed, and further that the beneficial party was a reservee, while Betsey Walker was not in fact a reservee, as is shown by the official reports of the Indian office. That there was a reservation made for the beneficial party is perfectly plain from the record. That white persons' names were entered as head of families is demonstrated by the 4th name below that of Betsey Walker, Emily Walker, who was enrolled as a head of a family, but is shown by the subsequent roll of 1851 to have been a white woman without Indian blood but married to a Cherokee Indian, and her children were entitled to enrollment, she representing them as the head of the family. The testimony in this case is somewhat uncertain as to the exact place of residence of the Betsey Walker ancestor of these claimants, but so far as the testimony goes it strongly tends to establish the fact that their ancestor was living in N.C., if living at all, in 1835, while as shown above the Betsey Walker enrolled in 1835 was living in Tennessee. There is also some uncertainty as to the date of the death of Betsey Walker, but if she was in fact living in 1835 she must have been extremely old. Harvey L. Moody, Application #32491, who was himself born in 1838 and who names a brother born in 1825, sets forth the fact that he is claiming as the great great grandson of Betsey Walker; Nancy T. McDaniel, Application #34979, who was born in 1830, likewise claims as the great great granddaughter of Betsey Walker; and Rebecca E. Ashe, Application #3597, who was born in 1883, claims as the great-great-great-great-granddaughter of Betsey Walker. These facts certainly go a long way toward establishing the extreme age of Betsey Walker, if living in 1835. Another inconsistency, though not a serious one, is the fact that Betsey Walker is alleged to have been the sister of Richard Walker, but her children were also known by the name of Walker. Who her husband was nowhere appears in either the applications or in the testimony. Various reasons are given by the claimants for the fact that they or their ancestors were not enrolled in 1835 and 1851, as will be seen from the following extracts from replies to letters to the claimants asking for their explanation: Joseph Burton Sherrill, Application #13882, on Dec. 4, 1907, states: "I have to say that they did not enroll on account of the Indian blood as it would have cut them out of the free schools among the whites at that time. My descendants were all white people, Anglo-Saxon, save the Indian blood shown from Elizabeth or Betsey Walker". Wm. B. Sherrill of Whittier, N.C., Application #11379, on Dec. 3, 1907, states: "It was from choice not to be enrolled at that time on account of the Cherokee blood. They were self-supporting and too high-minded at that time to claim the Cherokee blood, as it would have cut them out of the free scholl[sic] at that time in the white school". Laura Nations of Whittier, N.C., Application #2026, on Dec. 4, 1907, states: "So as I understand, when the Eastern Cherokees was wanted to be moved, or in other words was wanted to be moved West, those two little Indian children were caught by the soldiers and was given to an old citizen by the name of Felix Walker and afterwards they was allotted land and enrolled". Note: If Betsey Walker was captured at that time by the soldiers and was then a "little Indian", certainly she could not have been the ancestor of these claimants. The testimony in regard to these claims will be found in Miscellaneous Testimony, Pages 1538, 1657, 1658, 1704 and 1705. Mrs. Lillie Wiggins, 47 years of age, and testifying on behalf of Nora Rochester, Application #13867, states: "I don't think Nora's mother or grandmother ever lived with the Indians as members of the tribe. I never heard of any of Nora's ancestors being on any roll except that it is said that Elizabeth Leatherwood was on one of the early rolls way back, but don't know what one or when. The mother of Nora was recognized in the community as a white woman. Never heard of any of her ancestors receiving any money from the Government except Elizabeth Leatherwood but don't know when and where she received it. Never heard of any of Nora's ancestors taking part in any Indian deliberations or councils". Harvey L. Moody, 69 years of age, testifying at Whittier, N.C. in behalf of himself and his wife, who makes claim through the same source, Misc. Test. P. 1657 and 1758, says: "I claim Indian blood through my mother. She always claimed to have Cherokee blood. I have never received any money from the government and never have made application prior to this time. My mother never received any Indian money. My mother was a recognized white woman and was never enrolled. I have seen my grandparents John and Sallie Leatherwood. They lived in Haywood County, N.C. They both claimed Indian blood. They never lived with the Indians as Indians but lived amongst them. My grandfather was a recognized white man and a voter. I do not know why he was not enrolled. In 1835 my grandparents lived on Johnson's Creek, Haywood Co., N.C." And again: "Cordelia Moody is my wife. She claims Indian blood through the same line I do. She never received any Indian money from the Government and her parents never received any that I know of. I did not know Edward Leatherwood, nor his wife, Elizabeth Walker, and she was the daughter of Betsey Walker. I cannot say when Betsey Walker died. I do not know if she lived during my mother's life-time. I never heard my mother speak of having seen her. I cannot say if Betsey Walker was living in 1825. Do not know when she lived or when she died. I do not know where she was born but have heard that she lived somewhere near here and was supposed to have owned the land where Bryson City is now built. I do not know if she or her husband owned the land where Bryson City is now built.. I never heard what kind of Indian blood Betsey Walker had nor how much Indian blood. I heard others say that she was a full blood Cherokee. I never heard my mother say this. Never heard my grandfather say this. I have heard William P. Hyde say so. I do not recollect anybody else having said that Betsey Walker was a Cherokee Indian except (Wm) Penn Hyde. I heard him speak about this first six or eight years ago". William Penn Hyde, 65 years of age, (the one referred to above in the testimony of Harvey L. Moody) testified at Bryson City, N.C., as follows: "My grandmother moved here and was given land in the Indian boundary. This was my grandmother who was a Leatherwood. She married Ben Hyde. Betsey Walker was her mother. The evidence that I have according to the affidavits I have shows she was a full blood. Betsey Walker was captured by the soldiers and given to a white man named Walker who raised her. The man who raised her lived near Dillsboro, Jackson Co., N.C. He also raised Richard, her brother. When the treaty was made I think Betsey Walker's reservation was in Macon Co. I never saw Betsey Walker. Betsey Walker died in Macon Co. and was buried there. My grandmother lived and died in Swain Co., about a mile from Bryson City. She died about 1841. I do not know if my mother ever got any Indian money from the government. I have never received any Indian money. I remember when Chapman made the payment in 1852. I did not share in this payment. I remember when Hester enrolled the Indians. I did not make an effort to be enrolled then. I have lived among the Indians most of my life but was never admitted to tribal councils. My mother was a recognized white woman. I have always been recognized as a white man and a voter". Eliza J. Seay, 65 years of age, testified at Bryson City, N.C. as follows: "I claim Indian blood through my father, Uriah Burns. My father never received any Indian money from the Government. He claimed his Indian blood through his father, Hezekiah Burns. Hezekiah's father was Arthur Burns who married a daughter of Betsey Walker. I have always heard that she was a full-blood Cherokee and was captured at the time of the treaty. My grandfather lived in Georgia and Alabama and came and stayed with us when I was about 15 years old. My grandfather lived with the white people. We have always passed as white people yet I have always claimed Indian blood. The men in our family have always voted. Sam Burns went to Georgia and the sister lived on Johnathan Creek in Haywood Co., N.C. She was Sallie Leatherwood. My great grandfather lived in Haywood Co. when my mother was first married. I claim all my Indian blood through Betsey Walker". The testimony and the statements of the claimants in their applications and letters fail to establish the fact that they or their ancestors were recognized members of the Eastern Cherokee Tribe of Indians in 1835 or in 1846, and fails to overcome the negative fact that their immediate ancestors living in 1835 and 1851 were not enrolled with the Eastern Cherokees. The evidence taken in connection with the other facts would seem to establish the fact that the Betsey Walker whose name appears on the roll of 1835 was not the Betsey Walker the ancestor of these claimants. For the foregoing reasons all these claims are rejected.

App: 501 Thomas I. Helton and 4 children, Graysville, Tenn.
Rejected. Nephew of #504 and claims through the same source.

App: 502 Mary McGill, Graysville, Tenn.
Rejected. Niece of #504 and claims through same source.

App: 503 James H. Helton and 2 children, Rockwood, Tenn.
Rejected. Brother of #504 and claims through same source.

App: 504 Sarah M. Cross and 1 child, Graysville, Tenn.
Rejected. Applicant nor ancestors were never enrolled. Does not appear that they were living within the Cherokee Domain in 1835-6 and 1846 as recognized members of the tribe. Applicant and her father through whom she claims, never lived with the tribe. (Miscel. Test. P. 434).

App: 505 Floid Eanes, Day, Mo.
Rejected. Applicant claims through Alex Brown. See full report in #35.

App: 506 Lester Eanes, Day, Mo.
Rejected. Applicant claims through Alex Brown. See full report in #35.
App: 507 Lillie Eanes, Day, Mo.
Rejected. Applicant claims through Alex Brown. See full report in #35.
App: 508 Susan Trottingwolf and 4 children, Bartlesville, Okla.
Admitted. Applicant's mother enrolled in 1851 by Drenne[sic], Del. 654. (Miscel. Test. P. 2401).
App: 509 Coy Eanes, Day, Mo.
Rejected. Applicant claims through Alex Brown. See full report in #35.
App: 510 Lincoln Trottingwolf and 4 children, Bartlesville, Okla.
Admitted. Parents enrolled in 1851 by Drennen, Sal. 272. (Miscel. Test. P. 2400).
App: 511 Sabra A. Flint and 2 children, Coffeyville, Kans.
Admitted. Applicant's mother enrolled by Drennen in 1851, Dis. 14.
App: 512 John L. Miller,
Duplicate of #403.
App: 513 Tabitha Dockins, Clayton, Ga.
Admitted. Applicant's mother and grandmother enrolled in 1851 by Chapman #2084 and #2083.
App: 514 Stacy Cherokee Dickson and 3 children, Clayton, Ga.
Admitted. Sister of #513 and claims through same source. Applicant enrolled by Hester #2575.
App: 515 Samuel England, Locust Grove, Okla.
Admitted. Applicant enrolled in 1851 by Drennen, G.S. 687.
App: 516 Minnie Cochran, deceased and 3 children, Locust Grove, Okla.
Admitted. Applicant's mother, Lucy Locust, and grandparents, Chu-wa-lu-ke and Na-ke enrolled in 1851 by Drennen, Del. 261. (Miscel. Test. P. 3773).
App: 517 Annie Harry Oo-sa-wee, Eucha, Okla.
Admitted. Niece of #364 and claims through same source.
App: 518 Sallie Oo-sa-wee, Eucha, Okla.
Admitted. Sister of #518 and claims through same source.
App: 519 Jake Oo-sa-wee, Eucha, Okla.
Admitted. Nephew of #364 and claims through same source.
App: 520 Levi Childers and 4 children, Texanna, Okla.
Rejected. Applicant's father and brother on the Old Settler Roll, Sal. 29. Information in application relative to mother insufficient. Grandparents are not named. Mother born in Illinois. Her ancestors probably in Tennessee. There is nothing to show the right of applicant to participate through mother. There are no Whygles on the roll.
App: 521 Frank Littledave, Locust Grove, Okla.
Admitted. Brother of #189 and claims through same source.
App: 522 Henry Downing and 1 child, Locust Grove, Okla.
Admitted. Applicant's parents, Ta-goo-her and Car-tols-ter enrolled in 1851 by Drennen, Del. 249.
App: 523 Joe Vann and 3 children, Locust Grove, Okla.
Admitted. Applicant's parents, Ta-chee and Che-co-wee enrolled in 1851 by Drennen, Tah. 183.

App: 524 Mary Downing,
Duplicate of #189.

App: 525 Josiah Young, Locust Grove, Okla.
Deceased Dec. 21, 1906.

Admitted. Applicant's parents Youngbird or Ah-ne-tah enrolled in 1851 by Drennen, Del. 546.

App: 526 Adam Ridge, Eucha, Okla.

Admitted. Nephew of #366 and claims through same source.

(Note: Handwritten on the following page.)

Katy Jordan was also considered by Chapman and rejected by him. The following report being made by him in this case-"this woman is upon Siler's rejected list-she is illegitimate - her reputed father, Chas Ward, does not pretend to say that he believes himself to be her father, he is a half breed, her mother white". (Special report, #10, made by Chapman prior to Act of Congress roll and designated "Statement of an examination of the report and accompaning[sic] *papers submitted by A. Chapman, Special Agent.)*

App: 527 Alsy Ridge, Eucha, Okla.

Admitted. Niece of #364 and claims through same source.

App: 528 Lillie Bishop and 5 children, Murphy, N. C.

Rejected. Applicant claims through Catherine Jordan. Catherine Jordan's right to be enrolled as a Cherokee (Eastern) was considered by Agent Siler in 1851 and rejected. It is claimed that Catherine Jordan was the daughter of Charles Ward, and Charles Ward with wife and family are enrolled by Siler and Chapman (See Siler 1352 and Chapman 1390). As the claim of the mother through whom these parties trace their descent to Cherokee blood was thus considered and rejected, it would manifestly be improper to enroll these claimants now without a clear error was shown to have been made, but it does not so appear. With Charles Ward on the Chapman roll are found a wife, Polly, and 7 children – one son and 6 daughters, 2 of these being enrolled apart from him as Nos. 2132 and 2133, while Laura Mauldin (App. No. 15173) a daughter of Catherine Jordan, testified at Knoxville, Tenn. (Miscel. Test. P. 722) – "My mother never had any brothers and sisters". She also states in this testimony, first that she don't know when her mother's father died – "I think he died after the war", but at the close of her testimony, she swears: "Charles Ward was dead in 1851. Don't know whether he was living in 1835 or not." W. Clark Jordan (App. No. 1528) testified at Murphy, N.C. (Miscel. Test. P. 1563) – "My mother was an only child". The Charles Ward on the Chapman roll was enrolled from Cherokee Co., N.C., while W. Clark Jordan states that he remembers his grandfather; that he lived most of the time in Georgia and Swain Co., N.C. Also in response to office letters, Lillie Bishop (App. #528), Amanda Jordan (App. #530), Sis Fortner (App. 531) and Mark Jordan (App. #28056) – all children of Catherine Jordan, state that their mother, Catherine Jordan, had no brothers and sisters or half brothers and sisters. This would seem to make it certain that the Charles Ward, father of Catherine Ward, was not the Charles Ward enrolled by Chapman, and there is no other connection shown with the Cherokeee rolls of 1835 and 1851. (Handwritten on the bottom right; * *See opposite page)*

App: 529 William J. Mason, Buren, Ga.

Rejected. Applicant living in 1851 but not enrolled. No ancestor appears on either roll. Applicant and ancestors born in Macon Co., N.C. and probably not within the

Cherokee Domain. It seems they were not parties to the treaties of 1835-6 and 1846. Information in letters and applications insufficient.

App: 530 Amanda Jordan, Murphy, N.C.
Rejected. Sister of #528 and claims through same source.

App: 531 Sis Fortner, Isabella, Tenn.
Rejected. Sister of #528 and claims through same source.

App: 532 John A. Manar, Westville, Okla.
Rejected. Applicant and his mother, though living in 1851, were not enrolled at that time. He claims through Sallie Lowery, who was enrolled in 1835, but he fails to establish the fact that the Sallie Lowrey enrolled in 1835 was his ancestor. The testimony is very unsatisfactory. It does not appear that the applicant ever made any claim as an Eastern Cherokee prior to 1892. He does not appear to have affiliated with the tribe or to have been recognized as a member of the tribe. It would appear from the roll of 1835 that the Sallie Lowrey so enrolled was a white woman, while the claimant states that his mother was of Indian blood. He claims only through his mother and states that his grandmother was also an Indian. Applicant states that the Sallie Lowrey through whom he claims lived in N.C. in 1835 and the Sallie Lowrey enrolled in 1835 was enrolled in the State of Tennessee. (Miscel. Test. P. 4068).

App: 533 Sam Mathews and 1 child, Muskogee, Okla.
Rejected. Applicant not enrolled by the Dawes Commission. Parents born in Maryland and Missouri. Grandparents born in Pennsylvania, W. Va., Ga. and Kentucky. No ancestor enrolled either in 1851 or 1835. They probably never lived within the Cherokee domain and it appears they were not parties to the treaties of 1835-6 and 1846. Evidence insufficient. (Miscel. Test. P. 3117).

App: 534 Lizzie Trimble, Muskogee, Okla.
Rejected. Sister of #533 and claims through same source.

App: 535 Maggie Pendergrass, Muskogee, Okla.
Rejected. Sister of #533 and claims through same source.

App: 536 George Daniel and 4 children, Bartlesville, Okla.
Admitted. Applicant claims through Wah-yeh or Wolf, enrolled in 1851 by Drennen, Del. 810. Claimant also enrolled in same group. (Miscel. Test. P. 2431).

App: 537 Wm. Childers and 7 children, Wann, Okla.
Admitted. Applicant claims through mother, Sarah Bean, enrolled in 1851 by Drennen, Tah. 594.

App: 538 Nannie Maxwell, Wann, Okla.
Rejected. Applicant is on the Old Settler roll, Tah. 166. (Miscel. Test. P. 2426).

App: 539 Margaret Morris, Wann, Okla.
Admitted. Sister of #209 and claims through same source. Applicant enrolled as Peggy in 1851 by Drennen, Ill. #6.

App: 540 John Drywater, Oaks, Okla.
Admitted. Applicant enrolled in 1851 by Drennen, Sal. 66.

App: 541 Polly McPherson, Greenbrier, Okla.
Rejected. Claimant and both parents on Old Settler Roll, Fl. 52. (Miscel. Test. P. 3779).

App: 542 Emma Susan Rodgers and 1 child, Commerce, Tex. ~~Greenbrier, Okla.~~
Rejected. Claimant claims through father who was born in Tenn. in 1811. Never enrolled. Grandmother, Fannie Womack, through whom claim is made married David Weaver, who was a white man, prior to 1800, and she never lived with the Indians after she was married to him. Neither applicant nor any of her ancestors enrolled with Eastern Cherokees – left tribe, if ever connected with it) prior to 1800. (Miscel. Test. P. 2467).

App: 543 Mary E. Miller and 2 children, Grove, Okla.
Admitted. First cousin of #55. Applicant and her mother enrolled by Chapman in 1851, Nos. 1745 and 1744.

App: 544 Herbert A. Williams, Wagoner, Okla.
Admitted. Nephew of #929 and claims through same source.

App: 545 John Rowland and 3 children, Hayesville, N.C.
Rejected. Brother of #126 and claims through same source.

App: 546 Margret S. Bradley, Howe, Texas.
Rejected. Ancestors not on rolls. Does not establish genuine connection with Cherokee tribe. (Miscel. Test. P. 2267).

App: 547 Sherman Bell and 1 child, Leach, Okla.
Admitted. Nephew of #205 and claims through same source.

App: 548 Thos. L. Garrison, Montague, Texas.
Rejected. Brother of #375 and claims through same source.

App: 549 Isaac McClelland, Murphy, N.C.
Rejected. Brother of #197 and claims through same source.

App: 550 Wm. J. McDonald, Athens, Tenn.
Rejected. Applicant claims through Annie Blythe. See full report in #153.

App: 551 Edwin Lawson and 6 children, Keystone, Okla.
Rejected. It does not appear that applicant's parents were ever enrolled or were parties to the treaties of 1835-6 and 1846. Applicant claims his great grandfather was Dennis Wolfe and enrolled in 1835, but there is no proof presented to establish that fact, except that he was told that Dennis Wolfe was enrolled in 1835. Knows nothing about the Wolfe family. Applicant's father, mother, grandfather, George Wolfe, and two sisters and one brother were living in East Tenn. in 1835, but at least 100 miles away from the Cherokee Domain; and they lived in Arkansas in 1851, but none were ever enrolled. Under these circumstances, it seems extremely doubtful whether the Dennis Wolfe, the alleged great grandfather of claimant, is the same person as the Dennis Wolfe enrolled in 1835, and if he should have been, it is clear that the immediate ancestors of claimants had left the tribe prior to 1835. The William Martin on the roll of 1835 could not have been the father of claimant, as it is shown by testimony of Alfred M. Martin, that the father was a white man and they make no claim through him. (Miscel. Test. P. 2822).

App: 552 Alfred M. Martin, Garfield, Ark.
Rejected. Uncle of #551 and claims through same source.

App: 553 Elizabeth Constant, Ringgold, Ga.
Admitted. Applicant's father enrolled in 1851 by Chapman #1637.

App: 554 John Fields, Chattanooga, Tenn.
Admitted. Half-brother of #553 and claims through same source.

App: 555 Rannie Anderson and 7 children, Hill City, Tenn.
Admitted. Sister of #553 and claims through same source.
App: 556 Crocia A. Sivley and 5 children, Valdeau, Tenn.
Admitted. Sister of #553 and claims through same source.
App: 557 George Hammer Brown, Lenapah, Okla.
Admitted. Applicant, Abbie Brown and Perry Ross claim that their mother was a full blood Cherokee and their fathers (they had different fathers) were Negroes and slaves, but that they themselves were never slaves. They claim that they were enrolled in 1851 and George Hammer Brown states that his mother was dead at that time, and that Brise Martin's widow drew the money for them; that is, for George, June and Perry. Abbie being elder, drew for herself. George Hammer Brown is enrolled by the Dawes Commission on the roll of Cherokees by blood at #15967 as a half-blood. Abbie's name cannot be found in any of the Dawes Commission rolls under the name of Abbie Brown. Perry Ross was enrolled by the Dawes Commission on the Freedman roll at #2590 and he gives his explanation of the fact that he was enrolled upon that roll, that when he was asked by the Dawes Commission on which roll he wanted to go, he was scared and said "Freedman", "as they had told me I would have some trouble getting on the other although my mother was a full blood". (Miscel. Test. P. 2513). The names of George, June and Per-o appear on the Drennen roll, Sal. 464. Abigail in the same District #465, and it appears from the original roll that Sarah Martin received the money for these children. They also claim that their grandmother Susan Wilcox, and their aunt, Polly Wilcox, who was not married, were enrolled in 1851. Their names appear on the Drennen roll, F1. 353. George Hammer Brown states in affidavit that his mother had a brother by the name of John Brown, who was a full blood Cherokee Indian. He also states that he and his mother and sister came from Georgia with "Lige" Hicks and George Fields. The name John Brown appears on the Drennen roll, Sal. 531 and Elijah Hicks is the head of the preceding group #530. As these applicants, although their fathers were Negroes and slaves, claim through their mother, a full blood, and as they themselves are enrolled as above stated, they and their descendants are clearly entitled and should be admitted. See affidavit of George Hammer Brown of Feb. 29, 1908, and marked "Exhibit "A". Also Miscel. Test. P. 2135, 2136 and 2513.
App: 558 Abbie Brown, Lenapah, Okla.
Admitted. Sister of #557 and claims through same source. Applicant herself enrolled as "Abigal" in 1851 by Drennen, Sal. 465.
App: 559 Amanda M. Thornton, South West City, Mo., R.F.D. 3, Box 7.
Admitted. Aunt of #479 and claims through same source.
App: 560 Amanda M. Thornton,
Duplicate of #559 and #734.
App: 561 William I. Thornton, South West City, Mo.
Admitted. Brother of #330 and claims through same source. Applicant enrolled in 1851 by Drennen, S.B. 40.
App: 562 Henry Lowery and 4 children, Wann, Okla.
Admitted. Applicant's father and grandparents enrolled in 1851 by Drennen, Tah. 536.

App: 563 Archibald B. McCoy and 2 children Claremore, Okla.
Admitted. Applicant's mother, Lucy Clay, enrolled in 1851 by Drennen, F1. 634.

App: 564 Geo. W. Patrick and 5 children, Wann, Okla.
Admitted. Brother of #209. Is enrolled in 1851 by Drennen, Ill/6.

App: 565 James S. Hudson, Fairland, Okla.
Admitted. Brother of #312 and claims through same source.

App: 566 Perrie Lee Davis, Atlanta, Ga., R.F.D. 5, Box 86.
Rejected. Daughter of #725 and claims through same source.

App: 567 Mary F. Bradley and 6 children, Howe, Texas.
Rejected. Sister of #546 and claims through the same source.

App: 568 Mary E. Chastain, Fairland, Okla.
Admitted. Applicants mother enrolled in 1851 by Drennen, Del. 142.

App: 569 M. F. White and 3 children, Muskogee, Okla.
Rejected. Sister of #495 and claims through same source.

App: 570 Susan Allen and 4 children, Sleeper, Okla.
Admitted. Sister of #804 and claims through same source.

App: 571 Phenia Manley and 1 child, Muskogee, Okla.
Admitted. Sister of #804 and claims through the same source.

App: 572 Martha Ketcher and 5 children, Baptist, Okla.
Admitted. Applicant's father enrolled in 1851 by Drennen, S.B. 197.

App: 573 Lydia Scraper, South West City, Mo.
Admitted. Applicant claims through parents enrolled in 1851 by Drennen, Sal. 316.

App: 574 Marcus L. Janeway and 4 children, Wilburton, Okla.
Rejected. Applicants nor ancestors were never enrolled. Does not appear that they were living within the limits of the Cherokee Domain in 1835-6 and 1846, as recognized members of the tribe. Miscel. Test. P. 2564.

App: 575 Margret Odell, Nowata, Okla.
Admitted. Applicant's father enrolled in 1851 by Drennen, Del 1050.

App: 576 Sterling P. Cannon, Siloam Springs, Ark.
Admitted. Brother of #343 and claims through same source.

App: 577 Ida Lee Ballenger and 1 child, Coffeyville, Kans.
Admitted. First cousin of #201 and claims through same source.

App: 578 Bettie Sanders and 4 children, Stilwell, Okla.
Admitted. Applicant's parents enrolled in 1851 by Drennen, F1. 487.

App: 579 Andrew Jackson Countryman and 3 children, Needmore, Okla.
Admitted. Applicant enrolled in 1851 by Drennen, Dis. 24.

App: 580 Edith Bird Austin, Milton, Okla.
Rejected. Sister of #374 and claims through same source.

App: 581 Margaret Buttry, Pea Ridge, Ark.
Rejected. Aunt of #551 and claims through the same source.

App: 582 Allen Adams and 4 children, Presley, Ga.
Rejected. Applicant claims through Annie Blythe. See special report in #153.

App: 583 Susan Cook, Vinita, Okla.
Admitted. Applicant's parents enrolled in 1851 by Drennen, G.S. 157.

App: 584 Griffin Oxendine, Albuquerque, N.M.
Rejected. Applicant nor ancestors never enrolled. Applicant born in Robeson Co., N.C. in 1848 – 250 miles from Cherokee country. His parents and grandparents also born there and always lived in same country. Does not establish fact of descent from a person who was a party to the treaty of 1835-6 and 1846.

App: 585 Andrew J. Rowland and 4 children, Tomotla, N.C.
Rejected. Cousin of #126 and claims through same source.

App: 586 Mattie D. Lane and 7 children, Rockwood, Tenn.
Rejected. This group consists of about 223 applications representing the claims of persons who for the most part live in the state of Tennessee and in Monroe County. They all base their claim on the fact that they are descendants of the common ancestor whose name was Nathan Kirkland, and who they represent as being a Cherokee Chief, and because of the fact and for convenience, all of these cases have been grouped together, marked and designated as the Kirkland Group. After a careful investigation, it is found that none of the applicants nor any of the ancestors through whom they claim, are enrolled on the roll of 1835 or the roll of 1851, nor is there any one of said names on said rolls. It does not appear from Miscellaneous Testimony, P. 625-6 & 7, which was taken in the field in regard to this group of cases, that any of the applicants or the ancestors through whom they claim, were living within the Cherokee domain in 1835-6 and 1846 as recognized members of the Eastern Cherokee Tribe. Nor does it appear that they ever lived with the tribe as recognized members of it. Miscellaneous Testimony, P. 626 – Mr. Andrew Kirkland who was examined before the Special Commissioner at Madisonville, Tenn. on the 26th day of June 1908, testified in part as follows: "I was born in Monroe Co., Tenn. I am 57 years old. I knew James Kirkland, my grandfather. My mother was born about 1812. My father and mother were generally known as white people. I never received any money as an Indian. My father and mother never received any money that I ever heard of. I never heard of my father's mother leaving suddenly and going away anywhere so that people did not know where they were. I never heard of their hiding away in the mountains. I know of no reason why an enrolling officer of the U.S. could not have found them". Page 625 of Miscellaneous Testimony – the witness who was examined at the same time and place by the Special Commissioner, testified in part as follows: "My mother was married about 1855. My father and mother were generally known in the community as white people. I never heard of my grandparents living in the Nation, although they lived among them at times. My grandfather owned a little property at that time, and that was one of the reasons why they were not enrolled in 1851. My grandparents lived up here in the upper end of the county in 1835-6. They owned a place on Cane Creek. I have also heard my grandmother say that her father said he would rather die than be taken off. I never heard of their suddenly leaving this part of the county and the people around not knowing where they went". Page 627, Miscel. Test. – the witness examined at the same time and place by the Special Commissioner, testified in part as follows: "I am 77 years old and have lived in Monroe Co. all of my life. I remember the time of the enrollment in 1851. I do not know of any Indians being carried off in 1851. I never heard of the Kirklands hiding away in the mountains, and they were well known people in this country. I know of no reason why the enrolling agents could not have found them if they had tried". In view of the fact that none of the applicants nor their ancestors are enrolled, and that there is nothing showing that they or their ancestors were living within the Cherokee domain in 1835-6 and 1846 as recognized

members of the tribe, or that they ever lived with the tribe as recognized members of it, and from the fact that they were generally recognized as white people and were owning farms, it may be presumed that they were intruders in the domain, and although they may have had some trace of Cherokee blood, were not bona fide members of the tribe. Therefore, this group of cases is rejected.

App: 587 Richard E. Nicholson and 2 children, Talala, Okla.
Admitted. Applicant's father enrolled in 1851 by Drennen, Tah. 480.

App: 588 Lettie M. Brooking, Talala, Okla.
Admitted. Sister of #587 and claims through same source.

App: 589 Henry Nicholson, Talala, Okla.
Admitted. Brother of #587 and claims through same source.

App: 590 Daniel G. Nicholson Talala, Okla.
Admitted. Brother of #587 and claims through the same Source.

App: 591 Sarah Gage, Claremore, Okla.
Rejected. Applicant claims through husband who died Oct. 10, 1884.

App: 592 James Madison Zachary, Glendale, Ark.
Rejected. It does not appear that ancestors were ever enrolled or were parties to the treaties of 1835-6 and 1846. Applicant shows no real connection with the Eastern Cherokees. (Miscel. Test. P. 1933 and 1934).

App: 593 Mahala V.O. Rogers, Glendale, Ark.
Rejected. Niece of #592 and claims through the same source.

App: 594 Joseph U. Owen, Palmyra, Ark.
Rejected. Nephew of #592 and claims through the same source.

App: 595 Matilda C. Helton and 3 children, Hexon, Tenn.
Rejected. Niece of #504 and claims through the same source.

App: 596 Rachel A. Higdon, S. McAlister, Okla.
Rejected. A letter from W.W. Wright states that H.C. Freeland, an uncle, may be found on the rolls. Same cannot be found. Applicant was not enrolled by Dawes Commission. Evidence insufficient to establish a right to participate. No ancestor appears of[sic] the roll of 1851. There is a George Campbell on the roll of 1835 but nothing to show that he is the ancestor of applicant. Of the several uncles and brothers and sisters none appear on the 1851 roll. (Miscel. Test. P. 2679-2680).

App: 597 Ophela J. Harless and 4 children, Peggs, Okla.
Admitted. Sister of #343 and claims through the same source.

App: 598 Alfred P. Seabolt and 6 children, Muldrow, Okla.
Admitted. Applicants's mother and grandmother enrolled in 1851 by Drennen, S.B. 598.

App: 599 Luny Seabolt and 1 child, Maple, Okla.
Admitted. Sister of #598 and claims through the same source.

App: 600 James Seabolt, Maple, Okla.
Admitted. Brother of #598 and claims through the same source.

App: 601 Bean Seabolt and 1 child, Long, Okla.
Admitted. Brother of #598 and claims through the same source.

App: 602 Emma Sitton, Dawsonville, Ga.
Admitted. Applicant's father enrolled in 1851 by Chapman, #2005.

App: 603 Martin Hopper and 6 children, Stilwell, Okla.
Admitted. Applicant's parents enrolled in 1851 by Drennen, Fl. 220.

App: 604 Sallie Bigfeather and 1 child, Stilwell, Okla.
Admitted. Sister of #603 and claims through the same source.
App: 605 Annie Mouse and 2 children, Eucha, Okla.
Admitted. Applicant's grandfather and aunts, Ainnie and Judy, enrolled in 1851 by Drennen, Sal. 342.
App: 606 Darkey Mouse, Eucha, Okla.
Admitted. Sister of #364 and claims through same source.
App: 607 Peggy Mouse, Eucha, Okla.
Admitted. Applicant enrolled in 1851 by Drennen, Del. 39.
App: 608 Roll Mouse,
Admitted. Included in Application of father #627.
App: 609 Rachel Thompson,
Duplicate of #418.
App: 610 Jennie Starr, Eucha, Okla.
Duplicate of #419.
App: 611 Lydia Chuwalooky, Eucha, Okla.
Admitted. Applicant enrolled as "You-que" in 1851 by Drennen, Del. 39.
App: 612 Chick-a-le-le Chu-a-lu-ke and 5 children, Eucha, Okla.
Admitted. Brother of #364 and claims through same source.
App: 613 Joseph E. Smither, Claremore, Okla.
Admitted. Applicant's father enrolled by Chapman in 1851, #1366.
App: 614 Nancy M. Stephens and 5 children, Oolagah, Okla.
Admitted. Applicant's mother and grandparents enrolled in 1851 by Chapman #2040, #2038 and #2039.
App: 615 John Ross Trott, Virden, Ill.
Admitted. Applicant and parents enrolled in 1851 by Chapman, Nos. 1670, 1671 and 1672.
App: 616 William G. Rogers and 6 children, Dewey, Okla.
Admitted. Applicant's parents enrolled in 1851 by Drennen, Del. 937
App: 617 Sarah Ann Carr and 1 child, Bartlesville, Okla.
Admitted. Sister of #616 and claims through same source.
App: 618 Martha E. Flynn and 1 child, Dewey, Okla.
Admitted. Applicant's father and grandfather enrolled in 1851 by Drennen, Tah. 317.
App: 619 Nancy Miller and 6 children, Dewey, Okla.
Rejected. Applicant claims through John Tidwell, See full report in #16.
App: 620 John C. Childers, Copan, Okla.
Admitted. Brother of #537 and claims through the same source.
App: 621 Delila E. Fleetwood, (or Foreman) Copan, Okla.
Admitted. Niece of #51 and claims through the same source.
App: 622 Georgia Davidson and 6 children, Vallejo, Cal.
201 Ky. St.
Rejected. Neither applicant nor ancestors ever enrolled. Does not establish fact of descent from person who was a party to the treaty of 1835-6 and 1846.
App: 623 Nancy White, Los Angeles, Cal.
Admitted. Applicant enrolled in 1851 by Drennen, Ill. 279.

App: 624 Dick Chu-wa-loo-ky, Chloeta, Okla.
Admitted. Son of #364 and claims through the same source.
App: 625 Jennie O'Field, Eucha, Okla.
Admitted. Duplicate of #421.
App: 626 Ave Ridge, Eucha, Okla.
Admitted. Sister of #364 and claims through same source.
App: 627 Toney Mouse and 5 children, Eucha, Okla.
Admitted. Applicant's mother and maternal grandparents enrolled in 1851 by Drennen, Del. 38.
App: 628 Thomas Cowart, Hill City, Tenn., 300 Cowart St.
Admitted. Applicant enrolled in 1851 by Chapman #1635.
App: 629 Ta-kee Summerfield, Spavinaw, Okla.
Admitted. Applicant enrolled in 1851 by Drennen, Del. 288.
App: 630 Isaac Summerfield, Spavinaw, Okla.
Admitted. Applicant enrolled as Eh-se-ke in 1851 by Drennen, Del. 706.
App: 631 Lizzie Skah-gin-ne, Eucha, Okla.
Admitted. Sister of #630 and claims through same source.
App: 632 Margaret M. Rowland and 3 children, Tomotla, N.C.
Rejected. Aunt of #126 and claims through the same source.
App:633 William M. Rowland, Tomotla, N.C.
Rejected. Cousin of #126 and claims through the same source.
App: 634 Charles M. Rowland, Tomotla, N.C.
Rejected. Cousin of #126 and claims throught the same source.
App: 635 Mary A. Henderson, Tomotla, N.C.
Rejected. Aunt of #126 and claims through the same source.
App: 636 Bayless M. Henderson and 4 children, Copper Hill, Tenn.
Rejected. Cousin of #126 and claims through the same source.
App: 637 Susan Henderson, Tomotla, N.C.
Rejected Cousin of #126 and claims through same source.
App: 638 Viola G. Warren and 1 child, Wagoner, Okla.
Admitted. Niece of #929 and claims through same source.
App: 639 Sam Squirrel, Spavinaw, Okla.
Admitted. Applicant's parents enrolled in 1851 by Drennen, Del. 862.
App: 640 Lydia Ketcher and 3 children, Spavinaw, Okla.
Admitted. Niece of #639 and claims through the same source.
App: 641 George W. Smith, Rose, Okla.
Admitted. Father of applicant enrolled in 1851 by Drennen, G.S. 15. See App. #10271 for further information as to identity of father of applicant with name in G.S. 15.
App: 642 Rebecca Alice Boothe and 3 children, Lometa, Okla.
Admitted. Applicant's father enrolled in 1851 by Chapman #1686.
App: 643 Henry Julian Ward and 2 children, Muskogee, Okla.
Admitted. Applicant's mother enrolled in 1851 by Drennen, Dis. 39.
App: 644 Joe C. Fox, Jr., Eucha, Okla.
Admitted. Applicant's father enrolled in 1851 as Chu-wau-ye-cul-le by Drennen, Del. 310. (Miscel. Test. P. 2984).

App: 645 Lewis Mouse and 2 children, Spavinaw, Okla.
Admitted. Applicant's grandfather, Mouse, enrolled in 1851 by Drennen, Del. 38. (Miscel. Test. P. 3432).
App: 646 Cornelius Mouse, Eucha, Okla.
Admitted. First cousin of #645 and claims through same source.
App: 647 Nancy Runabout, Eucha, Okla.
Admitted. Applicant enrolled as "Wah-ne-wau" in 1851 by Drennen, Del. 39.
App: 648 Se-we Cornstalk, Eucha, Okla.
Admitted. Applicant's mother and maternal grandparents enrolled in 1851 by Drennen, Del. 766. Applicant's father and paternal grandparents enrolled in 1851 by Drennen, Del. 756.
App: 649 Watt Mouse and 2 children, Eucha, Okla.
Admitted. Brother of #645 and claims through same source.
App: 650 Quatie Chu-wa-loo-ke, Eucha, Okla.
Admitted. Sister of #364 and claims through same source.
App: 651 Annie Tanner, Eucha, Okla.
Admitted. Applicant's parents enrolled in 1851 by Drennen, Del. 589.
App: 652 Eliza Hair, Eucha, Okla.
Admitted. Sister of #648 and claims through same source.
App: 653 Jesse Starr, Eucha, Okla.
Admitted. Applicant's parents enrolled in 1851 by Drennen, Del. 184.
App: 654 Jennie Chopper, Eucha, Okla.
Admitted. Applicant and her parents enrolled in 1851 by Drennen, Del. 2.
App: 655 Daylight Chopper, Eucha, Okla.
Admitted. Applicant and his parents enrolled in 1851 by Drennen, Del. 756.
App: 656 Liza Smith, Rose, Okla.
Admitted. Applicant enrolled in 1851 by Drennen, Sal. 97. (Miscel Test. P. 3752).
App: 657 Lewis Budder, Eucha, Okla.
Admitted. Applicant's father enrolled in 1851 by Drennen, Sal. 251.
App: 658 Emma Fox and 2 children, Eucha, Okla.
Admitted. Sister of #648 and claims through the same source.
App: 659 Charley Galcatcher,
Duplicate of #368.
App: 660 John R. Mouse, Spavinaw, Okla.
Admitted. Brother of #645 and claims through the same source.
App: 661 Cornstalk, Eucha, Okla.
Admitted. Applicant, his mother and grandmother enrolled in 1851 by Drennen, Del. 765.
App: 662 Grant Fallingpot, Eucha, Okla.
Admitted. Applicant's mother and maternal grandparents enrolled in 1851 by Drennen, Sal. 271.
App: 663 Nancy Brown, Bartlesville, Okla.
Rejected. Applicant's ancestors were never enrolled. It does not appear that they were living within the Cherokee Domain in 1835-6 and 1846 as recognized members of the tribe. It does appear that they never lived with the tribe and were recognized white people. (Miscel. Test. P. 802 and 812).

App: 664 Sarah A. Mashburn, Andrews, N.C.
Rejected. Applicant claims through Edward Delozier, Alsey Fields, Alsey Spears, Elizabeth Delozier nee Poindexter, Pledge Poindexter, and his mother, Betty Pledge Poindexter. Her claim through the Deloziers is through Edward Delozier who was born in Blount Co., Tenn. about 1800 or prior thereto, and through his mother, Alsey Delozier nee Fields, who is claimed to have been 1/4 blood Cherokee, and her mother, Alsey Spears. Applicant #664 had a brother born in 1835. Neither Edward Delozier, Alsey Fields, Alsey Spears, nor applicants herein were ever enrolled, although the three persons named were living according to the statements of applicants, in Cherokee country in 1835 and 1851, and many of the applicants were living in or near Cherokee country in 1851 and, if Cherokees, would doubtless have been enrolled at least on one of those dates. The only evidence to the effect that Edward Delozier, Alsey Delozier nee Fields, and Alsey Spears were Cherokees in testimony of applicants to the following effect: "Edward Delozier, whose mother, Alsey Fields, was a Cherokee woman". (See Application #20088), and similar statements in other applications. Sarah A. Mashburn in an affidavit states as follows: "I live in Andrews, N.C. I have lived there for the last 18 or 20 years. I came from Swain Co., N.C. I am 65 (Note: Age blurred ?) years of age. I moved to Swain County a few years before the war when I was a child. We came to Swain Co. from Cherokee County, now Graham County, N.C. I was born in Cherokee Co., N.C. I claim my Indian descent through both parents. My father's name was Edward Delozier. He died just after the Civil War. He died in Swain Co., N.C. My father died in 1870. He was born in Blount Co., Tenn. I think he was in his seventies when he died. Edward Delozier came from Blount Co., Tenn. to Cherokee Co., N.C. His mother, Alsey Fields, claimed to be 1/4 Cherokee. Edward Delozier married a Poindexter. Her name was Elizabeth. She was Pledge Poindexter's daughter". Applicant's claim through the Poindexters brings her case into the large group of applicants claiming through Chief Donohoo. These may be divided into four classes: First, those claiming through Elizabeth (Betty) Pledge Poindexter; Second, those claiming through Frank Pledge; Third, those claiming through John Ayers, and Fourth, those claiming through Junalusky. These four individuals are alleged to have been the children of Elizabeth (or Betty) Pledge, who was said to have been the daughter of Chief Donohoo. There are about 800 or 1000 applications, representing probably 1500 individuals, claiming descent through these lines. The family history of those claiming through Betty Pledge Poindexter and Frank Pledge is comparatively clear, but that of those claiming through John Ayers and Junalusky is more involved, but, nevertheless, leads back to the common source, Chief Donohoo. As nearly as can be determined from the more or less conflicting statements contained in the numerous applications and the testimony taken, it would appear the Chief Donohoo was born in Va., probably near or on the James River, about the year 1700; that he married a white woman by the name of Mary Wentworth, and had a daughter who was given the name of Elizabeth, or Betty, who married a white man by the name of William, commonly called Bill.Pledge – that this Betty Pledge had two children who took the name of Pledge, to-wit, Elizabeth or Betty, the second, and Frank Pledge, and that she also, either before or after her marriage to William Pledge, had two other children, John Ayers and Junalusky. Betty Pledge, the second, sometime about the year 1760 or 1765, married Thomas Poindexter, a white man, who was born on the Rappahannock River, about 1733. They subsequently shortly after 1765 moved to what was known as the east bend of the Yadkin River, in what is not

Yadkin County, N. C., and there raised a large family, having twelve children, and their descendants are scattered through the counties of Stokes, Surry, Yadkin and Forsythe, North Carolina. It further appears that Frank Pledge removed to the same general locality with the Poindexters and his descendants are also located in that vicinity, as are also some of the descendants of Junalusky and John Ayers. It would appear further that Thomas and Elizabeth Pledge Poindexter took up a section of land on the Yadkin River sometime prior to 1770 and their descendants have occupied a portion of this tract from that day to this. It does not appear from the applications or from the testimony taken that any of the descendants of Chief Donohoo have lived in tribal relation to any band or tribe of Indians since the marriage of Betty Donohoo to William Pledge. There is nothing but the traditions of the family to show that Chief Donohoo was a Cherokee Indian, although it would seem from the testimony that there is a well recognized tradition in the family that he was of Cherokee blood. As against this tradition, however, are the equally well established facts that he came from Virginia, probably from the neighborhood of the James River, and that Betty Pledge Poindexter was born probably in the neighborhood of Louisa Co., Va., which was the locality from which Thomas Poindexter removed to North Carolina with his wife. There is nothing in the history of the Cherokee people that I have been able to discover that would indicate that they ever occupied the section of Virginia that appears to have been the home of Chief Donohoo and his immediate descendants, and it is certain, so far as the treaties between the Cherokees and the United States discloses, that the Cherokee Nation never undertook to cede to the United States any land in this section of Virginia or any lands in the vicinity of what is now Yadkin, Surry, Stokes and Forsythe Counties, N.C. In the year 1777, the Cherokee Indians made a treaty with Virginia and North Carolina, by which they ceded what they claimed as the lands in the extreme eastern limits of their domain, but the territory ceded did not extend to within forty miles of the east bend of the Yadkin River where Thomas and Elizabeth Pledge Poindexter were then living, and at the time of the treaty of 1835, the home of the Poindexters was from 150 to 200 miles the nearest point of the Cherokee domain as relinquished by that treaty, and between them and the Cherokee domain was interposed the Blue Ridge Mountains. There is no intimation in the testimony that any of those descendants or their ancestors back to the time of the Revolutionary War, have been regarded as Indians, but on the contrary, the testimony clearly seems to indicate that they have been living as white people and have passed in the communities in which they have resided as white people. They do no claim to have been enrolled as Indians or to have had any recognition by the Cherokee Tribe as Indians or to have received any benefits as members of the Eastern Cherokee Tribe of Indians or as members of any tribe of Indians. From the unquestioned tradition that is fully established in this large family, it would appear quite certain that there was an ancestor who was of Indian extraction, but from the history as given in the applications and in the testimony, it seems much more probable that this ancestor was a member of one of the Virginia tribes, rather than of Cherokee extraction, and certainly the applications and the testimony fail to show that any of these parties or their ancestors were recognized Cherokees by blood at the time of the treaties of 1835-6 or 1846. A brief summary of the testimony of the witnesses in support of these claims is subjoined. Charles M. Phelps (Poindexter Test. P. 1), 30 years of age, residing at Winston-Salem, N. C., claims through his grandmother, Sally Marion, who married a Houser, who was born in Surry Co. and was seventy odd years of age at that time of her death, which occurred about 2 years ago. He states: "I do not claim Cherokee blood through any other source than my mother and grandmother, back to Betty Pledge Poindexter. I cannot say when I first heard of my Indian blood, but as a boy I heard it spoken of in a general way. I did not hear of Donohoo at that time. I first heard of him about two years ago. I learned that Betty Pledge Poindexter was born in Louisa Co., Va., from Mr. Pleasant Poindexter. It would appear that Thomas and Betty Pledge Poindexter were originally from Va. I first learned that Donahoo was considered a Cherokee Indian, within the last 2 years. None of my people, so far as I know, ever lived with the Indians as Indians. As I understand it, Donohoo was an Indian chief who had a daughter who married a white man by the name of Pledge, and they had a daughter named Elizabeth or Betty Pledge, who married Thomas Poindexter, and through that source my Indian rights come. William Poindexter, the son of Thomas and Betty Pledge, was born Dec. 7, 1767. I think William P. Poindexter was born and lived in Surry Co., N.C. I was never enrolled as an Indian and never applied for enrollment before. I do not think my people claimed to be Indians, but simply claimed to be related to Betty Pledge Poindexter. None of my people that are living have ever claimed to be Indians as I know. They have always been admitted to the white schools without question." Ellen L. Dorsett (Poindexter Test. P. 2) gives her age at 53 years and states that she was born in Forsythe Co., N.C. and claims her Indians[sic] descent through her mother, Polly Scott. She testifies: "My mother was born in Forsythe Co. She was about 76 years old when she died in 1887. I can't tell for certain when I first heard of Chief Donohoo – over 12 months ago. I first heard of Donohoo in connection with this matter about 12 months ago, but had heard of him otherwise before that. I first heard of him when I was 17 or 19 years old. I don't remember what I heard; just heard of him talking about his land; heard that he was an Indian. I don't remember hearing anything about the tribe of Indians he belonged to at that time. I heard about 12 months ago about the tribe of Indians he belonged to, when this matter first came up". Sarah Catharine Ayers (Poindexter Test. P. 4), 56 years of age, testifies: "I was born in Surry Co. I never heard anything about being an Indian until this money matter came up. There were no Indians in Surry Co. while I lived there. I have heard my grandmother Phillips talk about the Indians, though. She lived in Surry County. She was ninety-some years old when she died and she died about 25 years ago. I was born in Surry County. I lived there until I was 29 years old, then moved to Watauga Co., N.C. and stayed there 12 years and moved back to Surry Co. and stayed there until coming here two years ago. I did not claim to be an Indian when in Watauga County. I did not know about being Indian blood until this came up. My grandmother never told me about any enrollments. I never heard my grandmother say she was an Indian, but she said she had seen Indians; there were a good many of them in here. My father has been dead 7 years, I don't think he ever knew anything about being an Indian". Peter A. Apperson (Poindexter Test. P. 5), testifies: "I live at East Bend, Yadkin Co., N.C. and I am 65 years of age. I have lived near Donnoha[sic] all my life. I am related to the Poindexter family. I only know what I have been told regarding my Indian blood. Uncle Sam Martin always said we were kin to the Indians through Donohoo, and they named the station after Indian Chief Donohoo. Martin was an uncle of my wife. Frank Pledge was my great grandfather. He was the brother of Betty Pledge Poindexter. The only Indian ancestor I have heard of was Donohoo. I first heard of my descent through Donohoo about 10 or 12 years ago when I made claim for land. My wife is a descendant of Betty Pledge, and I knew if one was kin, the other was. I did not put in a claim for land, but my wife did, but I knew if she was kin, I was. My grandfather Apperson came from Virginia with the Poindexters. My grandfather's mother was a Poindexter; I was under the impression that they married in Virginia. My grandmother was only 12 years old when she came into N.C. I think my great-grandfather, Frank Pledge, lived the great part of his life in Virginia. Betty Pledge Poindexter lived close to Donnoha[sic]. She died there. I think she lived in Virginia too. I heard my grandmother talk about coming from the James River. My grandmother, Nancy Pledge, was a daughter of Frank Pledge, and she was the one who spoke of coming from the James River. Frank Pledge was the grandson of Donohoo. I don't recall that Samuel Martin ever stated to what tribe of Indians we belong". John H. Scott (Poindexter Test. P. 6) testifies: "I am 48 years of age, I was born in Surry County. I never claimed to be an Indian until this matter came up. I had never heard that there was any Indian blood in my veins". Ida Clingman Humphrey (Poindexter Test. P. 7 and 8), states: "I am 62 years old. I was born in Yadkin Co., N.C. I claim as a Cherokee Indian through the Poindexters and Donohoo. I claim my Cherokee descent through my father, who died in June 1906 at 93 years of age. He was born at Huntsville, Yadkin Co., N. C., and his mother was born in Yadkin Co., and it was through her (Ann Poindexter) I claim. I belong to the Eastern Cherokee Indians. I trace my connection through Donohoo who was Chief of the Indian Cherokees. We don't know the date of his birth or death; it must have been nearly 200 years ago; he lived first in Va. we think, and then in N. C. I don't know what section of Va. His wife's name was Mary Wentworth, a white woman, who was born, we think, in Va. I don't know what tribe of Indians he lived with in Virginia. Elizabeth Poindexter was the grandmother of Ann Poindexter. Ann's father was Francis Poindexter, son of Thomas and Betty Pledge. I don't remember when Francis Poindexter was born. Francis Poindexter was a captain in the Revolutionary War, as was his father. The record is in Raleigh, N. C. I don't know whether they were living with any band of Indians during the Revolutionary War. They fought with the colonies. I don't now that Francis Poindexter ever lived among the Indians. I never heard that he did. I state in my application that Ann Poindexter was born in 1787, so I suppose that is correct. I do not know whether Ann was the oldest child of Francis Poindexter. I do not know that she ever lived among the Indians. I know she used to go out and hunt like the Indians. I first heard of Donohoo within the last two years. I have heard that there was a chief through who we traced our descent, but I did not know his name. I never heard anything about where Donohoo came from, although it is possible that he came from James River, as was stated in testimony yesterday. I always heard I was Cherokee and never heard of any other tribe of Indians associated with our name. I do not know that any of our people were recognized as Indians by the Government. So far as I know, we were known as citizens of the country, as white people. My father, so far as I know, never claimed any rights, nor my grandmother, I never heard that she made any claim at any time for any Cherokee funds". Frances A. Hunter (Poindexter Test. P. 9) testifies: "I am 64 years of age and live in Rural Hall, N. C., Forsythe Co., and was raised on the Yadkin River. My father was Thomas A. Poindexter. He has been dead about 25 years. He was born and raised in Yadkin Co. near Donoha[sic]. I have always heard that my family contains Indian blood. Thomas Poindexter was the son of John Poindexter, and his father was Thomas Poindexter. I don't know who Donohoo was. I do not know what kind of an Indian Betty Pledge was. I get this information as to my descent from my family Bible. There has not been very much said about our Indian descent in my family. To the best of my knowledge, I have heard my father say that he was related to the Indians. He did not say to what particular tribe, but mentioned Betty Pledge. Matthew D. Phillips (Poindexter Test. P. 10) testifies: "I am 56 years of age. I have lived in Stokes Co. all my life My grandparents on my mother's side were Robert and Mary Scott. They were both born in Yadkin Co. and died there. They never lived anywhere except in Yadkin County. I recall that my mother said that the Cherokees came to her father's house and exchanged gifts. That is all that I remember my mother said about my Indian descent. She never lived with the tribe; nor did my grandparents. My mother and my grandparents were never enrolled with the Indians, and never shared in any payments. I have never shared in any payments and have never been enrolled. My ancestors were always considered white people and the children attended the white schools. The kinship of the Poindexters as descendants of Chief Donohoo has always been accepted as a well established tradition". Isaac C. Poindexter (Poindexter Test. P 11) testifies: "I am 70 years of age. I have lived in Yadkin Co. all my life. My father wad Denson Poindexter, and his father was William P. Poindexter, who was a son of Thomas Poindexter and Betty Pledge Poindexter. My father was born in 1799. I can remember William P. Poindexter. I have never been enrolled with any tribe of Indians nor have I ever lived with any tribe of Indians. I cannot exactly say what I ever heard my father say that he belonged to any tribe of Indians. I do not know that I ever heard my father say that he had Indian blood. I do not know when I first heard of Betty Pledge; it must have been 40 or 50 years ago. I do not know when I first heard of Chief Donohoo, but is was not so long back. I did not know anything about Chief Donohoo being an ancestor of mine until this matter came up. I do not remember hearing my father speak of him as one of my ancestors. I have heard that Betty Pledge came from Va. on the James River, but I do not know any particulars. I have always passed as a white man. My father also passed as a white man. I never tried to be enrolled as a Cherokee Indian before this. I do not know of any tribes of Indians in Yadkin County or Surry County, as Indians in my time". John K. Martin (Poindexter Test. P. 12) who is not himself a claimant, testifies: "I live in Patrick Co., Va. I am 78 years of age. I was born and raised in Davis Co., N.C. I have known the Poindexters since I was a small boy. I remember John and Pleasant Poindexter. I knew John Poindexter as a boy would know an older man. I do not know what relation Jack Poindexter was to Thomas Poindexter. They were recognized as white people in the community but I have heard them spoken of as having Indian blood. They prided themselves on their Indian blood. Jack Poindexter was a middle-aged man when I first knew him as a small boy. I never heard him speak of Chief Donohoo. I know a Jennie Poindexter and heard her speak of the Cherokee Indians. She lived in Surry Co. at that time. I have heard her speak to the children incidentally about trouble with the Cherokee Indians and familiarity with some of them. I never heard her speak of Chief Donohoo. I never heard her speak of Betty Pledge. I never heard her say that she herself was an Indian. I never heard Jack Poindexter say that he was an Indian, except that he rather prided himself that he had some Indian blood. Jennie Poindexter was about the same age as Jack Poindexter when I first knew her. Jennie Poindexter married a Clingman and was the mother of General Clingman who was about my age". Martha M. Sharp (Poindexter Test. P. 13) testifies: "I live at East Bend, N. C. and am 77 years of age. My mother was 84 years of age at the time of her death, which occurred about 13 years ago at East Bend. She was born in Forsythe Co. My grandmother, Nancy Vest, lived with my mother and I was grown when she died. Nancy Vest was born in Virginia somewhere in the lower part of the state, and when her parents died she moved up into

Patrick County. She was about 85 or 86 years old at the time of her death. She died before the war. I do not recollect ever having heard her say that she was part Indian. I have heard her speak of her grandfather, Frank Pledge, but I have never heard her say that he was an Indian. I have never heard my mother say that she was an Indian. They both passed as white people. I never claimed to be an Indian before this matter came up". Abner P. Smitherman (Poindexter Test. P. 15) testifies: "I am 78 years of age and was born near the Yadkin River about four miles from East Bend, and have lived in Yadkin County all my life. My wife was a Truelove; her grandfather's name was J. G. Poindexter. I knew him quite well. He was close to 89 years of age when he died in 1883. I think I have heard J.G. Poindexter speak of his mother, Bettie Pledge Poindexter, and his grandmother. J. G. Poindexter passed in his community as a white man. I do not know that I ever heard him speak of having Indian blood. I do no remember ever hearing him speak of being descended from a Cherokee Indian chief. I first heard that the Poindexters had Indian blood when I was a little fellow. Some of the old folks spoke of it. I have never seen but two or three Indians in my life and never heard of any tribe living in this country in my life-time. The Indians I saw were with a show". Samuel A. Martin (Poindexter Test. P. 16) testifies- "I am 60 years of age, and live at East Bend, N. C. I am Chief of Police at this place. I could not tell you what kind of Indian Donohoo was but I always thought that he was a Cherokee. I have always heard and understood that the Indian settlement was right around this station here. I have always been recognized as a white man. I have never lived with a tribe nor has my father lived with a tribe". Thomas F. Matthews (Poindexter Test. P. 18) testifies: "I am 74 years of age and was born in what is now Yadkin Co. and have lived there all my life. I claim Indian blood from what I have been told. I have never received any money from the Government as an Indian. I have never lived with any tribe of Indians. I do not know that I have ever seen any Indians in this neighborhood, except in shows. I have always voted. I claim Indian blood through my mother, Mittie Poindexter, before her marriage. I remember my mother quite well. She has been dead about 18 years. I have heard my mother say that she was part Indian. She said she was Cherokee, and that her grandmother was a daughter of the Cherokee Chief. My mother never lived with the Indians as I know of. I do not suppose she ever received any money from the Government. I have always claimed that I thought I had a little Cherokee blood. I have always been recognized in the neighborhood as a white man. My mother and grandfather told me that I had some Indian blood, but it was never thrown up to me that I had Indian blood that I know of." Mary R. Marion (Poindexter Test. P. 19) testifies: "I am 62 years old. I live in Surry Co. I was born right across the mouth of the Ararat River in Surry Co. I am related to the Poindexters through my father, his mother being Sally R. Poindexter, the daughter of Thomas Poindexter and Elizabeth Pledge. Betty Pledge Poindexter, my father told me and he died a month ago at the age of 95, came from Va. and her father was William Pledge. He did not say where Betty Pledge was born. The wife of William Pledge was Betty Donohoo; I cannot tell you where Betty Donohoo was born; my father could not remember it. I have heard that the father of Betty Donohoo was Donohoo, a Cherokee Indian Chief, who lived finally in his last home in Yadkin (we think he did). I do not know where he lived before that. I am generally regarded in the community as a white woman and my father passed as a white man. I never enrolled as an Indian and my father never told me that he was enrolled. He never got any money from the Indians except what he worked for, as he was a doctor among the Western

Cherokees at Vinita, Ind. Ter. He practiced there for about 10 years; began practicing there in 1867. The Cherokees offered tribal rights if he would stay there, but he did not claim any rights at all. Then he moved to Mo. and died there. So far as I know he never made any claim. Sally R. Poindexter was born April 6, 1784". Pleasant Poindexter (Poindexter Test. P. 20 - 3) testifies: "My name if Pleasant Poindexter; I am 71 years old the 7th day of March past. My residence is East Bend, Yadkin Co. I was born in Surry Co., N. C. where I now live. Born there and raised there and spent my life there. My father was born July 14, 1788. He was born right the other side of my house about 150 yards.

Q. Do you claim any Indian blood through your grandfather, Thomas Poindexter?
A. No sir; none at all.
Q. He was a white man?
A. Yes sir; he was a white man.
Q. Do you know where Betty Pledge Poindexter was born?
A. I think she was born in Va. She died Feb. 29, 1816.
Q. Did you ever hear that she came from Louisa Co., Va?
A. Yes sir; that was my understanding.
Q. Who was the mother of Betty Pledge Poindexter?
A. It is said that Betty Donohoo Pledge was her mother.
Q. Did you ever hear where Betty Donohoo Pledge was born and lived?
A. No sir but I believe she was born in Virginia or North Carolina; it was in Virginia. I believe she married in Va.
Q. Who was the father of Betty Donohoo Pledge?
A. I was taught – it was said that a Cherokee Indian Chief was her father.
Q. Did the account, as you give it, indicate where Donohoo lived?
A. My impression is in Va.
Q. Do you understand that Betty Pledge married a white man – the daughter of Donohoo?
A. Yes sir; she married Bill Pledge, a white man.
Q. Did the account as you have it give any further information in regard to Chief Donohoo, as to the place of his death, or when he died, or when he was born?
A. No sir; a blank in there. But the woman, the mother of Betty Pledge, Mary Wentworth, I have a little knowledge that she was connected with the nobility of the country. Also about the oceans being connected – whether she came over with her mother because my uncle's grandmother came over the ocean.
Q. You have never been enrolled as an Indian yourself, have you?
A. No sir; never that I know anything about.
Q. Your father was not enrolled that you know of?
A. No sir; not that I know of.
Q. You have both pass in the neighborhood as white men?
A. Yes sir; never known anything else in my life.
Q. In the days of the muster, you were mustered the same as others?
A. Yes sir; yes sir.
Q. Did you ever know of any band or tribe of Indians in your time living in this vicinity?
A. No sir; no sir. I cannot remember that. Never saw but one or two and that was in my childhood. One ditched for my mother and another claimed to be a doctor.
Q. You have spoken of Thomas Poindexter and his wife, Elizabeth. Did you ever hear whether or not they took up any land in this vicinity? And if so, how much?

A. Yes sir; I cannot tell you only the one survey and that is in the bend of the river. That was 640 acres.
Q. Taken in what year?
A. Let's see; as well as I remember in 1760.
Q. Did you ever hear of this Thomas Poindexter's having a brother John?
A. Yes sir.
Q. What was his profession?
A. He was a preacher and county clerk
Q. Where?
A. Louisa County, Va. One of my relations in Mo. wrote that Thomas Poindexter, Jr. was born on the banks of the Rappahannock River in 1738".

In consideration of the premises, the application of this claimant and of all other persons claiming through Edward Delozier, Alsey Delozier nee Fields, Alsey Spears, Elizabeth Poindexter, Pledge Poindexter, and Betty Pledge Poindexter, are hereby rejected.

App: 665 Ollie Wright and 1 child, Topton, N.C.
Rejected. Cousin of #126 and claims through same source.
App: 666 Charles A. Pace, Topton, N.C.
Rejected. Uncle of #126 and claims through the same source.
App: 667 William Henry Martin, Tusquitee, N.C.
Rejected. Great uncle of #126 and claims through same source.
App: 668 Helen and Margaret Cummins, Walnut Grove, Mo.
Rejected. Applicant claims through Alex Brown. See full report in #35.
App: 669 Aaron Thomas Guy and 1 child, Richmond, Ind.
Rejected. It does not appear that any ancestor was ever enrolled or that any ancestor was party to the treaty of 1835-6 and 1846. Shows no real connection with the Eastern Cherokees. (Miscel. Test. P. 1811 and 1812).
App: 670 Anna Cummins, Walnut Grove, Mo.
Rejected. Applicant claims through Alex Brown. See full report in #35.
App: 671 Robert M. Hendricks and 1 child, Ochelata, Okla.
Admitted. Applicant's mother enrolled by Drennen in 1851, Tah. 364.
App: 672 Hattie E. Johnson and 1 child, Tomotla, N.C.
Rejected. Cousin of #126 and claims through same source.
App: 673 Eliza J. Jones and 6 children, Wilmot, N.C.
Rejected. Cousin of #126 and claims through same source.
App: 674 John Zachary and 4 children, Star City, Ark.
Rejected. Brother of #592 and claims through same source.
App: 675 Samuel T. Helton, Cordiff, Tenn.
Rejected. Nephew of #504 and claims through same source.
App: 676 M.C. Carroll, Rockwood, Tenn.
Rejected. Applicant claims through his wife who died in 1903 and makes claim through no other source.
App: 677 Silas M. Helton and 5 children, Sale Creek, Tenn.
Rejected. Nephew of #504 and claims through the same source.
App: 678 Sarah E. Smith, Rocky, Okla.
Rejected. Sister of #546 and claims through same source.

App: 679 Rosa Bruner and 3 children, Senora, Okla.
Rejected. Applicant states that his mother and father were both enrolled as Choctaws.
App: 680 Darthula McCoy, Madill, Okla.
Rejected. Neither applicant nor ancestors ever enrolled. Does not establish fact of descent from person who was a party to the treaty of 1835-6 and 1846.
App: 681 Melissa Keith, Little Rock, Ark.
Rejected. Sister of #669 and claims through the same source.
App: 682 Wash Swimmer and 1 child, Rose, Okla.
Admitted. Applicant and his father enrolled in 1851 by Drennen, Del. 689.
App: 683 David Oldfield, Locust Grove, Okla.
Admitted. Applicant and mother enrolled in 1851 by Drennen, Sal. 154.
App: 684 Joseph Sixkiller and 3 children, Locust Grove, Okla.
Admitted. Applicant's father enrolled as Redbird Sixkiller in 1851 by Drennen, G.S. 222.
App: 685 Eliza E. Brewer, Muskogee, Okla.
Rejected. Claimant was born in 1849. She derives her Indian blood, if any, from her mother. Neither she nor her mother have been enrolled on any Cherokee roll and no showing whatever is made that any of her ancestors were parties to treaties of 1835- 46. Her mother was born in Raleigh, N.C. which is nearly 200 miles removed from Cherokee domain as constitued[sic] in 1835. (Miscel. Test. P. 3059).
App: 686 Charles Harris and 2 children, Muskogee, Okla.
Admitted. Applicant enrolled in 1851 by Chapman #1759.
App: 687 Elizabeth Harden, Andrews, N.C.
Admitted. Applicant's father and paternal grandparents enrolled in 1851 by Chapman, Nos. 1250, 1251 and 1243. (Miscel. Test. P. 1557-8-9-60.)
App: 688 Harriet Lovingood and 2 children, Grandview, N.C.
Rejected. Applicant claims through Annie Blythe. See full report in #153.
App: 689 Alice Angel and 3 children, Andrews, N.C.
Rejected. Niece of #664 and claims through same source.
App: 690 Rachel Susan Ray, Waleska, Ga.
Rejected. Applicant claims Indian descent through both parents. Her father has filed application #2877. That group is rejected and the decision there made is here referred to as per grounds of rejecting claimant on the paternal side. Claimant's mother has filed application #2881, and as she was born in 1840 and as claimants mother had several brothers and sisters contained in this group, the mother of this is written up and decision made as to her case and all reference herein after made applies to #2881. Said claimant #2881 gets her Indian blood through her father, William Davis, who was born in Cherokee Co., N.C., probably along some time about 1800 to 1805 or 6, as applicant #12012 who is a sister of this claimant, gives her oldest brother's birth as 1828. There is a William Davis enrolled by Chapman in 1851, but there can be no doubt but that William Davis was some person other than the father of claimant, as his father was Daniel Davis, the same brothers and sisters are not given, and claimant's father was the head of a family. There is a Dr. William Davis on the roll of 1835, enrolled on Santah Creek, Ala., and as claimant's father was born in N.C. and apparently never lived anywhere else but there and in Ga., that William Davis could not have been claimant's father. Then too, the family as given on the 1835 roll could not have been that of

William Davis, as it does not tally up at all with the number in the family, nor the ages nor sexes. The claimant herself does not appear on any roll of Cherokees, nor do any of her brothers and sister. She and several of her brothers and sisters were living in and around the country where Hester made his roll in 1882 to 1884, and none of them are enrolled by him. None of the claimants who claim their Indian descent through the same source as does claimant, make any pretense of being on any roll themselves or of ever having had any Indian names, and consequently they and none of their ancestors not being found on the rolls under the simple name of Davis, and sufficient evidence not being furnished, identifying any of them or their ancestors with the Cherokees or as having been parties to the treaties of 1835-6 and 1846, this claimant and all claiming Indian blood through the same source are rejected.

App: 691 James P. Wicked and 2 children, Akins, Okla.
Admitted. Applicant's father enrolled in 1851, Chapman #1976.

App: 692 Minnie Boydston and 7 children, Akins, Okla.
Admitted. Sister of #691 and claims through same source.

App: 693 Samantha I. Jordan and 1 child, Akins, Okla.
Admitted. Sister of #691 and claims through same source.

App: 694 Annie A. Peters and 5 children, Sallisaw, Okla.
Admitted. Sister of #691 and claims through same source.

App: 695 Sarotho A. Lessley and 6 children, Akins, Okla.
Admitted. Sister of #691 and claims through same source.

App: 696 Nicholas Thomas, Vinita, Okla.
Admitted. Applicant enrolled in 1851 by Drennen, Del. 942.

App: 697 Sarah Foreman, Sallisaw, Okla.
Rejected. Applicant enrolled with Old Settlers in 1851. Claims right to participate in payment through husband who died in 1899.

App: 698 Charlie Davis, Sallisaw, Okla.
Admitted. Applicant's father enrolled in 1851 by Chapman #1611.

App: 699 Elizabeth Davis, Sallisaw, Okla.
Rejected. Applicant claims through husband who died in 1895.

App: 700 William Robbins, Oaks, Okla.
By N.L. Neilson, Gdn.
Admitted. Applicant's grandmother and great grandfather enrolled in 1851 by Drennen, G.S. 708. (Miscel. Test. P. 3259).

App: 701 Nancy Jane Robbins, Oaks, Okla.
Admitted. Grandmother of #700 and claims through same source.

App: 702 Nellie Walker, Kansas City, Okla.
Admitted. Applicant enrolled in 1851 by Drennen, Del. 535.

App: 703 Ollie Russell, Oaks Okla.
Admitted. Applicant enrolled by Drennen in 1851, G.S. 111.

App: 704 John T. Foreman and 2 children, Sallisaw, Okla.
Admitted. Applicant's father enrolled by Drennen in 1851, S.B. 192.

App: 705 Lizzie Kingfisher, Ochelata, Okla.
Admitted. Applicant's grandparents enrolled by Drennen in 1851, Sal. 336.

App: 706 Richard Daniels, Ochelata, Okla.
Admitted. Son of #536 and claims through same source.

App: 707 James C. Blythe, Bartlesville, Okla.
Admitted. Applicant enrolled as James C. Blythe in 1851 by Drennen, Del. 922.
App: 708 Susan K. Morrison and 9 children, Ochelata, Okla.
Admitted. First cousin of #411 and claims through the same source.
App: 709 Elmira Scott and 3 children, Coffeyville, Kans.
Admitted. Applicant's grandfather enrolled in 1851 by Drennen, G.S. 434.
App: 710 Mahala Smith, Wann, Okla.
Admitted. Claimant enrolled with her mother in 1851 by Drennen, Ill. 15. (Miscel. Test. P. 3458).
App: 711 Sarah Mizer and 2 children, Coffeyville, Kans.
Admitted. Applicant's father enrolled in 1851 by Drennen, G.S. 434.
App: 712 Blackfox Kingfisher, Peggs, Okla.
Admitted. Applicant enrolled by Drennen in 1851, Del. 525.
App: 713 Jacob Dick and 2 children, Ochelata, Okla.
Admitted. Applicant enrolled by Drennen in 1851, Sal. 224.
App: 714 Stand Suagee and 3 children, Coffeyville, Kans.
Admitted. Applicant enrolled in 1851 by Drennen, Del. 83 (Miscel Test. P. 2137).
App: 715 Texana Fields, Dewey, Okla.
Admitted. Applicant's father enrolled in 1851 by Drennen, Ill. 169 ½.
App: 716 Richard M. Fields and 4 children, Dewey, Okla.
Admitted. Applicant's father enrolled in 1851 by Drennen, Can. 10.
App: 717 Eva Henderson, Topton, N.C.
Rejected. Cousin of #126 and claims through same source.
App: 718 Ella M. Wilson, Marble, N.C.
Rejected. Cousin of #716 and claims through same source.
App: 719 William Parris and 2 children, Tulsa, Okla.
Admitted. Applicant's maternal grandparents enrolled in 1851 by Drennen, Tah. 277. (Miscel. Test. P. 4160).
App: 720 Chewanah Chualukee, Eucha, Okla.
Admitted. First cousin of #645 and claims through same source.
App: 721 Young Pigeon Wilson, Eucha, Okla.
Admitted. Applicant's mother enrolled in 1851 by Drennen, Del. 29.
App: 722 Samuel Dry and 4 children, Kansas, Okla.
Admitted. Son of #702 and claims through same source.
App: 723 John Sapsucker and 1 child, Eucha, Okla.
Admitted. Brother of #172 and claims through same source.
App: 724 Lillie A. Trull, Marble, N.C.
Rejected. Applicant claims through Annie Blythe. See full report in #153.
App: 725 Eliza Mandley, Spring Place, Ga.
Rejected. Neither applicant nor ancestors ever enrolled. Does not establish fact of decent from person who was a party to the treaty of 1835-6 and 1846. (Miscel. Test. P. ~~2839~~ (*Handwritten below marked out number: 1433*).
App: 726 Jonathan C. Hampton and 4 children, Hayesville, N.C.
Rejected. Applicant claims through Annie Blythe. See full report in #153.
App: 727 No application was given this number. It was omitted by mistake.

App: 728 Jake Concene, Robbinsville, N.C.
Admitted. Applicant enrolled in 1851 by Chapman #981.
App: 729 John D. Axe, Robbinsville, N.C.
Admitted. Applicant's father, George Axe, and mother enrolled in 1851 by Chapman #1260 and 1261. (Miscel. Test. P. 1684).
App: 730 John Ropetwister, Robbinsville, N.C.
Admitted. Applicant's father enrolled in 1851 by Chapman 995. (Miscel. Test. P. 1680).
App: 731 Eva Axe, Robbinsville, N.C.
Admitted. Sister of #730 and claims through same source.
App: 732 Robert L. Hauseman, St. Jo, Texas.
Rejected. Brother of #546 and claims through same source.
App: 733 Jeff Creech, deceased.
Duplicate of #759.
App: 734 Amanda Thornton, South West City, Mo. R.F.D. 3
Admitted. Duplicate of #559 and #560.
App: 735 Mary E. Alcorn and 2 grandchildren, Braggs, Okla.
Admitted. Applicant enrolled as Mary E. McCrary by Drennen in 1851, Del. 25.
App: 736 Taylor Hicks, and 5 children, Choteau, Okla.
Admitted. Applicant enrolled in 1851 by Drennen, Del. 940.
App: 737 Richard J. Parris, Bartlesville, Okla.
Admitted. Son of #1233 and claims through same source.
App: 738 Geo. W. Fawling and 5 children, Wann, Okla.
Admitted. Applicant's father, Ellis Fallen, enrolled by Drennen in 1851, Tah. 528.
App: 739 Geo. M. Harrison and 5 children, Bushyhead, Okla.
Rejected. Applicant claims through Keziah Vann. See full report in #276.
App: 740 Amanda D. Neale, Allegheny, Pa., 1611 Irwin Ave.
Rejected. Neither applicant nor ancestors ever enrolled. Does not establish fact of descent from person who was a party to the treaty of 1835-6 and 1846.
App: 741 Leonard E. Trainor and 3 children, ~~Bartlesville~~, Okla.
Admitted. Applicant's mother, Lucy Williams, enrolled in 1851 by Drennen, Fl. 525 (*Handwritten above Bartlesville, Chelsea*)
App: 742 James Kingfisher and 2 children, Bartlesville, Okla.
Admitted. Father "Squa-da-le-che" enrolled in 1851 by Drennen, Del. 525.
App: 743 Mary J. Hensley and 2 children, Tellico Plains, Tenn.
Admitted. Applicant's father enrolled in 1851 by Chapman #2100. (Miscel. Test. P. 560).
App: 744 Mary B. Lane and 2 children, Oklahoma City, Okla.
Rejected. Application #774 and others grouped therewith, alleged descendants of the common ancestor, William A. Duke, whose name appears on the roll of 1835. Of these claimants, the two oldest are Robert Avery, aged 81 years and Isaac N. Avery, aged 67 years. Applications #10484 and #14642, respectively. Robert Avery was born in Hall Co., Ga. in 1827, which was not at that time part of the Cherokee Domain. He was not

enrolled in 1835 or 1851. He claims Indian descent through his mother, Myrom Avery, who died as late as 1881. She was born in Greenville District, S.C. and lived in Bibb Co., Ala. in 1851, quite removed from the Cherokee domain. Myrom Avery was the daughter of Luke and Polly Crompton, and Polly Crompton was the daughter of William A. Duke, alleged to have been enrolled in 1835. "Neither Myrom Avery nor Polly Crompton were ever enrolled, and as they lived in Greenville Dist., S.C. at the time Myrom Avery was born, it is a natural presumption they lived there some time before. This locality is quite removed from the Cherokee domain. Isaac N. Avery, #14642, a brother of Robt. Avery, was born in Bibb Co., Ala. in 1841. In response to letter of inquiry, he wrote the Special Commissioner under date of Dec. 11, 1907, that his parents were married in Greenville District, S.C. in 1817 or 1818. That they lived in Georgia near the Cherokee line, and that they moved to Bibb Co., Ala. between 1828 and 1833, and were still living there in 1851. See letter marked "Exhibit A" in #14642. The William A. Duke enrolled in 1835 and living in Murray Co., Ga., who it is alleged is the great grandfather of Robert Avery, born in 1827, and the common ancestor of these claimants, had but 2 in his family at the time of the enrollment, himself and a female, presumably his wife. The enrollment of this small family further shows that one of the two was white and connected by marriage only, while the other was a quadroon. From the foregoing it appears that neither the applicant, Robert Avery, his parents nor grandparents ever lived in the Cherokee domain, were ever enrolled or were ever recognized as being members of the tribe, either by descent or association. If Myrom Avery and her husband moved to Bibb Co., Ala., between 1828 and 1833, and still lived in the middle of that state as late as 1851, they surely were not living in the Cherokee domain at the time of the treaty of 1835-6, and could not have been parties to this treaty. And the William A. Duke enrolled from Murray Co., Ga. in 1835 is not the William A Duke herein mentioned as the common ancestor of these claimants. These cases are accordingly rejected.

App: 745 Felix Payne and 7 children, Royston, Ga.
Admitted. Grandmother, Catherine Panther, enrolled in 1851 by Chapman #1344. Applicant a grand nephew of #6 and claims through that source.

App: 746 Alsie McKiney and 1 child, Andrews, N.C.
Rejected. Applicant a sister of #7 and claims through same source.

App: 747 Jasper P. Allison and 2 children, Choteau, Okla.
Admitted. Applicant's mother enrolled in 1851 by Drennen, Del. 945.

App: 748 Amanda Blair and 2 children, Cutler, Ill.
Rejected. It does not appear that any ancestor was a party to the treaties of 1835-6 and 1846, nor does it appear that any ancestor was ever enrolled. (Miscel. Test. P. 2055).

App: 749 Lidora A. Turner and 4 children, Claremore, Okla.
Admitted. ~~First~~ Sister of #47 and claims through same source.

App: 750 Nannie Parsley and 5 children, Claremore, Okla.
Admitted. First cousin of #47 and claims through same source.

App: 751 Nannie H. Rosenthal, Claremore, Okla.
Admitted. Niece of #107 and claims through same source.

App: 752 Virgil A. Garner and 5 children, Lowrey, Okla.
Admitted. First cousin of #614 and claims through same source.

App: 753 Mae Rich and 4 children, Prairie Grove, Ark.
Admitted. First cousin of #614 and claims through same source.

App: 754 Van Ward, Grove, Okla.
Admitted. Applicant enrolled by Chapman in 1851, #2093.
App: 755 David McN. Rogers, Adair, Okla.
Admitted. Half-brother of #400 and claims through same source.
App: 756 Arbazine Bailey and 1 child, Marshall, Texas.
Rejected. It does not appear that any ancestor was ever enrolled or that any ancestor was a party to the treaties of 1835-6 and 1846. Cannot relate applicant to any of the Albertys on the roll.
App: 757 Lewis Gaines and 4 children, Marshall, Texas.
Rejected. Applicant claims through the same source as #756.
App: 758 Sarah Beck, Clayton, Ga.
Admitted. Sister of #513 and claims through same source. Applicant enrolled by Hester #2570.
App: 759 Jeff Creech (Dead) Howe, Okla.
Admitted. Applicant's grandmother, Mary Ann Starns, enrolled in 1851 by Drennen, Ill. 28.
App: 760 Samuel Beck and 6 children, Clayton, Ga.
Admitted. Brother of #513 and claims through same source. Applicant enrolled by Hester #2580.
App: 761 Samuel Sixkiller and 3 children, Stilwell, Okla.
Admitted. Applicant's father enrolled in 1851 by Drennen, F1. 46. (Miscel. Test. P. 4019).
App: 762 Kiamintia C. McCullough and 1 child, Coffeyville, Kans.
Admitted. Applicant's mother and grandparents enrolled in 1851 by Drennen, Ill. 276.
App: 763 Barbra A. Presley.
Duplicate of #77.
App: 764 Jennie Henson and 3 children, Stilwell, Okla.
Admitted. Sister of #761. Claims through same source.
App: 765 John Skul-lor-le and 2 children Ochelata, Okla.
Admitted. Applicant's mother and maternal grandparents enrolled in 1851 by Drennen, Sal. 642.
App: 766 Ruth Mounts and 1 child, Dewey, Okla.
Admitted. Mother of #216 and claims through same source.
App: 767 Melissa Caroline Dooley, Catoosa, Okla.
Admitted. Applicant enrolled by Chapman in 1851, #1885.
App: 768 James M. Gravitt and 1 child, Catoosa, Okla.
Admitted. Applicant enrolled by Chapman in 1851, #1882.
App: 769 Lydia Quinton and 2 children, Bunch, Okla.
Admitted. Applicant's father enrolled in 1851 by Drennen, F1. 36.
App: 770 Walter Sixkiller and 4 children, Stilwell, Okla.
Admitted. Brother of #761. Claims through same source.
App: 771 John B. Stamper, Treadway, Tenn.
Rejected. Ancestors not on rolls. It is not proven that ancestors were parties to the treaties of 1835-6 and 1846.

App: 772 Mary Jane Stamper, Treadway, Tenn.
Rejected. It is not shown that the ancestors of applicant were parties to the treaties of 1835-6 and 1846. Parents' home 200 miles from Cherokee domain in 1835. Ancestors not on rolls.
App: 773 Jennie Akins and 6 children, Oolagah, Okla.
Admitted. Applicant's father enrolled in 1851 by Drennen, G.S. 325.
App: 774 Andrew T. Akin, Oolagah, Okla.
Admitted. Applicant and his mother enrolled in 1851 by Drennen, G.S. 412.
App: 775 Nancy Dotson, Blue Ridge, Ga.
Rejected. Half-sister of #776 and claims through same source.
App: 776 Malinda A. Ray, Blue Ridge, Ga.
Rejected. It does not appear that any ancestor was a party to the treaties of 1835-6 and 1846, nor does it appear that any ancestor was ever enrolled. (Miscel. Test. 1496).
App: 777 Amanda A. Dotson, Blue Ridge, Ga.
Rejected. Half-sister of #776 and claims through the same source.
App: 778 Joseph M. Mayfield and 4 children, Lenapah, Okla.
Admitted. Applicant's mother enrolled in 1851 by Chapman #1542. (Miscel. Test. P. 4139).
App: 779 William J. Foreman and 1 child, Westville, Okla.
Admitted. Son of #773 and claims through same source.
App: 780 Lula E. Reynolds and 3 children, Westville, Okla.
Admitted. Sister of #773 and claims through same source.
App: 781 Susan Robbins and 2 children, Ramona, Okla.
Admitted. Applicant's grandparents enrolled by Drennen in 1851, G.S. 451.
App: 782 Martha E. Lane,
Duplicate of #22565.
App: 783 William C. Smith, Chelsea, Okla.
Rejected. Claimant was born in Mo. in 1849. It does not appear that he or his mother or other ancestors lived with the Cherokees as members of the tribe and they are not identified on any Cherokee roll. Claimant is not enrolled by the Dawes Commission. (Miscel. Test. P. 4101).
App: 784 Ollie Bunch and 1 child, Stilwell, Okla.
Admitted. Applicant's grandfather on mother's side enrolled in 1851 by Drennen, S.B. 37 under the name of Little Deer Eagle.
App: 785 Gafford Tah-noo-wee and 4 children, Marble City, Okla.
Admitted. Applicant's father and grandparents on father's side enrolled in 1851 by Drennen, F1. 537.
App: 786 Nancy Sixkiller, Stilwell, Okla.
Admitted. Applicant's mother enrolled in 1851 by Drennen, F1. 512. (Miscel. Test. P. 3218).
App: 787 Ezekiel C. McLaughlin, Ardmore, Okla.
Rejected. Applicant enrolled by Dawes Commission on Choctaw by Marriage, Roll #1052.
App: 788 Edith H. Walker, Ft. Gibson, Okla.
Admitted. Applicant's father enrolled in 1851 by Drennen, Tah. 532.

App: 789 Emma I Hicks, Ft. Gibson, Okla.
Admitted. Sister of #788 and claims through same source.
App: 790 Noah Bunch, Stilwell, Okla.
Admitted. Applicant's father and paternal grandparents enrolled in 1851 by Drennen, F1. 74.
App: 791 Juliette Schrimpsher, Webbers Falls, Okla.
Admitted. Applicant and her father enrolled in 1851 by Drennen, F1. 276.
App: 792 Walter W. Tucker, et al Ramona, Okla.
Admitted. Cousins of #472 and claims through same source. Jacob D. Newport, Gdn. in this case.
App: 793 Elijah Blythe, Ramona, Okla.
Admitted. Applicant enrolled in 1851 by Drennen, Del. 917.
App: 794 Vandia L. Washington, Ramona, Okla.
Admitted. Nephew of #543 and claims through same source.
App: 795 Thomas T. Tucker, Ramona, Okla.
Admitted. Cousin of #472 and claims through same source.
App: 796 William Cole and 1 child, Dora, ~~Okla~~ *(Ga.* Handwritten*)*
Admitted. Applicant's parents and grandmother enrolled in 1851 by Chapman, Nos. 1431, 1432 and 1434.
App: 797 Elizabeth Baker and 1 child, Sweet Gum, Ga.
Admitted. Aunt of #796 and claims through same source.
App: 798 Elmira Baker and 4 children, Sweet Gum, Ga.
Admitted. Aunt of #796 and claims through same source.
App: 799 George W. Cole and 6 children, Sweet Gum, Ga.
Admitted. Uncle of #796 and claims through same source.
App: 800 Dora Sowther, Dora, Ga.
Admitted. Sister of #796 and claims through same source.
App: 801 Thomas Bruce, Culberson, N.C.
Admitted. Cousin of #796 and claims through same source.
App: 802 Robert and Emery Cole, Dora, Ga.
By Laura Cole, Gdn.
Admitted. Brothers of #796 and claim through same source.
App: 803 Ella Patterson and 6 children, Dora, Ga.
Admitted. Sister of #796 and claims through same source.
App: 804 Katie Cannon and 2 children, Sleeper, Okla.
Admitted. Applicant's mother's father, James Hammer, enrolled in 1851 by Drennen, Ill. 234. (Miscel. Test. P. 2688).
App: 805 Mary M. Sharper and 1 child, Ballard, Okla.
Admitted. Applicant's father and grandfather enrolled in 1851 by Chapman #1907 and #1902 respectively.
App: 806 Savannah G. Dickson, Clayton, Ga.
Admitted. Sister of #513 and claims through same source. Applicant enrolled by Hester #2572.
App: 807 Mary A. Beck and 1 child, Clayton, Ga.
Admitted. Niece of #513 and claims through same source. Applicant enrolled by Hester #2575.

App: 808 James Beck and 2 children, Clayton, Ga.
Admitted. Brother of #513 and claims through same source. Applicant himself enrolled in 1851by Chapman #2085 and by Hester #2574.
App: 809 Susannah Snyder, Sweden, Ga.
Admitted. Aunt of #273 and claims through same source.
App: 810 Ezekiel Fields and 3 children, Big Cabin, Okla.
Admitted. Applicant enrolled in 1851 by Drennen, Del. 137.
App: 811 Timothy Fields and 6 children, Grove, Okla.
Admitted. Brother of #810 and claims through same source.
App: 812 Francis S. Curry and 5 children, South West City, Mo.
Admitted. Sister of #390 and claims through same source.
App: 813 Eliza A. Strout, Vinita, Okla.
Admitted. Claimant's parents and older brothers and sister enrolled in 1851 by Drennen, Del. 158.
App: 814 Ally Swan and 1 child, Bushyhead, Okla.
Admitted. Applicant's father and half sister enrolled by Drennen in 1851, Tah. 572.
App: 815 Susan Swan, Foyil, Okla.
Admitted. Applicant enrolled in 1851 by Drennen, Sal. 132.
App: 816 Charles F. Mayes and 3 children, Pryor Creek, Okla.
Admitted. Applicant's mother and maternal grandfather enrolled in 1851 by Drennen, Sal. 452.
App: 817 Lucinda Tincup, Pryor Creek, Okla.
Rejected. It appears from the testimony of the applicant that her mother was born Nov. 10, 1835 at Ft. Leavenworth, Kans. and therefore she could not have been a party to the treaty of 1835-6. The father of applicant was a white man. The names of the ancestors of applicant through whom she claims her Cherokee blood, do not appear upon the rolls of 1835 or 1851, either Emigrant or Old Settler roll. While the applicant was enrolled by the Dawes Commission, it clearly appears from the testimony that if her ancestors were Cherokees, they left the Eastern Cherokee domain before 1835 and therefore were not parties to the treaties of 1835-6 and 1846. For information corroborating the finding herewith, see Miscel. Test. P. 2924, 4115 and 4369. See statements under "Remarks" in Applications #1398, Supl. #1398, #11894, Question 21, and Question 21, #10918. See also letter in #1398 written by Stephen D.C. Edwards, Chaffee, Okla.
App: 818 Martha W. Brown, deceased, Adair, Okla.
Rejected. Aunt of #817 and claims through same source.
App: 819 Noel B. Mayes, Pryor Creek, Okla.
Admitted. Half brother of #816 and claims through same source.
App: 820 Philo Harris, Lynch, Okla.
Admitted. Applicant enrolled as Phil Hall Harris in 1851 by Chapman #1762.
App: 821 Mary E. Dudley,
Duplicate of #22648.
App: 822 Lizzie Jackson and 1 child, Bartlesville, Okla.
Admitted. Applicant's parents enrolled in 1851 by Drennen, Sal. 642.

App: 823 Louisa J. Hastings, Maysville, Ark.
Admitted. Applicant enrolled in 1851 by Drennen under the name of Louisa J. Stover, Dis. 20. (Miscel. Test. P. 3408).
App: 824 Hannah L. Mundon and 1 child, Oklahoma City, Okla. 429 W. 3rd St.
Rejected. It does not appear that ancestors were ever enrolled or were parties to the treaties of 1835-6 and 1846. Shows no real connection with the Eastern Cherokees. (Miscel. Test P. 2060).
App: 825 Eliza E. Johnston, Tahlequah, Okla.
Admitted. Applicant's parents enrolled in 1851 by Drennen, G.S. 232. (Miscel. Test. P. 3236).
App: 826 John Humphrey and 5 children, Collinsville, Okla.
Admitted. Brother of #38 and claims through the same source. Applicant himself enrolled by Drennen in 1851, Dis. 26.
App: 827 Lucinda Ross, Stilwell, Okla.
Admitted. Sister of #163 and claims through same source.
App: 828 Wm. H. Miller and 8 children, Wimer, Okla.
Admitted. Brother of #163 and claims through the same source.
App: 829 Henry L. Waters and 6 children, Cole, Va.
Rejected. Applicant claims through Ned Sizemore. See full report in #417.
App: 830 John Sylvester Stubbs, Muskogee, Okla.
Admitted. Grandson of #623 and claims through the same source.
App: 831 Mary Elen Presson and 4 children, Francis, Okla.
Rejected. Neither applicant nor ancestors ever enrolled. Does not establish fact of descent from a person who was a party to the treaty of 1835-6 and 1846.
App: 832 William H.H. Mayes, Tip, Okla.
Admitted. Applicant enrolled in 1851 by Drennen, Fl. 354.
App: 833 Rena Ross Fair, Pryor Creek, Okla.
Admitted. Applicant's mother and maternal grandparents enrolled in 1851 by Drennen, Tah. 292.
App: 834 James P. Sneed and 2 children, Moody, Okla.
Admitted. Applicant's mother enrolled in 1851 by Chapman #2079.
App: 835 Jack Ragsdale, Metory, Okla.
Admitted. Applicant and parents enrolled in 1851 by Drennen, Tah. 538.
App: 836 Polly Crowder, Westville, Okla.
Admitted. Applicant enrolled in 1851 by Drennen, G.S. 325.
App: 837 Florence E. Edmondson, Maysville, Ark.
Admitted. Daughter of #623 and claims through same source.
App: 838 Charlotte T. Taylor, Muskogee, Okla.
Admitted. Daughter of #623 and claims through same source.
App: 839 William E. Helm and 1 child, Claremore, Okla.
Rejected. From the application of William S. Smith, a cousin of #839, and from his testimony (Miscel. Test. P. 2568) it appears that these claimants are endeavoring to prove their right to participate in this fund by and through John and Lewis Ross. William S. Smith states that his mother, Eliza J. Smith, was a daughter of Euphemia R. Perrin, who was a daughter of Benjamin Travis, who was a son of Jane Travis nee Jane Ross, who was a sister of John and Lewis Ross. From this it will be seen that the said Jane

Travis nee Ross, is the great-great grandmother of the claimant. Mr. Smith was born in Kentucky in 1861; his mother, Eliza J. Smith, was born in Kentucky in 1837. Euphemia R. Perrin was born in Tennessee, the section of the State not being given. None of these parties mentioned above appears on the roll of 1835 or on the roll of 1851. On the roll of 1835 there appears the name of John Ross, also the name of John G. Ross, and also the name of Lewis Ross, but these claimants offer nothing to prove that they are connected with either one of the Ross' on the roll. The applicants do not show that their ancestors ever resided within the Cherokee domain, either in the eastern or western section of the country. Mr. Smith states that he made application before the Dawes Commission, but his claim was rejected on the grounds that he had not furnished sufficient proof. Applicant #839, and all those claiming through the same ancestor, should be rejected because they have not shown that they or their ancestors were parties to the treaties of 1835-6 and 1846.

App: 840 Elna A. Helm et al, Claremore, Okla.
Rejected. Nieces and Nephew of #839 and claims through same source. This application is made by Ella L. Helm.

App: 841 Caroline P. Helm, Claremore, Okla.
Rejected. Mother of #839 and claims through same source.

App: 842 Louisa M. Arrowood, Peachtree, N.C.
Rejected. Applicant claims through Annie Blythe. See full report in #153.

App: 843 Mary E. Welch and 3 children, Marble, N.C.
Rejected. Applicant claims through Annie Blythe. See full report in #153.

App: 844 James F. Adams, Andrews, N.C.
Rejected. Applicant claims through Annie Blythe. See full report in #153.

App: 845 William B. Parker, Andrews, N.C.
Rejected. Applicant claims through Annie Blythe. See full report in #153.

App: 846 Thomas J. Golliger, Collinsville, Okla.
Admitted. Nephew of #38 and claims through same source.

App: 847 Sonora A. Pevehouse and 2 children, Collinsville, Okla.
Admitted. Aunt of #385 and claims through same source.

App: 848 Fannie Moore and 4 children, Tahlequah, Okla.
Admitted. Sister of #11 and claims through the same source.

App: 849 Daniel Downing, Locust Grove, Okla.
Admitted. Applicant probably enrolled as Tah-ga-nee-see in 1851 by Drennen, G.S. 630. (Miscel. Test. P. 3330 - 3729).

App: 850 Nellie Smith and 1 child, Peggs, Okla.
Admitted. Applicant's parents enrolled in 1851 by Drennen, Sal. 576. (Miscel. Test. P. 3532).

App: 851 James Smith, Peggs, Okla.
Admitted. Applicant enrolled in 1851 by Drennen, G.S. 14. (Miscel. Test. P. 3530).

App: 852 Sarah Swimmer, Tahlequah, Okla.
Admitted. Applicant's mother, Ah-kil-lo-hee, enrolled in 1851 by Drennen, Tah. 470. (Miscel. Test. P. 3424 - 3404[sic],). Died Aug. 8, 1908.

App; 853 Steeler Swimmer and 2 children, Tahlequah, Okla.
Admitted. Applicant's father enrolled in 1851 by Drennen, Fl. 239.

App: 854 James Dobbins, Gideon, Okla.
Admitted. Cousin of #833 and claims through same source.
App: 855 Betsy Parris, Gideon, Okla.
Admitted. Cousin of #833 and claims through same source.
App: 856 Peter C. Suagee and 2 children, Lenapah, Okla.
Admitted. Son of #714 and claims through same source.
App: 857 George B. Downing and 5 children, Westville, Okla.
Admitted. Applicant's mother and father enrolled in 1851 by Drennen, G.S. 322.
App: 858 Caroline Downing, Tahlequah, Okla.
Admitted. Sister of #857 and claims through same source. Applicant herself is enrolled in 1851 by Drennen as Caroline Faught, G.S. 329.
App: 859 Julia A. Bee and 2 children, Flint, Okla.
Admitted. Applicant claims through father and mother enrolled in 1851 by Drennen, Tah. 540, as Stephen P. and Mary Hildebrand.
App: 860 Polly Smith, Rose, Okla.
Admitted. Evidence shows that applicant is an Emigrant Cherokee and was enrolled as such in 1851. She never drew any Old Settler money. (See Miscel. Test. P. 4251).
App: 861 Mary Campbell, Peggs, Okla.
Admitted. Niece of #641 and claims through same source.
App: 862 John M. Sanders and 1 child, Wauhillau, Okla.
Admitted. Applicant's parents enrolled in 1851 by Drennen, Tah. 21.
App: 863 John M. Sanders.
Duplicate of #862
App: 864 Thomas Smith, Peggs, Okla.
Admitted. Applicant's mother enrolled in 1851 by Drennen, G.S. 29. (Miscel. Test. P. 3290).
App: 865 Mary J. Bitting, Tahlequah, Okla.
Admitted. Applicant enrolled in 1851 by Chapman #2116.
App: 866 John Beck, Flint, Okla.
Admitted. Applicant's father enrolled in 1851 by Drennen, Del. 569.
App: 867 Sabra Beck, Row, Okla.
Admitted. Applicant enrolled in 1851 by Drennen, G.S. 315.
App: 868 Susannah Chandler, Siloam Springs, Ark.
Admitted. First cousin of #867. Claims through same same[sic] source.
App: 869 Nancy Woodall and 2 children, Metory, Okla.
Admitted. Sister of #835 and claims through same source.
App: 870 Nellie Hendricks, Metory, Okla.
Admitted. Sister of #835 and claims through same source.
App: 871 William Risner, Bennington, Okla.
Rejected. Neither applicant nor ancestors ever enrolled. Does not establish fact of descent from person to the treaty of 1835-6 and 1846.
App: 872 Sarah L. Jackson and 2 children, Greenbrier, Okla.
Admitted. Applicant's mother enrolled in 1851 by Chapman #1713.

App: 873 Willie A. Cochran, Greenbrier, Okla.
Admitted. Applicant claims through father who was enrolled in 1851 by Drennen, Sal. 468.
App: 874 Martha J. Sanders and 1 child, Miles, Okla.
Admitted. Applicant's mother enrolled by Drennen in 1851, Del. 370.
App: 875 Ruth D. Atkins and 2 children, Russellville, Ky.
Admitted. Sister of #360 and claims through same source.
App: 876 Warren A. Miller and 1 child, Hudson, Okla.
Admitted. Brother of #402 and claims through same source.
App: 877 Jesse A. Thomas, Gdn for 4 children, Vinita, Okla.
Admitted. Grandmother of minor children enrolled by Drennen in 1851, Ill. 76.
App: 878 Daniel Buffington, Vinita, Okla.
Admitted. Applicant's mother enrolled by Drennen in 1851, Del. 905. Grandfather, Ave Miller, enrolled in 1835.
App: 878 1/2 Owen F. McNair, Tahlequah, Okla.
Admitted. Cousin of #816 and claims through same source.
App: 879 Emily J. Battles, Vinita, Okla.
Admitted. Applicant enrolled by Drennen in 1851, Dis. 33.
App: 880 Margaret E. Curry and 4 children, Coffeyville, Kans.
Admitted. Sister of #412 and claims through same source.
App: 881 Johnanah Garland and 2 children, Muskogee, Okla.
Rejected. Applicant enrolled by Dawes Commission as a Creek. (Miscel. Test. P #3468).
App: 882 Joseph Nave and 2 children, Tiawah, Okla.
Admitted. Brother of #102 and claims through same source.
App; 883 Sallie Thornton,
Duplicate of #382.
App: 884 Lucinda Falling, Collinsville, Okla.
Admitted. Applicant's mother enrolled in 1851 by Drennen, Tah. 34. (Miscel. Test. P. 4119 and 2435).
App: 885 Mollie Sanders, Childers, Okla.
Admitted. Claims through grandmother, Sally Downing, enrolled in 1851 by Drennen, Tah. 33. (Miscel. Test. P. 2295).
App: 886 James Smith, Bushyhead, Okla.
Admitted. Applicant's parents enrolled by Drennen in 1851 as Robbin and Sallie, Sal. 456.
App: 887 Joseph Cooper, Mark, Okla.
Admitted. Applicant's mother enrolled in 1851 by Drennen, F1. 213.
App: 888 William H.H. Scudder and 5 children, Chelsea, Okla.
Admitted. First cousin of #11 and claims through same source.
App: 889 Victoria Ware, Pawhuska, Okla.
Rejected. Applicant has affiliated with the Osage Tribe. He[sic] has received Osage payments and allotments. (Miscel. Test. P. 2521).
App: 890 Polly Duowah, Bartlesville, Okla.
Admitted. Niece of #536 and claims through same source.
App: 891 Cynthia Beck and 2 children, Owasso, Okla.
Admitted. Applicant's father enrolled in 1851 by Drennen, F1. 406.

App: 892 Mary G. Perry, Saline, Okla.
Admitted. This minor claims through her father enrolled in 1851 by Chapman #1982. Application made by Fannie D. Perry, Gdn.
App: 893 Ernest G. Perry, Welch, Okla.
Admitted. Half-brother of #892. Claimant's father enrolled in 1851 by Chapman #1982.
App: 894 Mary G. Perry, By Fannie D. Perry, Gdn.
Duplicate of #892.
App: 895 George Deerskin or Waters, Vian, Okla.
Admitted. Applicant enrolled as George Deerskin in 1851 by Drennen, Ill. 298. (Miscel. Test. P. 3016).
App: 896 Joseph Thornton and 3 children, Wauhillau, Okla.
Admitted. First cousin of #700 and claims through same source.
App: 897 Mattie Freels, Montague, Tenn.
Rejected. It does not appear that the applicant or any of her ancestors were ever enrolled. It does not appear that they were parties to the treaties of 1835-6 and 1846. It does not appear that they were recognized members of the tribe. (Miscel. Test. P. 258-9).
App: 898 Margaret J. Rayder and 3 children, Rockwood, Tenn.
Rejected. Applicant claims through the Kirklands. See full report in #576.
App: 899 T.F. Helton and 5 children, Spring City, Tenn.
Rejected. Niece of #504 and claims through same source.
App: 900 Nellie David, Tahlequah, Okla.
Admitted. Applicant and parents enrolled in 1851 by Drennen, Sal. 42.
App: 901 John E. Gunter, Muldrow, Okla.
Admitted. Applicant enrolled in 1851 by Drennen, S.B. 285.
App: 902 Arminta Pack, Muldrow, Okla.
Admitted. Sister of #901 and is enrolled in 1851 by Drennen, S.B. 285.
App: 903 Jenetta Barrow and 2 children, Muldrow, Okla.
Admitted. Sister of #901 and claims through same source.
App: 904 Florence V. Faulkner and 1 child, Muldrow, Okla.
Admitted. Niece of #901 and claims through same source. Daughter of #902.
App: 905 John W. McAlister, Choteau, Okla.
Admitted. Brother of #51 and claims through same source.
App: 906 Minnie Shay and 2 children, Henryetta, Okla.
Admitted. Applicant's mother and grandmother enrolled in 1851 by Drennen, Fl. 89.
App: 907 Martin Miller, Zena, Okla.
Admitted. Applicant enrolled in 1851 by Drennen, Sal. 557.
App: 908 Mary Brown and 3 grandchildren, Ketchum, Okla.
Admitted. Sister of #907 and enrolled in 1851 by Drennen, Sal. 557.
App: 909 Lucien B. Woodall, Wimer, Okla.
Admitted. Applicant's mother and grandmother enrolled in 1851 by Drennen, Del. 106.
App: 910 William Grass, Locust Grove, Okla.
Admitted. Brother of #81 and claims through same source.

App: 911 Cricket Cloud, Locust Grove, Okla.
Admitted. Applicant enrolled in 1851 by Drennen, G.S. 700 under the name Cricket. (Miscel. Test. P. 3791).
App: 912 Susie Pigeon, Locust Grove, Okla.
Admitted. Applicant's mother and father enrolled in 1851 by Drennen, G.S. 589. (Miscel. Test. P. 3776).
App: 913 Daniel Tilden, deceased, Locust Grove, Okla.
Admitted. Applicant's mother and grandfather enrolled in 1851 by Drennen, Del. 689. (Miscel. Test. P. 3792).
App: 914 Sarah Thompson, and 4 children, Eucha, Okla.
Admitted. Granddaughter of #87 and claims through same source.
App: 915 Adaline E. Battle and 2 children, Andrews, N.C.
Admitted. Sister of #361 and claims through same source.
App: 916 Lydia E. Wakefield, Andrews, N.C.
Admitted. Applicant enrolled in 1851 by Chapman #1235.
App: 917 Charles Fargo and 4 children, Muldrow, Okla.
Admitted. Applicant enrolled in 1851 by Drennen, S.B. 240.
App: 918 Susan McGhee, Grove, Okla.
Admitted. Applicant enrolled as Susan Beck in 1851 by Drennen, Del. 571.
App: 919 Syntha Barton, Grove, Okla.
Admitted. Sister of #918. Applicant enrolled as Scynthia Beck in 1851 by Drennen, Del. 571.
App: 920 Nick Byers, Evansville, Ark.
Admitted. Applicant enrolled in 1851 by Drennen, F1. 387 1/2.
App: 921 Joseph Harris and 4 children, Alluwee, Okla.
Admitted. Son of #820 and claims through same source.
App: 922 Polly David and 1 child, Tahlequah, Okla.
Admitted. Applicant's mother and maternal grandparents enrolled in 1851 by Drennen, Sal. 42.
App: 923 James M. Avants and 3 children, Antimony, Ark.
Rejected. It does not appear that ancestors were ever enrolled or were parties to the treaties of 1835-6 and 1846. Applicant shows no real connection with the Eastern Cherokees. (Miscel. Test. P. 2626).
App: 924 Betsy David, Tahlequah, Okla.
Admitted. Daughter of #900 and claims through same source.
App: 925 Richard Beck and 4 children, Flint, Okla.
Admitted. First cousin of #866 and claims through same source.
App: 926 Ida A. Beck, Flint, Okla.
Admitted. Grand niece of #132 and claims through same source.
App: 927 James R. Doherty and 2 children, Ramona, Okla. Box 82
Admitted. Applicant's mother enrolled as Winnie Love in 1851 by Drennen, G.S. 411.
App: 928 Minnie M. McKeehan and 3 children, Catoosa, Okla.
Admitted. Applicant's mother enrolled as Lucretia Key enrolled in 1851 by Drennen, Sal. 5. (Miscel. Test. P. 2538).

App: 929 Rebecca E. Creech and 1 child, Collinsville, Okla.
Admitted. Applicant's mother enrolled as Ruth Gann in 1851 by Drennen, Ill. 223. (Miscel. Test. P. 2536).
App: 930 Gilbert R. Ross and 3 children, Vera, Okla.
Admitted. Claimant enrolled in 1851 by Drennen, Tah. 157.
App: 931 Sarah Sullivan and 1 child, Proctor, Okla.
Admitted. Claimant's mother enrolled in 1851 by Drennen, Dis. 46.
App: 932 Mary Jane Casey and 6 children, Rockwood, Tenn.
Rejected. Ancestor not enrolled. Does not show any definite connection with Cherokee tribe. Is regarded as white in the community where she resides.
App: 933 Edward E. Bell, Milledgeville, Ga.
Admitted. First cousin of #11 and claims through same source.
App: 934 Daniel W. Lowery and 5 children, Lenapah, Okla.
Admitted. Brother of #562 and claims through same source.
App: 935 John Parker Collins, Moody, Okla.
Admitted. Claimant enrolled by Chapman in 1851, #1812.
App: 936 Wah-lee-yah or Peggy Thornton, Tahlequah, Okla.
Admitted. Applicant enrolled in 1851 by Drennen, Sal. 287.
App: 937 Johanna Jones and 2 children, Miami, Okla.
Admitted. Niece of #390 and claims through same source.
App: 938 Ezekiel P. Parris, Tahlequah, Okla.
Admitted. Uncle of #216 and claims through same source.
App: 938 1/2 E.P. Parris,
Duplicate of #938.
App: 939 Cynthia A. Welch and 1child, Miami, Okla.
Admitted. Applicant's father enrolled in 1851 by Drennen, Del. 142.
App: 940 Robert Tally, Jasper, Ga.
Rejected. It does not appear that applicant or ancestors were ever enrolled with the Cherokees, never lived with the tribe as members nor does it appear that applicant and ancestors were parties to the treaties of 1835-6 and 1846. (Miscel. Test. P. 1224, 1225, 1213, 1226).
App: 941 Susan E. Parris, Collinsville, Okla.
Rejected. Claimant, her mother and brothers enrolled on Old Settler roll in 1851, Del. 35. (Miscel. Test. P. 3234).
App: 942 William Sweetwater and 3 children, Zena, Okla.
Admitted. Applicant enrolled in 1851 by Drennen, Del. 472 under the name of Oo-chun-ter. (See letter in application).
App: 943 William Foreman, Moody, Okla.
Admitted. Applicant enrolled in 1851 by Drennen, Tah. 203. (Miscel. Test. P. 3518).
App: 944 W.H. Hampton, Spring Place, Ga.
Rejected. Applicant claims through Annie Blythe. See full report in #153.
App: 945 Ed L. Crawford, Pryor Creek, Okla.
Rejected. Neither applicant nor ancestors ever enrolled. Does not establish fact of descent from a person who was a party to the treaties of 1835-6 and 1846. Applicant's mother through whom he claims was probably born in Ky. prior to 1835 as she had a child born as early as 1848 and was herself born in Ky. (Miscel. Test. P. 2475).

App: 946 Jess Fallen, Collinsville, Okla.
Admitted. Brother of #27 and claims through same source.
App: 947 Perry Ross, Claremore, Okla.
Admitted. Brother of #557 and claims through same source.
App: 948 Samuel Sanders Tarpley, Quay, New Mexico.
Rejected. Claimant was born in 1845 in Tenn. He claims his Indian blood through his mother and her mother. Claimant's name nor none of his ancestors appear on any roll of Cherokees. Son of claimant testifies, Miscel. Test. P. 3567, that none of his people ever received any money from the Government by reason of their Indian blood. No showing is made that any ancestors ever lived with the Cherokees as a member of the tribe or were even located in any Cherokee domain at the time of the treaties of 1835-6 and 1846.
App: 949 Henry C. Maney and 5 children, Shooting Creek, N.C.
Rejected. Applicant claims through Keziah Vann. See full report in #276.
App: 950 Dock Anderson, Shooting Creek, N.C.
Rejected. Applicant claims through Keziah Vann. See full report in #276.
App: 951 Milton M. Maney and 8 children, Barefoot, Ga.
Rejected. Applicant claims through Keziah Vann. See full report in #276.
App: 952 Maggie Denton, and 1 child, Baldwin, Ga.
Rejected. Applicant claims through Keziah Vann. See full report in #276.
App: 953 Martin V. Maney and 6 children, Shooting Creek, N.C.
Rejected. Applicant claims through Keziah Vann. See full report in #276.
App: 954 William A. Maney and 6 children, Shooting Creek, N.C.
Rejected. Applicant claims through Keziah Vann. See full report in #276.
App: 955 William Maney and 1 child, Barefoot, Ga.
Rejected. Applicant claims through Keziah Vann. See full report in #276.
App: 956 Nancy Anderson, Shooting Creek, N.C.
Rejected. Applicant claims through Keziah Vann. See full report in #276.
App: 957 Rebecca Moss, Shooting Creek, N.C.
Rejected. Applicant claims through Keziah Vann. See full report in #276.
App: 958 Amanda Smith and 1 child, Shooting Creek, N.C.
Rejected. Applicant claims through Keziah Vann. See full report in #276.
App: 959 James W. Anderson, Shooting Creek, N.C.
Rejected. Applicant claims through Keziah Vann. See full report in #276.
App: 960 Sam Chuculate and 3 children, Sallisaw, Okla.
Admitted. Applicant's fathr enrolled in 1851 by Drennen, Fl. 51. (Miscel. Test. P. 2886).
App: 961 Allie Caler, Aquone, N.C.
Rejected. Half-sister of #126 and claims through same source.
App: 962 Calsina Gill, Rockwood, Tenn.
Admitted. Sister of #227 and claims through same source.
App: 963 George W. Fields, Fairland, Okla.
Admitted. Applicant's mother enrolled in 1851 by Drennen, Del 142.
App: 964 Mary Moose, Fairland, Okla.
Admitted. Aunt of #575 and claims through same source.
App: 965 Louella Fields and 4 children, Grove, Okla.
Admitted. Daughter of #543 and claims through same source.

App: 966 Rachel Edwards, Muldrow, Okla.
Rejected. Applicant was born in Montgomery Co., Ala. in 1827 which is nearly 100 miles removed from any Cherokee Domain as constitued[sic] in 1835 and 1846. Claimant claims through her father who died in 1827. Ancestors not found on any Cherokee roll nor no substantial connection with the tribe that would entitle claimant, is shown. (Miscel. Test. P. 4364 and 3920).
App: 967 Katy Price, Tahlequah, Okla.
Admitted. Applicant enrolled in 1851 by Drennen, F1. 185.
App: 968 Colonel J. Harris, Tahlequah, Okla.
Admitted. Brother of #686 and claims through same source.
App: 969 James R. Duncan, Echo, Okla.
Admitted. Applicant enrolled in 1851 by Drennen, Del. 969. (Miscel. Test. P. 3676).
App: 970 Mary Leach, Tahlequah, Okla.
Admitted. Applicant enrolled by Drennen in 1851, F1. 77.
App: 971 Eliza J. Baker and 2 children, Owasso, Okla. R. #1
Admitted. Applicant's mother, Louisa I. Trout, enrolled in 1851 by Chapman #2106.
App: 972 Mary A. Brown, Chance, Okla.
Admitted. Applicant's mother enrolled in 1851 by Chapman #1290.
App: 973 Eliza Brown, Chance, Okla.
Admitted. Applicant enrolled in 1851 by Chapman #1290.
App: 974 John W. Brown and 2 children, Chance, Okla.
Admitted. Applicant enrolled in 1851 by Chapman #1293.
App: 975 Narcissa Thompson and 1 child, Row, Okla.
Admitted. Sister of #972. Applicant enrolled in 1851 by Chapman #1292.
App: 976 Martin J. Raper, Chance, Okla.
Admitted. Great uncle of #211 and claims through same source. Applicant enrolled in 1851 by Chapman #1424.
App: 977 Vinita Crutchfield, Tulsa, Okla.
By Josephine A. Crutchfield, Gdn.
Admitted. Applicant's father enrolled in 1851 by Drennen, Del 498.
App: 978 Lucy Ann Hudson, Miami, Okla.
Admitted. Applicant's father enrolled in 1851 by Drennen, Del 142.
App: 979 Clara A. Ward, New York, N.Y. 29 W. 38th.
Admitted. Applicant's mother enrolled in 1851 by Drennen, Dis. 39.
App: 980 Sallie Stopp, Choteau, Okla.
Admitted. Sister of #464 and claims through same source.
App: 981 Lizzie Chuculate and 5 children, Sallisaw, Okla.
Admitted. Sister of #960 and claims through same source.
App: 982 Fannie E. Buffington and 1 child, Westville, Okla.
Admitted. Sister of #17 and claims through same source.
App: 983 Amanda P. Scales, Webbers Falls, Okla.
Admitted. Applicant enrolled as Amanda P. Morgan in 1851 by Drennen, Tah. 12.

App: 984 Peggy Beanstick, Stilwell, Okla.
Admitted. Applicant enrolled in 1851 by Drennen, F1. 376.
App: 985 James Neal, Jr. and 2 children, Inola, Okla.
Admitted. Nephew of #109 and claims through same source.
By Joe Willie Neal, wife.
App: 986 Rebecca Davis, Stoney, N.C.
Admitted. Applicant claims to be daughter of Charley Hornbuckle or Charlie Kah-whe-lih, enrolled in 1851 by Chapman #91. James W. Terrell formerly disbursing officer of the Treasury Dept. in an affidavit filed herein, states that he knows Rebecca Davis and knew Charley Hornbuckle and was told by the latter that he, Charley Hornbuckle, was the father of Rebecca Davis. Supt. Harris of the Cherokee Indian School, N.C. states that this case was investigated very fully by himself and Col. Churchill and that from the testimony of Capt. J.W. Terrell and a man by the name of Jenkins of Jackson Co. they established the fact that Rebecca Davis was the daughter of Pollie Wilkes and Charley Hornbuckle. Mr. Jenkins testified that Charley Hornbuckle lived with Pollie Wilkes in a little cabin fully a year while working for him on contract work, and that he furnished all the supplies for the home and that he acknowledge and recognized Rebecca Davis as his child. Confirmatory evidence was also given by Mr. Painter. The testimony and all the papers in the case were filed with Col. Churchill in the making of the Eastern Cherokee roll in the Qualla Boundary.
App: 987 Lizzie Wilkerson, Claremore, Okla.
Admitted. Sister of #27 and claims through same source.
App: 988 Charley Falling, Claremore, Okla.
Admitted. Nephew of #27 and claims through same source.
App: 989 John Falling, Collinsville, Okla.
Admitted. Nephew of #27 and claims through same source.
App: 990 Charles Towser, Claremore, Okla.
Admitted. Applicant's parents probably enrolled in 1851 by Drennen, Del. 703. (Miscel. Test. 4117).
App: 991 John Sanders and 7 children, Claremore, Okla.
Admitted. Applicant claims through father and mother Eli and Elvira Sanders, enrolled in 1851 by Drennen, G.S. 698. Applicant enrolled with parents in same group.
App: 992 Susan Cook,
Duplicate of #583.
App: 993 Arch Lookin, Claremore, Okla.
Admitted. Applicant enrolled by the Dawes Commission #32009, as a full-blood. Applicant testified that his father drew money in 1851 for himself and also for applicant, but never received any Old Settler money. John Sanders testified that applicant is recognized as an Emigrant Cherokee. (Miscel. Test. P. 2442).
App: 994 Bessie F. Summerlin and 1 child, Muskogee, Okla.
812 S. Cherokee St.
Admitted. Niece of #929 and claims through same source.
App: 995 Joseph Alice Dale, Nowata, Okla.
Admitted. Applicant's father, Joseph Crutchfield, enrolled in 1851 by Drennen, Del. 498.

App: 996 Sarah E. Boulden and 3 children, Webbers Falls, Okla.
Rejected. Reason for rejection on father's side found Case #10294. A name same as mother's of applicant is found on the Act of Congress roll but enrolled as the daughter of Sandell Still. Statement that Standill Still had no daughter named Mary, regarded as mistake in testimony. No ancestor on mother's side appears on the 1835 or 1851 roll. It appears not any of them were parties to the treaties of 1835-6 and 1846. (Miscel. Test. P. 3034 - 3038). (See #10294).
App: 997 Cloie Hambie and 3 children, Oktaha, Okla.
Rejected. Niece of #996 and claims through same source.
App: 998 Delia P. Jordan and 2 children, Vinita, Okla.
Admitted. Applicant claims through Mother, Caroline Lynch, enrolled in 1851 by Drennen, Sal. 373.
App: 999 Peggy Hawkins, Tahlequah, Okla.
Admitted. Applicant enrolled as Tsor-yook-ah in 1851 by Drennen, Sal. 308. (Miscel. Test. P. 3237).
App: 1000 John Sulteesky, Choteau, Okla.
Admitted. Applicant's mother, Nancy Stopp, enrolled in 1851 by Drennen, Sal. 167. Grandparents, Walter and Lucy Stopp, enrolled in 1851 by Drennen, Sal. 167. (Miscel. Test. P. 3592).
App: 1001 Takey Earbob and 5 children, Choteau, Okla.
Admitted. Half sister of #1000. Claims through mother Nancy Stop, Saline #167.
App: 1002 Sam Stopp, Choteau, Okla.
Admitted. Half brother of #1000. Claims through mother, Nancy Stop, Saline #167.
App: 1003 Gilbert Stopp and 1 child, Choteau, Okla.
Admitted. Half brother to #1000. Claims through mother, Nancy Stop, Saline #167. *(Handwritten for city below, Dragger)*
App: 1004 Paul Glass, (*Handwritten and 2 children*) ~~Tahlequah~~, Okla.
Admitted. Applicant claims through father and mother, enrolled as Tar-quar-te-he and Nancy Glass, Sal. #434.
App: 1005 Geo. Washington Ward and 5 children, Whiting, Mo.
Admitted. Brother of #106 and claims through same source.
App: 1006 Rufus Downing and 2 children, Baron, Okla.
Admitted. Applicant claims through Ooteeskahlee, who is his father and who is enrolled in G.S. #351, and through his mother, Polly Wilson, Tahl. #525.
App: 1007 Sarah J. Dooley and 1 child, McConnell, Ga.
Rejected. Cousin of #58 and claims through same source.
App: 1008 Henrietta W. Hunkler and 1 child, Atlanta, Ga.
Rejected. Daughter of #58 and claims through same source.
App: 1009 Jeremiah L. Pilgrim, Atlanta, Ga.
Rejected. Grandson of #58 and claims through same source.
App: 1010 Augustus J. Taylor, McConnell, Ga.
Rejected. Cousin of #58 and claims through same source.
App: 1011 Mrs. Albert W. Edwardy, Atlanta, Ga.
Rejected. Daughter of #58 an[sic] claims through same source.

App: 1012 Arabella F. Taylor and 1 child, McConnell, Ga.
Rejected. Cousin of #58 and claims through same source.
App: 1013 David Gallimore, Rockwood, Tenn.
Rejected. Ancestors not enrolled, were not living in the Cherookee[sic] domain in 1835-6 and 1846 and does not show genuine connection with Cherokee tribe.
App: 1014 Jim Bange, Rockwood, Tenn.
Rejected. It does not appear that any ancestor was ever enrolled. No ancestor was party to the treaties of 1835-6 and 1846. Shows no real connection with the Eastern Cherokees. Failed to appear to give testimony when summoned.
App: 1015 Fadina Jones, Cherokee, Kans.
Rejected. This applicant claims through the Sizemore's. See full report in #417.
App: 1016 Boyd Jones, Cherokee, Kans.
Rejected. This applicant claims through the Sizemore's. See full report in #417.
App: 1017 Mary Jane Jones, Cherokee, Kans.
Rejected. This applicant claims through the Sizemore's. See full report in #417.
App: 1018 Leta Bagley, Cherokee, Kans.
Rejected. This applicant claims through the Sizemore's. See full report in #417.
App: 1019 Clara Jones Bagby, Cherokee, Kans.
Rejected. This applicant claims through the Sizemore's. See full report in #417.
App: 1020 Winnie Staugh, Cherokee, Kans.
Rejected. This applicant claims through the Sizemore's. See full report in #417.
App: 1021 Nancy Jane Staugh, Cherokee, Kans.
Rejected. This applicant claims through the Sizemore's. See full report in #417.
App: 1022 Gwynn Jones, Cherokee, Kans.
Rejected. This applicant claims through the Sizemore's. See full report in #417.
App: 1023 Charlie Jones, Cherokee, Kans.
Rejected. This applicant claims through the Sizemore's. See full report in #417.
App: 1024 Alice Jones, Cherokee, Kans.
Rejected. This applicant claims through the Sizemore's. See full report in #417.
App: 1025 Florence Jones, Cherokee, Kans.
Rejected. This applicant claims through the Sizemore's. See full report in #417.
App: 1026 Neil Jones, Cherokee, Kans.
Rejected. This applicant claims through the Sizemore's. See full report in #417.
App: 1027 Lucy J. Green, Auburn, Ky.
Rejected. Cousin of #839 and claims through same source.

App: 1028 William J. Raper, Murphy, N.C.
Rejected. Information in application insufficient. Applicant failed to appear. None of the ancestors appear on the rolls. It appears they were not parties to the treaties of 1835-6 and 1846.
App: 1029 Vera Jones, Cherokee, Kans.
Rejected. This applicant claims through the Sizemore's. See full report in #417.
App: 1030 John Jones, Cherokee, Kans.
Rejected. This applicant claims through the Sizemore's. See full report in #417.
App: 1031 Wade Jones, Cherokee, Kans.
Rejected. This applicant claims through the Sizemore's. See full report in #417.
App: 1032 Callie Morrison and 1 child, Newport, R.I.
Rejected. Cousin of #126 and claims through same source.
App: 1033 Malinda McKiney, and 2 children, Tate, Ga.
Rejected. No ancestors on Rolls. It appears that no ancestor was a party to the treaties of 1835-6 and 1846. Proof of genuine connection with the Eastern Cherokees insufficient. (Miscel. Test. Page 1230.)
App: 1034 Nancy C Ransom, Needmore, Okla.
Admitted. Applicant enrolled by Chapman #2058. Parents, Louis and Elizabeth Rolston, Chapman #2053-2054.
App: 1035 Johnsanna Ragsdale and 3 children, Owasso, Okla.
Admitted. Niece of #901.
App: 1036 Isaac H. Ragsdale, Owasso, Okla.
Rejected. Claimant and his parents are on the Old Settler roll, Flt. 52. Claimant is a full brother of #541.
App: 1037 Minnie V. Adair and 1 child, Centralia, Okla.
Admitted. Applicant is a niece of John Hilderbrand, App. #2. Her grandparents, David and Elizabeth Hilderbrand, were enrolled by Drennen in Tahl. #136.
App: 1038 Martha Jane Vandever, Centralia, Okla.
Admitted. Sister of #1037. Mother probably not born until after 1851. Grandparents, David and Elizabeth Hilderbrand, enrolled Tahl. #136.
App: 1039 Amanda Martin and 1 child, Ruby, Okla.
Admitted. Sister of #363.
App; 1040 Dan Keith and 4 children, Dalton, Ga.
Rejected. Applicant's mother was born a slave. Ancestors not on rolls. Applicant probably has some Indian blood, but the proof which he offers is insufficient to entitle him to be enrolled. Does not show that his ancestors were ever members of the tribe, or were parties to the treaties of 1835-6 and 1846. Claimant was not enrolled by Hester. (Miscel. Test. Page 1337.)
App: 1041 Florence Mathews, Breen, Colo.
Rejected. Neither the applicant nor his father were ever enrolled. Does not know the names of grandparents. Father born in Miss. Unable to establish fact of descent through a person who was a party to the treaties of 1835-6 and 1846.
App: 1042 Emma Mathews, Breen, Colo.
Rejected. Sister of #1041 and claims through same source.

App: 1043 Abraham Mathews, Breen, Colo.
Rejected. Brother of #1041 and claims through same source.
App: 1044 Nancy J. Naranjo, Breen, Colo.
Rejected. Sister of #1041 and claims through same source.
App: 1045 Berrilla Rogers, Fairland, Okla.
Admitted. Great-aunt of #201 and claims through same source.
App: 1046 Maud M. England and 1 child, Fairland, Okla.
Admitted. First cousin once removed of #201 and claims through same source.
App: 1047 Mary L. McFarland and 3 children, Fairland, Okla.
Admitted. First cousin once removed of #201 and claims through same source.
App: 1048 John England and 2 children, Fairland, Okla.
Admitted. First cousin once removed of #201 and claims through same source.
App: 1049 Rachel Jane McCullough, Fairland, Okla.
Admitted. Applicant herself was enrolled by Drennen in Sal. 179 as Rachel J. Adair. Her father and mother, Geo W. and Martha Adair, are enrolled Sal. 179.
App: 1050 Thomas Blair, Tahlequah, Okla.
Admitted. Applicant himself was enrolled by Drennen in Flt. 641 1/2, as were also his father and mother, George and Nancy Blair, Flt. 641 1/2.
App: 1051 Connell Rogers, and 3 children, Fort Gibson, Okla.
Admitted. Applicant himself is enrolled by Chapman 1574. His mother, Cherokee Rogers, Chapman 1573.
App: 1052 Joseph Reese and 5 children, Chance, Okla.
Admitted. Applicant claims through his father, Andrew Reese, who was enrolled by Drennen Flt. 161 and also through his grandfather and grandmother, Johnson and Katty Reese, Flt. 161.
App: 1053 Margaret Blair and 1 child, Tahlequah, Okla.
Admitted. Applicant herself was enrolled by Drennen in Tahl. 32 as Peggy Sanders. Her mother and father, Jesse and Caroline Sanders also enrolled in Tahl. 32.
App: 1054 Charlotter Potts and 1 child, Muskogee, Okla.
Rejected. Applicant claims through mother, who was a slave. (Miscel. Test. Page 3476.)
App: 1055 Savannah McMakin, Muskogee, Okla.
Admitted. Applicant enrolled as Jane Savannah Harris by Chapman #1761. Sister of #686.
App: 1056 Thomas Ballard, Vian, Okla.
Admitted. Applicant himself was enrolled by Drennen in Del. 367. His mother, Sarah Ballard was also enrolled in Del. 367, and his grandfather, Alex Drumgold is on the 1835 roll.
App: 1057 William Sherill, Wolf Point, Mont.
Admitted. Son of Andy Ute, Application #15787, whose mother, Ne-qut-ti-ih, was enrolled by Chapman #133.
App: 1058 Laphila Lee and 2 children, Wimer, Okla.
Admitted. Sister of #319 and claims through same source.
App: 1059 Betsy Justice, Cookson, Okla.
Admitted. Applicant herself is enrolled as Cle-lun-na-che by Drennen in Fl. 119. Her mother, A-ally is also enrolled in Fl. 119.

App: 1060 John T. Ralston, Needmore, Okla.
Admitted. Brother of #1034 and claims through same source. Applicant himself enrolled by Chapman #2055.
App: 1061 Ben Dobkins and 1 child, Welch, Okla.
Admitted. Applicant claims through his grandfather and grandfather[sic] and grandmother, Benjamin and Polly Landrum, who were enrolled by Drennen in Del. 161.
App: 1062 Nora M. Strand and 3 children, Welch, Okla.
Admitted. Sister of #1061 and claims through same source.
App: 1063 Ada Durall and 3 children, Welch, Okla.
Admitted. Sister of #1061 and claims through same source.
App: 1064 Robert C. Parks and 2 children, Chelsea, Okla.
Admitted. Applicant himself was enrolled by Chapman #1603. His father, Richard T. Parks was also enrolled, Chapman #1602.
App: 1065 Lewis B. Hudson, Chelsea, Okla.
Admitted. Claims through self enrolled by Chapman as #1778, under the name of Lewis Blackburn Hudson.
App: 1066 Raleigh Caller and 2 children, Gatliff, Tenn.
Rejected. Half brother of #126 and claims through same source.
App: 1067 Henry A Ragle and 1 child, Wauchula, Fla.
Rejected. Nephew of #664 and claims through same source.
App: 1068 Becca Bunch, Stilwell, Okla.
Admitted. Applicant herself enrolled by Drennen as Ka-you-he-tah in F1. 5.
App: 1069 Mary J. Allen, Catoosa, Okla.
Admitted. Applicant enrolled by Drennen as Mary J. Price in Tahl. 287. Mother also enrolled as head of that group.
App: 1070 Silk Daugherty and 4 children, Stilwell, Okla.
Admitted. Applicant and his parents were enrolled by Drennen as Cornpsilk[sic] Daugherty and Eli and Lydia Daugherty in F1. 314. Applicant is the nephew of #984.
App: 1071 Louis Cochran and 4 children, Stilwell, Okla.
Admitted. Applicant claims through father, who was enrolled by Drennen as Wahty Cockran in F1. 334. Grandfather and grandmother enrolled as A-ally and John Cockran in same District.
App: 1072 Nancy Sixkiller,
Admitted. Duplicate of #786.
App: 1073 James Allen Thompson, Vinita, Okla.
Admitted. Applicant himself enrolled by Drennen in Tahl. #263. Also father and mother, Johnson and Eliza Thompson, enrolled in the same districts.
App: 1074 William R. Harris and 6 children, Muskogee, Okla.
Rejected. All have allotments in the Creek nation. Were enrolled by the Dawes Commission as Creeks. Wm. R. #4480. D.C.
App: 1075 Ellen R. Harris, Muskogee, Okla.
Rejected. Enrolled as a Creek, D.C. #4433.
App: 1076 Charles L. Harris, Muskogee, Okla.
Rejected. Enrolled as a Creek D.C. #4434.
App: 1077 Cheasquah Harris and 3 children, Muskogee, Okla.
Rejected. Enrolled as Creeks by Dawes Commission. Cheasquah enrolled D.C. #4483.

App: 1078 Daniel Ratliff, Cookson, Okla.
Admitted. Applicant enrolled by Drennen with his father, Richard Ratcliffee in Tahl. #1.
App: 1079 Lizzie B. Cookson and 3 children, Cookson, Okla.
Admitted. Applicant's father, George Spears, and her grandmother, Nancy Spears, enrolled by Drennen in Tahl. #152.
App: 1080 Elizabeth Keys, Cookson, Okla.
Admitted. Applicant enrolled by Drennen with mother, Margaret Catron, in Tahl. #36. Cousin of #859.
App: 1081 Mary H. Goforth, Caddo, Okla.
Rejected. Applicant enrolled with Choctaws. Intermarried #1381.
App: 1082 John Hicks and 7 children, Lynch, Okla.
Admitted. Nephew of #279 and claims through same source.
App: 1083 William H. Hicks, Spavinaw, Okla.
Admitted. Nephew of #279 and claims through same source.
App: 1084 Ruth K. Hawkins and 4 children, Vinita, Okla.
Admitted. Applicant's father, George W. Parks, enrolled by Chapman #1604.
App: 1085 Charles Work and 1child, Honey Creek, Okla.
Admitted. Applicant himself enrolled by Drennen in Del. #80.
App: 1086 William W. Caylor and 9 children, Whitewright, Tex.
Rejected. Half brother of #126 and claims through same source.
App: 1087 Susan C. Thompson, Vinita, Okla.
Admitted. Sister of #1084 and claims though[sic] same source. Applicant enrolled by Chapman #1605.
App: 1088 Thomas F. Thompson, Vinita, Okla.
Admitted. Brother of #1073 and claims through same source. Applicant enrolled in Tahl. #263.
App: 1089 Robt. L. Miller et al, Fairland, Okla.
By Martha Miller, Gdn.
Admitted. Minor's father, Andy J. Miller, and father's parents enrolled by Drennen in Del. #789. (Miscel. Test. P. 3719.)
App: 1090 Flora Stevens and 3 children, Fairland, Okla.
Admitted. Sister of #1089 and claims through same source.
App: 1091 Ida M. Cooley and 1 child, Fairland, Okla.
Admitted. Sister of #1089 and claims through same source.
App: 1092 Lucinda James and 5 children, Miami, Okla.
Admitted. Sister of #1089 and claims through same source.
App: 1093 Mahana Barber and 1 child, Afton, Okla.
Admitted. Sister of #1089 and claims through same source.
App: 1094 John O. Danderson, Catoosa, Okla.
By Frank F. Danderson, Gdn.
Admitted. Grandson of #447 and claims through same source.
App: 1095 Belle Poorboy, Tahlequah, Okla.
Rejected. Applicant's mother was a full blood Negro. Father and mother were never married. Father never recognized applicant as his child. Applicant's mother had children by 7 or 8 different men and was never married to any of them. Applicant enrolled as a freedman #887. (Miscel. Test. P. 4078.)

App: 1096 Tom Gritts and 1 child, Tahlequah, Okla.
Admitted. Brother of #936 and claims through same source.
App: 1097 Jack Squirrell and 4 children, Afton, Okla.
Admitted. (*Handwritten "Admitted"*). Applicant himself enrolled as Cha-wah-yoo-hah by Drennen in Del. #977. (Miscel. Test. P. 3667.)
App: 1098 William Wirt Ward, Miami, Okla.
Rejected. Applicant died Aug. 21, 1905, and this application is made by his brother on behalf of his widow. (See letter)
App: 1099 Martha C. Hall and 1 child, Afton, Okla.
Admitted. Claimant's father, Lemuel Childres, as an affliliated white, and mother as a quadroon, were enrolled on 1835 roll page #7. Grandfather Lemuel Paris, was enrolled in 1835 page #7 as an affiliated white. For full information for failure to be enrolled in 1851 see miscel. Test. Pages 4391-4387, 4102 and 4127. Also pages 2351 and 2590.
App: 1100 Emma Gritts and 1 child, Tahlequah, Okla.
Admitted. Applicant's father, Andrew Pelone, enrolled by Drennen in G.S. #89.
App: 1101 William Handle and 1 child, Zena, Okla.
Admitted. Applicant's father, Dempsey Handle, enrolled by Drennen in Del. #117.
App: 1102 Eliza Works, Needmore, Okla.
Admitted. Sister of #1097 and claims through same source.
App: 1103 Jennie C. Williams, Vinita, Okla.
Admitted. Applicant enrolled by Chapman #1634.
App: 1104 Martin McDaniel and 3 children, Catoosa, Okla.
Admitted. Half brother of #1059 and claims through same source.
App: 1105 Ida Albright and 2 children, Kiowa, Kans.
Rejected. Claims through Alexander Brown. See full report in #35.
App: 1106 Wm. and Lewis Carin, Kiowa, Kans.
Rejected. Claims through Alexander Brown. See full report in #35.
App: 1107 Nancy E. Forbes, Westville, Okla.
Admitted. Sister of #352 and claims through same source.
App: 1108 Ned Downing, Welling, Okla.
Admitted. Applicant's father enrolled by Drennen in Tahl. #14.
App: 1109 Ned Downing, Welling, Okla.
~~Admitted.~~ Duplicate of #1108.
App: 1110 Sallie Downing, Welling, Okla.
Admitted. Applicant's father enrolled by Drennen as High Bee Hunter in G.S. #652.
App: 1111 Sarah A. Nance and 6 children, Fairland, Okla.
Admitted. Applicant's father, James D. Vann, was enrolled by Chapman #1955.
App: 1112 Mrs. Lois Nash and 1 child, Kiowa, Kans.
Rejected. Claims through Alex. Brown. See full report in #35.
App: 1113 Lula R. Lee and 1 child, Needmore, Okla.
Admitted. Applicant is niece of #1034 and claims through same source.
(*Admitted - Handwritten*).

App: 1114 Eliza P. Ralston, Needmore, Okla.
Rejected. Claims only through deceased husband, who died in 1904. (See letter) (*Rejected - Handwritten*).
App: 1115 Betsy Cochran, Stilwell, Okla.
Admitted. Sister of #1070 and claims through same source.
App: 1116 Cephus K. Peak, Cleveland, Tenn.
Rejected. Neither applicant or ancestors were ever enrolled. Does not establish fact of descent from any person who was a party to treaties of 1835-6 and 1846.
App: 1117 John C. Sanders and 8 children, Wauhillau, Okla.
Admitted. Brother of #1055 and claims through same source.
App: 1118 Eliza Walker, Welling, Okla.
Admitted. Applicant claims through father, who was born about 1851. The grandfather, Oo-tee-scah-lee, was enrolled by Drennen in G.S. #351. (Miscel Test. P. 4083.)
App: 1119 John W. Thornton and 8 children, Welch, Okla. R.F.D. 1.
Admitted. Applicant's mother and grandfather enrolled by Drennen in Dis. #15.
App: 1120 Joseph V. Tasley, Catoosa, Okla.
Admitted. Cousin to #141-1120 and claims through same source.
App: 1121 Madison Sanders and 4 children, Tahlequah, Okla.
Admitted. Brother of #1053 and claims through same source.
App: 1122 Caleb S. Thompson, Ahniwake, Okla.
Admitted. Applicant enrolled by Chapman #2089 as Caleb Cass Thompson.
App: 1123 Ed Pritchett, Welling, Okla.
By Wm A. Evans, Gdn.
Admitted. Applicant's grandparents, Jack and Ah-ley Pritchett enrolled by Drennen in Fl. #642.
App: 1124 Betsy Greece and 4 children, Welling, Okla.
Admitted. Applicant's father enrolled by Drennen as head of Group #633 G.S.
App: 1125 Bird Gritts, Jr., Tahlequah, Okla.
Admitted. Applicant is the minor child of Tom Gritts #1096 and is enrolled with him.
App: 1126 Edna Gritts, Tahlequah, Okla.
Admitted. By Emma Gritts, Gdn. (see her mother's application #1100.)
App: 1127 Lucy J. Conner, Afton, Okla.
Admitted. Sister of #579 and claims through the same source.
App: 1128 Malinda N. Williams and 3 children, Afton, Okla.
Admitted. Sister of #579 and claims through the same source.
App: 1129 Katie Downing, Tahlequah, Okla.
Admitted. Applicant enrolled by Drennen in Tahl. #279 as Catherine Brewster.
App: 1130 Malzerine Hobbs and 4 children, Collinsville, Okla.
Admitted. Applicant's mother, Elizabeth (Betsy) Hair was enrolled by Drennen in G.S. #155. (Miscel. Test. P. 3521.)
App: 1131 Marsilla M. Plank and 6 children, Bartlesville, Okla.
Admitted. Applicant's mother, Amanda M. Ward enrolled by Chapman #2094.

App: 1132 Ida J. Harris and 3 children, Big Cabin, Okla.
Admitted. Aunt of #874 and half sister of #1572 and claims through same source.

App: 1133 Samuel J. Keys and 5 children, Owasso, Okla.
Admitted. First cousin of #642 and claims through same source. Father enrolled by Chapman #1680.

App: 1134 Samuel M. Donahoo and 7 children, Henryetta, Okla.
Rejected. Neither applicant nor ancestors were ever enrolled. It does not appear that they were living within the limits of the Cherokee domain in 1835-6 and 1846. It does not appear they were ever recognized as members of the tribe. (Miscel. Test. P. 2801.)

App: 1135 Mary L. Donahoo, Henryetta, Okla.
Rejected. Neither applicant nor ancestors were ever enrolled. Does not establish fact of descent from any person who was a party to the treaties of 1835-6 and 1846. (Miscel. Test. P. 2794.)

App: 1136 Catherine Green, Oscar, Okla.
Rejected. Cousin of #839 and claims through same source.

App: 1137 Daniel A. Brown and 1 child, Phoenix, Mo.
Rejected. Claims through Alex. Brown. See full report in #35.

App: 1138 James Parker, Marble, N.C.
Rejected. This applicant claims through Annie Blythe. See full report in #153.

App: 1139 John F. McGhee, Atmore, Ala.
Rejected. There are several hundred persons who have filed applications for participation in the distribution of the Eastern Cherokee fund, who for the most part, live in the extreme southern section of Alabama and the western section of Florida, who are not Cherokees at all, and most of them do not claim to be Cherokees, but are Creeks. Quite a number of these claim descent from such historic Creek characters as Billy Weatherford, Peggy Bailey, Willaim[sic] and Chilly McIntosh and Alexander McGillivray, and most of these applicant's claim only through the Hollinger, McGhee, McIntosh, Moniac, McGillivray, Franklin or Killian families, which are all of Creek origin. Some of these are recognized members of the Creek tribe, others while not recognized as members of the Creek tribe, claim as descendants of some Creek ancestor. Most of them state in so many words in their applications and in their testimony that they are Creeks, and they file their applications under the impression that descendants of Creek Indians are entitled to share in this fund. This idea was spread in certain sections of the south by some attorneys and claim agents, who were themselves under the impression that Eastern Creeks are entitled to share in this fund. Powers of attorneys have been received by the Special Commissioner, which provide for the payment to attorneys of a certain percent of any money recovered from these claims of "The Eastern and Emigrant Creeks."

There is absolutely no connection between any of these claimants and the Eastern Cherokees and no such connection is claimed by them. They never lived within the Cherokee domain. They were filed under the erroneous opinion that this fund was for Eastern and Emigrant Creeks instead of Cherokees. These cases have all been grouped together and for convenience marked "Creek file."

As they are not in any way connected or related to the Eastern Cherokees, and as most of them do not even claim to be so connected and related, of course none of them were ever enrolled with the Eastern Cherokees, nor were any of their ancestors parties to the treaties of 1835-6 and 1846. For particulars see "Creek Testimony" pp 1-12, taken Feb., 1908.

For the reasons above stated, all of these cases (in what is marked the "Creek file) are rejected.

App: 1140 Wm. L. McGhee, Atmore, Ala.
Rejected. This applicant claims through John F. McGhee one of the Creek claimants, and is claiming through the same source. See full report in #1139.

App: 1141 Emma McCauley, Pearch, Ala.
Rejected. This applicant is one of the Creek claimants. See full report in #1139.

App: 1142 Joseph Bailey Padget, Atmore, Ala.
Rejected. This applicant is one of the Creek claimants. See full report in #1139.

App: 1143 Henry Rollin, Atmore, Ala.
Rejected. This applicant is one of the Creek claimants. See full report in #1139.

App: 1144 Jospeh[sic] J. Deaux, Scranaga, Ala.
Rejected. This applicant is one of the Creek claimants. See full report in #1139.

App: 1145 Richard B. Padgett, Atmore, Ala.
Rejected. Applicant is a Creek claimant. See full report #1139.

App: 1146 David McGhee, Atmore, Ala.
Rejected. This applicant is one of the Creek claimants. See full report in #1139.

App: 1147 William Rollin, Atmore, Ala.
Rejected. This applicant is one of the Creek claimants. See full report in #1139.

App: 1148 Charles E. Bryars and 4 children, Scranage, Ala.
Rejected. This applicant is one of the Creek claimants. See full report in #1139.

App: 1149 John Rollin, Local, Ala.
Rejected. This applicant is one of the Creek claimants. See full report in #1139.

App: 1150 Mrs. Edwin Bryars and 1 child, Lottie, Ala.
Rejected. This applicant is one of the Creek claimants. See full report in #1139.

App: 1151 Oliver Rollin, Atmore, Ala.
Rejected. This applicant is one of the Creek claimants. See full report in #1139.

App: 1152 Neal McGhee, Atmore, Ala.
Rejected. This applicant is one of the Creek claimants. See full report in #1139.

App: 1153 David Gibson and 7 children, Atmore, Ala.
Rejected. This applicant is one of the Creek claimants. See full report in #1139.

App: 1154 Nettie Gibson, Atmore, Ala.
Rejected. This applicant is one of the Creek claimants. See full report in #1139.

App: 1155 Wm. M. Dees, Jeddo, Ala.
Rejected. This applicant is one of the Creek claimants. See full report in #1139.

App: 1156 Cannen F. McGhee, Henington, Ala.
Rejected. This applicant is one of the Creek claimants. See full report in #1139.

App: 1157 Sallie Hodges and 2 children, Atmore, Ala.
Rejected. This applicant is one of the Creek claimants. See full report in #1139.

App: 1158 Lee McGhee, Atmore, Ala.
Rejected. This applicant is one of the Creek claimants. See full report in #1139.

App: 1159 Bettie Gibson, Atmore, Ala.
Rejected. This applicant is one of the Creek claimants. See full report in #1139.

App: 1160 Drucilla McGhee, Atmore, Ala.
Rejected. This applicant is one of the Creek claimants. See full report in #1139.

App: 1161 Wm Henry Gibson, Atmore, Ala.
Rejected. This applicant is one of the Creek claimants. See full report in #1139.

App: 1162 Exena Prestley, Atmore, Ala.
Rejected. This applicant is one of the Creek claimants. See full report in #1139.

App: 1163 Nancy Rains and 1 child, Flowery Branch, Ga.
Rejected. Proof of genuine connection with the Eastern Cherokees insufficient. It appears that no ancestor was a party to the treaties of 1835-6 and 1846. No ancestor was ever enrolled. (Miscel. Test. P. 997.)

App: 1164 Altha DeLong, Flowery Branch, Ga.
Rejected. Proof of genuine connection with the Eastern Cherokees insufficient. No ancestor was ever enrolled. It appears that no ancestor was a party to the treaties of 1835-6 and 1846. (Miscel. Test. P. 997-8.)

App: 1165 1/2 Edwin O. Nash, Fort Gibson, Okla.
By Florian H. Nash, Gdn.
Admitted. Niece of #1051 and claims through same source.

App: 1165 Cherokee America Rogers, Fort Gibson, Okla.
Admitted. Applicant enrolled by Chapman #1573. Applicant is the mother of #1051.

App: 1166 Lucy Werther and 7 children, Nowata, Okla.
Rejected. Unable to locate ancestors on the 1851 roll. Applicant appeared and testified, but her knowledge of ancestry was not sufficient to connect them with the Eastern Cherokees, ~~the Emigrants~~. The testimony of G.W. Werther shows these people to be Old Settlers. (Miscel. Test. P. 2301-4132.)

App: 1167 Nelson Proctor, Stilwell, Okla.
Admitted. Applicant's parents, Na-sou-ee and Jenny, enrolled by Drennen in Fl. #501. (Miscel. Test. P. 3163.)

App: 1168 Lydia Proctor, Stilwell, Okla.
Admitted. Applicant and her parents, Ned and Jinny Duck, were enrolled by Drennen in Fl. #367.

App: 1169 Sallie Feather, Stilwell, Okla.
Admitted. Applicant and her brother and sister were enrolled by Drennen in G.S. #583. See testimony of James Feather taken at Stilwell, Mar. 22, 1909, pp 4012. (Also corroberative statement of J.B. Adair.)

App: 1170 Smith Fodder and 1 child, Uniontown, Ark.
Admitted. Applicant's parents were not born in 1851, but his grandfather Che-wee-skey, on his father's side, was enrolled by Drennen, in 1851 in G.S. #259. Applicant's grandfather, on h[sic] his mother's side, Screech-owl, was enrolled by Drennen #25, Skin Bayou. (Miscel. Test. P. 4009.)

App: 1171 Lewis H. Scruggs, Claremore, Okla.
Rejected. It does not appear that ancestors were ever enrolled, or were parties to the treaties of 1835-6 and 1846. Ancestors of applicant lived in Mo. in 1835 and 1851. They show no connection with the Eastern Cherokees. (Miscel. Test. P. 2284 and 3909.)

App: 1172 Eli Sanders and 2 children, Stilwell, Okla.
Admitted. Applicant's parents were enrolled by Drennen in Skin Bayou #23. (Cah-sah-low-ee and Cah-le-lo-lee.)

App: 1173 Saphronia Cooper, Mark, Okla.
Admitted. Applicant's mother was enrolled by Drennen in Tahl. #43.

App: 1174 James Sanders and 4 children, Long, Okla.
Admitted. Brother of #1172. Applicant enrolled in Skin Bayou #23 as "boy not named".

App: 1175 Ah-ley Lee, Evansville, Ark.
Admitted. Applicant enrolled herself in Fl. #366. Her mother and brothers in Fl. #365 and 367. (See testimony of Nick Byers taken Mar. 23, 1909—pp 4003.)

App: 1176 Mary Fenley and 6 children, Atlanta, Ga.
522 1/2 Decatur St.
Rejected. Sister of #1163 and claims through same source.

App: 1177 James Lyman, Moodys, Okla.
Admitted. Applicant's mother, Polly Lyman, was enrolled by Drennen in Tahl. #230.

App: 1178 Laura Bard and 1 child, Chelsea, Okla.
Admitted. Applicant was enrolled by Chapman #1836, and her parents were enrolled by Chapman #1834 and 1835.

App: 1179 William Moore and 4 children, Lometa, Okla.
Admitted. (*Admitted Handwritten*). Applicant's father, John Moore, and his grandparents, Mathew and Sarah Moore, were enrolled by Drennen Dis. #10.

App: 1180 Jennie M. Barnes, Chelsea, Okla.
Admitted. First cousin to #715 and claims through same source.

App: 1181 Myrtle Henry and 3 children, Chelsea, Okla.
Admitted. First cousin of #715, and claims through same source.

App: 1182 Augustus E. Ivey and 2 children, Stilwell, Okla.
Admitted. (*Admitted Handwritten*). First cousin of #998. Applicant's mother enrolled as "Charlotte Bell, 373 Saline", while visiting her Uncle Joseph Lynch.

App: 1183 Sallie Mouse,
Included in father's application #627.

App: 1184 Price Mouse, Eucha, Okla.
Admitted. Brother of #608 and claims through same source.

App: 1185 Lucy Mouse,
Admitted. Included in father's application #627.

App: 1186 Olkin Smith, Eucha, Okla.
Admitted. Sister of #608 and claims through same source.

App: 1187 Anna Snell, Oaks, Okla.
Admitted. Father and paternal grandmother of applicant were enrolled by Drennen under the names of Isaac and Che-le-you-me in G.S. #541. Mother enrolled in G.S. #212.

App: 1188 Charlotte Dry, Kansas, Okla.
Admitted. Grandparents enrolled as Tsoo-le-or-woh and Lucy by Drennen in Saline #245.

App: 1189 Youngdeer, Oaks, Okla.
Admitted. The applicant and his father were enrolled by Drennen in G.S. #17 under the names of Big Tel-choo-lau-eh[sic] and Youngdeer.

App: 1190 Lila Smith and 2 children, Oaks, Okla.
Admitted. The father of applicant was enrolled by Drennen in Del. #913. Mother and maternal grandparents were enrolled in Tahl. #388.

App: 1191 Jennie Wofford, Stilwell, Okla.
Admitted. Applicant was enrolled in G.S. #272 by Drennen under the name of Che-wah-sah.

App: 1192 Anna Murphy, Sapulpa, Okla.
Admitted. Daughter of #72 and claims through same source.

App: 1193 Mary M. Alexander and 2 children, Mannford, Okla.
Rejected. Cousin of #551 and claims through same source.

App: 1194 Alfred W. Stephens, Mannford, Okla.
Rejected. Cousin of #551 and claims through same source.

App: 1195 Mahala Ihrig and 7 children, Mannford, Okla.
Rejected. Cousin of #551 and claims through same source.

App: 1196 Eli Snell and 1 child, Kansas, Okla.
Admitted. Half brother of #469 and claims through same source.

App: 1197 Nancy Youngbird, Kansas, Okla.
Admitted. Applicant's mother, Ta-ya-ne, was enrolled by Drennen in Saline #156. (Miscel Test. P. #4237.)

App: 1198 Isaac Youngbird and 2 children, Kansas, Okla.
Admitted. Applicant enrolled by Drennen in Del. #697 as Kah-na-ne-ske.

App: 1199 Joe Chopper, Eucha, Okla.
By Emma Fox, Gdn.
Admitted. Brother of #648. Mother enrolled by Drennen in Del. #766.

App: 1200 Nancy Blackbird and 4 children, Uniontown, Ark.
Admitted. The mother of applicant enrolled by Drennen in Del. #513 under the name of Che-lou-e-che. Grandmother enrolled in same[sic] group as Co-te-ca-me.
App: 1201 Ruth Hampton, Troy, Ill.
Rejected. Claimant was born in 1847. She, her parents or other ancestors do not appear on any Cherokee roll and no substantial connection with Cherokee tribe is shown. Claimant and others grouped with her have failed to appear twice when summoned for examination in the field.
App: 1202 Jennie Pann and 1 child, Hulbert, Okla.
Admitted. Niece of #900 and claims through same source.
App: 1203 Annie Tahquitte, Hulbert, Okla.
Admitted. The father of the applicant and his paternal grandparents are enrolled by Drennen in Tahl. #354.
App: 1204 Henry L. Cloud and 2 children, Wellston, Okla.
Admitted. The mother of the applicant and maternal grandparents were enrolled by Drennen in Tahl. #345 under the names of John, Lucretia and Lucy Tadpole.
App: 1205 Mary J. Keys and 4 children, Childers, Okla.
Admitted. Applicant's mother and maternal grandfather were enrolled by Drennen in Skin Bayou #45. Grandfather, Ellis Sanders on 1835 roll.
App: 1206 Lillie W. Lint and 2 children, Muskogee, Okla.
Admitted. Aunt of #759 and claims through same source.
App: 1207 Thomas J. Taylor, Tahlequah, Okla.
By Rebecca A. Johnson, daughter and Gdn.
Admitted. Applicant himself enrolled by Drennen in F1. #661.
App: 1208 Birdie Bates Tahlequah, Okla.
Admitted. Applicant's maternal grandfather, and maternal great grandparents were enrolled by Chapman #1857-1858-1859.
App: 1209 Jessie Webb, Tahlequah, Okla.
By Col. J. Harris, Gdn.
Admitted. Sister of #1208 and claims through same source.
App: 1210 Mary Foreman, Lowery, Okla.
Admitted. Applicant enrolled as Mary Lowery by Drennen in Saline xxxx 171. Great aunt of #465.
App: 1211 Amanda Hair, Proctor, Okla.
Admitted. Applicant, her mother, and maternal grandparents were enrolled by Drennen in Tahl. #335 under the names of Ta-ku-ne, Cha-wa-you-car, Se-cah-me and Cah-se-car.
App: 1212 Nancy Charles, Stilwell, Okla.
Admitted. Sister of #1200 and claims through same source.
App: 1213 Kire Coleman, Bushy, Okla.
Admitted. Applicant's mother and sisters were enrolled by Drennen in Skin Bayou #189 under the names of Quaty, Sagee and Patsy Coleman. The applicant is enrolled as Hezekiah Charles Killer in the same group.
App: 1214 George W. Silk and 5 children, Akins, Okla.
Admitted. Applicant's grandparents, ?og[sic] Silk and Ah-ne-wa-ke, were enrolled by Drennen (15) n[sic] Skin Bayou #212.

App: 1215 Leona A. Riddle, Ramona, Okla.
Admitted. Sister of #927 and claims through same source.
App: 1216 Sarah E. Carson, Ramona, Okla.
Admitted. Sister of #927 and claims through same source.
App: 1217 Zenie Brown and 5 children, Council Hill, Okla.
Rejected. Applicant and children enrolled by the Dawes Commission as Creeks.
App: 1218 Joel A. Harris, Tahlequah, Okla.
By Col. J. Harris, Gdn.
Admitted. Applicant is Nephew of #1049 and claims through same source.
App: 1219 Callie Harris, Tahlequah, Okla.
By Col. J. Harris, Gdn.
Admitted. Grand niece of #1049 and claims through same source.
App: 1220 Charles H. Harris, Tahlequah, Okla.
By Col. J. Harris, Gdn.
Admitted. Grand nephew of #1049 and claims through same source. Mother, Nannie E. Adair enrolled in Saline #477.
App: 1221 Nelson Hicks and 5 children, Moodys, Okla.
Admitted. Applicant himself enrolled by Drennen in Saline #170.
App: 1222 Daniel Batt, Oaks, Okla.
Admitted. Mother, Eliza Lowery, enrolled by Drennen in Sal. #171 First cousin once removed of #465.
App: 1223 Betsy Smith, Tahlequah, Okla.
Asmitted. Half sister of #1211 and claims through same source.
App: 1224 George Smith and 2 children, Tahlequah, Okla.
Admitted. Applicant's parents were enrolled by Drennen in Tahl. #290 as Tom and Susanna Smith. (Miscel. Test. P. 3422.)
App: 1225 Dave Downing and 2 children, Peggs, Okla.
Admitted. Brother of #178. Enrolled himself by Drennen in Tahl. #558.
App: 1226 Thompson Downing and 2 children, Peggs, Okla.
Admitted. Half brother of #178 and claims through same source.
App: 1227 Celestia A. Glover, Adair, Okla.
Rejected. Claims through same source as #966.
App: 1228 William Carter, Springplace, Ga.
Rejected. Neither applicant nor any of his ancestors are on any rolls of the Eastern Cherokee except Siler, who rejects them and states that it is doubtful if they are of Cherokee blood. It is not shown that applicant's ancestors were parties to the treaties of 1835-6 and 1846.
App: 1229 William L. Cowart and 6 children, Stilwell, Okla.
Admitted. Father, Lemuel Cowart, enrolled by Chapman #1633.
App: 1230 Jesse D. Thompson and 8 children, Stilwell, Okla.
Admitted. Mother of applicant enrolled by Drennen in Dis. #62 under name of Mary Dammon. Applicant is first cousin of #5793.
App: 1231 Peter Adair, Stilwell, Okla.
Admitted. Applicant's father, Chu-noo-lees-kie, enrolled by Drennen in Fl. #203. Grandfather, Ke-nah, Fl. #205. (*Handwritten Misc. Test P. 3312.)*

App: 1232 Mary E. Collins, Tahlequah, Okla.
Admitted. Grandfather, aunts, and uncles were enrolled by Chapman #1808-1809-1811.
App: 1233 Noah Parris and 1 child, Tahlequah, Okla.
Admitted. Applicant, parents, brothers and sisters enrolled by Drennen in Dis. #45. Father of #737.
App: 1234 Walter Bigbey and 2 children, Ahniwake, Okla.
Admitted. Father of Applicant enrolled by Drennen in F1. #611. Mother enrolled Tahl. #535.
App: 1235 Eva M. Bigham and 1 child, Ramona, Okla.
Admitted. First cousin of #587 and claims through same source. Applicant's father, Richard L. Nicholson, enrolled in Tahl. #480.
App: 1236 Annie Keener, Ahniwake, Okla.
Admitted. Applicant's father, Stu-e-stee, was enrolled by Drennen in Tahl. #362.
App: 1237 Lucy Jane Wells and 1 child, Grove, Okla.
Admitted. First cousin of #1746 and claims through same source.
App: 1238 Maud Webb, Tahlequah, Okla.
By Col. J. Harris, Gdn.
Admitted. Sister of #1208 and claims through same source.
App: 1239 Bascom Webb, Tahlequah, Okla.
By Col. J. Harris, Gdn.
Admitted. Brother of #1208 and claims through same source.
App: 1240 Olin Webb, Tahlequah, Okla.
By Col. J, Harris, Gdn.
Admitted. Brother of #1208 and claims through same source.
App: 1241 Paul Webb, Tahlequah, Okla.
By Col. J. Harris, Gdn.
Admitted. Brother of #1208 and claims through same source.
App: 1242 Mary Webb, Tahlequah, Okla.
By Col. J. Harris, Gdn.
Admitted. Niece of #1208 and claims through same source.
App: 1243 Clarence Webb, Tahlequah, Okla.
By Col. J. Harris, Gdn.
Admitted. Brother of #1208 and claims through same source.
App: 1244 Charotte Hogner and 1 child, Stilwell, Okla.
Admitted. Applicant, her brother and her parents were enrolled by Drennen in G.S. #735.
App: 1245 Black Bat, Stilwell, Okla.
Admitted. Applicant enrolled by Drennnen in Sal. #105 as Ar-ne-ka-yar Bat.
App: 1246 James Fishinghawk and 1 child, Stilwell, Okla.
Admitted. Brother of #1244 and claims through same source.
App: 1247 David Chu-a-lu-kee and 2 children, Eucha, Okla.
Admitted. Duplicate of #364.
App: 1248 Robert Ofields and 2 children, South West City, Mo.
Admitted. Brother of #651. Father enrolled in Del. #589.

App: 1249 Susannah Edmonds, South West City, Mo.
Rejected. Duplicate of #215.
App: 1250 Josiah Young, Locust Grove, Okla.
Duplicate of #525.
App: 1251 Richard Glory, Pryor Creek, Okla.
Admitted. Nephew of #967 and claims through same source.
App: 1252 George Russell, Sallisaw, Okla.
Admitted. Son of Polly Russell, #10397, whose father, George Guess, was enrolled by Drennen in S.B. #320. (Miscel. Test. P. 2934.)
App: 1253 William Young, Locust Grove, Okla.
Admitted. Son of #525 and claims through same source.
App: 1254 Eliza J. Hilderbarand[sic], Benton, Tenn.
Admitted. Applicant her self enrolled by Chapman #1539. Her father also enrolled by Chapman #1536.
App: 1255 Amelia E. Hilderbrand, Benton, Tenn.
Admitted. Daughter of #1254 and claims through same source.
App: 1256 John W. Hilderbrand, Benton, Tenn.
Admitted. On 1835 roll as John V. Hilderbrand, on Chapman #1536 as John W. Hilderbrand, and on Hester as #2699. Cousin once removed of #859.
App: 1257 Lizzie Shoemaker and 8 children, Teonigh, Ga.
Rejected. Sister of #1163 and claims through same source.
App: 1258 Mary Thompson and 5 children, Culberson, N.C.
Admitted. Mother, Rachel Raper enrolled by Chapman #1430. (Miscel. Test. P. 1553.)
App: 1259 Rachel A. Webster, Culberson, N.C.
Admitted. Enrolled by Chapman as Rachel Raper #1430.
App: 1260 Lula Paterson and 2 children, Culberson, N.C.
Admitted. Sister of #1258 and claims through same source.
App: 1261 Wm. L. Webster and 4 children, Culberson, N.C.
Admitted. Brother of #1258 and claims through same source.
App: 1262 Martha Thompson and 8 children, Culberson, N.C.
Admitted. Sister of #1258 and claims through same source.
App: 1263 Richard Pann,
Duplicate of #376.
App: 1264 Richard Pann,
Duplicate of #376.
App: 1265 John A. Arledge and 2 children, Catoosa, Okla.
Admitted. Applicant's maternal grandparents, Anderson and Sallie or Sarah Springston, with several children were enrolled by Drennen in Del. #748. (Miscel. Test. P. 2443.)
App: 1266 Maud Arledge, Catoosa, Okla.
Admitted. Sister of #1265 and claims through same source.
App: 1267 Ada Henderson and 2 children, Catoosa, Okla.
Admitted. Sister of #1265 and claims through same source.
App: 1268 Sarah W. Sequoyah and 1 child, Choteau, Okla.
Admitted. Applicant's father enrolled by Drennen in Del. #74. (Miscel. Test. P. 3587.)

App: 1269 John A. Bird or Doublehead, Texanna, Okla.
Admitted. Claimant's mother and maternal grandparents enrolled by Drennen in Saline #320. Father enrolled in Del. #17.
App: 1270 Lovie Beltch and 1 child, Galena, Kans.
Rejected. Claims through same source as #966.
App: 1271 Lawrence Hyde and 1 child, Flowery Branch, Ga.
Rejected. Brother of #1164 and claims through same source.
App: 1272 Mike and Adam Proctor, Pryor Creek, Okla.
By A.L. Brown, Gdn.
Admitted. Father, Charles Proctor, enrolled in G.S. #324 by Drennen.
App: 1273 A.L. Brown, Pryor Creek, Okla.
Rejected. Applicant was claiming for deceased wife. Wife died in 1905.
App: 1274 Nannie B. Smith and 6 children, Rose, Okla.
Admitted. Claimnant's father, uncle and paternal grandparents enrolled by Drennen in Del. #58. (Miscel. Test. P. 3859.)
App: 1275 William A. Downing and 8 children, Rose, Okla.
Admitted. Brother of #857 and claims through same source.
App: 1276 Downing Riley, Locust Grove, Okla.
Admitted. Nephew of #408 and claims through same source.
App: 1277 William Isaac, Locust Grove, Okla.
Admitted. Nephew of #641 and claims through same source.
App: 1278 Rat Sanders, Choteau, Okla.
Admitted. Brother of #407 and claims through same source.
App: 1279 John Sanders and 5 children, Locust Grove, Okla.
Admitted. Son of #407 and claims through same source.
App: 1280 Skilley Vann, Locust Grove, Okla.
Admitted. Father of applicant was enrolled by Drennen in Sal. #160 under the name of Yar-tun-ee Vann. Brother of #380.
App: 1281 Lucullus Vann and 2 children, Locust Grove, Okla.
Admitted. Brother of #380.
App: 1282 Rachel Vann, Locust Grove, Okla.
Admitted. Applicant and her parents were enrolled by Drennen in Saline #37 under the names of Rachel Turner, Turner and Betsy Turner.
App: 1283 Mary Stopp and 2 children, Choteau, Okla.
Admitted. Sister of #380.
App: 1284 George Suteer and 1 child, Marble City, Okla.
Admitted. Applicant evidently a full blood Cherokee; enrolled as a full blood by the Dawes Commission. (*Handwritten roll number written between sentences #25768*). Is a first cousin of John Noisywater and claims through maternal grandmother, Ah-ley, enrolled by Drennen in Fl. #616. (Mis. Test. P. 2927-3144-3977.)
App: 1285 Joe Fishinghawk and 4 children, Stilwell, Okla.
Admitted. Brother of #1244 and claims through same source.
App: 1286 Aka White, Stilwell, Okla.
Admitted. Sister of #1245 and claims through same source. Applicant was enrolled in Saline #103 by Drennen under the name of Agga Bat.

App: 1287 Jack Batt, Stilwell, Okla.
Admitted. Brother of #1245 and claims through same source. Applicant enrolled by Drennen in Sal. #103 under the name of Oo-soh-tsar-na-tah.

App: 1288 Jennie Blossom and 4 children, Locust Grove, Okla.
Admitted. Maternal grandmother and maternal great grandparents enrolled by Drennen in Tahl. 451.

App: 1289 Dick Pan,
Duplicate of #376.

App: 1290 Katie Littlebird,
Duplicate of #181.

App: 1291 Joe Shade, Peggs, Okla.
Admitted. Claimant was living in 1851 and testifies that he, his brothers and sisters with their mother drew Emigrant money in 1851. (see Miscel. Test. P. 3283.) His brother, Isaac Shade, testified at Tahlequah Mar. 30, 1909 to the same effect. (see Miscel. Test. P. 4100.) The name of the claimant and his immediate ancestors cannot be found on the pay roll of 1851, and they must have been enrolled under some Indian name now unknown. He is a full blood Cherokee and did not draw Old Settler money in 1896. He is enrolled and allotted in the Cherokee Nation. Applicant's grandmother was enrolled by Drennen in Tahl. #501.

App: 1292 Joe Spade[sic],
Admitted. Duplicate of #1291.

App: 1293 Mariah A Deatherage and 3 children, Tahlequah, Okla.
Admitted. Cousin of #671 and claims through same source.

App: 1294 Writer Hogner and 1 child, Stilwell, Okla.
Admitted. Claimant enrolled by Drennen in F1. #101 under the name of Ton-naw-who-lau-neh. Parents and brother ~~a~~and[sic] sisters in same group. (Miscel. Test. P. 3343.)

App: 1295 George Deer-in-water, Evansville, Ark.
Admitted. Claimant enrolled by Drennen in F1. #511 under the name of Wal-a-ne-tah.

App: 1296 Jennie Bat, Stilwell, Okla.
Admitted. Claimant's father and paternal grandfather enrolled by Drennen in G.S. #672. (Miscel. Test. P. 3352.)

App: 1297 Wm. McLemore and 2 children, Stilwell, Okla.
Admitted. Applicant's father enrolled by Drennen in F1. #212 (Miscel. Test. P. 3138.)

App: 1298 Arch Casey and 1 child, Carthage, Mo.
Admitted. Applicant claims through Elizabeth Fields enrolled by Drennen in Dis. #32. (Miscel. Test. P. 4180-4162-4163.)

App: 1299 James Harris, Ketchum, Okla.
Admitted. Applicant enrolled as James Harris Chapman #1755. Brother of #686.

App: 1300 Silas D. Ross and 4 children, Tahlequah, Okla.
Admitted. Applicant's father, George W. Ross, enrolled by Drennen in Tahl. #242.

App: 1301 Sarah C. Ghormley, Cove, Okla.
Admitted. Applicant and her mother enrolled by Drennen in Fl. #251. Father on 1835 roll.
App: 1302 Irene Kirksey, Owasso, Okla.
Admitted. Niece of #901 and claims through same source.
App: 1303 Melvina Nicholson, Grandview, N.C.
Rejected. This applicant claims through Annie Blythe. See full report in #153.
App: 1304 Martha J. Dockery, Grandview, N.C.
Rejected. This applicant claims through Annie Blythe. See full report in #153.
App: 1305 Catherine Dockery, Murphy, N.C.
Rejected. This applicant claims through Annie Blythe. See full report in #153.
App: 1306 Joanna Barber and 1 child, Crowell, Texas.
Rejected. It does not appear that any ancestor was a party to the treaties of 1835-6 and 1846. Nor does it appear that any ancestor was ever enrolled, or that any ancestor lived within the Cherokee domain. (Miscel. Test. P. 3393.) (*Handwritten, applicant born in Arkansas in 1835.*)
App: 1307 Jefferson D. Stratton, Blue Ridge, Ga.
Rejected. First cousin once removed of #32 and claims through same source.
App: 1308 Argelia Quin and 3 children, Passover, Ga.
Rejected. No ancestor ever enrolled. The Aaron Thompson on 1851 roll is not the grandfather of the applicant. The Tom Thomas on 35 is not enrolled. (Miscel. Test. P. 1455-56.)
App: 1309 Thomas J. Smith and 5 children, Ada, Okla.
Rejected. Cousin of #839 and claims through same source.
App: 1310 Belle Jones and 8 children, Andrews, N.C.
Rejected. Sister of #7 and claims through same source.
App: 1311 Annie Martin, Paris, Texas.
Rejected. It does not appear that any ancestor was ever enrolled or that any ancestor was a party to the treaties of 1835-6 and 1846. Shows no connection with the Eastern Cherokees.
App: 1312 Ira Benton Moore and 3 children, Collinsville, Okla.
Rejected. Claimant was born in 1868 and claims his Indian blood through his mother, who has filed application #3272 and who was born in 1849. Claimant, his mother and none of the claimants grouped herewith make claim that they or any of their ancestors were ever enrolled, except the great (*Handwritten great)*, grandfather, Thomas Barnes, who they claim was on the 1835 roll. The family of Thomas Barnes is enrolled on the roll of 1835—pp3, but the Thomas Barnes there enrolled was evidently a white man and there are no males over 18 in the family and one white is given as connected by marriage. Claimant's mother made application to the Dawes Commission and was evidently rejected as she does not appear on that roll. Claimant's mother was born in the State of Iowa, and she and her parents were living there in 1851 as also were her grandparents, and if any of the family were ever connected with the Cherokees, they must have left the tribe long prior to 1835, and consequently were never parties to the treaties of 1835-6 and 1846.
App: 1313 George H. Moore, Collinsville, Okla.
Rejected. Brother of #1312 and claims through same source.

App: 1314 Key Ketcher and 3 children, Tahlequah, Okla.
Admitted. Father of #1236. Applicant enrolled by Drennen in Tahl. #362.
App: 1315 Ida Williams, Cleburn, Texas.
Rejected. Cousin of #58 and claims through same source.
App: 1316 Clara M.W. Forrest, Mt. Ranier, Md.
Rejected. Daughter of #58 and claims through same source.
App: 1317 Barbara A. Condreay and 6 children, Westville, Okla.
Admitted. First cousin once removed of #180 and claims through same source.
App: 1318 Eunice M. Madden, Edna, Kans.
Admitted. Niece of #1177. Mother, Eleanor Lyman, enrolled by Drennen in Tahl. #230.
App: 1319 Everett H. Johnson, Edna, Kans.
Admitted. Brother of #1318. Mother enrolled by Drennen in Tahl. #230. (*Admitted Handwritten*).
App: 1320 Constance Madden, Edna, Kans.
Admitted. Sister of #1318 and claims through same source.
App: 1321 Andrew Lowery and 7 children, Tahlequah, Okla.
Admitted. Brother of #562 and claims through same source.
App: 1322 Maria Wicked, Evansville, Ark.
Admitted. Applicant was enrolled under the name of Oo-ka-yoo-star with her mother, Coo-ti-e, and step-father in Flint #370. (Miscel. Test. P. 3989.)
App: 1323 Alex. Bunch and 5 children, Stilwell, Okla.
Admitted. Father of applicant enrolled by Drennen under the name of Jack in Fl. 74. Cousin of #790.
App: 1324 Manervia Countryman, Needmore, Okla.
Admitted. Sister of #1056 and claims through same source.
App: 1325 George W. Countryman, Needmore, Okla.
Admitted. Brother of #579 and claims through same source.
App: 1326 Jennie D. Chambers and 4 children, Claremore, Okla.
Admitted. Claimant's parents and oldest sister enrolled by Drennen in Tahl. #422.
App: 1327 John Noisywater and 2 children, Stilwell, Okla.
Admitted. Claimant's father enrolled by Drennen in Fl. #221. Claimant's mother enrolled in Fl. 616. (miscel. Test. P. 3144.)
App: 1328 Betsey Johnson and 1 child, Stilwell, Okla.
Admitted. Claimant's mother and maternal grandparents enrolled by Drennen in Fl. #203. (Miscel. Test. P. 3134.)
App: 1329 Joanna Ruth Lewis and 6 children, Afton, Okla.
Admitted. Claimant's mother and maternal grandparents enrolled by Drennen in Del. #393.
App: 1330 John M. Countryman and 1 child, Afton, Okla.
Admitted. Brother of #579 and claims through same source.
App: 1331 Delila Flint and 5 children, Fairland, Okla.
Admitted. Sister of #1056 and claims through same source.
App: 1332 William L. Howdeshell and 6 children, Catoosa, Okla.
Admitted. Claimant's mother and maternal grandparents enrolled by Drennen in Del. #390.

App: 1333 Edward Crutchfield, Spavinaw, Okla.
Admitted. Applicant's father, John Crutchfield, enrolled by Drennen in Del. #947.
App: 1334 Dondenah P. Couch and 1 ~~father~~, (*Handwritten Child.)* Vinita, Okla.
Admitted. Applicant's father enrolled by Chapman #1604. Sister of #1084.
App: 1335 Ellie M. Eaton and 3 children, Claremore, Okla.
Admitted. Applicant's father enrolled by Drennen in G.S. #314.
App: 1336 Wm W. Miller and 5 children, Claremore, Okla.
Admitted. First cousin of #1089 and claims through same source.
App: 1337 Eliza Downing, Claremore, Okla.
Admitted. Claimant born in 1855. Father Old Settler. Mother and sister, Annie, enrolled by Drennen in Tahl. #393.
App: 1338 Charlotte W*atie* (*Handwritten "atie"*) Sanders and 4 children, Chauteau[sic], Okla.
Admitted. Father enrolled by Drennen in Del. 689 under the name of Ah-de-was-kee, and grandfather under the name of Ga-ga-wee.
App: 1339 Sallie Bill, Stilwell, Okla.
Admitted. Grandmother of #1328. Applicant is enrolled as Lochimna by Drennen in Fl. #203.
App: 1340 Martha E. Horsley, Maysville, Ark.
Admitted. Applicant enrolled by Drennen in Del. #432.
App: 1341 Sarah P. Smith and 3 children, Maysville, Ark.
Admitted. Sister of #1340. Applicant enrolled by Drennen in Del. #432. The children applicant claims for, are, one adult son, who is insane and two grandchildren, whose father, Jefferson D. Smith, died Feb. 17, 1888. Applicant applies as guardian and individually.
App: 1342 Nina I Keith and 1child, Maysville, Ark.
Admitted. Niece of #1340. Mother, Laura Yearger (Fields) was enrolled by Chapman in Del. #432.
App: 1343 Claude W. Yeargar, Maysville, Ark.
Admitted. Nephew of #1340. Mother enrolled Del. #432.
App: 1344 Lizzie Swimmer and 1 child, Stilwell, Okla.
Admitted. Applicant's father under the name of Yellowbug (*very blurred, difficult to read, type-over on first and last letters*) and both grandparents were enrolled by Drennen in Fl. #239. (Miscel. Test. P. 4011.)
App: 1345 Mabelle Hornbuckle and 4 children, Claremore, Okla.
Admitted. Niece of #218 and claims through same source.
App: 1346 Joseph Trapp, Catoosa, Okla.
Rejected. Claimant evidently not born in 1851. Dawes Commission gives him as 45 in 1902. Claimant's mother and mother's brother and sister on Old Settler roll Ill. #10. Claimant has failed twice to appear in response to summons in the field. Evidence insufficient to establish Eastern Cherokee descent on father's side.
App: 1347 Virginia Powell, Monatta, Okla.
Rejected. It does not appear that applicant's ancestors were parties to the treaties of 1835-6 and 1846, never shared in payments to the Cherokees nor were enrolled with them. (Miscel. Test. P. 2370.)

App: 1348 Charley C. Pinion, Lehigh, Okla.
Rejected. Son of #9774 and claims through same source. (*Handwritten, Misc. Test. P. 2363)*
App: 1349 Charlotte Adair and 3 children, Stilwell, Okla.
Admitted. Father enrolled by Drennen in G.S. #534 under the name of William Hummingbird. (Note: In applicant's testimony her parents were confused. She is without doubt entitled through G.S. 534. (Miscel. Test. P. 3311-3335-3272.)
App: 1350 Lula Rohr and 4 children, Claremore, Okla.
Admitted. Applicant's father enrolled by Drennen in Tahl. #200 1/2.
App: 1351 Lucy Miller, Needmore, Okla.
Admitted. Applicant enrolled in 1851 by Drennen in Del. #378. Claims through Peter Hilderbrand same number.
App: 1352 James L. Kell, Chelsea, Okla.
Admitted. Applicant's mother enrolled in 1851 by Drennen in Fl. #341.
App: 1353 Webster W. Weir and 1 child, Sacremento, Calif.
Admitted. Applicant enrolled by Drennen in 1851 in Del. #78.
App: 1354 Mittie A. Bazzell and 4 children, Vinita, Okla.
Admitted. Cousin of #201 and claims through same source.
App: 1355 Lucinda Hornbuckle and 4 children, Inola, Okla.
Admitted. Niece of #51 and claims through same source.
App: 1356 Samuel I. Fields and 1 child, Maysville, Ark.
Admitted. Brother of #1340. Applicant was enrolled by Drennen in 1851 in Del. #432.
App: 1357 Margaret Smith, Maysville, Ark.
Admitted. Sister of #1340. Applicant enrolled by Drennen in 1851 in Del. #432.
App: 1358 Sophronia Milligan, Maysville, Ark.
Admitted. Sister of #1340. Applicant was enrolled by Drennen in 1851 in Del. #432 as Serfronia Fields.
App: 1359 John M. Miller and 2 children, Needmore, Okla.
Admitted. Uncle of #1089. Enrolled by Drennen in Del. #789.
App: 1360 Sarah A. Duncan, Afton, Okla.
Admitted. Aunt of #1089. Applicant enrolled by Drennen in Del. #789 as Sarah Miller.
App: 1361 William D. Ross, Fort Gibson, Okla.
Admitted. Applicant enrolled by Drennen in 1851 in Tahl. #592.
App: 1362 Hubbard Ross and 3 children, Fort Gibson, Okla.
Admitted. Brother of #1361 and claims through same source.
App: 1363 Henry C. Meigs, Fort Gibson, Okla.
Admitted. Applicant and his mother, Jane Nave nee Ross, were both enrolled by Drennen in Tahl. #225.
App: 1364 Mary Jane Ross, Fort Gibson, Okla.
Admitted. Mother of #1361. Applicant enrolled by Drennen in Tahl. #592.
App: 1365 Emma L. Ross, Fort Gibson, Okla.
Admitted. Sister of #1361 and claims through same source.
App: 1366 Mollie Howard, Fort Gibson, Okla.
Admitted. Niece of #1361 and claims through same source.

App: 1367 Nancy Holland, Westville, Okla.
Admitted. Mother of #334. Applicant enrolled by Chapman #1995.
App: 1368 Rutha C. Ross and 3 children, Rose, Okla.
Admitted. Sister of #334 and claims through same source.
App: 1369 Edward B. McNair, Tahlequah, Okla.
Admitted. Cousin of #816 and claims through same source.
App: 1370 Eliza Howel and 2 grandchildren, Oseuma, Okla.
Admitted. Applicant sister of #1056 and claims through same source.
App: 1371 William W. Chambers and 2 children, Tiawah, Okla.
Admitted. Applicant mother and brother all enrolled by Drennen in Tahl. #240. (See also app. #11265.)
App: 1372 Martha Pope and 2 children, Hemp, Ga.
Admitted. Aunt of #211 and claims through same source.
App: 1373 Joseph Vann, Peggs, Okla.
Admitted. Applicant, his mother, and brother and sisters all enrolled by Drennen in G.S. #292.
App: 1374 Cook Still and 4 children, Peggs, Okla.
Admitted. Father, John Still, and paternal grandparents enrolled by Drennen in G.S. #323.
App: 1375 Cyntha Vann and 1 child, Peggs, Okla.
Admitted. Father enrolled as James Downing by Drennen in G.S. #252. (Miscel. Test. P. 4223.)
App: 1376 Marshall Daly, Webbers Falls, Okla.
Admitted. Father, Rufus Daley, and grandmother, Rachel Daley, enrolled by Drennen in Skin Bayou #194.
App: 1377 Maggie Strickler and 4 children, Hadley, Okla.
Admitted. Sister of #1375 and claims through same source.
App: 1378 Julia Wallace and 2 children, Tahlequah, Okla.
Admitted. First cousin of #227 and claims through same source.
App: 1379 Cicero Johnson and 1 child, Tahlequah, Okla.
Admitted. Applicant, his mother, and brothers and sisters enrolled by Chapman #1322 to 1326 inclusive.
App: 1380 Laura Newton and 1 child, Tahlequah, Okla.
Admitted. Sister of #1379 and claims through same source.
App: 1381 Levi Keener and 6 children, Ahniwake, Okla.
Admitted. Mother, Sallie Ross, and grandmother, Caty Ross, enrolled by Drennen in Tahl. District #485. (Miscel. Test. P. 3848.)
App: 1382 David Taylor, Dawson, Okla.
Admitted. Nephew of #52 and claims through same source.
App: 1383 Jonia Pleasant, Cleveland, Ohio
Rejected. It does not appear that any ancestor was ever enrolled or that any ancestor was a party to the treaties of 1835-6 and 1846. Shows no connection with the Eastern Cherokees. It does not appear that any ancestor ever lived within the Cherokee domain. (*Handwritten See also #435.*)
App: 1384 Hattie Herndon and 1 child, Cleveland, Ohio.
Rejected. Sister of #1383 and claims through same source.

App: 1385 Thomas A. Foreman and 1 child, Oolagah, Okla.
Admitted. Brother of #773 and claims through same source.
App: 1386 Lutitia Corntassel and 3 children, Westville, Okla.
Admitted. Applicant's father, John Te-cah-ne-ye-skee enrolled with his father, Big Te-cah-ne-ye-skee by Drennen in Tahl. #508.
App: 1387 Ruth Mounts and 1 child, Dewey, Okla.
Admitted. Duplicate of #766.
App: 1388 Uphaney Poorbear, Fort Gibson, Okla.
Admitted. Aunt of #216 and claims through same source.
App: 1389 Benjamin Whitfield, Wauhillau, Okla.
Admitted. Grandfather, William A. Foreman, and great grandfather, Johnson Foreman, were enrolled by Drennen in Tahl. #278. (*Handwritten, Misc. Test. P. 3253.*)
App: 1390 Luke Whitfield and 1 child, Wauhillau, Okla.
Admitted. Brother of #1389 and claims through same source.
App: 1391 Tah-yu-ne-se Twist, Dutch Mills, Ark.
Admitted. Applicant enrolled as Toh-ga-ne-se Twist, together with his father, Twist, and his brother John Twist, were enrolled by Drennen in G.S. #402, 403 and 404. (Miscel. Test. P. 3001.)
App: 1392 Parker Collins Harris and 8 children, Muskokee, Okla.
Admitted. Applicant enrolled by Chapman #1760. Brother of #686.
App: 1393 Lafayette Teel, (*Handwritten and 6 children,*) Claremore, Okla.
Rejected. Half brother of #817 and claims through same source.
App: 1394 Ezekiel Fields, South West City, Mo.
Admitted. Uncle of #242. Enrolled as Ezekiel Fields Del. #135.
App: 1395 Margret Gates and 2 children, Catoosa, Okla.
Admitted. Sister of #1265 and claims through same source.
App: 1396 Hiram Elliott and 6 children, Big Cabin, Okla.
Admitted. Applicant claims his Indian descent through his mother and father and is enrolled by the Dawes Commission #8422. His father was Arch Elliott and Arch Elliott derives his Indian (*Handwritten, blood*) through his mother, whose maiden name was Elizabeth Foreman. Elizabeth married one John Elliott, who came to the Indian Territory from Georgia about 1838. John Elliott was a white man and was killed in the Territory in the forties. He had several children among them were James, Walter, Abigail, George, Nannie (who married a Carter) and Sallie or Sarah (who married a Springston). They have a son living by the name of John L. Springston, who has filed application #447 (see Del. 748). It does not appear that any of the other children of John and Elizabeth Elliott were enrolled in 1851, but in 1835 John Elliott was enrolled in the State of Georgia, page 51, as an affiliated white and his wife was evidently a half breed, as there is one half breed enrolled, and the others were apparently children living at that time and are given as quadroons. It appears that the grandchildren of John Elliott have shared in all the recent payments of the Cherokees, and it is shown by the testimony of a number of witnesses, that the children of John Elliott and Elizabeth were considered and recognized as Eastern or Emigrant Cherokees, and were probably left off of the roll of 1851 by reason of some political difference existing at that time. (see Miscel. Test. P. 3674-4363-4350-4356 and the affidavits of D.W.C. Duncan and James M. Bell, filed herewith.) No. 1396 is the cousin of James Elliott, #2993 on their father's side. It would

also appear that the mother of #1396 and the mother's brother, Jesse, were enrolled by Drennen in 1851 in Del. #547.

App: 1397 Sena Howell Vinita, Okla. R.F.D.#3.
Admitted. Grandniece of #1351 and claims through same source. Grandfather enrolled by Drennen in Del. #378.

App: 1398 Stephen D.C. Edwards and 1 child, Chaffee, Okla.
Rejected. Half brother of #817 and claims through same source.

App: 1399 Thomas L. Landrum ~~and 2 children~~, Foyil, Okla.
Admitted. First cousin of #265 Applicant's father enrolled by Drennen in Del. #43. (*Handwritten, Two minor children rejected, as they are enrolled by Dawes Com. with Chickasaws, and are affiliated with that tribe.)*

App: 1400 Nancy Edins and 3 children, Wann, Okla.
Admitted. Father enrolled as Joseph Vann and grandfather as Hon. JohnVann by Drennen in 1851 in Saline #207. (Miscel. Test. P. 2402.)

App: 1401 Emma L. Crotzer and 6 children, Fairland, Okla.
Admitted. Sister of #1111 and claims through same source.

App: 1402 James Ketcher and 1 child, Christie, Okla.
Admitted. Brother of #1386 and claims through same source.

App: 1403 Miles S. Milles, Tulsa, Okla.
Rejected. It does not appear that applicant or any ancestor was ever enrolled. It does not appear that they were living within the limits of the Cherokee domain in 1835-6 and 1846, or were recognized members of the tribe. (Miscel. Test. P. 2537-2581.)

App: 1404 Andrew M. Thornsberry and 2 children, Tulsa, Okla.
Rejected. half[sic] brother of #1403 and claims through same source.

App: 1405 Susan C. Byrd and 1 child, Tulsa, Okla.
Rejected. Sister of #1403 and claims through same source.

App: 1406 Martha Mills, Tulsa, Okla.
Rejected. Mother of #1403 and claims through same source.

App: 1407 Artie Cheney and 3 children, Collinsville, Okla.
Admitted. Sister of #326 and claims through same source.

App: 1408 Thos. Sanders, Stilwell, Okla.
Duplicate of #203.

App: 1409 Gilbert Snell and 3 children, Kansas, Okla.
Admitted. Half brother of #469 and claims through same source.

App: 1410 Jennie Noisywater, Stilwell, Okla.
Admitted. Applicant's mother enrolled by Drennen as Cut-toy-ye-heh in Fl. #338.

App: 1411 Robert L. Ralston and 3 (sis & bro.) Cleora, Okla.
Admitted. Nephew of #1034. Grandfather and grandmother, Lewis and Elizabeth Ralston, enrolled by Chapman #2053 and #2054.

App: 1412 Margaret E. Keys and 3 children, Cookson, Okla.
Admitted. Cousin of #859. Mother Elizabeth Keys and grandmother Margaret Catron enrolled by Drennen in Tahl. #36.

App: 1413 Lydia Goback, Stilwell, Okla.
Admitted. Applicant herself enrolled by Drennen in Fl. #461. Father enrolled in Fl. #447.

App: 1414 Eli Tadpole and 4 children, Wellston, Okla.
Admitted. Uncle of #1204 and claims through same source.

App: 1415 Mary Wilson, Dayton, Tenn.
Admitted. Sister of #553 and claims through same source.

App: 1416 Elizabeth Cate, Hill City, Tenn.
Admitted. Applicant herself enrolled by Chapman #1679 under the name of Elizabeth Hail. Father enrolled by Chapman #1678.

App: 1417 Grandville Martin and 2 children, Greenbrier, Okla.
Admitted. Brother of #873 and claims through same source.

App: 1418 John Twist, Dutch Mills, Ark.
Admitted. Brother of #1391. Applicant enrolled by Drennen in G.S. #404.

App: 1419 Sut Cooley and 1 child, Stilwell, Okla.
Admitted. Father and mother, Doctor and Wutty Cooley, enrolled by Drennen in 1851 in Fl. #315.

App: 1420 Watta Beanstick, Stilwell, Okla.
Admitted. Mother of #1419. Applicant enrolled in Fl. #315.

App: 1421 Robert V. Steele, Tahlequah, Okla.
Admitted. Applicant himself enrolled with mother, Mary Steele, by Drennen in Tahl. #353.

App: 1422 John Lovett, Gans, Okla.
Admitted. Grandfather and grandmother, Robert and Polly Lovett enrolled by Drennen in Ill. #125.

App: 1423 Che-ka-yoo-ee Youngdeer, Oaks, Okla.
Admitted. Enrolled by Drennen in G.S. #269 together with her husband Kah-na-see-ta-skee. (Misc. Test. P. #4235.)

App: 1424 Caroline Wolfe and 5 children, Claremore, Okla.
Admitted. ~~Grand~~Mother and grandfather, Ah-noo-wa-kie and Ah-tah-goo-lee-skie, and grandmother, Sally, all enrolled by Drennen in G.S. #111.

App: 1425 Watt Russell, Oaks, Okla.
Admitted. Father and Uncle, Aaron and Samuel, enrolled by Drennen in Del. #641. (Miscel. Test. P. 4236.)

App: 1426 Bessie Smith
By Lila Smith, Gdn.
Duplicate of child in #1190.

App: 1427 Wm Cline and 4 children, Bunch, Okla.
Admitted. Applicant's mother, Caty Soap, was enrolled by Drennen in G.S. #374.

App: 1428 Nellie Soap, Stilwell, Okla.
Admitted. Applicant herself enrolled as Nellie ~~Rector~~[sic] by Drennen in Fl. #125. Grandfather, William Grimmett, also enrolled in same group.

App: 1429 Josephine Hulsey, Needmore, Okla.
Admitted. Sister of #1034 and claims through same source.

App: 1430 Sarah Ketcher, Westville, Okla
Admitted. Sister of #1386 and claims through same source.

App: 1431 Rosa Bruner, Senora, Okla.
Duplicate of #679.

App: 1432 John Ketcher and 1 child, Westville, Okla.
Admitted. Brother of #1386 and claims through same source.
App: 1433 Andy Linn and 2 children, Philadelphia, Tenn.
Rejected. This applicant claims through Nathan Kirkland. See full report in #586.
App: 1434 Susannah Grant and 4 children, Roeckwood[sic], Tenn.
Rejected. This applicant claims through Nathan Kirkland. See full report in #586.
App: 1435 Francis M. King, Union Star, Mo.
Rejected. Applicant born in 1836 in Iowa. His mother born in Va. in 1803. Moved west to Ky. And Ill. prior to 1830 and was living in Iowa in 1834-5-6, so that she could not have been a member of the Eastern Cherokee tribe in 1835 or a party to the treaty of 1835-6. Applicant nor any of his ancestors were ever enrolled. (Miscel. Test. P. 3890.)
App: 1436 Mary Sanders, Bunch, Okla.
Admitted. Applicant's father and mother and applicant herself enrolled respectively as John, Ue-te-yah, and Ah-haw-cah Rogers by Drennen in S.B. #204.
App: 1437 Nakie Sanders, Bunch, Okla.
Admitted. Applicant enrolled as Na-key, together with her father, mother, brothers and sisters by Drennen in F1. #575.
App: 1438 Lizzie Sanders, Bunch, Okla.
Admitted. Sister of #1437 and claims through same source.
App: 1439 Jolly Sanders, Bunch, Okla.
Admitted. Brother of #1437, applicant enrolled by Drennen Fl. #575.
App: 1440 Aggie Sanders and 3 children, Bunch, Okla.
Admitted. Sister of #1437 and claims through same source.
App: 1441 Jennie Sanders, Bunch, Okla.
Admitted. Sister of #1437 and claims through same source.
App: 1442 John W. Jordan and 5 children, Cleveland, Okla.
Admitted. Applicant enrolled by Drennen in Tahl. #58 together with grandfather and grandmother, John and Susan Riley.
App: 1442 1/2 Wm. Owen Jordan et al, Turley, Okla.
By Nancy E. Downs, Gdn.
Admitted. Grandchildren of #1442 and claim through same source.
App: 1443 Cyntha Loudermilk and 2 children, Culberson, N.C.
Admitted. Father, William Raper, enrolled in 1851 by Chapman #1433.
App: 1444 Jane Anderson and 2 children, Culberson, N.C.
Admitted. Sister of #1443 and claims throug[sic] same source.
App: 1445 Alcy Foster and 4 children, Culberson, N.C.
Admitted. Sister of #1443 and claims through same source.
App: 1446 John Loudermilk and 2 children, Culberson, N.C.
Admitted. Grandson of #1443 and claims through same source.
App: 1447 Sunday Hogtoter, Vian, Okla.
Admitted. Applicant enrolled as Sunday together with his father, mother, brothers and sisters by Drennen in #284 Flint.

App:1448 Coowie Blackhawk, Sallisaw, Okla.
Admitted. Applicant's mother enrolled as Salsey by Drennen in Fl. #60. Her great grandparents enrolled at the head of same group.
App: 1449 Na-key Baldridge, Akins, Okla.
Admitted. Applicant enrolled as Na-a-ky by Drennen in F1. #24. Her father enrolled at the head of same group.
App: 1450 Mose Chuculate, Sallisaw, Okla.
Admitted. Applicant is father of #960 and was enrolled by Drennen in F1. #51.
App: 1451 Calvin Lee and 6 children, Sallisaw, Okla.
Admitted. Applicant's father enrolled at Skin Bayou #60.
App: 1452 John Childers, Sallisaw, Okla.
Admitted. Applicant enrolled with his mother Akey Creeson enrolled by Drennen in F1. #551 under the name of John Childress.
App: 1453 Linda Duval and 1 child, Sallisaw, Okla.
Admitted. Great niece of #202. Applicant's mother Tsau-gau-he, who was born since 1851, was the daughter of Akey, enroll[sic] by Drennen in F1. #321. Akey's father was enrolled in F1. #314 under the name Eli Daugherty.
App: 1454 Aggie Silk, Akins, Okla.
Admitted. Applicant enrolled by Drennen as Aly Baldridge in Skin Bayou #33.
App: 1455 Armstrong Elmore and 2 children, Brent, Okla.
Admitted. Brother of #1453 and claims through same source. Grandnephew of #202.
App: 1456 Nancy Childers, Sallisaw, Okla.
Admitted. Sister of #1454. Applicant enrolled in S.B. #33.
App: 1457 Jennie Christie and 2 children, Sallisaw, Okla.
Rejected. Applicant is an Old Settler. Nothing shown to establish an Emigrant Cherokee claim. Applicant formally withdrew claim at Sallisaw, Okla. Mar. 12, 1909.
App: 1458 Cherokee Christie, Sallisaw, Okla.
Admitted. Applicant's grandfather Dieck[sic] Christie, enrolled by Drennen in F1. #627.
App: 1459 Nannie Woods and 2 children, Sallisaw, Okla.
Admitted. Sister of #1458 and claims through same source.
App: 1460 William Young and 1 child, Marble City, Okla.
Admitted. Brother of #1124. Father enrolled in 1851 by Drennen in G.S. #633.
App: 1461 Wm. Young,
Duplicate of #1460.
App: 1462 Sunday Hogtoter,
Duplicate of #1447,
App: 1463 Nick Soap (deceased) and 1 child, Stilwell, Okla.
Admitted. Applicant enrolled at Flint #304, by Drennen.
App: 1464 Thomas J. Bradley and 3 children, Whitmire, Okla.
Rejected. Neither applicant nor any of his ancestors were ever enrolled. Does not establish the fact of descent from any person who was a party to the treaties of 1835-6 and 1846.
App: 1465 Arthur Caudill, Grayson, N.C.
Rejected. This applicant is one of the Sizemore Claimants. See full report in #417.

App: 1466 Elizabeth Caudill and 6 children, Grayson, N.C.
Rejected. This applicant claims through the Sizemore's. See full report in #417.
App: 1467 Amanda Eggers and 1 child, Hemlock, N.C.
Rejected. This applicant claims through the Sizemore's. See full report in #417.
App: 1468 Emily C. Webb, Knoxville, Tenn. 716 N. 3rd Ave.
Admitted. Sister of #1254 and claims through same source. Enrolled by Chapman #1540.
App: 1469 Susan E. Kelly and 4 children, Grove, Okla.
Admitted. Niece of #496 and claims through same source.
App: 1470 Leonard Spade and 3 children, Moodys, Okla.
Admitted. Applicant's father, Kar-ta-ske, enrolled in 1851 in Saline #540 by Drennen. Applicant's daughter, Emma, enrolled with Linnie F. Younger app. #30362. (Miscel. Test. P. 3288.)
App: 1471 Noah Cloud, Tahlequah, Okla.
Admitted. Brother of #1204 and claims through same source.
App: 1472 Simon McKinzey and 3 children, Pryor Creek, Okla.
Rejected. Applicant enrolled as W.R. McKenzie on the Old Settler roll Saline #104. (see letter herein)
App: 1473 Betsey Ketcher, Tahlequah, Okla.
Admitted. Applicant's father enrolled by Drennen in Del. #81. Applicant's mother enrolled by Drennen in Del. #95.
App: 1474 George Roach, Tahlequah, Okla.
Admitted. Brother of #931 and claims through same source. Applicant himself enrolled in Dis. #46.
App: 1475 Annie Dick, Peggs, Okla.
Admitted. Applicant's father and mother enrolled by Drennen as Coming Deer and Ause in Del. #313.
App: 1476 Dick Pann,
Duplicate of #376.
App: 1477 Ruth Wofford and 1 child, Moody*s*, Okla.
Admitted. Sister of #1221. Applicant's parents enrolled by Drennen in Saline #170. (*Handwritten "s" after Moody*)
App: 1478 Lafayette Catron and 2 children, Wauhillau, Okla.
Admitted. Applicant enrolled in 1851 by Drennen in Tahl. 36. Mother also enrolled in same group.
App: 1479 Margaret P. Cromwell, Andrews, N.C.
Admitted. Sister of #361. Enrolled by Chapman in 1851 as #1237.
App: 1480 Sarah A. Whitaker, Andrews, N.C.
Admitted. Sister of #361. Enrolled by Chapman #1239.
App: 1481 James M. Whitaker, Andrews, N.C.
Admitted. Brother of #361. Enrolled by Chapman #1238.
App: 1482 Mack Cooper and 1 child, Andrews, N.C.
Admitted. Nephew of #361 and claims through same source.

App: 1483 Stan Watie Winton (deceased) Peggs, Okla.
By W.M. Winton, Gdn.
Rejected. Parent claims for his son Stan, who died in 1899. He does not claim for himself.
App: 1484 John Catron and 8 children, Wauhillau, Okla.
Admitted. Applicant's father Lafayette Catron enrolled by Drennen in Tahl. #36. First cousin once removed of #859.
App: 1485 Almira Stephens, Park Hill, Okla.
Admitted. Applicant's father, Lafayette Catron, enrolled by Drennen in Tahl. #36.
App: 1486 Nellie Holland (E), Centralia, Okla.
Admitted. Granddaughter of #1207 and claims through same source.
App: 1487 Eliza J. Dunaway, Estella, Okla.
Admitted. Applicant's father and paternal grandparents enrolled by Drennen in Del. #97.
App: 1488 Charles Hunter, Estella, Okla.
Admitted. Applicant's mother enrolled as Susannah Connor by Drennen in Del. #369.
App: 1489 Nancy McDaniel, Muskogee, Okla.
Admitted. Applicant enrolled as Nancy Ross by Drennen in Dis. #4. Mother enrolled as Rachel Hickey in Dis. #3.
App: 1490 Richard Henson and 4 children, Foyil, Okla.
Admitted. First cousin of #326. Grandfather, Wm. Henson, enrolled by Chapman #1307.
App: 1491 Karl Webb, Tahlequah, Okla.
Admitted. Brother of #1208 and claims through same source.
App: 1492 Callie Ridge and 6 children, Rose, Okla.
Admitted. First cousin of #737. Applicant's father enrolled as Moses Paris by Drennen in Dis. #45.
App: 1493 Ida V. Coleman, Fort Gibson, Okla.
Admitted. Mother and grandmother enrolled as Fanny and Araminta Vann by Drennen in Tahl. #243.
App: 1494 Lewis R. Nash and 4 children, Fort Gibson, Okla.
Admitted. Brother of #1493 and claims through same source.
App: 1495 William Cochran and 3 children,
Duplicate of #150.
App: 1496 Emily Bird and 5 children, Wagoner, Okla.
Admitted. Daughter of #151 and claims through same source.
App: 1497 Emily Bird and 5 children,
Duplicate of #1496.
App: 1498 Carrie Alkin[sic] and 4 children, Wagoner, Okla.
Admitted. Mother and maternal grandfather enrolled by Chapman respectively as #1385 and #1378. (Note: *Alkin has a, U, mixed with what looks like an* A.)
App: 1499 Carrie Beach, Needmore, Okla.
Admitted. Applicant niece of #1034 and claims through same source.
App: 1500 Martha E. Flynn,
Duplicate of #618.

App: 1501 Victoria R. Rogers Nowata, Okla.
Admitted. Sister of #873 and claims through same source.
App: 1502 Sarah Snell, Oaks, Okla.
Admitted. Father, Blackfox, and mother, Na-key, both enrolled by Drennen in Del. #679.
App: 1503 Coming Snell, Oaks, Okla.
Admitted. Brother of #1502 and claims through same source.
App: 1504 Mattie Dial, Oaks, Okla.
Admitted. Grandson of #702 and claims through same source.
App: 1505 Barker Dry, Oaks, Okla.
By Lizzie Stover, Gdn.
Admitted. Grandson of #702 and claims through same source.
App: 1506 Quatie Bunch and 2 children, Stilwell, Okla.
Admitted. Sister of #790 and claims through same source.
App: 1507 Ollie Thompson, Oaks, Okla.
Admitted. Applicant enrolled by agent Drennen together with her brothers and sisters, Le-se, Ste-ne and Na-chil-ly, in Del. #652.
App: 1508 Charley Bunch, Stilwell, Okla.
Admitted. Brother of #790 and claims through same source.
App: 1509 Ruben W. Moore, Sapulpa, Okla.
Rejected. Brother of #1312 and claims through same source.
App: 1510 Euphemia R. Harvey, Biardstown, Texas.
Rejected. Cousin of #839 and claims through same source.
App: 1511 Robert B. Hampton and 1 child, Blue Ridge, Ga.
Rejected. This applicant claims through the Blythe group. See full report in #153.
App: 1512 James A. Hampton and 3 children, McCays, Tenn.
Rejected. This applicant claims through Annie Blythe. See full report in #153.
App: 1513 Wm A. McDonald and 6 children, Grandview, N.C.
Rejected. This applicant claims through Annie Blythe, see full report in #153.
App: 1514 Matilda South, (*Handwritten above, Wagoner, Okla.*) ~~Waco, Texas~~.
Rejected. Claims Cherokee descent through her mother Lettie Grass, who lived in Smyth Co. Virginia, far removed from the Cherokee domain and who was never enrolled. There is no testimony to show that she ever lived with the tribe or was ever recognized as being a member of the tribe at the time of the treaty of 1835-6 or since. Claimant's grandmother, Rachel Smock, was never enrolled, and nothing to show Cherokee recognition or affiliation. Claimant herself born in 1846 was not enrolled in 1851. (Miscel. Test. P. 2535.)
App: 1515 Matilda A. Courtney and 1 child, Bartlesville, Okla.
Rejected. Claimant was born in Polk County, Mo., in 1842 far removed from the Cherokee domain. Her mother, Dicey Fender, through whom she claims, died as late as 1890 and was not enrolled in 1835 nor 1851, nor did she ever receive any Cherokee recognition as far as the records in this case show. Claimant herself was not enrolled in 1851. Has lived in Oklahoma 20 years, and there is no evidence to show Cherokee recognition wither by association or descent. (*Handwritten Alexander Brown case. See No. 35)*

App: 1516 John Smith and 8 children, Madola, Ga.
Admitted. Grandson of #423 and claims through same source. Mother, Rebecca Smith, enrolled by Chapman #1890.
App: 1517 Bettie Rogers and 4 children, Tomotla, N.C.
Rejected. This applicant claims through Annie Blythe. See full report in #153.
App: 1518 Sophie E. Witt and 2 children, Peachtree, N.C.
Rejected. This applicant claims through Annie Blythe. See full report in #153.
App: 1519 Monte A. Hampton, McCays, Tenn.
Rejected. This applicant claims through Annie Blythe. See full report in #153.
App: 1520 Eddie E. Hampton, McCays, Tenn.
Rejected. This applicant claims through the Annie Blythe group. See full report in #153.
App: 1521 Nancy Goble, Quarles, Ga.
Admitted. Grandmother of #24. Applicant enrolled by Chapman #1913.
App: 1522 Ann Morrison and 1 child, Dennis, Ga.
Rejected. It does not appear that any ancestor was a party to the treaties of 1835-6 and 1846. Nor does it appear that any ancestor was ever enrolled. Shows no real connection with the Eastern Cherokees. (Miscel. Test. P. 1486.)
App: 1523 George W. Wright and 1 child, Galloway, Ga.
Admitted. Mother enrolled on Act of Congress roll. Applicant enrolled by Swetland—see data herein. (Miscel. Test. P. 1733-4-5-6.)
App: 1524 Sarah A. Hart, Lawrence, Ala.
Rejected. This applicant claims through Annie Blythe. See full report in #153.
App: 1525 Evan (?) Howell, Marietta, Ga.
312 Kennesaw Ave
Admitted. Son of #29 and claims through same source.
App: 1526 Dela Quarles, Dennis, Ga.
Rejected. Sister of #1522 and claims through same source.
App: 1527 John M. Ditmore and 7 children, Hydro, Okla.
Rejected. This applicant claims through Annie Blythe. See full report in #153.
App: 1528 W. Clark Jordan and 5 children, Murphy, N.C.
Rejected. Brother of #528 and claims through same source.
App: 1529 Polly A. Baldwin and 3 children, Brighton, Mo.
Rejected. This applicant claims through Alex. Brown. See full report in #35.
App: 1530 William A. Henry, Bartlesville, Okla.
Admitted. Son of #5003 and claims through same source.
App: 1531 Jacob E. Martin and 7 children, Lookout, N.C.
Rejected. Cousin of #126 and claims through same source.
App: 1532 Martha E. James and 3 children, ~~Bourne~~, Texas.
(*Handwritten above, Bowie.*)
Admitted. Sister of #1111 and claims through same source.
App: 1533 John C. Seitz, Bartsboro, Ga.
Admitted. First cousin of #98 and claims through same source.
App: 1534 Jennie Lynn Seitz and 2 children, Bartsboro, Ga.
Admitted. First cousin of #98 and claims through same source.
App: 1535 Georgia A. Seitz, Bartsboro, Ga.
Admitted. First cousin of #98 and claims through same source.

App: 1536 Amanda E. Satterfield and 1 child, Hedwig, Ga.
Admitted. First cousin (*Handwritten once removed*) of #98 and claims through same source.

App: 1537 Arthur A. Bible and 1 child, Alluwe, Okla.
Admitted. Claims Cherokee descent through his mother, Ruth Nicholson—(enrolled Luretta)—who with his aunts, Harriet, Martha and Eleanor, were enrolled by Drennen in Tahl. #535. (see testimony of his sister, Ella Coon, #12420.)

App: 1538 Martha House and 3 children, Alluwe, Okla.
Admitted. Sister of #1537 and claims through same source.

App: 1539 John Sixkiller, Stilwell, Okla.
Admitted. Claimant was enrolled with his father, Cricket Sixkiller, by Drennen in 1851 in G.S. #221.

App: 1540 Marcus L. Tucker and 3 children, Stilwell, Okla.
Admitted Nephew of #423 and claims through same source. Applicant himself enrolled by Hester #1947 and father enrolled by Chapman #1900.

App: 1541 Judge K. Clingan, Chelsea, Okla.
Admitted. Applicant and his mother, Martha Clingan, were enrolled by Chapman ~~in~~ #1586 and #1580 respectively.

App: 1542 Emma Blair and 1 child, Catoosa, Okla.
Admitted. Father, Joseph Ruddle, enrolled by Chapman #1404.

App: 1543 Florence J. Boyd, Catoosa, Okla.
Admitted. Sister of #1542 and claims through same source.

App: 1544 Moses Oldfields and 3 children, Eucha, Okla.
Admitted. Brother of #344 and claims through same source.

App: 1545 Lille C. Lowe and 1 child, Aquone, N.C.
Rejected. Cousin of #126 and claims through same source.

App: 1546 Isaac N. Bruner and 3 children, Stilwell, Okla.
Admitted. First cousin of #642. Mother of applicant enrolled by Chapman #1685.

App: 1547 Dicey Beanstick and 1 child, Stilwell, Okla.
Admitted. Applicant's father, Thomas Fourkiller, and two sisters Sookey and Jensey Fourkiller, were enrolled by Drennen in G.S. #354.

App: 1548 Martha E. Leatherwood, Stilwell, Okla.
Admitted. Niece of #423. Applicant herself enrolled by Chapman #1901.

App: 1549 Esther Nelson and 1 child, Porum, Okla.
Admitted. Evidence shows that applicant's mother is an Emigrant Cherokee and considered such by every one who knows her. (Miscel. Test. P. 4218.)

App: 1550 Wm Dyer Walls, Peachtree, N.C.
Rejected. This applicant claims through Annie Blythe. See full report in #153.

App: 1551 Jennie Smith, Union Town, Ark.
Rejected. Cannot find names of ancestors given in application on rolls. Applicant fails to answer letters of inquiry from office and failed to appear when notified to give testimony. Rejected from want of proof.

App: 1552 Thomas Splitnose and 3 children, Porum, Okla.
Admitted. Half brother of #1549 and claims through same source.

App: 1553 Susan Splitnose and 3 children, Porum, Okla.
Admitted. Father and paternal grandparents of applicant were enrolled by Drennen in Del. #715 under the names of James, John Anderson and Dah-ne. (see letter in #1553.)

App: 1554 George Wilkerson, Webbers Falls, Okla.
Admitted. Half brother of #1549 and claims through same source.

App: 1555 Thomas Sunday and 3 children, Porum, Okla.
Admitted. Claimant's mother, Betsy Walker, and half brother, Stephen Walker, were enrolled by Drennen in 1851 in Del. #206 and #207 respectively.

App: 1556 Malinda Sunday and 3 children, Porum, Okla.
Admitted. Father enrolled by Drennen in G.S. #371 under the name of John Coon. (Miscel. Test. P. #4216.)

App: 1557 John M. Mathis and 7 children, Ranger, Ga.
Rejected. In his application the applicant states that he was born in Gilmer Co., Ga. in 1864; that he claims his Cherokee Indian blood through his mother, Jane Mathis, whose maiden name was Jane McDaniel. He states that his mother was born in Cherokee Co. *N.C.* (*N.C. Handwritten)* in 1828; that his mother claims her Indian blood through her father, John McDaniel. No information is submitted as to the date and place of birth of said John McDaniel. In his testimony taken at Calhoun, Ga. on the 9th of July 1908, the applicant states that his mother and grandfather through whom he claims lived in Cherokee Co. N.C. in 1835; that in 1851 his mother was living in Union Co. Ga., and his grandfather was living in the Cherokee Nation in the Indian Territory. The applicant states further in his testimony that his mother was enrolled in 1851 in Union Co., Ga. The applicant has a sister, Sarah C. Brackett, who resides at Sallisaw, Okla. (application #8023) who states that her grandfather's name was Thomas McDaniel instead of John McDaniel. A thorough examination of the Eastern Cherokee rolls taken in 1851 fails to show the name of Jane Mathis. The applicant has two sisters and one brother, who were old enough to be enrolled in 1851. Their names do not appear on any roll taken in 1851. The name of John McDaniel, the grandfather of the applicant, does not appear on any Cherokee roll as the head of a family. In 1884 the applicant, his mother and his sister were enrolled by Hester, who gave the name of the ancestor on the previous rolls as Thomas McDaniel. Granting that Thomas McDaniel is the correct name of the Grandfather of the applicant, the Thomas McDaniel enrolled in 1835 was living at that time in Cass Co., Ga., while the applicant states in his testimony that his grandfather was living in Cherokee Co. N.C. on that date. (See miscel. test. P. 1302.) In the testimony of Sarah Brackett, as sister of the applicant, the following statement appears, "I was enrolled by the Dawes Commission, but they afterwards refused to allow my claim and took all my papers. They claimed that I was an adopted citizen". (See misc. Test. P. 2941.) As the names of the ancestors given by the applicant do not appear upon the Eastern Cherokee rolls in such a way as to connect him with the Eastern Cherokee tribe, and further, as his testimony fails to prove that he is a descendant by blood of Cherokees who were parties to the treaties of 1835-6 and 1846, his claim is hereby rejected.

App: 1558 Betsy Tanner, Grove, Okla.
Admitted. Father, Eu-nau-le, and grandfather, Cul-lau-noo-las-ke, were enrolled by Drennen in Del. #320.

App: 1559 Jesse Budder and 5 children, Eucha, Okla.
Admitted. Brother of #6?7 (*?-Difficult to read, could be #637 or 657*) and claims through same source.

App: 1560 Moses O'Fields, Eucha, Okla.
Admr. John Rider Estate.
Rejected. John Rider died May 10, 1904. See testimony in application.

App: 1561 Eve Wolfe, Eucha, Okla.
Admitted. Applicant enrolled in 1851 together with her father and mother and brother in Saline #313.

App: 1562 Sarah A. Wright and 2 children, Albany, Texas.
Rejected. Niece of #77 and claims through this same source.

App: 1563 Charley Tanner and 3 children, Grove, Okla.
Admitted. Brother of #420 and claims through same source.

App: 1564 Sarah Wickett and 3 children, Zena, Okla.
Admitted. Half sister of #3?8 (*?- could be #378 or 388*) and claims through same source.

App: 1565 James Wilkerson and 5 children, Peggs, Okla.
Admitted. Father, John Wilkerson, and paternal grandparents were enrolled by Drennen in G.S. #631.

App: 1566 Wm D. Wilkerson, Peggs, Okla.
Admitted. Brother of #1565 and claims through same source.

App: 1567 George W. Wilkerson, Jr. and 4 children, Peggs, Okla.
Admitted. Brother of #1565 and claims through same source.

App: 1568 Joe Fox and 2 children, South West City, Mo.
Admitted. Father of #644 and claims through same source.

App: 1569 Katie Snell, South West City, Mo.
Admitted. Aunt of #644 and claims through same source.

App: 1570 Sparrow Sulrah, South West City, Mo.
Admitted. Uncle of #1569 and claims through same source.

App: 1571 Agnes Jones, Cleora, Okla.
Admitted. Applicant's mother enrolled by Chapman #2063. Niece of #1034.

App: 1572 Mary J. Bachtel and 3 children, Hudson, Okla.
Admitted. Mother of #874. Applicant herself is enrolled by Drennen in Del. #370.

App: 1573 Henry Muskrat, Kansas, Okla.
Admitted. Claims through his grandmother, Chic-co-nel Da-nee-ski, who was enrolled by Drennen in Del. #666. See testimony of Annie BL[sic] Ridge, #5606, mother of claimant.

App: 1574 Young Beaver Ridge, Kansas, Okla.
Admitted. Brother of #366 and claims through same source.

App: 1575 Catherine M. Leadford and 4 children, Culberson, N.C.
Admitted. Mother, Jennette Rogers, enrolled by Chapman #1354.

App: 1576 George W. Wilkerson Sr., and 5 children, Peggs, Okla.
Admitted. Uncle of #1565 and claims through same source.

App: 1577 Emerson A. Metcalf and 3 children, Little Creek, N.C.
Rejected. This applicant claims through Keziah Vann. See full report in #276.

App: 1578 Wiley E. Metcalf and 3 children, Little Creek, N.C.
Rejected. This applicant claims through Keziah Vann. See full report in #276.
App: 1579 Tilden Cramp and 2 children, Porum, Okla.
Admitted. Father, Watt Cramp, enrolled by Drennen in Del. #750.
App; 1580 Lizzie Rattler, Porum, Okla.
Admitted. Niece of #1579 and claims through same source. Paternal grandfather enrolled by Drennen in Del. #750.
App: 1581 Rider Rattler and 4 children, Porum, Okla.
Duplicate of #345.
App: 1582 Percy W. Hicks, Fort Gibson, Okla.
Admitted. Brother of #788 and claims through same source.
App: 1583 John Graves and 1 child, Porum, Okla.
Admitted. Father, Isaac Graves, was enrolled by Drennen in 1851 in Tahl. #304.
App: 1584 Mary Olive Adler, Adair, Okla.
Admitted. Grandparents, Alexander and Martha Clingan, were enrolled by Chapman #1579 and 1580.
App: 1585 Mary E. Graham, Cobb, Okla.
Rejected. It does not appear that ancestors were ever enrolled or were parties to the treaties of 1835-6 and 1846. Applicant shows no real connection with Eastern Cherokees. (Misc. Test. P. 2373.)
App: 1586 Martha Ann Graham, Weleetka, Okla.
Rejected. Sister of #1585 and claims through same source.
App: 1587 M. A. Stamper and 3 childen, Park, Va.
Rejected. This applicant claims through the Sizemore's. See full report in #417.
App: 1588 Jug Bunch and 4 children, Bunch, Okla.
Admitted. Brother of #1323 and claims through same source.
App: 1589 Annie Bunch, Bunch, Okla.
Admitted. Father, George Manus, was enrolled by Drennen in G.S. #636. (Misc. Test. P. 2922.)
App: 1590 Adam Corntassel, Westville, Okla.
Admitted. Father, Corntassel, was enrolled by Drennen in G.S. #274. (Misc. Test. P. 3226.)
App: 1591 Betsy Fodder, Westville, Okla.
Admitted. Sister of #1590 and claims through same source.
App: 1592 Anna Whitmire, Westville, Okla.
Admitted. Sister of #1590 and claims through same source.
App: 1593 Charlotte Whitmire and 2 children, Baron, Okla.
Admitted. Sister of #1590 and claims through same source.
App: 1594 Jennie Scott and 4 children, Chance, Okla.
Admitted. Sister of #1590 and claims through same source.
App: 1595 Tom Corntassel, Westville, Okla.
Admitted. Brother of #1590 and claims through same source.
App: 1596 Artemiza E. Ethridge and 1 child, Claremore, Okla.
Admitted. Father, Alexander Ballard, and mother, Rachel Ballard, both enrolled by Drennen in Ill. #7.

App: 1597 Florence Patrick, Claremore, Okla.
Admitted. Niece of #1596 and claims through same source.
App: 1598 John M. Thompson, Sherman, Texas.
Admitted. Applicant enrolled by Drennen in #1047. (Misc. Test. P. 2266.)
App: 1599 Cynthia Lynch and 1 child, Ketchum, Okla.
Admitted. Sister of #879 and claims through same source.
App: 1600 Wm A. Smith and 3 children, Cleora, Okla.
Admitted. Half Brother of #879 and claims through same source.
App: 1601 Richard F. Glenn and 4 children, Miles, Okla.
Admitted. Mother, Jennie Glenn, was enrolled by Drennen in F1. #40.
App: 1602 Nancy Proctor, Stilwell, Okla.
Admitted. Father, Isaac Proctor, was enrolled by Drennen in F1. #420. See testimony taken at Stilwell, Okla., Mar. 23, 1909.
App: 1603 Nannie E. Walker, and 7 children, Chloeta, Okla.
Admitted. Sister if #1332 and claims through same source. Supl. application for minors lost and children supplied by reference to Dawes Com. and letter marked "A".
App: 1604 Joella Nall and 4 childen, Pensacola, Okla.
Admitted. Mother, Frances Thompason[sic], and her father, James Kell, who with applicant's uncle and aunts were enrolled by Drennen in Del. #866. (Misc. Test. P. 2711.)
App: 1605 Jennie Hanson and 4 children, Nowata, Okla.
Admitted. Grandmother and uncles and aunts were all enrolled by Drennen in Ill. #4 and 5.
App: 1606 Crawler Proctor, Stilwell, Okla.
Admitted. Applicant's parents enrolled by Drennen in S.B. #10.
App: 1607 Rachel C. Garrett and 4 children, Centralia, Okla.
Admitted. First cousin of #1601 and claims through same source.
App: 1608 Sophie King, McKay, Okla.
Admitted. Mother, Caty Osman, and sisters were all enrolled by Drennen in Ill. #256. (Misc. Test. P. 3932.)
App: 1609 Rachel Spade, Proctor, Okla.
Admitted. Mother of Applicant, Jennie Wolfe, enrolled by Drennen in F1. #235 1/2. (Misc. Test. P. 3388-9.)
App: 1610 Nancy E. Kates and 3 children, Hulbert, Okla.
Admitted. Grandmother of applicant was enrolled by Drennen in Tahl. #364 under her maiden name, Mary Jane Fish. (*Handwritten - Misc. Test. P. 3332.*)
App: 1611 Acie Woodall, Hulbert, Okla.
Admitted. Applicant's father enrolled by Drennen in Sal. #339.
App: 1612 Henry Woodall, Hulbert, Okla.
Admitted. Claims through same source. As #671. Nephew of #12656.
App: 1613 Dolly E. Galloway, Vinita, Okla.
Admitted. Aunt of #562. Applicant herself enrolled by Drennen in Tahl. #536.
App: 1614 Mary Osage and 1 child, Westville, Okla.
Admitted. Applicant's grandparents were enrolled by Drennen in G.S. #26. (*Handwritten- Minor child Philip Jr., enrolled with claimants former husband Stephen Osage #17010.)*

App: 1615 Jennie Shell, Stilwell, Okla.
Admitted. Mother enrolled by Drennen in Fl. #571. (Misc. Test. P. 3136 & 3067.)

App: 1616 Polly Morris, Ballard, Okla.
Admitted. Parents of applicant enrolled by Drennen in G.S. #400 under the names of Cah-nel-sy and Wutty Cah-nel-se. (See letter in #1616.)

App: 1617 Samuel Shell, Stilwell, Okla.
Admitted. Son of #1615 and claims through same source.

App: 1618 Sarah Taylor, Stilwell, Okla.
Admitted. Daughter of #1615 and claims through same source.

App: 1619 Helen D. White and 1 child, Oolagah, Okla.
Admitted. Mother enrolled as Mary Elizabeth McLaughlin by Drennen in 1851 in Del. #857.

App: 1620 Saladen A. Fargo, Muldrow, Okla.
Admitted. Nephew of #917. Applicant's father, Calvin Fargo, enrolled in S.B. #240.

App: 1621 Joel Fargo et al, Muldrow, Okla.
By Delia Fargo, Gdn.
Admitted. Nephew of #917. Applicant's father enrolled in S.B. #240, by Drennen.

App: 1622 Myrtle Fargo, Muldrow, Okla.
Admitted. Niece of #917. Father enrolled in S.B. #240, by Drennen.

App: 1623 Elizabeth Patton, Muldrow, Okla.
Admitted. Half sister of #917 and applicant herself enrolled in S.B. #240 as Elizabeth Richardson, by Drennen.

App: 1624 Cora H. Fargo, Muldrow, Okla.
Admitted. Niece of #917. Applicant's father, Calvin Fargo, enrolled in S.B. #240.

App: 1625 William L. Fargo and 2 children, Muldrow, Okla.
Admitted. Nephew of #917. Father enrolled in S.B. #240.

App: 1626 Nancy Holland, Centralia, Okla.
Admitted. Sister of #406 and claims through same source.

App: 1627 Galuga Reed, Clarksville, Ark.
Admitted. Niece of #1084 and claims through same source.

App: 1628 Richard Oskison and 2 children, Estella, Okla.
Admitted. First cousin of #1488 and claims through same source. Applicant's mother, Rachel Connor, enrolled by Drennen in Del. #368.

App: 1629 Oce P. Benge and 4 children, Adair, Okla.
Admitted. Applicant's father enrolled by Drennen in 1851 in Tahl. #368.

App: 1630 James F. Benge, Lynch, Okla.
Admitted. Brother of #1629. Applicant enrolled by Drennen in Tahl. #368.

App: 1631 Mollie Fields, Texanna, Okla.
Admitted. Grandfather enrolled as Te-tah-nah-skee Hornet and great uncle Peter Hornet enrolled by Drennen in Tahl. #297-1/2 and #297 respectively. (Misc. Test. P. 4219.)

App: 1632 Herman V. Lipe and 1 child, Oolagah, Okla.
Admitted. Father enrolled by Drennen in 1851 in Tahl. #479.

App: 1633 Josephine G. Bass and 2 children, Ramona, Okla.
Admitted. Mother enrolled as Eliza M. Blythe by Drennen in Del. #922.
App: 1634 John E. Foreman, Ramona, Okla.
Admitted. Brother of #1633 and claims through same source.
App: 1635 Earl Davis and 6 children, Dahlonega, Ga.
Admitted. First cousin of #98 and claims through same source.
App: 1636 Harriett Pitts, Indianola, Okla.
Rejected. Neither applicant nor ancestors ever enrolled. Does not establish fact of descent from any person who was a party to the treaty of 1835-6 and 1846.
App: 1637 Annie B. Snider and 4 children, Chelsea, Okla.
Admitted. Father enrolled by Chapman #1703.
App: 1638 Alice Beamer, Moody*s*, Okla.
Admitted. Parents enrolled by Drennen in 1851 in Del. #746.
App: 1639 Katie Fodder, Westville, Okla.
Admitted. Applicant enrolled in 1851 by Drennen in G.S. #264.
App: 1640 Joseph L. Williams and 4 children, Chelsea, Okla.
Admitted. Brother of #874 and claims through same source.
App: 1641 George W. Fields, South West City, Mo.
Admitted. Uncle of #242 and himself enrolled by Drennen in Del. #135.
App: 1642 Joseph Reese and 4 children, Hulbert, Okla.
Admitted. Applicant's father enrolled by Drennen in 1851 in Tahl. #253.
App: 1643 Milton M. Caulk and 1 child, Chelsea, Okla.
Rejected. Uncle of #255 and claims through same source.
App: 1644 Nancy Wadkins and 1 child, Dodge, Okla.
Admitted. Niece of #252. Mother enrolled as Lucy ~~Smith~~ (*Note: Handwritten below, Snail*), by Drennen in Del. #128.
App: 1645 Samantha Summerfield, South West City, Mo.
Admitted. Niece of #252. Mother enrolled by Drennen in Del. #128.
App: 1646 Lizzie Vann and 6 children, Chloeta, Okla.
Admitted. Niece of #252. Mother enrolled by Drennen in Del. #128.
App: 1647 Mary White, South West City, Mo.
Admitted. Niece of #252. Mother enrolled by Drennen in Del. #128.
App: 1648 Margaret Crow, Tahlequah, Okla.
Admitted. Applicant enrolled by Chapman #1311.
App: 1649 James Buffington and 3 children, Caney, Kansas.
Admitted. Brother of #22 and claims through same source.
App: 1650 Minnie B. Holland, Foyil, Okla.
Admitted. Niece of #405. Daughter Lucinda Hampton, who married Dr. B.F. Buckner.
App: 1651 Charlotte Foyil and 1 child, Foyil, Okla.
Admitted. Father, James B. Choate, was enrolled by Drennen in Dis. #75.
App: 1652 Richard M. Dannenburg and 2 children, Tahlequah, Okla.
Admitted. Brother of #384. Applicant himself enrolled by Drennen in G.S. #719.
App: 1653 Louisa H. Emerson, Decatur, Texas.
Admitted. Applicant herself and her parents enrolled by Drennen in Del. #859.

App: 1654 Josephine C. Rasmaus, Tahlequah, Okla.
Admitted. Sister of #384. Claimant enrolled by Drennen in 1851 in G.S. #719.

App: 1655 John H. Dannenburg, Stilwell, Okla.
Admitted. Brother of #384. Claimant enrolled by Drennen in G.S. #719.

App: 1656 Susan A. Walker, Fort Gibson, Okla.
Admitted. Sister of #384. Claimant enrolled by Drennen in G.S. #719.

App: 1657 John Tylor McPherson and 1 child~~ren~~, Warner, Okla.
Admitted. Claimant is Nephew of #1653. Paternal grandparents enreolled[sic] by Drennen in G.S. #436.

App: 1658 Sallie Bennett, Muskogee, Okla.
Rejected. It does not appear that applicant's ancestors were parties to the treaties of 1835-6 and 1846. Never shared in payments to the Cherokees nor were enrolled with them. (*Handwritten - Misc. Test. P. 3058.*)

App: 1659 David M. Caldwell and 1 child, Park, Va.
Rejected. This applicant claims through the Sizemore's. See full report in #417.

App: 1660 James A. Osborn, Jr. and 4 children, Park, Va.
Rejected. This applicant claims through the Sizemore's. See full report in #417.

App: 1661 Columbus A. Bell and 6 children, Isabella, Tenn.
Rejected. Applicnat[sic] fails to establish genuine connection with the Cherokee tribe. Ancestors were not parties to the treaties of 1835-6 and 1846. (Misc. Test. P. 1318.)

App: 1662 Thomas J. Parris and 4 children, Tahlequah, Okla.
Admitted. Brother of #825 and claims through same source.

App: 1663 Eliza E. Johnson,
Duplicate of #825.

App: 1664 Emma Sixkiller, Afton, Okla.
Admitted. Claimant born in 1855. Father, Ellis Blythe and older brother, William, enrolled by Drennen in Del. #956.

App: 1665 Charlotte Hughgin, Peggs, Okla.
Admitted. Great aunt of #1288. Claimant enrolled by Drennen in Tahl. #451. (Misc. Test. P. 4228.)

App: 1665 1/2 Decksie Hughgins, Peggs, Okla.
By Charlotte Hughgins, Gdn.
Admitted. Great grandparents enrolled as Money and Sallie Hunter by Drennen in Tahl. #553. Grandfather and father were not living in 1851. (Misc. Test. P. *4228.*) (*Handwritten Number for Misc. Test. P.*)

App: 1666 Mary E. Oliver and 7 children, Durant, Okla.
Rejected. Applicant enrolled by Dawes Commission as a Choctaw. Minor children enrolled with Choctaws.

App: 1667 Lena Smallwood and 2 children, Porum, Okla.
Admitted. Applicant claims through great grandmother, Annie Fool, who with her sisters, Caty, Akey, Alsey and Wutty were enrolled by Drennen in S.B. #208. (Misc. Test. P. 2766.)

App: 1668 Samuel Smallwood and 2 children, Porum, Okla.
Admitted. Applicant's grandfather was enrolled by Drennen in 1851 in G.S. #26. (Misc. Test. P. 2692.)

App: 1669 William Smallwood and 1 child, Porum, Okla.
Admitted. Brother of #1668 and claims through same source.

App: 1670 Mary Sunday and 1 child, Porum, Okla.
Admitted. Sister of #345 and claims through same source.

App: 1671 Josiah Eddings, Chouteau, Okla.
Rejected. Claims through Elizabeth Eddings, daughter of Dave Weaver. See #45.

App: 1672 Andrew S. Eddings, Chouteau, Okla.
Rejected. Claims through Elizabeth Eddings, daughter of Dave Weaver. See #45.

App: 1673 Thomas J. Parris, Gdn.
Duplicate of #1662. (Wife dead. Died 1902. Children inc. with father.)

App: 1674 Lydia Woolly, Conway, Okla.
Rejected. It does not appear that applicant's ancestors were parties to the treaties of 1835-6 and 1846 and never shared in any payments to the Cherokees nor were enrolled with them. (*Handwritten - Misc. Test. P. 2201.*)

App: 1675 James A. Woolly and 1 child, Conway, Okla.
Rejected. Claims through same source as #1674.

App: 1676 Newton Williams and 2 children, Vinita, Okla.
Admitted. First cousin of #741. Father of David Williams, enrolled by Drennen in F1. #525.

App: 1677 Lydia Foreman, Proctor, Okla.
Admitted. Applicant's mother enrolled in 1851 by Drennen in G.S. #171. (Misc. Test. P. 3220.)

App: 1678 Jemima S. Blythe, Vinita, Okla.
Admitted. Applicant enrolled by Drennen in 1851 in Del. #922.

App: 1679 Sara A. Webb, Athol, Idaho.
Rejected. It does not appear that any ancestor was a party to the treaties of 1835-6 and 1846. Nor does it appear that any ancestor was ever enrolled. Shows no connection with the Eastern Cherokees.

App: 1680 Mrs. Julia Taylor Smith, Frontenac, Kans.
Rejected. This applicant claims through the Sizemore's. See full report in #417.

App: 1681 Mrs. Rose M. Ware, Frontenac, Kans.
Rejected. This claimant claims through the Sizemore's. See full report in #417.

App: 1682 Mary I. Howie, Vinita, Okla.
Admitted. Applicant was enrolled by Drennen in Sal. #451 under the name of Mary Steadman.

App: 1683 William H. Glenn, Miles, Okla.
Admitted. Applicant's grandmother enrolled by Drennen in 1851 in F1. #40.

App: 1684 Milo A. Hoyt and 4 children, Hoyt, Okla.
Rejected. Enrolled as a Choctaw on the Dawes Commission roll.

App: 1685 Laura B. Long, Carbon, Okla.
Rejected. This applicant claims through the Sizemore's. See full in #417.

App: 1686 Pigeon Hanson and 1 child, Estella, Okla[sic] Estella, Okla.
Admitted. Maternal grandfather of applicant was enrolled in 1851 under the name of Pigeon Halfbreed in Del. #405. (*Handwritten Miscel. Tes. P. 4371.*)

App: 1687 Caroline Jackson, Ochelata, Okla.
Admitted. Applicant claims through mother, Eliza Jackson, who was not living in 1851, but whose father and older brothers and sisters were enrolled by Drennen in Sal. #365 as Oo-wor-her-tser, Sallie, Stephen and Adam.

App: 1688 Cynthia P. Harmon, Webbers Falls, Okla.
Admitted. Applicant herself enrolled in Fl. #233 by Drennen together with mother and brother and sister.

App: 1689 Nellie Humanstricker, Evansville, Ark.
Admitted. Mother, Sarah, enrolled by Drennen in Fl. #512. (Misc. Test. P. 3257.)

App: 1690 Ollie Sunshine and 1 child, Evanville, Ark.
Admitted. Parents, Oo-gua-loh-cah and Watty, enrolled by Drennen G.S. #382.

App: 1691 Mary J. Martin and 1 child, Gans, Okla.
Admitted. Sister of #1866 and claims through same source.

App: 1692 Mary Riley, Gans, Okla.
Admitted. Sister of #901. Claimant enrolled by Drennen in S.B. #230 as Mary Jack.

App: 1693 Peggy Thompson and 2 children, Siloam Springs, Ark.
Admitted. Aunt of #1374. Father enrolled by Drennen in G.S. #323.

App: 1694 Katy Kizer and 6 children, Row, Okla.
Admitted. Aunt of #1374. Father of applicant enrolled in 1851 in G.S. #323.

App: 1695 Lucinda Martin, Cherokee City, ~~Okla.~~ (*Handwritten Ark. Above.*)
Admitted. Aunt of #1374. Enrolled as Lucinda Still in G.S. #323.

App: 1696 Julia D. Perry and 4 children, Tate, Ga.
Admitted. Sister of #341 and claims through same source.

App: 1697 Peggy Sellers, Evansville, Ark.
Admitted. Sister of #1690 and claims through same source.

App: 1698 Arle Alex, Eucha, Okla.
Admitted. Applicant enrolled as Arl-ser by Drennen in Del. #282. Applicant's parents, Te-la-he-la and Tar-ke, also enrolled in same group. (Deceased) Misc. Test. P. 2997-2967.)

App: 1699 Jack Budder, Eucha, Okla.
Admitted. Brother of #657 and claims through same source.

App: 1700 Lacy Skuck-inne and 2 children, Eucha, Okla.
Admitted. Claims through parents, Skuck-in-ne and Rachel, enrolled by Drennen in Del. #275. (*Handwritten ~~Miscel. Tes. P. 2948.~~*)

App: 1701 Peggy Galcatcher, Eucha, Okla.
Admitted. Sister of #657 and claims through same source.

App: 1702 Johnnie A. Brown and 7 children, Collinsville, Okla.
Admitted. Mother, Ellen King, enrolled by Drennen in S.B. #132. Grandmother, Oney King, enrolled in same group. (*Handwritten Miscel. Tes. P. 2948.*)

App: 1703 Anna Welch, Eucha, Okla.
Admitted. Claims through mother and grandfather enrolled by Drennen in Sal. #264.
App: 1704 Eliza Morris and 3 children, Vinita, Okla.
Admitted. Sister of #651. Father enrolled by Drennen in Del. #589.
App: 1705 Susie Davis, and 2 children, Kansas, Okla.
Admitted. Sister of #1573 and claims through same source.
App: 1706 Peter Wolfe, Eucha, Okla.
Admitted. Son of #1561 and claims through same source.
App: 1707 Fixing Davis and 1 child, Spavinaw, Okla.
Admitted. Uncle of #648. Father enrolled by Drennen in Del. #766.
App: 1708 Samuel Coleman and 1 child, Eucha, Okla.
Admitted. Father, Ah-ma-ya-ha, enrolled by Drennen in Del. #716.
App: 1709 Joseph Hyder, Eucha, Okla.
Admitted. Father, Andy Hyder, and grandparents, Daniel Ku-sku-lea-sky and Can-te-ca-we, enrolled by Drennen in Del. #219.
App: 1710 Eliza Sixkiller and 4 children, Maysville, Ark.
Admitted. Sister of #420 and claims through same source.
App: 1711 Nancy Tanner and 1 child, Eucha, Okla.
Admitted. Sister of #645 and claims through same source.
App: 1712 Susan Ridge, Spavinaw, Okla.
Admitted. Aunt of #651. Parents of applicant were dead in 1851, but claims through same source as #651.
App: 1713 Mary Mouse, Eucha, Okla.
Admitted. Sister of #645 and claims through same source.
App: 1714 Thomas Tanner and 2 children, Eucha, Okla.
Admitted. Son of #339 and claims through same soure.
App: 1715 Jennie Kettle, Porum, Okla.
Admitted. Mother of #1167 and claims through same source. (Deceased)
App: 1716 John Kettle, Porum, Okla.
Admitted. Applicant enrolled as John Big Kettle by Drennen in Can. #76. Brother Stephen in Can. #7? (*Second too blurry to read.) (Handwritten Miscel. Tes. P. 2806.)*
App: 1717 Wilson Muskrat, Webbers Falls, Okla.
Admitted. Claimant and his mother enrolled by Drennen in Del. #851.
App: 1718 Sallie Muskrat, Webbers Falls, Okla.
Admitted. Cousin of #1667 and claims through same source.
App: 1719 William Fool and 3 children, Porum, Okla.
Admitted. Cousin of #1667 and claims through same source.
App: 1720 Sarah Towser and 1 child, Claremore, Okla.
Admitted. Father enrolled under the name of Te-ga-se by Drennen in Sal. #241. Grandfather enrolled as head of same group.
App: 1721 Nancy Falling (deceased) and 4 children, Dragger, Okla.
Admitted. Father enrolled by Drennen in Del. #774. Mother in Del. #604. See testimony in #27 as to death of claimant as well as supplemental. Died July, 1907. (Misc. Test. P. 3233.)

App: 1722 Lee Toney, Webbers Falls, Okla.
Admitted. Applicant's grandfather enrolled as Levi Toney in Sal. #23, by Drennen.
App: 1723 Fanny E. Chandler and 4 children, Ogeechee, Okla.
Admitted. Mother, Eliza B. McKee enrolled by Chapman #1188. Grandmother, Rebecca Morris enrolled by Chapman #1181.
App: 1724 Aggie Alexander, Porum, Okla.
Admitted. Parents, George and Jane Owens, enrolled by Drennen in Del. #327. (See letter)
App: 1725 Cornelia C. Chandler and 8 children, Fairland, Okla.
Admitted. Sister of #1723 and claims through same source.
App: 1726 Martha I. Evans, Fairland, Okla.
Admitted. Aunt of #55. Applicant enrolled by Chapman #1741 under the name of Martha Paden.
App: 1727 Rebecca T. Angel and 2 children, Ogeechee, Okla.
Admitted. Sister of #1723 and claims through same source.
App: 1728 Robert Daniel, Vinita, Okla.
Admitted. Applicant probably enrolled as R.B.M. Daniel in Del. #52 by Drennen. Father, Ezikiel[sic] Daniel, enrolled in same group. Mother enrolled as Nicy in same group.
App: 1729 Mary J. Charlesworth and 3 children, Vinita, Okla.
Admitted. Father, Isaac Woodall, enrolled by Drennen in G.S. #234. Mother, M.J. Daniel, enrolled in Del. #36. (see remarks in app.)
App: 1730 Rebecca J. Wilkerson, Peggs, Okla.
Rejected. Applicant claims through her deceased husband.
App: 1731 Elizabeth Newton and 4 children, Peggs, Okla.
Admitted. Sister of #1565 and claims through same source.
App: 1732 Thomas Gritts, Jr. Tahlequah, Okla.
Admitted. Nephew of #936 and claims through same source.
App: 1733 William Riley Wolfe and 2 children, Ruby, Okla.
Admitted. Applicant's grandmother, Martha Stansell, who was enrolled by Drennen in S.B. #117. (Mother of Applicant is #3925.)
App: 1734 George Washington Hail and 3 children, Hanson, Okla.
Admitted. Applicant himself enrolled as Geo. W. Hail by Chapman #1664. Grandmother and father enrolled by Chapman #1662-3.
App: 1735 Katie Silver-Smith and 5 children, South West City, Mo.
Admitted. Father, Jackson England, enrolled by Drennen as Rabbitt in Del. #308. (Misc. Test. P. 2584-2966.)
App: 1736 Claudie Hanna, Grove Okla.
Admitted. Mother's mother, Polly or Wah-ly, was enrolled by Drennen in Del. #319. Great grandmother, Wa-le-se and several children were enrolled in same group. (Misc. Test. P. 3000-2990-2991.)
App: 1737 James Wright and 4 children, South West City, Mo.
Admitted. Applicant enrolled by Drennen in Del. #15.
App: 1738 Emma Smith and 1 child, Grove, Okla.
Admitted. Niece of #390 and claims through same source.

App: 1739 Nancy Hanna and 2 children, Grove, Okla.
Admitted. Mother of applicant and her maternal grandparents were enrolled by Drennen in 1851 in Del. #323. (Misc. Test. P. 2993.)
App: 1740 Aggie Bucket and 4 children, Grove, Okla.
Admitted. Aunt of #1739 and claims through same source.
App: 1741 Sarah Ketcher, Grove, Okla.
Admitted. Aunt of #1739 and claims through same source.
App: 1742 Ella Leach, Tahlequah, Okla.
Admitted. Grandniece of #2494 and claims through same source.
App: 1743 Ben Crittenden and 5 children, Proctor, Okla.
Admitted. Uncle of #1677 and claims through same source.
App: 1744 Tommie Foreman, Westville, Okla.
Admitted. Nephew of #773 and claims through same source.
App: 1745 Lizzie Moore and 1 child, Estella, Okla.
Admitted. Parents, Cul-lot-ca and Rachel Smith, enrolled by Drennen in Del. #798. Brother of applicant also enrolled in same group.
App: 1746 Emina J. Davidson and 3 children, Woodly Okla.
Admitted. Father, Felix J. Nidiffer not old enough to be enrolled in 1851, but grandmother, Lucy Nidiffer was enrolled by Drennen in Dis. #9.
App: 1747 Enoch B. Browning, Byars, Okla.
Rejected. Applicant born in 1849 but not enrolled. Applicant's father living in 1851 and must have been in 1835, but not enrolled on either roll. There is a Qua-tee Moore on the 1851 roll in G.S. District, but applicant states that he saw his grandmother when he was 8 or 9 years old and at that time she was living in Alabama. Besides her name should have been Browning in 1851. There is a Peggy Moore on the 1835 and also on the 1851 roll G.S., but not to show any connection between these and applicant. It appears that they were not parties to the treaties of 1835-6 and 1846. (Misc. Test. P. 2697.)
App: 1748 William Shory Pack, Muldrow, Okla.
Admitted. Brother of #1688 and claims through same source. Applicant enrolled in F1. Dist. #233.
App: 1749 Mary E. Caldwell and 1 child, Park, Va.
Rejected. This applicant claims through the Sizemore's. See full report in #417.
App: 1750 Noah Osborn, Park, Va.
Rejected. This applicant claims through the Sizemore's. See full report in #417.
App: 1751 Daniel Davis, Hedwig, Ga.
Admitted. First Cousin of #98 and claims through same source.
App: 1752 Lorenzo N. Davis and 1 child, Hedwig, Ga.
Admitted. First cousin once removed of #98 and claims through same source.
App: 1753 Jetta A. Davis Hedwig, Ga.
Admitted. First cousin once removed of #98 and claims through same source.
App: 1754 William E. Davis and 3 children, Hedwig, Ga.
Admitted. First cousin one[sic] removed of #98 and claims through same source.
App: 1755 Susan Wilson and 2 children, Tahlequah, Okla.
Admitted. Sister of #930 and claims through same source.

App: 1756 Samuel Foreman and 3 children, Tahlequah, Okla.
Admitted. Son of #1210 and claims through same source.
App: 1757 Eliza Comingdeer, Tahlequah, Okla.
Admitted. Applicant enrolled by Drennen in 1851 in G.S. #29 as Ah-ye-kah.
App: 1758 William B. Foreman, Lowery, Okla.
Admitted. Son of #1210 and claims through same source.
App: 1759 Thomas Shade, Melvin, Okla.
Admitted. Son of #1291 and claims through same source.
App: 1760 Thomas Shade,
Duplicate of #1759.
App: 1761 Vasse M. Fisher, Tahlequah, Okla.
Rejected. This applicant claims through Keziah Vann. See full report in #276.
App: 1762 John Cicero Manney, Peggs, Okla.
Rejected. This applicant claims through Keziah Vann. See full report in #276.
App: 1763 Major Shade, Melvin, Okla.
Admitted. Brother of #1291 and claims through same source.
App: 1764 Major Shade,
Duplicate of #1763.
App: 1765 Clark L. Collins and 1 child, Moody, Okla.
Admitted. Nephew, of #935 and claims through same source.
App: 1766 Jeremiah Orchard, Moody, Okla.
Admitted. Grandnephew of #935 and claims through same source.
App: 1767 Addie Leatherwood and 3 children, Blue Ridge, Ga.
Admitted. Niece of #423. Mother enrolled by Hester in #1942, and by Chapman #1901.
App: 1768 William S. Smith, Ardmore, Okla.
Rejected. Cousin of #839 and claims through same source.
App: 1769 G.W. Blaylock and 1 child, Talona, Ga.
Rejected. Evidence to establish right to fund insufficient. In 1851 applicant's father and mother lived in Georgia, but neithter[sic] appears on the roll. Grandparents appear neither in the 1835 or 1851 (*Handwritten "roll"*), though born in N.C. (Misc. Test. P. 1400)
App: 1770 Josephine Loudermilk, Culberson, N.C.
Rejected. Ancestors not on rolls. Does not establish genuine connection with the Cherokee tribe. (Misc. Test. P. 1492-3.)
App: 1771 Mayfield H. Fisher, Miller, Mo.
Rejected. Neither applicant nor ancestors ever enrolled. Does not establish fact of descent from any person who was a party to the treaties of 1835-6 and 1846. Parents born in Ky. or Mo. prior to 1835.
App: 1772 Martha Orr and 5 children, Calhoun, Ga.
Rejected. Sister of #24876 and claims through same source.
App: 1773 John H. Adams, Siboney, Okla.
Rejected. This applicant claims through Annie Blythe, see full report in #153.
App: 1774 Anderson Green Franklin, Dalton, Ga.
Rejected. Father of #315 and claims through same source.
App: 1775 Cisco McKinney and 6 children, Presley, Ga.
Rejected. This applicant claims through Annie Blythe. See Full report in #153.

App: 1776 Jack Bean, Baron, Okla.
Admitted. Father and mother enrolled by Drennen in 1851 in G.S. #346.
App: 1777 George Fisher, Ballplay, Tenn.
Admitted. Nephew of #423. Applicant enrolled by Hester #1941. Mother enrolled by Chapman #1891.
App: 1778 William T. Wishon and 8 children, Cherry Log, Ga.
Admitted. Nephew of #423. Mother enrolled by Chapman #1891.
App: 1779 Samantha N. Key and 2 children, Cherry Log, Ga.
Admitted. Grand niece of #423. Grandmother enrolled by Chapman #1891.
App: 1780 John W. Wishon and 2 children, Cherry Log, Ga.
Admitted. Nephew of #423. Mother enrolled by Chapman #1891.
App: 1781 James Sanders and 1 child, Baron, Okla.
Admitted. Applicant's father enrolled by Drennen in G.S. #165.
App: 1782 Aggie Knight and 4 children, Baron, Oka.
Admitted. Father and paternal grandparents enrolled by Drennen in 1851 in G.S. #270. (see #11536 herewith, question 7. See G.S. 266, 269 and 271. These parties are relatives of the applicants.)
App: 1783 Mary England, Baron, Okla.
Admitted. Applicant's father enrolled by Drennen in 1851 G.S. #348. (Applicant's mother has filed #8318.)
App: 1784 Rachel Soap, Baron, Okla.
Admitted. Applicant aunt of #1427 and was herself enrolled by Drennen in G.S. #374.
App: 1785 Susan Bean, Baron, Okla.
Rejected. Ancestors not enrolled. Were not parties to the treaties of 1835-6 and 1846. Does not show genuine connection with the Cherokee tribe. No official testimony taken in this case.
App: 1786 John Looney and 1 child, Westville, Okla.
Admitted. Applicant enrolled by Drennen in G.S. #337 under the name of Noo-char-we. Father, Kar-lo-nah-stee-skee, enrolled in same group.
App: 1787 Isaac Crittenden and 4 children, Baron, Okla.
Admitted. Brother of #1783 and claims through same source.
App: 1788 Rebecca L. Chattin and 6 children, Jasper, Ga.
Rejected. No Ancestor was ever enrolled. It does not appear that any ancestor was a party to the treaties of 1835-6 and 1846. Proof of genuine connection with the Eastern Cherokees insufficient. (Misc. Test. P. 1235.)
App: 1789 Mary Jane Weiss, Cherokee, Kans.
Rejected. This applicant claims through the Sizemore's. See full report in #417.
App: 1790 Olive E. Weiss, Cherokee, Kans.
Rejected. This applicant claims through the Sizemore's. See full report in #417.
App: 1791 Wave Weiss, Cherokee, Kans.
Rejected. Sizemore claimant. See full report in #417.

App: 1792 Lulie E. McDaniel, Madola, Ga.
Admitted. Granddaughter of #423 and claims through same source.

App: 1793 Pearlie Ann Rogers, Cherry Log, Ga.
Admitted. Grandniece of #423 and claims through same source.
App: 1794 Robert C. Wishon, Cherry Log, Ga.
Admitted. Great nephew of #423 and claims through same source.
App: 1795 Thos. J. Wishon, Cherry, Log, Ga.
Admitted. Great nephew of #423 and claims through same source.
App: 1796 William Boot and 1 child, Estella, Okla.
Admitted. Grandmother, Aincey, enrolled by Drennen in Del. #1024. Mother also enrolled in same group. (Misc. Test. P. 3646.)
App: 1797 Eliza Boot, Estella, Okla.
Admitted. Mother of #1796. Applicant herself enrolled by Drennen in Del. #1024 as Oo-te-was-ke.
App: 1798 Biddy Hart and 5 children, Weasel, N.C.
Rejected. This applicant claims through the Sizemore's. See full report in #417.
App: 1799 Amanda Hart and 2 children, Weasel ,N.C.
Rejected. This applicant claims through the Sizemore's. See full report in #417.
App: 1800 Rebecca Wilcox and 1 child, Weasel, N.C.
Rejected. This applicant claims through the Sizemore's. See full report in #417.
App: 1801 Wm O. Lewis and 1 child, ~~Weasel, N.C~~.
(Handwritten above, Park, Va.)
Rejected. This applicant claims through the Sizemore's. See full report in #417.
App: 1802 Martha E. Haga and 3 children, Azen, Va.
Rejected. This applicant claims through the Sizemore's. See full report in #417.
App: 1803 Thomas M. Osborne, Park, Va.
Rejected. This applicant claims through the Sizemore's. See full report in #417.
App: 1804 Manda A. Lewis, Park, Va.
Rejected. This applicant claims through Sizemore's. See full report in #417.
App: 1805 Maggie C. Osborne, Park, Va.
Rejected. This applicant claims through the Sizemore's. See full report in #417.
App: 1806 Mary Lewis, Park Va.
Rejected. This applicant claims through the Sizemore's. See full report in #417.
App: 1807 William L. French, Tahlequah, Okla.
Admitted. Second cousin of #377 and claims through same source.
App: 1808 Amanda M. Wofford, Tahlequah, Okla.
Admitted. Aunt of #741. Mother of applicant enrolled by Drennen in F1. #525.
App: 1809 Jack Neugin, Proctor, Okla.
Admitted. Father enrolled by Drennen in G.S. #305. Father's father and mother enrolled in G.S. #142. Jack Crittendens wife Annie is a sister of claimant's father. See

G.S. #301. Jack Crittenden is a brother of claimant's maternal grandmother. (Misc. Test. P. 4055.)

App: 1810 Sarah J. Wofford, Tahlequah, Okla.
Admitted. Aunt of #741. Applicant herself enrolled by Drennen in 1851 in Fl. #525.

App: 1811 Arabella Southerland, Vinita, Okla.
Admitted. Aunt of #874. Mother of applicant enrolled by Drennen in Del. #370.

App: 1812 Laura J. Kelley and 2 children, Centralia, Okla.
Admitted. Mother enrolled by Drennen in 1851 in Del. #430.

App: 1813 Samuel Nidiffer and 5 children, Fairland, Okla.
Admitted. Uncle of #1746 and claims through same source. Applicant is enrolled by Drennen in Dis. #9.

App: 1814 Freeman Nidiffer and 2 children, Fairland, Okla.
Admitted. Uncle of #1746. Applicant enrolled by Drennen in Dis. #9.

App: 1815 Vinia Adams and 2 children, Marble, N.C.
Admitted. Father, Andrew J. Taylor, enrolled by Drennen in Fl. #522. Andrew J. Taylor was the son of David and Mary Taylor, enrolled by Chapman #1251 and 1243.

App: 1816 John A. Foreman and 1 child, Talala, Okla.
Admitted. Applicant enrolled by Drennen in 1851 in Tahl. #234.

App: 1817 Jennie Bailey, Christie, Okla.
Admitted. Parents enrolled by Drennen in 1851 in G.S. #682.

App: 1818 Malinda J. Kuhn, Chelsea, Okla.
Admitted. Applicant enrolled by Drennen in 1851 in G.S. #723.

App: 1819 Mary Bennett, Chelsea, Okla.
Admitted. Mother of #1818 and claims through same source.

App: 1820 Martha Graizer and 5 children, Narcissa, Okla.
Admitted. Mother enrolled by Drennen in 1851 in Del. #346.

App: 1821 Lucy Campbell, Collinsville, Okla.
Admitted. Aunt of #562. Herself enrolled in 1851 by Drennen in Tahl. #536 as Lucy Lowery.

App: 1822 Levi Doublehead, Vinita, Okla.
Admitted. Grandson of #1717 and claims through same source.

App: 1823 Celie Alex Skah-gin-nee, Eucha, Okla.
Admitted. Daughter of #1698 and claims through same source.

App: 1824 Peter Soldier and 2 children, Eucha, Okla.
Admitted. First cousin of #64? (*Handwritten last two numbers, last number illegible, could be an, "8" but very blurred.*) (Applicant claims father was on the 1851 roll. There are two persons by the name of Chu-war-ye-cul-le, but it is impossible to decide which one is correct.)

App: 1825 Nancy Hyder and 1 child, Eucha, Okla.
Admitted. Mother enrolled by Drennen in 1851 in Del. #49. Father, Jack Tanner, in Del. #885. (*Handwritten - Miscel. Tes. 2744-2972.*)

App: 1826 Henry Goddard, (*Handwritten "and5 children"*) Kinnison, Okla.
Admitted. Mother, Elizabeth Goddard, enrolled by Drennen in 1851 in Del. #932.
Roberson

App: 1827 James Goddard, Centralia, Okla.
Admitted. Brother of #1826 and claims through same source.
App: 1828 Susie Swimmer, Cookson, Okla.
Admitted. Parents enrolled by Drennen in 1851 in G.S. #564.
App: 1829 Betsy Young, Wauhillau, Okla.
Admitted. Sister of #1828 and claims through same source.
App: 1830 Nancy J. Shell and 4 children, Baron, Okla.
Admitted. Sister of #1781 and claims through same source.
App: 1830 1/2 Roach Young, Wauhillau, Okla.
Admitted. Grandson of #3979 and claims through same source.
App: 1831 Charlie Young and 1 child, Wauhillau, Okla.
Admitted. Son of #3979. Father enrolled by Drennen in 1851 in G.S. #633.
App: 1831 1/2 Callie Young, Wauhillau, Okla.
Admitted. Granddaughter of #3979 and claims through same source.
App: 1832 Mary Ann Ward, Hollow, Kans.
Admitted. Sister of #579 and claims through same source.
App; 1833 Jackson K. Pearse and 3 children, Coffeyville, Kans.
Admitted. Half *(Handwritten brother)* of #1702 and claims through same source.
App: 1834 Sarah C. Jones and 3 children, Bartlesville, Okla.
Rejected. Sister of #1312 and claims through same source.
App: 1835 Delilah J. Davis, Atlanta, Ga.
259 Rawson, Ga.
Admitted. First cousin of #98 and claims through same source.
App: 1836 Annie C. Bennett and 2 children, Muskogee, Okla.
Admitted. Sister of #741 and claims through same source.
App: 1837 Cherokee Hudson and 5 children, Westville, Okla.
Admitted. Sister of #201 and claims through same source.
App: 1838 Nevermore Trainor, Muskogee, Okla
Admitted. Sister of #741 and claims through same source.
App: 1839 Eliza Smith, Stilwell, Okla.
Admitted. Mother of #10711. Applicant herself enrolled by Drennen in F1. #102
App: 1840 Eliza Pheasant, Stilwell, Okla.
Admitted. Applicant claims through her own right, being enrolled with her first husband, Joe, in 1851 by Drennen in F1. #117. See testimony of J.B. Adair taken at Stilwell, Okla. March 23d. 1909. P. 3981.
App: 1841 Charley Smith and 2 children, Stilwell, Okla.
Admitted. Applicant enrolled by Drennen in 1851 in F1. #137.
App: 1842 Winnie Sixkiller,
Duplicate of #177.
App: 1843 James Tincup and 4 children, Pryor Creek, Okla.
Admitted. Brother of #654 and claims through same source.
App: 1844 Annie L. Pace. And 5 children, Welch, Okla.
Admitted. Applicant's grandfather enrolled by Drennen in 1851 in F1. #244. (Misc. Test. P. 3663.)

App: 1845 Johnson Harris, Greenbrier, Okla.
Admitted. Applicant's mother enrolled by Drennen in G.S. #423.
App: 1846 Betsy Phillips and 1 child, Baron, Okla.
Admitted. Sister of #1781 and claims through same source.
App: 1847 Eli H. Whitmire and 1 child, Westville, Okla.
Admitted. Mother, Elizabeth Whitmire, together with sisters and brother enrolled by Drennen in G.S. #713.
App: 1848 Charlotte Wright and 1 child, Christie, Okla.
Admitted. Sister of #1847. Applicant enrolled as Charlotte Whitmire, in G.S. #713.
App: 1849 Delila Sanders, Baron, Okla.
Admitted. Sister of #1847. Applicant enrolled as Delila Whitmire in G.S. #713.
App: 1850 Katie Wolfe and 1 child, Stilwell, Okla.
Admitted. Applicant herself enrolled as Ja-noo-la together with her mother, Cah-na-hee, by Drennen in F1. #223. (Misc. Test. P. 3256.)
App: 1851 James Osborn, Park, Va.
Rejected. This applicant claims through the Sizemore's. See full report in #417.
App: 1852 Emiline Osborn and 3 children, Park, Va.
Rejected. This applicant claims through the Sizemore's. See full report in #417.
App: 1853 Ruben K. Baldwin and 3 children, Park, Va.
Rejected. This applicant claims through the Sizemore's. See full report in #417.
App: 1854 Martha Baldwin, Park, Va.
Rejected. This applicant claims through the Sizemore's. See full report in #417.
App: 1855 Wiley Baldwin, Park, Va.
Rejected. This applicant claims through the Sizemore's. See full report in #417.
App: 1856 Malissa Wyatt and 6 children, Park, Va.
Rejected. This applicant claims through the Sizemore's. See full report in #417.
App: 1857 Raby H. Osborn and 5 children, Kipling, Va.
Rejected. This applicant claims through the Sizemore's. See full report in #417.
App: 1858 James C. Trott, Vinita, Okla.
Admitted. Brother of #615 and claims through same source.
App: 1859 Frank Pettit and 1 child, Edna, Kansas.
Admitted. Claimant, his mother, brothers and half sister were enrolled by Drennen in 1851 in Ill. #86.
App: 1860 Martha C. Rogers and 1 child, Culberson, N.C.
Admitted. Sister of #1575 and claims through same source.
App: 1861 Thomas Robertson and 1 child, Peachtree, N.C.
Admitted. Grandmother, Polly Ann Payne and aunts, Catherine, Elizabeth and Eleanor Payne enrolled by Chapman #1351-1355 inclusive.

App: 1862 Gita Roberson, Culberson, N.C.
By James B. Roberson, Gdn.
Admitted. Sister of #1861 and claims through same source.
App: 1863 Edward C. Roberson and 1 child, Culberson, N.C.
Admitted. Brother of #1861 and claims through same source.
App: 1864 James Smith and 2 children, Moodys, Okla.
Admitted. Brother of #1224 and claims through same source.
App: 1865 Sarah Vann, Moodys, Okla.
Admitted. Parents and one brother enrolled by Drennen in 1851 in Tahl. #248. (*Handwritten, Paternal grandfather on 1835 roll P. 59.*)
App: 1866 Minnie A. Springwater and 6 children, Gans, Okla.
Admitted. Father, Anderson Choate enrolled by Drennen in S.B. #120. Niece of #1651.
App: 1867 Eli Snell and 1 child, South West City, Mo.
Admitted. Parents and older brothers enrolled in 1851 by Drennen in Del. #669.
App: 1868 Sarah Fields and 3 children, South West City, Mo.
Admitted. Mother enrolled by Drennen in 1851 in Del. #127.
App: 1869 Ida Six, South West City, Mo.
Admitted. Sister of #252 and claims through same source.
App: 1870 Mary Dannenburg, Manard, Okla.
Admitted. Niece of #562, and claims through same source. (*Handwritten, Grandfather, Henry Lowery, Tahl. 536*)
App: 1871 Tennessee Schell and 2 children, Nowata, Okla.
Admitted. Maternal grandmother and uncle of applicant enrolled by Drennen in 1851 in Fl. #53 under the names of Elizabeth and Benjamin Pettit.
App: 1872 Lizzie Downing and 1 child, Estella, Okla.
Admitted. Applicant herself and mother, Ah-quah-lah, enrolled by Drennen in 1851 in Del. #96. (Misc. Test. P. 3650.)
App: 1873 John Corntassell, Vinita, Okla.
Admitted. Brother of #1872 and claims through same source.
App: 1874 Evans Roberson and 2 children, Tahlequah, Okla.
Admitted. Father, paternal grandparents, one uncle and aunt enrolled by Drennen in 1851 in Tahl. #178.
App: 1875 Mary Smith, Moody, Okla.
Admitted. Mother and half sister enrolled by Drennen in 1851 in Tahl. #421. (Misc. Test. P. 3359.)
App: 1876 Hollie Blackwood and 4 children, Baron, Okla.
Admitted. Nephew of #177 and claims through same source.
App: 1877 Emma J. Samuels, Collyer, Kans.
Admitted. Parents, brother and sister enrolled by Drennen in 1851 in Tahl. #267.
App: 1878 Nancy A. Ballard and 5 children, Vinita, Okla.
Admitted. Sister of #1877 and claims through same source.
App: 1879 Richard L. Martin, Pensacola, Okla.
Admitted. Brother of #873 and claims through same ource[sic].
App: 1880 Susie McKnight and 5 children, Alluwee, Okla.
Admitted. Niece of #188 and claims through same source.

App: 1881 Polly Manus, Peggs, Okla.
Admitted. Father enrolled as Jim Scott and grandmother, Rachel Scott, by Drennen in 1851 in #327. See letter filed herein marked exhibit A.
App: 1882 Betsy Goingsnake, Row, Okla.
Admitted. Sister of #1189 and claims through same source.
App: 1883 Annie Downing, Locust Grove, Okla.
Admitted. Daughter of #522 and claims through same source.
App: 1884 Daniel Backbone,
Duplicate of #464.
App: 1885 Jim Wilson, Locust Grove, Okla.
Admitted. Parents and brothers and sisters enrolled by Drennen in 1851 in Saline #57. See Misc. Test. P. 3731.
App: 1886 Peter Rogers, (*Handwritten- and 2 children*), Locust Grove, Okla.
Admitted. Claimant born in 1876 and his mother was not born in 1856 or later (see app. #5286). Claimant's maternal grandmother is still living and has filed application #22006. Grandmother and her brothers and sisters enrolled by Drennen in 1851 Del. #800 and 801. (Misc. Test. P. 3438 and 3814.)
App: 1887 Wilson Coming, Locust Grove, Okla.
Admitted. Brother of #1885 and claims through same source.
App: 1888 George W. Johnson and 5 children, Uniontown, Ark.
Admitted. Father and grandmother, Anna Johnson, enrolled by Drennen in 1851 in Dis. #85. See testimony of Alta V. Theurer taken at Stilwell, Okla. Mar. 22, 1909. Also Misc. Test. P. 4015.
App: 1889 John Roastingear and 2 children, Uniontown, Ark.
Admitted. Brother of #202 and claims through same source.
App: 1890 Julia Middlestriker and 1 child, Uniontown, Ark.
Admitted. Mother and maternal grandparents enrolled by Drennen in 1851 in Fl. #470.
App: 1891 George Shakingbush and 4 children, Uniontown, Ark.
Admitted. Nephew of #202 and claims through same source.
App: 1892 Annie Holt and 1 child, Long, Okla.
Admitted. Applicant, her father and mother enrolled by Drennen in 1851 in S.B. #17.
App: 1893 Nancy Seabolt, Long, Okla.
Admitted. Claimant, her husband and two children enrolled by Drennen in 1851 in S.B. #38.
App: 1894 Caroline Rogers and 2 children, Uniontown, Ark.
Admitted. Father enrolled by Drennen in 1851 S.B. #31. Brother of applicant's father enrolled in Sal. #500. (See group of applications #2669.)
App: 1895 William Miller, Long, Okla.
Admitted. Applicant claims through Jack Miller and sister, Betsy both enrolled by Drennen in 1851 in Fl. #230-1/2 (Misc. Test. P. #2925.)
App: 1896 Sarah Daylight and 1 child, Short, Okla.
1 Admitted and 1 rejected.
Applicant's mother and maternal grandparents enrolled by Drennen in 1851 in S.B. #63. Applicant's minor child, Jesse Daylight, for whom additional

application is made in app. #40045, is rejected. It appears from letter (exhibit A) filed herewith that Jesse died Oct. 24, 1899.

App; 1897 Mose Downing and 4 children, Uniontown, Ark.
Admitted. Parents were not living in 1851. See app. and misc. test. pp 2812. Paternal grandfather and two aunts enrolled by Drennen in 1851 in F1. #428.

App: 1898 Nancy Rattler, Uniontown, Ark.
Admitted. Claimant enrolled by Chapman #683 together with her mother, Chapman #681 and step father Chapman #680. (Misc. Test. P. 1685 and 2808.)

App: 1899 Joseph M. Johnson and 5 children, Uniontown, Ark.
Admitted. Cousin of #1888 and claims through same source.

App: 1900 Robert Czarnikow and 10 children, Dora, Okla.
Admitted. Applicant, his mother, brother, and stepfather were all enrolled by Drennen in 1851 in S.B. #153. (See letter herein dated Dec. 23, 1907.)

App: 1901 Amus Langly and 1 child, Long, Okla.
Admitted. Mother, Darkey, S.B. #7 by Drennen and also grandfather, Cho-co-a, enrolled by Drennen in S.B. #129. (Misc. Test. P. 2914.)

App: 1902 Lydia Waters and 3 children, Uniontown, Ark.
Admitted. Parents were not living in 1851. Paternal grandparents and one aunt enrolled by Drennen in 1851 in S.B. #66. App. #1894 is probably mother of claimant and is also O.K. through same source. Applicant's daughter, Maggie, is enrolled with her father, Alex Welch, #10727.

App: 1903 John R. Vann and 2 children, (*Handwritten +1 niece +1 nephew)* Uniontown, Ark.
Admitted. Applicant's mother, Nancy Baldridge, enrolled by Drennen in 1851 in S.B. #33.

App: 1904 Linnie J. Crail and 6 children, Wagoner, Okla.
Admitted. Sister of #642. Father enrolled by Chapman #1686.

App: 1905 Lizzie Cornstalk and 1 child, Maysville, Ark.
Admitted. Nephew of #653 and claims through same source.

App: 1906 Richard Russel and 1 child, Oaks Okla.
Admitted. Brother of #1425 and claims through same source.

App: 1907 Blossom Falling and 3 children, Eucha, Okla.
Admitted. Father enrolled by Drennen in 1851 in Del. #724.

App: 1908 Sarah Hogshooter and 1 child, Maysville, Ark.
Admitted. Father, paternal grandparents and aunts enrolled by Drennen in 1851 in Del. #275.

App: 1909 Johnson Manning and 2 children, Tahlequah, Okla.
Admitted. Father, paternal grandmother and uncles and aunts enrolled by Drennen in Tahl. #247 and 248.

App: 1910 Narcissus Duncan and 4 children, Chotopa, Kans.
Admitted. Father enrolled by Drennen in 1851 in Dis. #31. Grandfather enrolled in Dis. #27.

App: 1911 Cora D. Martin and 4 children, Welch, Okla.
Admitted. Father, through whom she claims her Indian blood, was not born until 1857. Father's mother, Malinda J. Lane, and father's half sister, Samantha, enrolled by Drennen in Del. #935. (Misc. Test. P. 4390.)

App: 1912 Thomas J. Rogers and 4 children, Kinnison, Okla.
Admitted. Father, Lewis, and grandmother, Diannah Rogers, enrolled by Drennen in Del. #952. (Misc. Test. P. 3645.)
App: 1913 George Hilderbrand, Webbers Falls, Okla.
Admitted. Applicant enrolled by Drennen in 1851 in Tahl. #294.
App: 1914 Jack Sawney, Stilwell, Okla.
Admitted. Parents enrolled as Tah-lah-se-nah and Sally, by Drennen in Fl. #514. (Misc. Test. P. 3141.)
App: 1914 1/2 Jack Sawney, (*Handwritten 1/2.*)
Duplicate of #1914.
App: 1915 Eliza J. Coney, Vinita, Okla.
Admitted. Father, William Seabolt, enrolled by Drennen in Fl. #526. (*Handwritten Misc. Tes. P. 2881*)
App: 1916 Jennie Daniel, Evansville, Ark.
Admitted. Sister of #1689 and claims through same source.
App: 1917 Annie Ketcher, Evansville, Ark.
Admitted. Half sister of #1913 and claims through same source.
App: 1918 Nancy Alberty, Baron, Okla.
Admitted. Niece of #177 and claims through same source.
App: 1919 Alice Payne, Welch, Okla.
Admitted. Grandfather, Henry Nave, enrolled on 1835 roll #64. Grandmother, Susannah Nave, and claimants uncles and aunts enrolled by Drennen in Tahl. #143. Cousin of #102.
App: 1920 Joe Hilderbrand and 2 children, Estella, Okla.
Admitted. Nephew of #1351. Father, Benjamin Hilderbrand, enrolled by Drennen in Del. #378.
App: 1921 Jane Walkingstick, Baron, Okla.
Admitted. Niece of #177 and claims through same source.
App: 1922 Caroline Sanders, Baron, Okla.
Admitted. Niece of #177 and claims through same source.
App: 1923 William R. Harris, Greenbrier, Okla.
Admitted. Brother of #1845 and claims through same source.
App: 1924 Martin Blackwood, Baron, Okla.
Admitted. Nephew of #177 and claims through same source.
App: 1925 George Snell, Kansas, Okla.
Admitted. Half brother of #469 and claims through same source.
App: 1926 Rachel Collins, Oaks, Okla.
Admitted. Father enrolled as Edward Lowery, Sal. #171, by Drennen.
App: 1927 Mollie Fields, Moody, Okla.
Admitted. Sister of #1926 and claims through same source.
App: 1928 Jennie Murphy and 3 children, Oaks, Okla.
Admitted. Sister of #1926 and claims through same source.
App: 1929 George Still, Leach, Okla.
Admitted. Uncle of #1374. Applicant himself enrolled by Drennen in G.S. #323.
App: 1930 Sallie Arch, Evansville, Ark.
Admitted. Mother of #1689. Herself enrolled by Drennen in 1851 in Fl. #512.

App: 1931 Lucy Duck, Evansville, Ark.
Admitted. Father enrolled by Drennen in Dis. #64. (Misc. Test. P. 3208.)
App: 1932 Nannie B. Smith,
Duplicate of #1274.
App: 1933 Archilla Baldridge and 4 children, Locust Grove, Okla.
Admitted. Father enrolled by Drennen in 1851 in G.S. #2.
App: 1934 Tylor Tilden and 2 children, Locust Grove, Okla.
Admitted. Brother of #913 and claims through same source.
App: 1935 William Coats and 3 children, Miami, Okla.
Admitted. Mother, Annie Spears, and grandmother, Lucinda Davis or Dennis, enrolled by Drennen in 1851 in Sal. #201. (*Handwritten Miscel. Tes. P. 3119.*)
App: 1936 Lydia Wilson and 3 children, Rowe, Okla.
Admitted. Half sister of #8006 and claims through same source.
App: 1937 Runabout Ar-mer-teas-ky, Peggs, Okla.
Admitted. Father enrolled as Ah-ma-de-ske and mother, Che-na-ye, by Drennen in 1851 in Del. #837. (*Handwritten Miscel. Tes. P. 3435.)*
App; 1938 Peggy Sunday or Wakee Deerin-water, Locust Grove, Okla.
Admitted. Mother, Susannah Deer-in-water and also applicant herself enrolled by Drennen in Tahl. #141. (Misc. Test. P. 3788.)
App: 1939 Clabran Manus, Peggs, Okla.
Admitted. Mother enrolled by Drennen in 1851 in G.S. #636.
App: 1940 Maggie Frye and 6 children, Mark, Okla.
Admitted. Sister of #1939 and claims through same source.
App: 1941 William Johnson, Cookson, Okla.
Admitted. Brother of #1328 and claims through same source.
App: 1942 Peggy Shade, Peggs, Okla.
Admitted. Sister of #1881 and claims through same source.
App: 1943 Katy Hosea and 3 children, Locust Grove, Okla.
Admitted. Sister of #189. Father enrolled by Drennen in Sal. #212.
App: 1944 Lydia Blackwood, Baron, Okla.
Admitted. Niece of #177 and claims through same source.
App: 1945 Cecil Presson, Francis, Okla.
Rejected Son of #831 and claims through same source.
App: 1946 Gracie Presson, Francis, Okla.
Rejected. Daughter of #831 and claims through same source.
App: 1947 George Presson, Francis Okla.
Rejected. Son of #831 and claims through same source.
App: 1948 Wm E. Presson, Francis, Okla.
Rejected. Son of #831 and claims through same source.
App: 1949 William W. Foreman and 3 children, Centralia, Okla.
Admitted. First cousin once removed of #1683. Father enrolled by Drennen in Fl. #633.
App: 1950 Andrew J. Griffin, Muskogee, Okla.
Admitted. Applicant himself enrolled as Andrew Seabolt together with mother in Fl. #621, by Drennen.
App: 1951 Ruth B. Evans, and 4 children, Tulsa, Okla.
Admitted. Daughter of #447 and claims through same source.

App: 1952 Beulah M. Beard, Claremore, Okla.
Admitted. Grandfather enrolled by Drennen in Tahl. #133.
App: 1953 Sarah Stevens, Lometa, Okla.
Admitted. Applicant enrolled by Drennen together with her husband in 1851 in G.S. #429.
App: 1954 Susan D. Haralson, Atlanta, Ga. 137 Spring St.
Admitted. First cousin of #98 and claims through same source.
App: 1955 Stewart Mongrain and 3 children, Burbank, Okla.
Rejected. Enrolled as Osages. See letter from Indian office.
App: 1956 Allen B. Slaughter, Elgin, Kans.
Rejected. Applicant enrolled as an Osage. See letter herein Marked Exhibit A.
App: 1957 Harry S. Slaughter Jr. Elgin, Kans.
Rejected. Enrolled as an Osage and brother of #1956.
App: 1958 Amanda Slaughter, Elgin, Kans.
Rejected. Enrolled as an Osage and sister of #1956.
App: 1959 Mary A. Mongrain, Springfield, Mo. Loretta Academy
Admitted. Applicant enrolled by Drennen in Del. #950.
App: 1960 Mary E. Harris, Elgin, Kans.
Rejected. Sister of #1956 and claims through same source.
App: 1961 James D. and Nellie Overtaker, Sallisaw, Okla. By Maggie McKinney, Gdn.
Rejected. John Overtaker, alleged father not enrolled. Charles and Nellie Overtaker, the grandparents not enrolled. Nothing shown to establish Eastern Cherokee descent. (See letter of Maggie McKinney and Misc. Test. P. 3933 and 3934.)
App: 1962 Wallace Thornton, Vian, Okla.
Admitted. Mother, Quaty Thornton, enrolled by Drennen in 1851 in Ill. #251. (Misc. Test. P. 2893.)
App: 1963 Fannie Cummings or Cummins and 4 children, Vian, Okla.
Admitted. Applicant's grandfather, Lewis Tyner, was enrolled in 1835 in Tennessee. It appears that about 1850 the family moved west, some of them residing in Mo., and some of them in Ark. For this reason they were not enrolled, either by Chapman in the East or by Drennen in the West. Several of the younger generation were enrolled as Cherokees and have received allotments, while others have not been so enrolled and allotted, but they are recognized as being of Cherokee Indian descent, and there is no reason why they should not have been allotted if they had made the same effort. The children of Fannie Cummins would be entitled as the descendants of Allen and Wallis Ratley, who are enrolled in Ill. #74. See testimony of Fannie Cummins, John W. Tyner and Martha Smith taken at Vian, Okla. Mar. 15, 1909. (Misc. Test. P. 3958 and 3959 and 3657.)
App: 1964 James Hair, Vian, Okla.
Admitted. Uncle of #1130. Father enrolled in G.S. #155, by Drennen.
App: 1965 Smith Thornton and 1 child, Vian, Okla.
Admitted. Brother of #1962 and claims through same source.
App: 1966 Evans Cummings and 1 child, Vian, Okla.
Admitted. Son of #1963 and claims through same source.

App: 1967 Charles F. Patton and 3 children, Paw Paw, Okla.
Admitted. Mother enrolled by Drennen in 1851 in S.B. #240.
App: 1968 Joe Young, Vian, Okla.
Admitted. Nephew of #1124. Father enrolled by Drennen in G.S. #633.
App: 1969 Austin Ofields and 2 children, Needmore, Okla.
Admitted. Father enrolled by Drennen in 1851 in Del. #590.
App: 1970 John Silversmith, South West City, Mo.
Admitted. Half brother of #1868 and claims through same source.
App: 1971 Bettie Fields and 7 children, South West City, Mo.
Admitted. Half sister of #1868 and claims through same source.
App: 1972 Mary J. Yeargin, Maysville, Ark.
Admitted. Applicant enrolled by Drennen in Del. #499.
App: 1973 Nick Snipp and 4 children, Westville, Okla.
Admitted. Grandfather, Deer-in-water, on mother's side, and mother's sister, Lucy, were enrolled by Drennen in Tahl. #555. (Misc. Test. P. 4062.)
App: 1974 Ruth Morgan, (*Handwritten and 8 children),* Tahlequah, Okla.
Admitted. Cousin of #671 and claims through same source. (*Handwritten For children see suppl. #6055.*)
App: 1975 Abbie King, Tahlequah, Okla.
Admitted. Applicant enrolled by Drennen in 1851 in Ill. #305.
App: 1976 Ellis Rattlinggourd and 4 children, Tahlequah, Okla.
Admitted. Nephew of #278. Father, Ellis R. Gourd, enrolled in Tahl. #478.
App: 1977 James Evans Parris and 4 children, Gideon, Okla.
Admitted. Uncle of #737. Applicant born in 1851, but does not seem to have been enrolled. Father and mother, George and Matilda Parris enrolled by Drennen in Dis. #45.
App: 1978 Margaret Parris, Tahlequah, Okla.
Admitted. Niece of #278. Applicant's father, Ellis R. Gourd enrolled in Tahl. #478.
App: 1979 Samantha Terrell and 1 child, Eureka, Okla.
Admitted. Niece of #278. Father, Ellis R. Gourd, enrolled in Tahl. #478.
App: 1980 Elias Rattlinggourd and 3 children, Tahlequah, Okla.
Admitted. Nephew of #278. Father, James Rattlinggourd, enrolled in Tahl. #478.
App: 1981 Nick Commingdeer, Tahlequah, Okla.
Admitted. Applicant enrolled by Drennen in 1851 in Sal. #295.
App: 1982 Susan R. Gourd, Moodys Okla.
Admitted. Applicant enrolled by Drennen in Tahl. #368 as Susann[sic] Benge.
App: 1983 Harriet Hubbard, Tahlequah, Okla.
Rejected. Claims for husband who died in 1900. See application.
App: 1984 Jesse R. Gourd and 1 child, Moodys, Okla.
Admitted. Brother of #1865 and claims through same source. Applicant himself is also enrolled in Tahl. #249.
App: 1985 Joannan Hart and 3 children, Manard, Okla.
Admitted. Niece of #562. Mother born in 1858, but maternal grandfather, Henry Lowery, enrolled in #536 Tahl., by Drennen.

App: 1986 Anderson Richey, Metory, Okla.
Admitted. Applicant's grandfather enrolled by Drennen in Dis. #48.
App: 1987 Delilah Miller and 4 children, Tahlequah, Okla.
Admitted. Duplicate of #5020.
App: 1988 Cherokee Bread, Hulbert, Okla.
Admitted. Lewis Bread, father, and grandparents, Bread and Aincy, all enrolled by Drennen in 1851 in Fl. #641.
App: 1989 Annie E. Blackwell, Meridian, Okla.
Rejected. Sister of #367 and claims through same source.
App: 1990 Charles Levi and 1 child, Leach or Peggs, Okla.
Admitted. Father enrolled as Gah-lah-stee-hus-ke, grandmother as Eu-ne-ke and aunt Gah-ne-yaw-e, all enrolled by Drennen in 1851 in Del. #799. (Misc. Test. P. 3733.)
App: 1991 Andrew J. Rogers, Uniontown, Ark.
Admitted. Mother, Lydia, grandparents, Wa-a-ky and Charlotte-te-hee, all enrolled by Drennen in 1851 in Fl. #485. (Misc. Test. P. 2815 and 3735.)
App: 1992 Joe Blackbird, Uniontown, Ark.
Admitted. Father and mother, William B. and Anne B. Bird, enrolled by Drennen in 1851 in S.B. #100.
App: 1993 Jack Middlestricker, Uniontown, Ark.
Admitted. Father Ar-ya-le-no-no-yah-kee and mother, Lakee, enrolled by Drennen in 1851 in S.B. #47.
App: 1994 Sallie Welch and 2 children, Short, Okla.
Admitted. Evidence shown that applicant's mother was an emigrant Cherokee and was recogonized as such. Never received any Old Settler money. (Misc. Test. P. 2814 and 4013.)
App: 1995 Katie Roastingear and 2 children, Uniontown, Ark.
Admitted. Applicant and her mother and brother and sister were enrolled by Drennen in Fl. #330, under the names of Ka-he-tah, Joster, Lacy, and Achinna.
App: 1996 Malinda Eagle and 5 children, Long, Okla.
Admitted. Daughter of #1898 and claims through same source.
App: 1997 Henry P. Wood and 4 children, Zena, Okla.
Admitted. Brother of #1131 and claims through same source.
App: 1998 Nancy M. Reed and 2 children, Zena, Okla.
Admitted. Sister of #1131 and claims through same source.
App: 1999 Francis M. Wood and 2 children, Zena, Okla.
Admitted. Brother of #1131 and claims through same source.
App: 2000 James F. Wood and 4 children, Zena, Okla.
Admitted. Brother of #1131 and claims through same source.
App: 2001 Nama W. Newman and ~~5~~ children, Welch, Oklahoma
Admitted. Applicant's grandfather "Stephen Hildebrand" enrolled "540 Tahlequah". Niece of #859.
App: 2002 Charlotte~~e~~[sic] C. Martin and 1 child, Vinita, Oklahoma.
Admitted. Niece of #1301.
App: 2003 Junaluska Standingdeer, Paintown[sic], N.C.
Admitted. Claims through grandfather enrolled as Lu-ih. Grandmother enrolled

as Yeh-kin-nih. Both of whom were enrolled by Chapman in 1851. Numbers 183 and 184.

App: 2004 James M. Gunter and one child, Redland, Oklahoma
Admitted. Nephew of #901. Claimant's father enrolled in 1851 by Drennen, S.B. 285.

App: 2005 Thos. P. Sawyer, Almond, N.C.
Rejected. It does not appear that any ancestor was ever enrolled or that any ancestor was party to the treaties of 1835-6 and 1846. Shows no connection with the Eastern Cherokees. Misc. Test P. 1706, 1729 and 1730.

App: 2006 Etna D. Looney and four children, Ozark, Mo.
Rejected. Claims through Alex Brown. See #35. (Special Report #35)

App: 2007 Martha Raper, Murphy, N.C.
Rejected. Ancestors not parties to treaties of 1835-6 and 1846. Show no affiliation or association with Cherokees. Not enrolled by Hester 1884.

App: 2008 Polly Stiles, Sylva, N.C.
Rejected. Betsy Walker case. See special report in #500.

App: 2009 Isaiah U. Hambleton and 7 children, Gainesville, Mo.
Rejected. Claims through Alex. Brown. See #35. (Special Report #35)

App: 2010 Alfred D. Ellis and 3 children, Aurora, Mo.
Rejected. Duplicate of #5419.

App: 2011 Etna Poindexter and three children, Ranger, N.C.
Rejected. Claims only as a descendant of Polly Murphy. (*Handwritten See #119.*)

App: 2012 James E. Barber, Ramona, Oklahoma.
Rejected. Grandson of Joanna Barber. Application #1306 and claims through the same source.

App: 2013 Emma L. Murphy and 5 children, Ramona, Oklahoma.
Rejected. Grabddaughter[sic] of Joanna Barber #1306 and claims through the same source.

App: 2014 Joel A. Barber and 5 children, Ramona, Oklahoma.
Rejected. Son of Joanna Barber #1306 and claims through the same source.

App: 2015 William L. Constant, Breyson City, N.C.
Rejected. Nephew of #664 and claims through the same source.

App: 2016 Ollie E. Presley and 4 children, ~~Salyer~~, Mo.
(*Handwritten above, Lockwood*)
Rejected. Claims through Alex Brown. (See special report #35).

App: 2017 James R. Constant, Andrews, N.C.
Rejected. Nephew of #664 and claims through the same source.

App: 2018 Joseph N. Mason and 7 children, Flats, N.C.
Rejected. Brother of #529 and claims through the same ancestors.

App: 2019 Mary Amis and 2 children, Dayton, Ohio.
Rejected. Niece of #197 and claims through the same source.

App: 2020 Emma Eggers and 2 children, Peachtree, N.C.
Rejected. Niece of #664 and claims through the same source.

App: 2021 James L. Sawyer, Judson, N.C.
Rejected. Brother of #2005 and claims through the same source.

App: 2022 Sidney C. Hambleton and 5 children, Fay, Mo.
Rejected. Claims through Alex Brown. See special report #35.
App: 2023 James N. Hambleton, Gainesville, Mo.
Rejected. Claims through Alex. Brown. See special report #35.
App: 2024 Minnie M. Stansburg (*Handwritten over g is a y*) Almond, N.C.
Rejected. Niece of #664 and claims through the same source.
App: 2025 Sylvester A. Smith, Blue Ridge, Ga.
Admitted. Nephew of #423 and claims through the same source.
App: 2026 Laura C. Nations, Ocona Lufty, N.C.
Rejected. Mother of 29330 and claims through the same source.
App: 2027 Bryson Kell) Blue Ridge, Ga.
Arthur B. Kell)
Admitted. Claimed through grandfather enrolled by Chapman in 1851 as mix. Kell, No. 2100. applicant's father was enrolled by Hester #2603. By Mary E. Buchanan, Gdn. and mother.
App: 2028 Sarah Poe and 5 children, Kansas City, Mo.
Rejected. Claims through Alex. Brown. (Gen. Del.) see special report #35.
App: 2029 James D. Lane and 2 children, Keokuk Falls, Oklahoma.
Rejected. Son of #744.
App: 2030 Benjamin T. Smith, Hennepin, Oklahoma.
Rejected. Cousin of #839, and claims through the same ancestors.
App: 2031 John U. Hambleton, Gainesville, Mo.
Rejected. Claims through Alex. Brown. See special report #35.
App: 2032 Susan Morrow and 4 children, Blue Ridge, Ga.
Rejected. It does not appear that any ancestors was party to the treaties of 1835-36 or 1846. Nor does it appear that any ancestors were ever enrolled. Misc. Test #1422.
App: 2033 Martha R. Brown, Calhoun, Ga.
Rejected. Sister of #315. Claims through the same source.
App: 2034 Dick Ka-Ka-wee, Oaks, Oklahoma.
Admitted. Half brother on father's side of #682 and is admitted for same reasons.
App: 2035 Katie Ka-Ka-wee and 2 children, Oaks, Oklahoma.
Admitted. Claims through Grandparents, Alexander Love and Susan Love, enrolled in 1851, by Drennen, in Delaware District No. 659. Misc. Test. P. 3184.
App: 2036 Katie Wolfe, Oaks, Oklahoma.
Admitted. By Minnie Isreal, Guardian. Grand niece of #1245 and claims through the same source. Grandfather of applicant, enrolled in 1851 under name of Ter-ger-wor-se, in Saline District, No. 103.
App: 2037 Minnie Israel, Oaks, Oklahoma.
Admitted. Grand niece of #1245 and claims through the same ancestors. Grandfather of applicant enrolled in 1851 under name of Ter-ger-wor-see. No. 103. (*Handwritten Saline Dist.*)
App: 2038 Charles Deal, Stilwell, Oklahoma.
Admitted. A once removed cousin of Wilson Morris. (C. 1194).
App: 2039 Celia Parnell and 1 child, Cookson, Oklahoma.
Admitted. Applicant was enrolled as Ceily in #413 G.S. District 1851 and her

father and mother Mary. Appl. #17277 were also enrolled in the same district and under the same number.

App: 2040 Nellie Clevenger, Vinita, Oklahoma.
Admitted. The parents of applicant were enrolled in 997 Delaware District in 1851 by Drennen. See Misc. Test P. 4307.

App: 2041 Eli Batt, Oaks, Oklahoma.
Admitted. Applicant claims through his father Blue Bat, who was enrolled in 1851, by Drennen, in Saline District, No. 82. Also claims through his mother, who was enrolled as Susan, in same district and group.

App: 2042 Lewis Stover, Oaks, Oklahoma.
Admitted. Claims through mother enrolled as Aikey. Grandfather enrolled as Tah-qua-noo-shah-lah-kee. Grandmother enrolled as Maria. Uncle and Aunt enrolled as Ne-goo-cha-kee and Kah-lon-eh-skee. All of whom were enrolled by Drennen in 1851 in Going Snake District, Group #71. See Misc. Test P. 3765.

App: 2043 Nancy Vann, Oaks, Oklahoma.
Admitted. Aunt of #2207.

App: 2044 Sarah Smith, Kansas, Oklahoma.
Admitted. Sister of #2041, and claims through the same ancestors.

App: 2045 Ella Rusk and 3 children, Oaks, Oklahoma.
Admitted. Claims through father enrolled as David Israel. Grandfather enrolled as Kah-sah-lah-nee (or Kah-sah-lah-wee). Grandmother enrolled as Nelly (or Molly). Aunts and uncles enrolled as Ah-nee-wa-kee, Inee-lee-koo and Josiah Israel. All of whom were enrolled by Drennen in 1851 in Going Snake District. Group #10.

App: 2046 Emma Jackson and 4 children, Kansas, Oklahoma.
Admitted. Sister of #2045 and claims through same source.

App: 2047 David Israel and 2 children, Oaks, Oklahoma.
Admitted. Brother of #2045 and claims through the same source.

App: 2048 William Israel and 2 children, Oaks, Oklahoma.
Admitted. Brother of #2045 and claims through the same source.

App: 2049 Rufus B. Cobb, Muskogee, Oklahoma.
Admitted. Claims through self enrolled as Rufus Cobb. Mother enrolled as Susan Cobb. Brother enrolled as James Henry Cobb. All were enrolled by Chapman in 1851. No's. 1872 to 1874 inc.

App: 2050 Albert W. Harlan, Fairland, Oklahoma.
Admitted. Claims through self enrolled as Albert Harlin. Brothers and sister enrolled as Lafayette, Ezekiel, Lucinda and David Harlin. All of whom were enrolled by Drennen in 1851 in Delaware District, Group #934.

App: 2051 David L. Harlin and 1 child, Fairlabd[sic], Oklahoma.
Admitted. Brother of #2050. Applicant enrolled as David Harlin. Del. #934.

App: 2052 Samantha Hillen, Fairland, Oklahoma.
Admitted. Claims through self enrolled as Samantha Lane. Mother enrolled as Melinda J. Lane. Sister enrolled as Tennessee Lane. All were enrolled by Drennen in 1851 in Del. District. Group #935.

App: 2053 Tennessee A. James and 2 children, Fairland, Okla.
Admitted. Enrolled as Tennessee Harlin. Del. #935. Sister of #2052.

App: 2054 Joseph Downing for Lewis Downing. Hadley, Oklahoma.

Admitted. Nephew of #1374. Cannot identify father upon rolls of '51.

App: 2055 Elizabeth Williams and 7 children, Chouteau, Oklahoma.
Admitted. Father enrolled as Jack Downing. Tahl. #577 See Misc. Test P. 4224.

App: 2056 Joseph Downing for Geo. Downing, Hadley, Oklahoma.
Admitted. Nephew of #1374. Cannot identify father of applicant on rolls of '51.

App: 2057 Joseph Downing for Druscilla Downing, Hadley, Oklahoma.
Admitted. Niece of #1374. Mother of applicant not living in 1851.

App: 2058 Joseph Downing for Reggie Downing. Hadley, Oklahoma.
(Blank) Niece of #1374. Mother of applicant not living in 1851.

App: 2059 Joseph Downing and 3 children, Hadley, Oklahoma.
Admitted. Enrolled as Joseph Woodhall. Sister enrolled as Lucy Woodhall. Grandmother enrolled as Nancy Woodhall. Aunt and uncle enrolled as Celia and Thomas G.S. #237. The applicant is also making a claim for an insane sister Lucy-enrolled as Lucy Woodhall. G.S. #237. See Misc. Test P. 4225.

App: 2060 Ezekiel Still and 4 children, Hadley, Oklahoma.
Admitted. Uncle of 3609.

App: 2061 Benjamin Smith, Eucha, Oklahoma.
Admitted. Claims through grandmother enrolled as Warl-se. Saline #248. Great-greatfather enrolled as Oo-dee-geo-ste. Great grandmother enrolled as Noo-yor-he. Saline #229. See Misc. Test P. 3884.

App: 2062 Martha Lee Choate, Chouteau, Oklahoma.
Rejected. Applicant is a white woman claiming through her husband who died April 3, 1902, leaving no children.

App: 2063 Henry L. Coats and 4 children, Welch Oklahoma.
Admitted. Brother of #1935 and claims through the same source.

App: 2064 Pleasant Fields, Fairland, Oklahoma.
Admitted. Nephew of #390. Applicant's mother enrolled by Drennen in 1851. Del. 142.

App: 2065 Bettie Hendricks and 1 child, Vinita, Oklahoma.
Admitted. Niece of #651. Parents of applicant not living in 1851.

App: 2066 Eliza Morris, Vinita, Oklahoma.
Admitted. Duplicate of #1704.

App: 2067 Geo. O. Sanders, Wauhillau, Oklahoma.
Admitted. Brother to #862. Claimant himself enrolled in Tah. 21.

App: 2068 George O. Sanders, Wauhillau, Okla.
Duplicate of 2067.

App: 2069 Ellen Morris Stilwell, Okla.
Rejected. Applicant claims through her husband. She was living in 1835 and 1851 but does not appear on either roll. Neither parents or grandparents appear on the above mentioned rolls nor any of their children.

App: 2070 Joseph H. Morris and 6 children, Stilwell, Oklahoma.
Admitted. Cousin to Fannie E. Chandler (1723) and son of Wilson Morris.

App: 2071 Land Morris, Stilwell, Oklahoma.
Admitted. A two times removed cousin of Fanny E. Chandler (1723) and grandson of Wilson Morris.

App: 2072 Wilson E. Morris and 3 children, Ballad, Oklahoma.

Admitted. Cousin of Fannie E. Chandler (1723) and son of Wilson Morris.
App: 2073 Robert L. Russell and 5 children, Clarence, Oklahoma.
Admitted. Nephew #159, and claims through the same ancestors. Applicant enrolled by Hester No. 2452. Mother of applicant enrolled by Chapman. No. 2029.
App: 2074 Sarah M. Beavers, Claremore, Oklahoma.
Admitted. Sister of #343.
App: 2075 William H. Russell, Owasso, Oklahoma.
Admitted. Nephew of #159 and claims through the same ancestors. Applicant enrolled by Chapman, No. 2031. Applicant enrolled by Hester, No. 2458. Mother of applicant enrolled by Chapman, No. 2029.
App: 2076 Lena Brown and 2 children, Murphy, N.C.
Rejected. Applicant's mother was a slave and this claim is made through her. See letter.
App: 2077 Thos. M. Delozier and 3 children, Almond, N.C.
Rejected. Nephew of #664 and claims through the same source.
App: 2078 Amanda L. Delozier Almond, N.C.
Rejected. Niece of #664 and claims through the same source.
App: 2079 Sarah C. Hyde, Almond, N.C.
Rejected. Niece of #664 and claims through the same source.
App: 2080 Mary A. Patterson, Almond, N.C.
Rejected. Niece of #664 and claims through the same source.
App: 2081 Tom Brown, Greenfield, Mo.
Rejected. Claims through Alex. Brown (See special report No. 35).
App: 2082 Alexander Robertson, Hayden, Mo.
Rejected. It does not appear that any ancestor was ever enrolled or that any ancestor was party to the treaties of 1835-6 or 1846. Shows no connection with the Eastern Cherokees.
App: 2083 Sarah E. Downing, Bushyhead, I.T.
Rejected. Kaziah[sic] Vann case. See special report #276.
App: 2084 Joahne I. Garlingham and 4 children, Rivera, Cal.
Rejected. Granddaughter of Joana Barber #1306 and claims through the same source.
App: 2085 Jos. P. Parker, Grove, I.T.
Rejected. Blythe case. See special report #153.
App: 2086 Mary E.R. Delozier, Almond, N.C.
Rejected. Claims as wife of Jesse R. Delozier who died Oct/22/1886. who was a brother of #664.
App: 2087 Ida S. Tate and 2 children, Tuttle, I.T.
Rejected. Ancestor not on rolls. Does not establish geniue connection with Cherokee tribe. Misc. Test P. 2049.
App: 2088 Rebecca Hughes, Norman, Oklahoma.
Rejected. Mother of #2087.
App: 2089 Dalton Stewart, Decautur, Illinois.
Rejected. It does not appear that any ancestor was ever enrolled or that any ancestor was a party to the treaties of 1835-6 and 1846. Shows no connection with the Eastern Cherokees. Ancestors did not live in the Cherokee domain. Misc. Test P. 2657.
App: 2090 Roby Blevins and 3 children, Brandon, N.C.

Rejected. Sizemore case. See special report of #417.

App: 2091 Rutha Jane Jones and 3 children, Silas Creek, N.C.

Rejected. Sizemore case. See special report of #417.

App: 2092 Charley M. Blevins, Silas Creek, N.C.

Rejected. Sizemore case. See special report of #417.

App: 2093 Martha Barker and 4 children, Silas Creek, N.C.

Rejected. Sizemore case. See special Report of #417.

App: 2094 Ader Mcloore, Silas Creek, N.C.

Rejected. Sizemore case. See special Report of #417.

App: 2095 Lettie Stuart, Silas Creek, N.C.

Rejected. Sizemore case. See special Report of #417.

App: 2096 Mary Dickson and 4 children, Silas Creek, N.C.

Rejected. Sizemore case. See special report of #417.

App: 2097 G.D. Blevins and 1 child, Silas Creek, N.C.

Rejected. Sizemore case. See special report of #417.

App: 2098 Susannah Blackburn, Silas Creek, N.C.

Rejected Sizemore case. See special report of #417.

App: 2099 John W. Blevins, Silas Creek, N.C.

Rejected. Sizemore case. See special report of #417.

App: 2100 Cordelia Howell and 2 children, Silas Creek, N.C.

Rejected. Sizemore case. See special report of #417.

App: 2101 Mary A.F. Parker, and 1 child, Hulbert, Oklahoma.

Admitted. Cousin of #671 and claims through the same source.

App: 2102 Sallie Cox and 1 child, Hulbert, Oklahoma.

Admitted. Cousin of #671 and claims through the same source.

App: 2103 Alice Campbell and 1 child, Hulbert, Oklahoma.

Admitted. Cousin of #671 and claims through the same source.

App: 2104 Eddy Fish and 3 children, Claremore, Oklahoma.

Admitted. Cosuin[sic] of #671 and claims through the same source.

App: 2105 Eliza Jane Hendricks, Talequah[sic], Oklahoma.

Admitted. Aunt of #671 and claims through the same source.

App: 2106 Annie E. Fields, Muskogee, Oklahoma.

Rejected. Applicant was a slave. Misc. Test P. 3480.

App: 2107 Nellie Raper and 2 children, Eucha, Oklahoma.

Admitted. Mother of #2061, and claims through the same source.

App: 2108 Norris Ruddles, Catoosa, Oklahoma.

Admitted. Brother of #1542.

App: 2109 John E. Dean, Turnesville, Ga.

Rejected. It does not appear that any ancestor was a party to the treaties of 1835-6 or 1846 nor does it appear that any ancestor was enrolled. Misc. Test P. 1523.

App: 2110 James B.Raper and 9 children, Ivy Log, Ga.

Admitted. Brother of #1443 and claims through the same source.

App: 2111 Catherine I. Wasson, Welch, Oklahoma.

Admitted. Applicant's mother, Elizabeth Harlin, was enrolled by Drennen Disputed #54.

App: 2112 Mary A. Clark and 3 children, Talala, Oklahoma.

Admitted. First cousin once removed of No. 1683 and claims through the same source. Applicant's father enrolled by Drennen, Flint #633, as Daniel Foreman.

App: 2113 Jane Patton, Muskogee, Oklahoma.

Admitted. First cousin of #98 and claims through the same source.

App: 2114 Joseph Pettit and six children, Edna, Kansas.

Admitted. 1st. cousin of #866.

App: 2115 Wm. P. Goddard and 1 child, Chetopa, Kansas.

Admitted. Son of #2111.

App: 2116 Wm. R. Storer and 5 children, Needmore, Oklahoma.

Admitted. Brother of #823 and claims through the same source.

App: 2117 Susie Price and 6 children, Sallisau[sic], Oklahoma.

Admitted. First cousin of #1130. Father of applicant enrolled in 1851 in Going Snake #155.

App: 2118 Mary C. Waters and 2 children, Vian, Oklahoma.

Admitted. Applicant's grandparents, Jack Miller was enrolled by Drennen. in Flint 230 1/2. See Misc. Test of James Still and Mary C. Waters taken at Vian, Okla. Mar. 15/09. Misc. Test 3960-3961.

App: 2119 G.W. Pettit and six children, Cookson, Oklahoma.

Admitted. Applicant's grandmother, Nelly Lovett, was enrolled by Drennen in Illinois District #81, and his mother was enrolled in Skin Bayou District #310.

App: 2120 Nellie Majors and 2 children, ~~Vinita~~, Oklahoma
(*Handwritten above, Afton.*)

Admitted. Niece of #511, and claims through the same ancestors.

App: 2121 Emily L. Clark and ~~2~~ Children, Chelsea, Oklahoma.

Admitted. Applicant and her mother were enrolled by Drennen in Illinois District #288.

App: 2122 Christopher C. Seabolt and three children, Hanson, Oklahoma.

Admitted. Brother of #598; claims through the same source.

App: 2123 Gibson W. Alberty, Christie, Oklahoma.

Rejected. Ancestors were enrolled as old settlers. See O.S. Flint 58. Misc. Test 3263 and 4056.

App: 2124 Wiley R. Mulkey, Warner, Oklahoma.

Admitted. Nephew of No. 277 and claims through the same source.

App: 2125 Eliza A. McCamish and 1 child, Vinita, Oklahoma.

Admitted. Niece of #1353 and claims through the same ancestors. Mother of applicant, Edosia Clark (Weir) enrolled in 1851 in Delaware District No. 78.

App: 2126 Anisia M. Payne and 4 children, Blue Jacket, Oklahoma.

Admitted. Niece of #1353 and claims through the same ancestors. Grandmother of applicant, Edosia Clark (Weir) enrolled in 1851 in Delaware District No. 78.

App: 2127 Nathaniel J. Holden, Aquone, N.C.

Rejected. Cousin of #126 and claims through the same ancestors.

App: 2128 Leonard Bolin, Locust Grove, Oklahoma.

Admitted. Applicant's mother, Akee, and his grandparents Co-tak-quah-skee & Quc~~a~~tsy (or Quatsy) were enrolled by Drennen in Tahl. District #23.

App: 2129 Mary Sanders, Locust Grove, Oklahoma.

Admitted. Half sister of #641 and claims through the same source.

App: 2130 Annie Feeling and 3 children, Locust Grove, Oklahoma.

Admitted. Daughter of #407.

App: 2131 Jim Sanders, Locust Grove, Oklahoma.
Admitted. Nephew of #407.
App: 2132 Tom Blossom, Locust Grove, Oklahoma.
Admitted. Brother of #78 and claims through the same source.
App: 2133 Jack Blossom, Locust Grove, Oklahoma.
Admitted. Brother of #78 and claims through the same source.
App: 2134 Cynthia Downing, Locust Grove, Oklahoma.
Admitted. Niece of #178 and claims through the same source.
App: 2135 Ned Downing, Peggs, Oklahoma.
Admitted. Nephew of No. 178 and claims through the same source.
App: 2136 Mollie Wilkerson, Locust Grove, Oklahoma.
Admitted. Niece of #178 and claims through the same source.
App: 2137 Nancy Goingsnake and 3 children, Rose, Oklahoma.
Admitted. Daughter of James Rowe. Appl. #195, who was enrolled by Drennen, Group #22 Flint.
App: 2138 Betsy Rowe, Rose, Oklahoma.
Admitted. Daughter of James Rowe, Appl. No. 195, who was enrolled by Drennan[sic], Group No. 22 Flint.
App: 2139 Thomas Goingsnake, Rose, Oklahoma.
Admitted. Claimant's father and paternal grandparents enrolled by Drennan[sic]-Delaware No. 835.
App: 2140 Susie Smith, Locust Grove, Oklahoma.
Admitted. Sister of #189. Father of applicant enrolled in 1851 Saline #212.
App: 2141 Dora Vann, Locust Grove, Oklahoma.
Admitted. Applicant's father was not living in 1851. Grandmother was enrolled as Oo-te-ee Vann. Great grandfather was enrolled as We Vann. Great Uncle enrolled as Ca-gou-cah Vann. Tahl. #569. See Misc. Test No. P. 4264.
App: 2142 Josphine Ross and 2 children, Locust Grove, Okla.
Admitted. Niece of #1859.
App: 2143 Nancy Nolen and 1 child, Big Cabin, Oklahoma.
Admitted. Claimant's father enrolled by Dreennen[sic] in 1851. Del. #81. Father's brother and sister enrolled in Del. #103 and 104. See Misc. Test. P. 4382.
App: 2144 Charley Hughes, Rose, Oklahoma.
Rejected. Applicant was enrolled with his mother, Mary Hughes and sisters, Group 57 on the old Settler roll. Misc. Test P. 3579.
App: 2145 Martha J. Ward, Grove, Oklahoma.
Admitted. Aunt of #1746 and claims through the same ancestors. Mother of applicant, Lucy Nidiffer, enrolled in Disputed District No. 9.
App: 2146 Geo. M. Ward, Grove, Oklahoma.
Admitted. Claims through self enrolled as George Melton. Mother enrolled as Narcissa Melton. Sisters enrolled as Nancy, Lucy and Mary Melton. Dis. #28.
App: 2146-1/2 Nellie M. Blevins, Grove, Oklahoma.
By A. Blevins, Gdn.
Admitted. Granddaughter of #2146. Claims through the same source.

App: 2147 William Clark, and 4 children, Grove, Oklahoma.
Admitted. Nephew to William T. Melton (2158) and claims from the same

source. Mother of Applicant enrolled in 1851, as Nancy Melton, in Disputed District #28.
App: 2148 William H. Parsons for his children, Silas Creek, N.C.
Rejected. Sizemore case. See special report #417.
App: 2149 Charlotte F. Johnson, Afton, Oklahoma.
Admitted. Sister of #615 and claims through the same source.
App: 2150 Susan M. Carr, Grove, Oklahoma.
Admitted. Sister of #2150.
App: 2151 Johnson C. Parks and 3 children, Cowskin, McDonald Co., Missouri.
Admitted. Brother of #1877.
App: 2152 Richard T. Parks, Chelsea, Oklahoma.
Admitted. Applicant is the father of #1064. " enrolled " Chapman 1602".
App: 2153 Ruth A. Tyler and 5 children, Bluejacket, Okla.
Admitted. Aunt of #874. Half sister of #1572.
App: 2154 Mary Falling, Vinita, Oklahoma.
Admitted. Applicant's father, Thirsty Tiger, was enrolled by Drennen in Delaware District #842.
App: 2155 Martha J. Mitchell and 7 children, Blue Jacket, Oklahoma.
Admitted. Cousin of #1601. R.F.D. 1.
App: 2156 Nellie Hoskin, Vinita, Oklahoma.
Admitted. Half-Sister of #1231 and claims through the same father, Chu-noo-lees-kie.
App: 2157 Amanda Cherokee Scott and 2 children, Vinita, Oklahoma.
Admitted. Applicant and her mother, Sina Duncan, were enrolled by Drennen in G S. District #361.
App: 2158 William T. Melton and 7 children, Love, Oklahoma.
Admitted. Applicant claims through Mother, Norcissa Melton enrolled in Disputed District, Group 28. Applicants Grand mother Nancy Carroll enrolled Dis. 25. Misc. Test. P. 3692.
App: 2159 Aggie Cookson and 4 children, Cookson, Oklahoma.
Admitted. Sister of #2119.
App: 2160 John C. Goodrich and 1 child, Stilwell, Oklahoma.
Admitted. Applicant's grandparents, Sar-ta-Gah & Ki-hu-Gah were enrolled by Drennen in Flint District. #391.
App: 2161 Mr. Joe Russel, Oaks, Oklahoma.
Admitted. Son of #6601. Grandmother of app. Dorcas Foster, was enrolled by Drennen in Delaware District #793. Misc. Test P. 3721, 3718.
App: 2162 Daniel Russell and 1 child, Oaks, Oklahoma.
Admitted. Son of #6601. Brother of #2161.
App: 2163 Katie Bolyn and 5 children, Cookson, Oklahoma.
Admitted. Sister of #970.
App: 2164 Eliza Cookson and 4 children, Cookson, Oklahoma.
Admitted. Sister of #2119
App: 2165 Thomas J. Pettit, Cookson, Oklahoma.

Admitted. Brother of #2119.

App: 2166 Alex (Tuxy) Ballard and 8 children, Braggs, Oklahoma.

Admitted. Brother of #1596 and claims through the same ancestors.

App: 2167 Richard Lovett and 4 children, Cookson, Oklahoma.

Admitted. First Cousin of #2119.

App: 2168 William W. Fields and 10 children, Las Animas, Col.

Admitted. Nephew of #1353 and claims through the same ancestors. Mother of applicant, Malvina Fields, (Weir) enrolled in 1851, in Delaware District, No. 78.

App: 2168 1/2 Edward Fields, Chetopa, Kansas.

Admitted. By Nellie Fields, Guardian. Son of App. #2168. Grand-nephew of #1353, and claims through the same ancestors.

App: 2169 John R. Pettit, Cookson, Oklahoma.

Admitted. Brother of #2119.

App: 2170 Albert Fields and 8 children, Blue Jacket, Oklahoma.

Admitted. Nephew of #1353 and claims through the same ancestors. Mother of applicant Malvina Fields, (Weir) enrolled in 1851, in Delaware District No. 78.

App: 2171 Sarah Jane Martin and 6 children, Manard, Oklahoma.

Admitted. Sister to #562. Claims through exactly same source. "536 Tahl."

App: 2172 Alice Smith, Grove, Oklahoma.

Admitted. Niece to William T. Melton, (2158) and claims from the same source. Mother of applicant enrolled in 1851, as Nancy Melton, in Disputed District #28.

App: 2173 Mary Parkhurst and 4 children, Grove, Oklahoma.

Admitted. Niece to William T. Melton (2158) and claims from the same group. Mother of applicant enrolled in 1851 as Nancy Melton, in Disputed District #28.

App: 2174 Dollie E. Martin and 3 children, Manard, Oklahoma.

Admitted. Sister to #562. Claims through same source. "536 Tahl.".

App: 2175 Washington H. Eiffeit Ft. Gibson, Oklahoma.

Admitted. Mother of applicant, Margaret A.W. Eiffeit or Morgan enrolled in 1851 on Chapman #1558. Applicant enrolled by Chapman #1564. Misc. Test. P. 3454.

App: 2176 Margaret P. McClelland, We~~b~~ber Falls, Oklahoma.

Admitted. Sister of #217(?) (*Last number looks like a Handwritten 5.*) Applicant enrolled in 1851 by Chapman No. 1561.

App: 2177 Bettie J. Lindsey, Texana, Oklahoma.

Admitted. Sister of #2175. Applicant enrolled in 1851 by Chapman #1559.

App: 2178 Robert T. Hanks and 1 child, We~~b~~ber Falls, Oklahoma.

Admitted. Brother of #2175. Applicant enrolled in 1851 on Chapman No. 1562.

App: 2179 Elizabeth Walker, Ft. Gibson, Oklahoma.

Admitted. Mother of #13 and admitted for same reasons.

App: 2180 Jack Walker, Ft. Gibson, Oklahoma.

Admitted. Brother of #13 and claims through the same source.

App: 2181 Kate Flenoye nee Phillips and 1 child, Ft. Gibson, Oklahoma.

Admitted. Admitted through Illinois 87. See special report below:

Application #2181 and others grouped therewith.

By comparing the application of Kate Flenoye, nee Osage, #2181, with that of Charles Osage, #13762, we find that they are brother and sister, their parents being Sam Osage and Lesey Osage. Referring to the application of Charles Osage, #13762, for the reason that there is more information contained therein than in the application of his sister #2181, we find that the grandmother of the said Charles Osage on his mother's side was Rachel U-ne-nu-de or Oo-na-noo-te and that he has an uncle by the name of Jim Phillips living at Braggs, Oklahoma and an aunt, Lucy U-ne-nu-di. Referring to application #11189 we find it to be that of James Phillips of Braggs, Oklahoma, the uncle of the applicant #13762. The mother of James Phillips was Rachel Phillips, nee Cornsilk. His grandfather was U-na-nude or U-ne-nu-de or Oo-na-noo-te. He has one sister living in 1851 by the name of Lucy Crawford and a brother born in 1856 by the name of Steve Phillips. Referring to application #12512 we find it to be the application of Nellie Phillips Christie, who was the daughter of the said Steve Phillips. In a letter on file in application #12512 applicant states that her father has a brother by the name of James Phillips living at Braggs, Oklahoma. Then applicant #12512 is the niece of applicant #11189. Referebee[sic] to the index of the rolls of 1851 shows that U-na-nude or U-ne-uude or Oo-na-noo-tee translated to English is Cornsilk.

In Illinois District, Group 87, the following persons were enrolled: Cornsilk, who was the great grandfather of applicant #2181, 13762 and 12512 and the grandfather of applicant #11189. Also enrolled in Group 87 is Nancy Cornsilk, who was the great aunt of applicant #2181, 13762 and 12512 and she is the aunt of applicant #11189. In the same group is enrolled Rachel Cornsilk, who was the grandmother of (*Handwritten between lines, applicants 2181, 13762 and 12512 and she is the mother of*) #11189. In Group 87 is also enrolled Lucinda Crawford, who is the first cousin once removed of applicant #2181 and 13762, the aunt of the applicant #12512 and the sister of applicant #11189.

These applicants being descendants of the persons enrolled in group 87 Illinois are therefore admitted.

App: 2182 William Vann, Ft. Gibson, Oklahoma.
Admitted. Claimant's father, supra 2183, and grandparents on the father's side, enrolled by Drennen in 1851, Tahl. 569. Paternal grandfather on the roll of 1835, page 51. Mother was going by the name of Thornton in 1851 and was enrolled with her son Thomas, S.B. 188. (See application #14040).

App: 2183 David Vann, Ft. Gibson, Oklahoma.
Admitted Father of #2182. Claims through the same source. Applicant enrolled in Tahl. District #569.

App: 2184 John Casey, Ft. Gibson, Oklahoma.
Admitted. Brother to 1298 and claims through the same source. Mother enrolled as Elizabeth Fields in Disputed District 32.

App: 2185 Samuel Hilderbrand and 3 children, Estella, Oklahoma.
Admitted. Nephew of #1351 and claims through the same ancestors. Father of applicant, Benjamin Hilderbrand, enrolled in 1851, in Delaware District No. 378.

App: 2186 Ezra Hilderbrand, White Oak, Oklahoma.
Admitted. Nephew of #1351 and claims through the same source. Father of applicant, Benjamin Hilderbrand enrolled in 1851 in Delaware District #378.

App: 2187 Lucinda Hilderbrand, Estella, Oklahoma.
Admitted. Niece of #1351 and claims through the same ancestors. Father of applicant, Benjamin Hilderbrand enrolled in 1851 in Delaware District #378.

App: 2188 Eli Wilson and 2 children, Welling Oklahoma.
Admitted. Nephew of 936.

App: 2189 George Wilson and 1 child, Welling Oklahoma.
Admitted. Nephew of #936.

App: 2190 Dick Pann.
Duplicate of #376.

App: 2191 William C. Wilson, Wichita, Kansas.
Rejected. It does not appear that any ancestor was ever enrolled or that any ancestor was a party to the treaties of 1835-6 and 1846. Ancestors did not live in the Cherokee domain. Rejected by the Dawes Commission. Misc. Test. #2026.

App: 2192 Jacob Wilson and 3 children, Wichita, Kansas.
Rejected. Nephew of #2191.

App: 2193 Lifus Rains and five children, Hightower, Ga.
Rejected. Brother to Nancy Rains, #1163.

App: 2194 G. Thomas Ridge and 7 children, Whitewell, Tenn.
Rejected. It does not appear that applicant or any of his ancestors were ever enrolled. It does not appear that they were living within the Cherokee Nation in 1835-6 and 1846 as recognized members of the tribe. Misc. Test P. 164.

App: 2195 James D. Ridge and 1 child, Whitewell, Tenn.
Rejected. Brother of #2194.

App: 2196 William J. Ridge and 8 children, Whitewell, Tenn.
Rejected. Brother of #2194.

App: 2197 Charles Ridge and 2 children, Whitewell, Tenn.
Rejected. Cousin of #2194.

App: 2198 Ida Locust, Stilwell, Oklahoma.
Admitted. Applicant is proven to be an immigrant Cherokee through Misc. Test. of Locust (Ida), P. 3260. (*Handwritten and 4018 and also thru that of Sawney taken at Stilwell*) Mar. 20, 1909. p. 4018.

App: 2199 Susan Carnes and 4 children, Kansas, Oklahoma.
Admitted. Cousin of #866.

App: 2200 John William Pierce, Nowata, Oklahoma.
Admitted. Claimant is a first cousin once removed to #614 and claims through the same source.

App: 2201 Sarah Josephine Beck, Kansas, Oklahoma.
Admitted. Niece of #132.

App: 2202 Diannah Carnes, Flint, Oklahoma.
Admitted. Sister of #132.

App: 2203 Elizabeth Carnes, Flint, Oklahoma.
Admitted. Niece of #132.

App: 2204 Mary F.S. Bell, Vinita, Oklahoma.
Admitted. Applicant herself was enrolled by Drennen in G.S. Dist. #309.

App: 2205 Lucian B. Bell, Vinita, Oklahoma.
Admitted. Applicant's father, John A. Bell, enrolled in 1851, Del. 868. Sister of applicant, Ann Bell, enrolled in 1851, Del. 868. Applicant enrolled in 1851 Delaware #868. Dawes Commission #8673. Misc. Test #P[sic]. 3641.

App: 2206 Moses Welch, Siloam Springs, Ark.
Admitted. Grandnephew of #132.

App: 2207 Jane Sunday and 1 child, Oaks, Oklahoma.
Admitted. Claims through grandfather as Jesse Sunday, Saline 77; great-grandfather, Sunday, Saline 81; great uncle William Sunday Saline 80; David and Thomas, great uncles, Saline 81. Great aunts, Jane and Nelly Sunday, all enrolled by Drennen in 1851, Saline District, Group #77-80-81.
App: 2208 Lucy Hilderbrand, Oaks, Oklahoma.
Admitted. Cousin to #2207.
App: 2209 William Sunday, Oaks, Oklahoma.
Admitted. Brother to #2209[sic].
App: 2210 Maria Feelin, Oaks, Oklahoma.
Admitted. Claims through the same source as #2207.
App: 2211 Lewis Feeling and 2 children, Kansas, Oklahoma.
Admitted. Applicant's father enrolled by Drennen 1851 Del. #594. Misc. Test P. 3876.
App: 2212 Laura Sunday, Oaks, Oklahoma.
Admitted. Sister to #2207.
App: 2213 Susie Hart and 1 child, Oaks, Oklahoma.
Admitted. Sister of #2207.
App: 2214 Reese Thornton and 3 children, Chance, Oklahoma.
Admitted. Nephew to #130.
App: 2215 Maggie Ragsdale and 1 child, Chance, Oklahoma.
Admitted. Niece of #130.
App: 2216 Mary M. Brown, Chance, Oklahoma.
Admitted. Applicant's mother enrolled by Drennen 1851. G.S. #409.
App: 2217 Margaret Proctor, Ballard, Oklahoma.
Rejected. Applicant enrolled as an old settler. G.S. #41.
App: 2218 Polly Morris and 3 children, Chance, Oklahoma.
Admitted. Niece of #130.
App: 2219 Sarah Bird and 2 children, Stilwell, Oklahoma.
Admitted. Sister of 2198.
App: 2220 Taton L. Ray and 1 child, Wilscot, Ga.
Rejected. Son of #776 and claims through the same source.
App: 2221 Susie Mayes and 9 children, Afton, Oklahoma.
Admitted. Sister of #1820.
App: 2222 Mary Carter, Muskogee, Oklahoma.
Admitted. Applicant enrolled by Drennen 1851. Ill. #179.
App: 2223 Lucy Lynch Muskogee, Oklahoma.
Admitted. Sister of #2222. Applicant enrolled in 1851 in Ill. #179.
App: 2224 Walter Youngwolf, Proctor, Oklahoma.
Admitted. Applicant's mother enrolled by Drennen 1851-Del. #165. Misc. Test No. P. 3355.
App: 2225 Job. Alexander and 5 children, Westville, Oklahoma.
Admitted. Son of #1639 and claims through the same source.
App: 2226 Betsy Walkingstick and 2 children, Baron, Oklahoma.
Admitted. Sister of #2224. Mother of applicant enrolled in 1851 in Goingsnake #165.

App: 2227 Sarah Sixkiller, Tahlequah, Oklahoma.
Admitted. Niece of #1129. Mother of applicant enrolled in 1851 Tahlequah #279.
App: 2228 Jesse Sixkiller, Gdn. Tahlequah, Oklahoma.
Admitted. Grandmother of Fay Dew enrolled by Drennen 1851. Ill. #238.
App: 2229 Fannie Morris and 7 children, Ballard, Oklahoma.
Admitted. Cousin of #1601.
App: 2230 Susan Hawk and 2 children, Melvin, Oklahoma.
Admitted. Aunt of #618.
App: 2231 John Hawk, Melvin, Oklahoma.
Admitted. Applicant's mother enrolled by Drennen 1851. Del. #660.
App: 2232 Alexander Raper and 1 child, Culberson, N.C.
Admitted. Applicant enrolled by Chapman #1435 in 1851 under name of Alexander Raper.
App: 2233 Kathleen Wilkes and 1 child, Tahlequah, Oklahoma.
Admitted. Applicant's mother enrolled by Drennen 1851. G.S. #217.
App: 2234 Jennie Marrs, Welling, Oklahoma.
Admitted. Applicant's mother enrolled by Drennen 1851. Flint #283.
App: 2235 Charles Marrs, Welling, Oklahoma.
Admitted. Applicant is grandchild of Lydia Goback. Nos. 9387 and #1413.
App: 2236 Ethel Sixkiller, Tahlequah, Oklahoma.
Admitted. (*Handwritten Admitted.*) Sister of #2233. Sarah Sixkiller, applicant's mother is guardian of same and enrolled in G.S. #217.
App: 2237 Webster M. Vann and 2 children, Pryor Creek, Oklahoma.
Admitted. Applicant's father, James Vann, enrolled in 1851 in Delaware District #854. Applicant enrolled in 1851 in Delaware District #854. Misc. Test. p. 3615.
App: 2238 Ermina C. Mayes, Pryor Creek, Oklahoma.
Admitted. Sister #2237.
App: 2239 Mary L. Jones and 3 children, Murphy, N. C. R.F.D. #1
Rejected. Cousin of #126, and claims through the same source.
App: 2240 John Davis, Wilscot, Ga.
Rejected. Claims through same source as #690.
App: 2241 Ada Myrtle Tuck and 2 children, Brighton, Mo.
Rejected. Claims through Alex Brown. See special report #35.
App: 2242 Marvilla O. Sharp and 2 children, Brighton, Mo.
Rejected. Claims through Alex Brown, See special report #35.
App: 2243 Alice Sampson and 2 children, Montague, Texas.
Rejected. Also Myrtle Garrison. Nieces of #375. Daughters of #548.
App: 2244 Walter Manar, Westville, Oklahoma.
Rejected. Son of #532.
App: 2245 James A. Manar, Westville, Oklahoma.
Rejected. Son of #532.
App: 2246 Emery F. Sharp and 2 children, Brighton, Mo.
Rejected. Claims through Alex Brown. See special report #35.

App: 2247 Susan Tanner, Claremore, Oklahoma.
Rejected. Cousin of #551, and claims through the same ancestors.
App: 2248 David McKinney and 3 children, Presley, Ga.
Rejected. Blythe case. See special Report #153.
App: 2249 Wm. E. Franklin and 5 children, Dalton, Ga.
Rejected. Brother of #375 and claims through same source. (Note: number is not clear, could be #375 or #315.)
App: 2250 Dovis M. Jones and 3 children, Tulsa, Oklahoma.
Rejected. Sister of #1312.
App: 2251 Mary C. Payne, Coffeyville, Kansas.
Rejected. First cousin of #1312.
App: 2252 Dorcus L. Kephart and 5 children, Grandview, N.C.
Rejected. Blythe case. See special report #153.
App: 2253 Ellen E. Howell, 69 North 48th Street, New York, N.Y.
Admitted. Daughter of #29 and claims through the same source.
App: 2254 Amanda Holbrook and 5 children, Buren, Ga.
Rejected. Daughter of #529 and claims through the same ancestors.
App: 2255 Lillie Sneed and 5 children, Grandview, N.C.
Rejected. Blythe case. See special report #153.
App: 2256 Nancy C. Sandlin and 1 child, Andrews, N.C.
Rejected. Daughter of #664 and claims through the same source.
App: 2257 Vernon E. Tanner, Claremore, Oklahoma.
Rejected. Cousin of #551 and claims through the same ancestors.
App: 2258 Charles C. Lane and 5 children, Roff, Oklahoma.
Rejected. Son of #744.
App: 2259 William A. Parker, Grove, I.T.
Rejected. Blythe case. See special report #153.
App: 2260 Lillie A.F. Broyden and 3 children, Atlanta, Ga.
Rejected. Blythe case. See special report #153.
App: 2261 John A Nicholson and 1 child, Grandview, N.C.
Rejected. Blythe case. See special report #153.
App: 2262 Lucy Turpin and 4 children, Hiawassie, Ga.
Rejected. Blythe case. See special report #153.
App: 2263 Boudinot Swan, Bushyhead, Oklahoma.
Admitted. Son of #815.
App: 2264 George W. Goble and 4 children, Quarles, Ga.
Admitted. Uncle to #24. Son of #1521.
App: 2265 James Starr and 6 children, Evansville, Arkansas.
Admitted. Applicant's mother enrolled by Drennen 1851. Flint #407. Misc. Test P. 3300.
App: 2266 Lydia Duck and 3 children, Stilwell, Oklahoma.
Admitted. The grandparents of the applicant were enrolled in Flint District 322 by Drennen in 1851 under the names of Feather and Quaity.

App: 2267 Annie Spade, Christie, Oklahoma.
Admitted. Applicant's mother, Ta-kee enrolled in 1851 in Going Snake #544. Brother of applicant Oo-squa-lu-sker enrolled in Going Snake #544. Dawes Commission No. 29105. Misc. Test P. 3264.

App: 2268 Nannie Horner, Kansas, Oklahoma.
Admitted. Daughter of #721 and claims through grandmother Sarah Keener or Sallie Wilson. 29 Del.

App: 2269 Charlotte French and 2 children, Stilwell, Oklahoma.
Admitted. Applicant's father (De-gah-ne-ye-sky-Jackson Killer) was enrolled in Flint #472. See testimony of Charlotte French taken at Stilwell, Oklahoma. March 20, 1909 p. 4017.

App: 2270 Fannie Starr and 1 child, Stilwell, Oklahoma.
Admitted. Sister of #2265. Mother of applicant enrolled in Flint #407.

App: 2271 Jennie Cornsilk, Stilwell, Oklahoma.
Admitted. Applicant's mother enrolled by Drennen 1851. G.S. #544.

App: 2272 Nancy Swimmer, Stilwell, Oklahoma.
Admitted. Applicant enrolled by Drennen 1852. Cah-ta-ky, Flint 153.

App: 2273 Hugh M. Adair, Stilwell, Oklahoma.
Admitted. Applicant enrolled by Drennen 1851. Flint #237.

App: 2274 Sarah Ganzilas and 4 children, Stilwell, Oklahoma.
Admitted. Sister of #2266, and claims through same source.

App: 2275 Oodahye Weavel and 1 grandchild, Stilwell, Oklahoma.
Admitted. Aunt of #2266, claims through same source.

App: 2276 Sallie Feather,
Duplicate of #1169.

App: 2277 Jennie Daughty, Stilwell, Oklahoma.
Admitted. Daughter of #2272.

App: 2278 Lossie Jones and 4 children, Stilwell, Oklahoma.
Admitted. Cousin of #2266 and claims through the same source.

App: 2279 Necked French, Stilwell, Oklahoma.
Admitted. Cousin to #2266.

App: 2280 Jennie Feather, Stilwell, Oklahoma.
Admitted. Aunt of #2266 and claims through same source.

App: 2281 Annie Feather and 1 child, Stilwell, Oklahoma.
Admitted. Cousin of #3296 and claims through the same source.

App: 2282 Cora Kingfisher, Oaks, Oklahoma.
Admitted. Applicant's mother enrolled by Drennen 1851. Sal. 297. See Misc. Test 3750.

App: 2283 Lydia Santafee, Oaks, Oklahoma.
~~Rejected~~. (*Handwritten Admitted.)* Claims through self enrolled as Lydia Sleeve. Mother and Father enrolled as Na-hee and Robert Sleeve. Brothers and sisters enrolled as Fesse[sic], Daniel, Wa-kee and Te-wo-yee and Jenny. Tahl. #388.

App: 2284 Lula Fluke and 6 children, Cleora, Oklahoma.
Admitted Applicant's grandmother enrolled by Drennen 1851. Del. #319.

App: 2285 Vennie, Minnie and Evalys Grass, ~~Afton~~, Oklahoma.
Louis More. Guardian (*Handwritten above, Collinsville*)

Rejected. Minors claim their Indian blood through their father who derived his Indian blood from his mother Katy Grass. Katy Grass was first married to a man named Goodwin and is enrolled as an old settler on Roll Flint 17. Minors are first cousins to number 23589, which see for children of Katy Grass by former marriage to Goodwin. See Misc. Test. p. 4384.

App: 2286 William H. Donaldson and 3 children, Afton, Oklahoma.
Admitted. (Ola M., Jessie A. and Arthur Donaldson, through their father and gdn.) Half nephew and nieces of Sarah E. McLaughlin #250.

App: 2287 David W. Vann and 6 children, Fairland, Oklahoma.
Admitted. Brother of #1111 and claims through the same source.

App: 2288 Charmer M. Jones, Cleora, Oklahoma.
Admitted. Applicant is nephew of No. 1034 and admitted for same reasons. Applicant's mother #2063 Chapman.

App: 2289 Victoria Barks and 3 children, Vinita, Oklahoma.
Admitted. Applicant's grandparents enrolled by Drennen 1851. Del. #929. Applicant's father enrolled in same group.

App: 2290 Laura Hilderbrand and 6 children, Vinita, Oklahoma.
Admitted. Niece of #8741 and claims through the same source.

App: 2291 Wallace Hilderbrand and 3 children, Vinita, Oklahoma.
Admitted. Nephew of #1351 and claims through the same ancestors.

App: 2292 Lovie M. Green, Vinita, Oklahoma.
Admitted. Sister of #377.

App: 2293 Nelson Foreman and 6 children, Chelsea, Oklahoma.
Admitted. Brother of #773 and claims through the same source.

App: 2294 Peggie Sullivan, Claremore, Oklahoma.
Admitted. Niece of #1333; claims through the same source.

App: 2295 Frank Sullivan and 1 child, Claremore, Oklahoma.
Admitted. 1st. cousin of #709. Grandfather Geo. McPherson, G.S. 434. Mother, Mary McPherson, 434 G.S.

App: 2296 Frances R. [illegible]s(*Handwritten above, Edens*) Needmore, Oklahoma.
Admitted. Applicant is niece of #1034 and admitted for same reasons. Applicant's father enrolled as "2059 Chapman".

App; 2297 George Proctor and 2 children, Stilwell, Oklahoma.
Admitted. Applicant's father enrolled by Drennen 1851. Flint 420. Misc. Test p. 3308.

App: 2298 Susie Frogg and 1 child, Stilwell, Oklahoma.
Admitted. Aunt of #2266, claims through the same source.

App: 2299 Jennie Scullowe and 3 children, Bartlesville, Okla.
Admitted. Applicant claims through Judge Bottle enrolled in Tahl. Dist. Group #370.

App: 2300 Ollie Morrison and 4 children, Marble, N.C.
Admitted. Niece of #1815 and claims through the same source.

App: 2301 Floda M. Tuck and 1 child, Brighton, Mo.
Rejected. Claims thru Alex. Brown. See special report #35.

App: 2302 Ben M. Dockey and 5 children, Grandview, N.C.
Rejected. Blythe case. See special report #153.

App: 2303 Sarah A. Fender, Brighton, Mo.
Rejected. Claims thru Alex. Brown. See special report #35.
App: 2304 Susan A. Mooney and 6 children, Andrews, N.C.
Rejected. Sister of #7 and claims through the same source.
App: 2305 Nancy C. Presley and 2 children, Willard, Mo. R.F.D. #2.
Rejected. Claims thru Alex Brown. See special report No. 35.
App: 2306 Fannie Presley, Presley, Ga.
Rejected. Blythe case. See special report #153.
App: 2307 Letitia F. Colding, Savannah, Ga. (213 Thirty-second St.)
Admitted. Enrolled by Hester, #2348, as Letitia Pooler and by Chapman under some name at #2121. Applicant is daughter of Williamina Cleland, Chap. #2118. Applicant is a sister of #29.
App: 2308 Linder Pendergrass, Culberson, N.C.
Rejected. Daughter of #529 and claism[sic] through the same ancestors.
App: 2309 Dovie M. Jones,
Rejected. Same as #2250.
App: 2310 Maybell Stroud, Presley, Ga.
Rejected. Blythe case. See special Report #153.
App: 2311 Victoria Cathey and 2 children, Maysville, Ga.
Rejected. Blythe case. See special Report No. 153.
App: 2312 Sarah J. Davis and 2 children, Grandview, N.C.
Rejected. Blythe case. See special report #153.
App: 2313 Nancy Comwell and 3 children, Murphy, N.C.
Rejected. Blythe case. See special report #153.
App: 2314 Phoebe Dockery, Murphy, N.C.
Rejetced[sic]. Blythe case. See special report #153.
App: 2315 Martha E. White and 5 children, Grandview, N.C.
Rejected. Blythe case. See special report #153.
App: 2316 John J. Carter and 3 children, Padena, Ga.
Rejected. nephew of #32 and claims through the same source.
App: 2317 Mary M. Young and 3 children, x Grandview, N.C.
Rejected. Blythe case. See special report #153.
App: 2318 Dona Bell Hendricks and 4 children, Claremore, Oklahoma.
Rejected. Cousin of #551 and claims through the same source.
App: 2319 Albert L. Tanner, Claremore, Oklahoma.
Rejected. Cousin of #551 and claims through the same ancestors.
App: 2320 Eli Crutchfield, et al, Claremore, Oklahoma.
Sarah Crutchfield.
Rejected. There is a Joseph Crutchfield #498 Del. but application #3010 shows this case has no connection with the #498 Del. The grandfather, Joseph, was living in 1851 but not enrolled at that time. There is and[sic] Edward Crutchfield enrolled but nothing in testimony to show any connection. The John Crutchfield is the father of Joseph in 498 Del. and not of Joseph, the grandfather of the applicant. Misc. Test. p. 4123.

App: 2321 Julia Holbrook and 4 children, Buren, Ga.
Rejected. Daughter of #529 and claims through the same ancestors.
App: 2322 Mary Crutchfield, Claremore, Oklahoma.
Rejected. Sister to Eli Crutchfield (2320) and claims from the same source.
App: 2323 Charlie W. Avery and 6 children, Lamasco, Texas.
Rejected. Nephew to #744.
App: 2324 Sarah J.T. McClintock, Roff, Oklahoma.
Rejected. It does not appear that applicant's ancestors were parties to treaties of 1835-6 or 46. Never shared in payments to Cherokees, nor enrolled with them. Misc. Test. p. 2203.
App: 2325 James M. Loveless, Moneta, Cal.
Rejected. Claims thru Elizabeth Eddings, daughter of Dave Weaver. See Special report #45.
App: 2326 Jessie V. Brown, Aldrich, Mo.
Rejected. Claims thru Alex Brown. See special report #35.
App: 2327 Frankie Garrison, c/o Belva A. Lockwood, Wash. D.C.
Rejected. Nephew of #375. Son of #10146.
App: 2328 Asa Eliz. Fender Brighton, Mo.
Rejected. (*Handwritten Rejected.*) Claims thru Alex. Brown. See special report #35.
App: 2329 Joseph Dockery and 4 children, Murphy, N.C.
Rejected. Blythe case. See special report #153.
App: 2330 Harriet L. Avery, Sulphur, Oklahoma.
Rejected. Sister-in-law of #744.
App: 2331 Lillian Brock, Maysville, Ga.
Rejected. Blythe case. See special report #153.
App: 2332 Martin V. York and 1 child, Mena, Arkansas.
Rejected. It does not appear that any ancestor was ever enrolled or that any ancestor was party to the treaties of 1835-6 and 1846. Shows no connection with the Eastern Cherokees; ancestors did not live in the Cherokee domain. Misc. Test pp. 2085 and 2291.
App: 2333 Jane Ralings and 1 child, Buren, Ga.
Rejected. Daughter of #529 and claims through the same ancestors.
App: 2334 Eliza Elmer and Olie Brown and 3 children, Aldrich, Mo.
Rejected. Claims thru Alex Brown. See special report No. 153.
App: 2335 Charley D. Franklin and 2 children, Spring Place, Ga.
Rejected. It does not appear that any ancestor was a party to the treaties of 1835-6 or 1846, nor does it appear that any ancestor was ever enrolled; shows no real connections with the Eastern Cherokees. Misc. Test. p. 1428.
App: 2336 Timothy Daley and 2 children, Brushy, Oklahoma.
Admitted. Brother of #1376. Father of applicant enrolled in 1851 in Skin Bayou #194.
App: 2337 Missouri R. Gains (or Goins) and 3 children, Vian, Oklahoma.
Admitted. Sister of #1376. Father of applicant enrolled in Skin Bayou #194.
App: 2338 Homer (or Hamer) Daley, Vian, Oklahoma.
Admitted. Brother of #1376. Father of applicant enrolled in 1851 in Skin Bayou #194.

App: 2339 Franklin Gritts, Gritts, Oklahoma.
Admitted. Applicant enrolled by Drennen 1852. Flint District 102.
App: 2340 Mary M. Young, Peggs, Oklahoma.
Rejected. Applicant or ancestors were never enrolled. Does not appear that they were living within the limits of the Cherokee domain in 1835-6 or 1846 as recognized members of the tribe. Does not appear that they ever lived with the Cherokees as recognized members of the tribe. Misc. Test p. 4226.
App: 2341 Cora L. Gerboth and 1 child, Collinsville, Oklahoma.
Rejected. Sister of #1312. Claims thru same source.
App: 2342 William Buzzard and 2 children, Afton, Oklahoma.
Admitted. Claims through father enrolled as Keel-sah-ler-ke Del. #319.
App: 2343 Martha Taylor and 2 children, Afton, Oklahoma.
Admitted. Sister of #1375; claims thru same source.
App: 2344 Thompson Frogg and 2 children, Stilwell, Oklahoma.
Admitted. Applicant's parents enrolled by Drennen 1851. Flint 266. Misc. Test p. 3353.
App: 2345 Joshua Choate, Sallisaw, Oklahoma.
Admitted. Nephew of No. 1452 and claims thru the same source.
App: 2346 John C. Choate and 1 child, Tahlequah, Oklahoma.
Admitted. Nephew of #1452 and claims thru the same source. Applicant's mother, Liza Childress enrolled by Drennen, Flint #551.
App: 2347 Richard B. Choate and 2 children, Bunch, Oklahoma.
Admitted. Nephew of #1452 and claims thru the same source. Applicant's mother, Liza Choate enrolled by Drennen, Flint #551.
App: 2348 Laura M. Hunt and 4 children, Coffeyville, Kansas.
Admitted. Niece of #1178. Mother of applicant enrolled in 1851 by Chapman #1837.
App: 2349 Mollie Welch, By John Welch, Gdn. Ballard, Oklahoma.
Admitted. Grandniece of #132.
App: 2350 Bruce Welch, By Jno. Welch, Ballard, Oklahoma.
Admitted. Grandnephew of #132.
App: 2351 May (or Nay) Welch, by John Welch, Gdn. Ballard, Oklahoma.
Admitted. Grandnephew of #132.
App: 2352 David C. Davis, Hurlburt, Oklahoma.
Admitted. First cousin of #651. Mother of applicant enrolled Del. #589.
App: 2353 David C. Davis, Hurlburt, Oklahoma.
Admitted. Duplicate of #2352.
App: 2354 David C. Davis, Hurlburlt[sic], Oklahoma.
Admitted. Duplicate of #2352.
App: 2355 Martha Jane Houston, Tallequah[sic], Oklahoma.
Rejected. Applicant is a white woman claiming only through her husband who died Jan. 7, 1906.
App: 2356 Margaret Hartsell, Sanders, Ark.
Rejected. See report on Brumbello case below:

There are quite a number of persons who have filed application for participation in the Eastern Cherokee fund who base their claims solely on their relationship to one Elizabeth Brumbello, who, they allege, was a full blood Cherokee Indian.

The name Brumbello does not appear on the roll of 1835 or on the roll of 1851 nor do the names of any of these applicants appear on the Hester or any other subsequent roll.

The number of affidavits all to the same effect have been filed with these applications. These affidavits are sworn to by William E. Furr, a man 80 years old and George Washington Huneycupp, a man 75 years old, both residents of North Carolina, and the latter now dead. These affidavits state that the affiants were both personally acquainted with Elizabeth Brumbello, who married a white man by the name of Ezekiel Morton. They further allege that Elizabeth Brumbello was a full blood Cherokee Indian and that she lived in Stanly County, North Carolina?[sic] Stanly Co., is fully 200 miles from the Cherokee domain and there is nothing whatever to show that this Elizabeth Brumbello ever affiliated with the Cherkee tribe or in fact that she was a Cherokee at all. The evidence shows that she married Morton, who was a white man prior to 1835, and there is no evidence that she lived with the Cherokee tribe thereafter. In fact, there is no evidence whatever, that she ever lived with the Cherokee tribe. On the contrary, the only evidence there is shows that she was living at least 200 miles away from the Cherokee domain.

There seems to be no merit in these cases, as no ancestor of any of the applicants was ever enrolled, nor was any ancestor parties to the treaties of 1835-6 and 1846, nor is it shown that any ancestor ever lived with the tribe and it is shown that Elizabeth Brumbello, through whom all these applicants claim, never lived within the Cherokee domain.

For these reasons all of the applicants who base their claims upon Elizabeth Brumbello and her descendants are rejected.

App: 2357 Jackson L. Hartsell and 6 children, Malvern, Ark.
Rejected. Brumbello case. See special report #2356.

App: 2358 Jonas L. Hartsell and 5 children, Sanders, Ark.
Rejected. Brumbello case. See special report #2356.

App: 2359 Josephus Tucker, Sanders, Ark.
Rejected. Brumbello case. See special report #2356.

App: 2360 Ella Rogers and 1 child, Mountain Seam, Ga.
Rejected. Blythe case. See special report #153.

App: 2361 Mary E. Black and 4 children, McCays, Tenn.
Admitted. Great (*Handwritten niece)* of #423 and claims thru the same source. Applicant's father on Hester roll #1951 and grandmother on Chapman roll #1890.

App; 2362 Ishmael S. Fisher and 2 children, El Paso, Texas.
Rejected. Brother of #2324. (400 W. Boulevard).

App: 2363 Jacob M. Dockery and 5 children, Grandview, N.C.
Rejected. Blythe case. See special report No. 153.

App: 2364 Sarah J. Tucker, Athens, Tenn.
Rejected. Blythe case. See special report No. 153.

App: 2365 Green Cardell, Talking Rock, Ga.
Rejected. Kaziah[sic] Vann case. See special report #376.

App: 2366 Cicero K. Smith and 2 children, Marietta, Ga.
Admitted. Great nephew of #423 and claims thru same source. Applicant's father enrolled by Hester #1951.

App: 2367 John Brown, Murphy, N.C.
Rejected. Son of #2076 and shows no conection with the Eastern Cherokees; ancestors not being on the rolls and it not appearing that any ancestor was party to the treaties of 1835-6-or 46.

App: 2368 Austin C. Barber and 4 children, Wilson Creek, Wash.
Rejected. Son of Joanna Barber #1306 and claims thru the same source.

App: 2369 Isena J. House, Holly, Colorado
Rejected. Daughter of Jeana Barber #1306 and claims thru the same source.

App: 2370 Levi R. Eddings and 3 children, Vaness, Oklahoma.
Rejected. Claims thru Elizabeth Eddings, daughter of Dave Weaver. See special Report #45.

App: 2371 Vinney Deavers and 1 child, Presley, Ga.
Rejected. Blythe case. See special report ~~#35~~ #153.

App: 2372 Nancy Jane Datson and 4 children, Tomotla, N.C.
Rejected. Sister of #22626.

App: 2373 Lucena Long, Welch, Oklahoma.
Rejected. Aunt of #1312.

App: 2374 Lillie A. Chadwick, Oran, Ga.
Rejected. Kesiah Van[sic] case. See special report of #276.

App: 2375 Anie Longbird, Bunch, Oklahoma.
Admitted. Minor child of #2381. Enrolled with mother in #2381.

App: 2376 Spencer Stephens, Lometa, Oklahoma.
Admitted. Applicant enrolled by Drennen 1851. G.S. #429.

App: 2377 John J. Lovett, Cookson, Oklahoma.
Admitted. Nephew of #2119.

App: 2378 John Silk and 1 child, Maple, Oklahoma.
Admitted. Uncle of #1214. Father of applicant is on Drennen roll #212.

App: 2379 Maud Lane and 4 children, Chelsea, Oklahoma.
Admitted. This applicant's grandmother, Elizabeth Schrimsher and her mother, Mary Schrimsher, are enrolled by Drennen from Tahl. District under group #374.

App: 2380 Sallie C. McSpadden and 7 children, Chelsea, Oklahoma.
Admitted. Sister of Maud Lane, appl. #2379 and is admitted for the same reasons.

App: 2381 Jennie Longbird and 1 child, Bunch, Oklahoma.
Admitted. Applicant enrolled as Ti-ya-nih. Father and mother enrolled as Kaw-stah-nis-teh and Ah-nee-tuh. Sister of applicant enrolled as E-yah-nih. All were enrolled by Chapman in 1851. No's. 966 to 969 inc. See Misc. Test P. 3159.

App: 2382 James M. Wilson and 2 children, Turley, Okla.
Admitted. Claims thru mother enrolled as Rebecca Wilson. Sisters enrolled as Susannah and Isabella Wilson. Tahl. #59.

App: 2383 Ruby Rice. By Isabella Rush, Gdn. Muskogee, Oklahoma.
Admitted. Grandniece of #5322. Claims thru the same source.

App: 2384 Isabella Rush, Muskogee, Oklahoma.
Admitted. Sister of #2382. Enrolled as Isabella Wilson. Tahl. #59.

App: 2385 Lewis W. Coodey, Fawn, Oklahoma.
Admitted. Nephew of #71 and claims thru the same source. By Martha L. Coodey, Gdn.
App: 2386 Benj. L. Coodey, Fawn, Oklahoma.
Admitted. By Martha L. Coodey, Gdn. Brother of #71 and claims thru the same source.
App: 2387 Myrtle U.Coodey, Fawn, Oklahoma.
Admitted. By Martha L. Coodey, Gdn. Sister of #71 and claims thru the same source.
App: 2388 Miriam M. Ballard and 3 children, Needmore, Oklahoma.
Admitted. First cousin to William T. Melton (2158) and claims from the same source. Father of applicant, Fincher Monroe, enrolled in Disputed District No. 30.
App: 2389 Annie Warneke and 7 children, Black Gumm, Oklahoma.
Admitted. Claims thru father, David Alexander. Tal. #60 Grand parents and their children. Tahl. #60. Misc. Test. P. 2898.
App: 2390 Charles F. Watt, Cookson, Oklahoma.
Admitted. First Cousin once removed of #700.
App: 2391 Pheasant Christie, Stilwell, Oklahoma.
Admitted. Nephew of #1841.
App: 2392 Mary Redbird, Stilwell, Oklahoma.
Admitted. Applicant's father enrolled by Drennen 1851. Del. #777.
App: 2393 Smith Longbird, Bunch, Oklahoma.
Admitted. Son of #2381 and claims thru the same source.
App: 2394 Charles Wolfe, Stilwell, Oklahoma.
Admitted. Applicant claims thru mother, Elizabeth Jones, G.S. #239 (now Elizabeth Wolfe) #2492.
App: 2395 Jonathan M. Taylor, Nina, N.C.
Rejected. Applicant clams[sic] to be son of James Taylor, son of Daniel and Polly, nee Bigley, and claims Cherokee blood thru him only. Applicant, however, is not child of James Taylor, as James secured divorce from wife and did not live with her after 1870. Applicant was born in 1874. (See evidence in application, marked "Exhibit A".)
App: 2396 Lucy Christie, Stilwell, Oklahoma.
Admitted. Sister to #2394. Claims thru Mother, Elizabeth Jones, enrolled #329 G.S. (now Elizabeth Wolf).
App: 2397 Emiline Good, Collinsville, Oklahoma.
Admitted. Great aunt of #180.
App: 2398 Wiley Long, Sr. Higdon's Store, Ga.
Rejected. Applicant claims thru Cheasquaha. There is a Cheasquaha on Chapman's Roll, but applicant fails to prove genuine relationship to this party. Ancestors were not enrolled. Were not parties to treaties of 1835-'36 or '46. Does not prove that ancestors were ever recognized members of Cherokee tribe. Evidence not of sufficient strength to entitle applicant's claim to be admitted. Misc. Test. p. 1434, 1435 and 1580.
App: 2399 Peggy A. Harlow and 5 children, Chetopa, Oklahoma.
Admitted. Applicant's grandmother enrolled by Drennen 1851. Del #927? (Last number looks like a seven over a six.)
App: 2400 Geo. W. Ewers and 6 children, Hollow, Oklahoma.
Admitted. Brother of #2399 and claims thru the same source.

App: 2401 Oden C. Hill and 1 child, Perryville, W. Va.
Admitted. Niece of #361.
App: 2402 Neoma E. Booker, Chilhowie, Va.
Rejected. Sizemore case. See special report #417.
App: 2403 Myrtle B. Baldwin, White Top, Va.
Rejected. Sizemore case. See special Report #417.
App: 2404 Cecero M. Baldwin and 7 children, White Top, Va.
Rejected. Sizemore case. See special Report #417.
App: 2405 Walter E. Trainor, Amarillo, Texas.
Admitted. Brother of #741 and claims through the same source.
App: 2406 Susan Hall and 1 child, Big Cabin, Oklahoma.
Admitted. Niece of #1473 and claims thru the same source. Applicant's mother, Nancy Guess, enrolled by Drennen Del. #103.
App: 2407 Joseph W. Davis and 4 children, Adair, Oklahoma.
Admitted. First cousin of #98 and claims thru the same source.
App: 2408 Jennie H. Rogers, Greenbriar, Oklahoma.
Admitted. Applicant enrolled by Drennen 1851. Tahl. #464. (*Handwritten Misc. Test. P. 4357.*)
App: 2409 Madison Carey, Porum, Oklahoma.
Admitted. Applicant's father enrolled by Drennen 1851. Tahl. #506. (*Handwritten Mother enrolled as "I-yoo-que". Can. #86.*)
App: 2410 John L. Ward and 3 children, Maysville, Ark.
Admitted. Brother to #9 and claims thru the same source.
App: 2411 Charlotte Ballard, Echo, Oklahoma.
Admitted. Applicant enrolled by Drennen 1851. Flint #284.
App: 2412 William Ballard and 3 children, Echo, Oklahoma.
Admitted. Brother of #1820.
App: 2413 Randolph Ballard, Needmore, Oklahoma.
Admitted. Brother of #1820.
App: 2414 Mary E. Payne and 3 children, Tahlequah, Oklahoma.
Admitted. Sister of #2045 and claims thru the same source.
App: 2415 Harry Sisson and 5 children, Rex, Oklahoma.
Admitted. 2nd. Cousin of #1208. and claimants mother is on Chapman Roll #1861.
App: 2416 Annie Hair, Eucha, Oklahoma.
Admitted. Niece of #364.
App: 2417 Walker Mitchell, South West City, Mo.
Admitted. Nephew of #2915 and claims thru the same source.
App: 2418 Noma Ofield, South West City, Mo.
Admitted. Sister of #252 and claims thru the same source.
App: 2419 Nancy Snell, South West City, Mo.
Admitted. Sister of #252 and claims thru the same source.
App: 2420 Charles Whitmire and 2 children, Proctor, Oklahoma.
Admitted. Brother of #1847. Enrolled as Charles Whitmire, G.S. #713.
App: 2421 Eliza Ann Lawrence, Dallas, Ga.
Rejected. Claims through John Tidwell. See #16. Duplicate of #14593.

App: 2422 Andromache Bell Shelton, Vinita, Oklahoma.
Admitted. Sister of #2205.
App: 2423 Lafayette Tanner and 4 children, Claremore, Oklahoma.
Rejected. Cousin of #551, and claims through the same ancestors.
App: 2424 Susan V. Needham, Aldrich, Mo.
Rejected. Claims through Alex. Brown. See special Report #35.
App: 2425 Ada Q.V. Lee and 3 children, Patrick, N.C.
Rejected. It does not appear that any ancestor was a party to the treaties of 1835-'36 or '46. Nor does it appear that any ancestor was ever enrolled. Shows no real connection with the Eastern Cherokees. Misc. Test. 1629.
App: 2426 John A. Needham, Gdn. for four children, Aldrich, Mo.
Rejected. Claims thru Alex. Brown. See special report #35. Minors. – Harrison L., Loma P., Yolder R., and Della M. Needham.
App: 2427 Jackey L. Doke, Morrisville, Mo.
Rejected. Claims through Alex. Brown. See special report #35.
App: 2428 Barnette L. Hinsley and 8 children, Talona, Ga.
Rejected. Kesiah Van[sic] case. See special report #276.
App: 2429 Jas. A. Harralson and 3 children, Morrisville, Mo.
Rejected. Claims thru Alex. Brown. See special report #35.
App: 2430 Jacob R. Kephart, Grandview, N.C.
Rejected. Blythe case. See special Report #153.
App: 2431 Eliza C. E. O'Neal and 3 children, Kosh, Ala.
Admitted. Sister of #642. Father of applicant enrolled by Chapman #1686.
App: 2432 Lydia Conley and 4 children, Buren, Ga.
Rejected. Daughter of #529 and claims through the same ancestors.
App: 2433 Cordelia Sneed and 4 children, Grandview, N.C.
Rejected. Blythe case. See special Report #153.
App: 2434 Canders Moore and 5 children, Newholland, Ga.
Rejected. Blythe case. See special Report #153.
App: 2435 Henry B. Quarles and 2 children, Quarles, Ga.
Admitted. 1st cousin to #24. Son of #3022. Grabdson[sic] of #1521.
App: 2436 James R. Long, Chetopa, Kansas.
Rejected. First cousin of #1312.
App: 2437 William Cordry, Kaw City, Oklahoma.
Admitted. Half brother of #671 and claims thru the same source.
App: 2438 Ida B. Cantwell and 2 children, Needmore, Oklahoma.
Admitted. Applicant is niece of #1034 and admitted for same reasons. Applicant's father "#2059 Chapman".
App: 2439 Francis M. Moore, Skiatook, Okla.
Rejected. Brother of #1312. Claims thru same source.
App: 2440 Joe Glory, Tahlequah, Oklahoma.
Admitted. This applicant's mother, Nancy Glory, appl. #2442 and also his grandfather and grandmother are enrolled by Drennen from Tahl. Dis. under Group #423. Misc. Test. p. 3372.
App: 2441 William Glory, Tahlequah, Oklahoma.
Admitted. Brother of Joe Glory, Appl. #2440. Admitted for the same reasons.

App: 2442 Nancy Glory, Tahlequah, Oklahoma.
Admitted. Mother of Joe Glory, appl. #2440 and is admitted for same reasons.
App: 2443 Rachel Neugin, Hulbert, Oklahoma.
Admitted. Sister of #1894.
App: 2444 Allie Downing, Hadley, Oklahoma.
Admitted. 1st. cousin of #1386. Applicant Alley Vann, 292 G.S. Mother, Linny Vann (Ketcher) 292 G.S.
App: 2445 Katie Rackloff, Hulbert, Oklahoma.
Admitted. 1st. cousin to #1386. Daughter of #2448, who was enrolled as "Wa-kee-" Tahl. #508.
App: 2446 Sabra McKee and 1 grandchild, Hulbert, Oklahoma.
Admitted. 1st. cousin to #1386. Daughter of #2448, Rebecca Neugin, enrolled as "Wa-kee" Tahl. #508.
App: 2447 Henry Neugin, Locust Grove, Oklahoma.
Admitted. 1st. cousin to #1386. Son of #2448, enrolled as "Wa-kee" 508 Tahl.
App: 2448 Rebecca Neugin, Locust Grove, Oklahoma.
Admitted. Aunt of #1386. Applicant enrolled as "Wa-kee". 508 Tahl.
App: 2449 William A. Langley and 7 children, Rober, Ga.
Admitted. Nephew of #205 and claims thru same source.
App: 2450 Mary E. Adams and 4 children, Altus, Oklahoma.
Rejected. Blythe case. See special report #153.
App: 2451 Zillah Smith, Warrier, Alabama.
Rejected. Aunt of #58 and claims thru the same source.
App: 2452 Elrilda Candill and 1 child, Grove, Oklahoma.
Admitted. Applicant enrolled as Alwilda Panther C. #1348. Cousin of #6.
App: 2453 M.M. Belle Norris and 1 child, Grandview, N.C.
Rejected. Blythe case. See special report #153.
App: 2454 Mary J. Matherly and 3 children, Springfield, Mo.
Rejected. Claims thru Alex. Brown. See special Report #35.
App: 2455 Neal Neugin and 3 children, Hadley,Oklahoma.
Admitted. 1st. cousin to #1386. Son of #2448 Rebecca Neugin, enrolled as "Wa-kee" Tahl. #508.
App: 2456 Bryant Hughes and 4 children, Hulbert, Oklahoma.
Admitted. Applicant's grandparents enrolled by Drennen 1851, Saline #21.
App: 2457 Wiley H. Stamper, Park, Va.
Rejected. Sizemore case. See special report #417.
App: 2458 Ora Madden and 1 child, Coffeyville, Kan.
Admitted. Grandfather enrolled as Wm. Riley Blythe, Del. #920.
App: 2459 Nellie Boot, Estella, Oklahoma.
Admitted. Granddaughter of #1717. Claims through same source.
App: 2460 Jennie W. Timberlake, Vinita, Oklahoma.
Admitted. Applicant's father enrolled by Drennen 1851. Fl. #262. Grandfather Levi Timberlake enrolled 1835.
App: 2461 Martha C. Wolfe and 5 children, Vinita, Oklahoma.
Admitted. Sister of #2460 and claims thru the same source.

App: 2462 William W. Whitmire, Westville, Oklahoma.
Admitted. Applicant's grandmother enrolled by Drennen 1851. G.S. #714. Misc. Test 3062.
App: 2463 Dave Downing, Baron, Oklahoma.
Admitted. Nephew of #256 and claims through the same source.
App: 2464 Margaret Hammer and 1 child, Westville, Oklahoma.
Admitted. Claims through Mother, Qual-la-you-kee and grandfather Chicken Roost, who were enrolled in 1851 by Drennen in Flint Dis. No. 470. Misc. Test pp. 4050 and 4051.
App: 2465 John Hammer, Westville, Oklahoma.
Admitted. Applicant's father and mother enrolled by Drennen 1851 Del. #769.
App: 2466 Betsy Fodder, Westville, Oklahoma.
Admitted. Sister of 1590. Duplicate of #1591.
App: 2467 Lizzie Bell, Westville, Oklahoma.
Admitted. Sister of #2465. applicant is enrolled by Drennen from Del. Dis. on 1851 Roll #769.
App: 2468 William Downing and 1 child, Baron, Oklahoma.
Admitted. Nephew of #256 and claims thru the same source.
App: 2469 William S. Sneed, Nina, N.C.
Admitted. Brother to #834.
App: 2470 Miller Davis and 4 children, Dahlonega, Ga.
Admitted. First cousin of #98 and claims thru the same source.
App: 2471 Cynthia Smith, Nina, N.C.
Admitted. Sister to #834.
App: 2472 Mary Roberson, Sint, Oklahoma.
Admitted. Sister of #1861; claims thru same source.
App: 2473 Willis O. Roberson, Culberson, N.C.
Admitted. Brother of #1861, claims thru same source.
App: 2474 Narcissa Chase, Chatanooga[sic], Tenn.
33 East End Ave.
Rejected. See special report below:

Application of Narcissa Chase, et al, #2474, claiming thru Noah Raper. Applicant was born Cherokee Co., N.C. in 1842, and her sister, Louisa or Eliza Robinson (app. #20469) was also born in Cherokee Co. in 1846 or 1848 – certainly prior to 1851. Eliza and Narcissa also claim that they have a sister Dovie who was born in 1849 or 1850, and a sister Tiny or Margaret (app. #2475.) who was born in 1857. Tiny states in one application that she was born in Union Co., N.C. and in another that she was born in Indian Territory. In the testimony, Narcissa states that Tiny is her full sister, while, while[sic] Tiny states that Narcissa is her half sister. Narcissa gives the name of her mother as Minerva Raper, formerly Minerva Taylor and Louisa gives her mother's name as Minerva Raper, formerly Minerva Brown, Tiny in her first application also states that her mother's name was Jane Ward, maiden name Jane McDaniel. In her testimony she says that her mother's maiden name was Ward and not McDaniel. In Tiny's first application she states that she claims thru her father only, while in her second application she states that she claims also thru her mother. The names of Noah Raper, Minerva Raper, and Jane Raper, Louisa Narcissa Raper do not appear on the Chapman Roll of 1851, nor does the name of any one of these nor of their descendants, appear on the

Hester Roll of 1884. These parties claim back thru Noah Raper to a Thomas Raper. Narcissa and Tiny in her first application giving the names of their grandparents as Thomas Raper and Jane Raper, formerly Jane McDaniel, while Louisa and Tiny, in her second application give the names of her grandparents as Thomas and Katy Raper. Thomas and Katy Raper were enrolled by Chapman in 1851, but the number of children, all of whose names are given in English, and the descendants of the children so named are enrolled by Hester and have made application here, and they failed to mention as one of the children of Thomas and Katy Raper any child by the name of Noah. It appears further from the testimony that Thomas Raper was himself a white man, and this also appears from the roll of 1835, where he is put down as an affiliated "white". It would appear therefore that Noah Raper, if the son of this Thomas Raper, must have been his son by a white woman, and as such not given the status as an Indian either in 1835 or 1851. If he had had such a status, as it is shown that he was living in the Cherokee Country with his family in 1851, he would certainly have been enrolled at that time and his descendants would have been enrolled by Hester

As is referred to above there is some claim on the part of Tiny Pendleton to Indian blood thru her mother, but the rolls failed to disclose any party of the name given as her mother or grandparents on her mother's side and in view of the fact that in her original application she distinctly states that she claims thru her father only, this claim thru her mother may be disregarded (See pp.122, 3 and 4, Misc. Test.)

In addition to the facts given above, claimants have filed an affidavit executed by Alexander Raper who was a son of Thomas Raper, which was executed in 1893, in which Alexander Raper states that he is then 70 years of age, and in support of the application of Margaret or Tiny Pendleton for enrollment as a Cherokee citizen states that she is the daughter of Noah Raper, who was his affiant's first cousin by Cherokee blood. If this statement is true, as seems probable that Noah was the first cousin of Alexander Raper, then he was not the son of Thomas Raper as Thomas was the father of Alexander Raper and it is more probable that Noah was the son of William, who is shown to have been another brother of Thomas Raper, and William does not appear ever to have been adopted by the Cherokees and is shown to have been a white man. These claimants are therefore rejected.

App: 2475 Tyne Pendleton, Chattanooga, Tenn.
Rejected. Sister of #2474 and claims thru the same source.

App: 2476 Maggie L. Thompson and 2 children, Centralia, Oklahoma.
Admitted. Niece of #1812.

App: 2477 Bark F. Celveland[sic], Blue Jacket, Oklahoma.
Admitted. Cousin of #1601.

App: 2478 Charlotte B. Dupree, Vinita, Oklahoma.
Admitted. Aunt of #2205.

App: 2478 1/2 A.M. Clinkscales for 2 children, Vinita, Oklahoma.
Admitted. First cousin once removed of #2205. This application is filed by father of these children, who is their legal guardian. They claim thru their mother, Annie Dupree, Cherokee Indian, who is deceased. Their application was filed as supplemental to #2478.

App: 2479 Margaret Tanner and 5 children, Albuquerque, N.M.
Admitted. Sister of #1812.

App: 2480 Agnes Pfaunkche, Vinita, Oklahoma.
Admitted. Applicant is a sister of #1034. Applicant "2061 Chapman".
App: 2481 Moses O. Fields and 3 children, Collinsville, Oklahoma.
Admitted *(Handwritten Admitted.)* Nephew of #1340 and claims thru same ancestors. Father of applicant, James S. Fields, enrolled in Del. Dis. #432.
App: 2482 Benj. F. Goss, Stilwell, Oklahoma.
Admitted. Applicant was enrolled by Drennen 1851. G.S. #725.
App: 2483 Lydia Eli, Evansville, Arkansas.
Admitted. Applicant's father enrolled by Drennen 1851. Flint #394.
App. 2484 Sarah Dallar (or Dollar), Stilwell, Oklahoma.
Admitted. Applicant's father enrolled by Drennen 1851. Flint #110. Mother enrolled by Drennen in 1851 as Ca-the-claiv-hee. Flint #117. Mother's application #2486.
App: 2485 Lizzie Hunter, Evansville, Arkansas.
Adnitted. Applicant enrolled by Drennen. C. #1091. Misc. Test. p. 3293.
App: 2486 Ceily Teller, Stilwell, Oklahoma.
Admitted. Claims thru self, enrolled as Ca-tle-claw-hee. Father, Joe, Mother, Lizy, enrolled by Drennen in 1851. Flint District, Group #117.
App: 2487 Lucinda Deerinwater and 4 children, Evansville, Arkansas.
Admitted. Applicant's father enrolled by Drennen 1851, Flint #412. Misc. Test p. 3173.
App: 2488 Nancy Duck and 2 children, Evansville, Arkansas.
Admitted. Half sisters on mother's side.
App: 2489 James Taylor and 2 children, Evansville, Arkansas.
Admitted. Nephew of #1689. Claims through Sallie Arch, Flint #512, grandmother. Mother #1911 born in 1855.
App: 2490 Beulah Ralston, Needmore, Oklahoma.
Admitted. First cousin, once removed of William T. Melton (2158) and claims from the same source. Father of applicant, James Monroe, enrolled in 1851, in Disputed District #30.
App: 2491 John Ralston and 1 child, Needmore, Oklahoma.
Admitted. Applicant is nephew of #1034 and admitted for same reasons. Applicant's father "Lewis Ralston 2059 Chapman".
App: 2492 Elizabeth Wolf, Stilwell, Oklahoma.
Admitted. Mother of #2394. App. enrolled as "Elizabeth Jones" G.S. #329. Applicant claims for minor grandchildren whose fathers are in prison; but they are mentioned on both father's and mother's applications, #19822, 11162, #2394, 22525 #1231.
App: 2493 Richard L. Taylor, Stilwell, Oklahoma.
Admitted. First cousin of #1428. Mother of applicant enrolled in Flint #125.
App: 2494 Betsey Christy, Locust Grove, Oklahoma.
Admitted. Applicant enrolled by Drennen 1851. Saline #314. Misc. Test p. 3833 and 3751.
App: 2495 Niecer Hosea and 1 child, Locust Grove, Oklahoma.
Admitted. Sister of #1886.
App: 2496 David C. Rowe, Rose, Oklahoma.
Rejected. Brother of #190 and claims thru the same source.

App: 2497 Nelson Murphy, Locust Grove, Oklahoma.
Admitted. Applicant's father enrolled by Drennen 1851 Tahl. #414.
App: 2498 Elizabeth Grass, Locust Grove, Oklahoma.
Admitted. Half sister of #2233. Mother of applicant enrolled in 1851 in G.S. #217.
App: 2499 Rachel Sack and 1 child, Peggs, Oklahoma.
Admitted. Daughter of #522 and claims through the same ancestors.
App: 2500 Annie Sanders, Locust Grove, Oklahoma.
Admitted. This applicant's father Young Mulberry and also the applicant are enrolled by Drennen, from Saline District under group #182. Misc. Test 3716.

App: 2501 Nancy Littledave, Locust Grove, Oklahoma.
Admitted. Niece of #5288. Claimant's paternal grandfather enrolled in 1851 by Drennen. Saline #151.
App: 2502 Jesse Henson and 3 children, Locust Grove, Oklahoma.
Admitted. Brother of #627 and claims through the same source.
App: 2503 Nellie Rowe, Locust Grove, Oklahoma.
Admitted. This applicant's father Henry or Cah-tah-quah-lah Downing is enrolled by Drennen from Tahl. District. under Group #412. Misc. Test P. 3784.
App: 2504 Susie Oo-loo-lah, Vinita, Oklahoma.
Admitted. Grand-daughter of #1717. Claims through same source. (See #2459 for ancestors).
App: 2505 Jesse Duck or Charley tee hee, Evansville, Arkansas.
Admitted. Claimant's parents and oldest sister or brother et al., enrolled by Drennen in 1851, Tahl. #300.
App: 2506 Jennie Duck and 4 children, Evansville, Arkansas.
Admitted. Half sister of #2160.
App: 2507 Annie Taylor, Evansville, Arkansas.
Admitted. Applicant's mother was Emigrant Cherokee See Test, of J.B. Adair taken at Stilwell, Oklahoma. March 22, 1909, p. 4010.
App: 2508 Yose Duck, Evansville, Arkansas.
Admitted. Half-brother of #2160.
App: 2509 Sidney S. Hinkle and 3 children, Morrisville, Mo.
Rejected. Claims thru Alex. Brown. See special Report #35.
App: 2510 Dennis C. Hinkle and 3 children, Morrisville, Mo.
Rejected. Claims thru Alex Brown. See special Report #35.
App: 2511 Lenora Hinkle and 3 children, Morrisville, Mo.
Rejected. Claims thru Alex. Brown. See special Report #35.
App: 2512 Sarah L. Moody and 9 children, Robbinsville, N.C.
Rejected. Kesiah Vann case. See special Report #276.
App: 2513 Rosa Lee Langston and 6 children, Cass Station, Ga.
Admitted. Cousin of #319 and claims through the same source.
App: 2514 Elijah Payne and 1 child, Cincinati[sic], Ohio.
Rejected. Brother of #9199 and claims through the same source.
App: 2515 Samantha Nichols, Kansas, I.T.
Rejected. Betsey Walker case. See special report #500.

App: 2516 Sarah Hogan and 5 children, Cass Station, Ga.
Rejected. Whitmire Case. (Below)

Whitmire File #2516.

The applicants who claim their right to share in the Eastern Cherokee fund because they are descendants of Samuel and Polly Whitmire or of some of their children, especially Delilah Corbin must all be rejected for the following reasons:

None of their ancestors were enrolled in 1835 or in 1851 or at any other time. No evidence has been submitted which would tend to show that any ancestor of these claimants was party to the treaties of 1835-6 and 1846.

It appears from the applications that Samuel and Polly Whitmire through whom these applicants claim to trace their connection with the Eastern Cherokee Tribe were born sometime prior to the year 1800. A number of these persons now claiming to share in this fund were living in 1835 and a greater number were living in 1851, and yet none of them or their ancestors appear on the rolls made on these dates. The name of Delilah Whitmire does appear on the roll of 1851 but it is manifest considering these applications with the roll that this cannot be the Delilah Whitmire who was the daughter of Samuel and Polly Whitmire, as the one on the roll lived in the Going Snake District in 1851 and was enrolled by Drennen, while the Delilah Whitmire through whom these claimants claim lived in the east. Delilah Whitmire was married to John Corbin certainly prior to 1830 while the Delilah Whitmire whose name appears on the roll of 1851 was apparently a minor child. The Delilah Whitmire who was the daughter of Samuel and Polly Whitmire did not reside anywhere near the locality in which the Delilah Whitmire who was enrolled lived in 1851.

On October 26, 1907, a letter was sent from this office to Mr. J. C. DePutron, who is attorney for most of these claimants and in that letter Mr. J.C. DePutron was informed that unless affidavits of the strongest character clearly showing the connection of these Whitmire claimants or some of their ancestors with the Eastern Cherokee tribe could be furnished, this office would not be justified in putting the firm to the expense of taking the testimony of these claimants.

Certain affidavits were filed in compliance with this letter, but none of these affidavits indicate that the Delilah Whitmire, who was enrolled in 1851 was the daughter of Samuel and Polly Whitmire, nor do these affidavits show any genuine connection on the part of the Whitmire family with the Cherokee tribe, either in 1835 or '51. On the contrary the affidavits are extremely general and there is noticeable absence of the mention of any dates in them. The applicants as a general rule make no claim of ever having been enrolled.

For the reasons stated above all the claimants in this group must be rejected.

App: 2517 John Shelton, Rome, Ga.
Rejected. 1. No ancestor ever enrolled. 2. No ancestor was ever party to treaties of 1835-6 and 1846. 3. Shows no connection to Eastern Cherokees.

App: 2518 William W. Howell and 1 child, Lindale, Ga.
Rejected. It does not appear that any ancestor was ever enrolled or that any ancestor was a party to the treaties of 1835-6 and 1846. Failed to appear to give testimony when summoned and shows no real connection with the Cherokee tribe.

App: 2519 Jeanette Rogers, Culberson, N.C.
Admitted. Aunt of #1861.

App: 2520 Henrietta Givens, East Birmingham, Ala.
Rejected. 1. No ancestor ever enrolled. 2. No ancestor party to treaties of 1835-6 and 1846. 3. Shows no connection with Eastern Cherokees. 4. Ancestors were slaves and also applicant.
App: 2521 Matilda Garrein, Wolf Creek, N.C.
Rejected. Sister of #1661.
App: 2522 Boze H. Deck and 3 children, Millspairag[sic], N.C.
Rejected. Son of #9199 and claims thru the same source.
App: 2523 Dorah Floyd and 2 children, Flat Rock, N.C.
Rejected. Its does not appear that any ancestor was ever enrolled or that any ancestor was party to the treaties of 1835-6 or '46. Shows no genuine connection with the Eastern Cherokees.
App: 2524 James A. Jones and 1 child, Blue Ridge, Ga.
Rejected. It does not appear that any ancestor was a party to the treaty of 1835, 36 or 1846. Nor does it appear that any ancestor was ever enrolled. Shows no real connection with the Eastern Cherokees. Misc. T. 1419.
App: 2525 D.H. Crow and 2 children, Allatoona, Ga.
Rejected. Neither applicant nor ancestors was ever enrolled. Does not establish fact of being descendants of any person who was ever a party to the treaty of 1835, 6 or '46. Misc. Test p. 1209.
App: 2526 Margaret M. Culver, Sylvania, Ala.
Rejected. Ancestors not on rolls. Does not prove any genuine connection with Cherokee tribe. Very evident they are white people. (*Handwritten Misc. 715)*
App: 2527 Perrie Thomas Bugg, Athens, Ga.
Rejected. No ancestor ever enrolled. No ancestor ever party to treaties of 1835, 6 or 1846. Shows no connection to Eastern Cherokees. Party and ancestors were slaves.
App: 2528 Sarah J. Webb, Kings Creek, Oklahoma[sic].
Rejected. It does not appear that applicant's ancestors were parties to treaties of 1835-6 or 1846. Never shared in payments to Cherokees, nor enrolled with them. Misc. Test. p. 2411.
App: 2529 A.J. Webb and 5 children, Kings Creeks, N.C.
Rejected. Husband of #2529. See applicantion #2528.
App: 2530 Silas Jolly, Gdn. and 3 children, Kings Creeks, N.C.
Rejected. Applicant claims through his wife, Lucy Jolly, nee Dyson who is a niece of #2540.
App: 2531 Lucy J. Jolly and 3 children, Kings Creeks, N.C.
Rejected. Niece of #2540.
App: 2532 John Dyson, Beaver Creek, N.C.
Rejected. Duplicate of #2540.
App: 2533 Lousinda Dyson, Kings Creeks, N.C.
Rejected. Cousin of #2540.
App: 2534 Susan Dyson, Beaver Creek, N.C.
Rejected. Cousin of #2540.
App: 2535 Marcus Dyson, Beaver Creek, N.C.
Rejected. Cousin of #2541.
App: 2536 Violet Dyson, Beaver Creek, N.C.
Rejected. Cousin of #2540

App: 2537 Elizabeth Dyson, Beaver Creek, N.C.
Rejected. Cousin of #2540.

App: 2538 James Dyson, Beaver Creek, N.C.
Rejected. Nephew of #2540.

App: 2539 Zero Dyson, Beaver Creek, N.C.
Rejected. Nephew of #2540.

App: 2540 John Dyson and 6 children, Beaver Creek, N.C.
Rejected. Ancestors not on rolls. Were not parties to treaties of 1835-6 or '46. Does not establish genuine connection with the Cherokee tribe. Misc. Test p. 1601.

App: 2541 Cynthia Dyson, Kings Creeks, N.C.
Rejected. Daughter of #2540.

App: 2542 Jos. B. Blackwell and 3 children, Whetstone, S.C.
Rejected. Nephew of #21023 and claims through the same source.

App: 2543 Mrs. Mary Blackwell, Raburn, Ga.
Rejected. Sister of #21023 and claims through the same source.

App: 2544 Mary Norton, Clayton, Ga.
Rejected. Blythe case. See special report #153.

App: 2545 Elias P. Norton and 5 children, Pine Mountain, Ga.
Rejected. Blythe case. See special report #153.

App: 2546 Lillie Calhoun, Clayton, Ga.
Rejected. Blythe case. See special report #153.

App: 2547 ~~Nancy~~ Russell and 3 Children, Blue Ridge, Ga.
Rejected. (*Handwritten above, Mary*) Neither applicant nor ancestors was enrolled. Does not establish fact of descent from a person who was a party to the treaties of 1835-6 or '46. (*Handwritten Misc. Test. 534, 1321 and 1532.)*

App: 2548 Nancy Golden and 8 children, Higdon's Store, Ga.
Rejected. Cousin of #2547 and claims thru same source.

App: 2549 Hiram F. Dudley and 6 children, Dallas, Texas.
Rejected. Claims through John Lidwell. See #16.

App: 2550 Albert B. Ledford, Jr. Gay, N.C.
Rejected. Nephew of #2551 and claims through the same source.

App: 2551 Pressfield S. Ledford and 5 children, Isabella, Tenn.
Rejected. Neither applicant nor ancestors was enrolled; does not establish fact of descent from person who was party to the treaty of 1835-6 or '46. (*Handwritten See 2547. Mis. Test 5311* (or *5312*))

App: 2552 Richard Ledford and 15 children, Isabella, Tenn.
Rejected. Brother of #2551 and claims through the same source.

App: 2553 Julius Ledford, Gay, N.C.
Rejected. Brother of #2551 and claims through the same source.

App: 2553-1/2 Elbert B. Ledford, Gay, N.C.
Rejected. Father of #2551 and claims through the same source.

App: 2554 Tina Tidwell (*Handwritten Suggs*) and 2 children, Cartersville, Ga.
Rejected. Claims through John Langley and Sally Langley nee Tidwell. See special report below:

IN RE APPLICANTS CLAIMING THROUGH JOHN
LANGLEY AND SALLIE TIDWELL, APPL. #2554, et al.

ooOoo

These applicants claim to be descendants of John Langley and Sallie Langley, nee Tidwell. (See application #2617 et al.) They claim that Sallie Langley, nee Tidwell and John were married and lived together as man and wife; that John left Sallie and the children took the name of their mother, Tidwell; that in 1851 they were living in Forsythe Co., Ga.

John Langley is enrolled by Chapman #1902 in Gilmer Co., Ga., with his wife Susannah, age 40 and a family of children. He was married twice. His first wife being Sallie Parrish. He had several children by her, one of whom, Nancy Goble, is living and has filed application #1521, and she, herself, is enrolled by Chapman #1913. His second wife was Sussanah[sic] Langley, nee Dougherty. See applications (#805 and 12626. with 805).

Siler at pages 93-4 of his roll mentions a Sarah Saunders, age 48 whose real name he states, is Sarah Tidwell; that she was a white woman who claimed to have been the wife of a Cherokee and had a large family of Cherokee children; that she was never married, but lived with the Cherokees. Siler rejected the woman and her family of children. It is impossible to determine certainly whether this woman was the same person as applicant's ancestor, who they claim was the wife of John Langley. She could not have been the lawful wife of John as he had a wife, as above shown with whom he was enrolled by Chapman. It would appear, therefore, that applicants herein, if in fact the descendents of John Langley, C. #1902, or the descendants of illegitimate children of John whom he did not recognize; and it is quite probable that the Sallie Saunders, nee Tidwell, mentioned by Siler was the same person as applicants' ancestor. This conclusion is substantiated by the fact that none of the applicants herein nor their ancestors, with the exception of John Langley (whom they allege was their ancestor) have ever been enrolled with the Eastern Cherokees, altho in 1851 and since that time they have lived in Georgia in localities where other persons were enrolled and where they would have had ample opportunity to have been enrolled if they had been entitled.

It is a matter of record that John Langley, C. #1902, was a white man. (See Siler Roll p. 65 No. 1797, also see appl. Nancy Goble, #1521, and also that of Ana M. Tovey, #2899.) John Langley was enrolled because he had married a woman with Cherokee blood, prior to 1835, and all his descendants who are entitled inherit their Cherokee blood thru his wife.

Applicants herein make no claim thru Sallie Langley, nee Tidwell. (she may possibly belong to the John Tidwell family). (For any claiming thru him see special Report with Group #16.)

In consideration of the premises, therefore, the applications of all persons claiming thru John Langley and Sallie Tidwell are hereby rejected.

--oOo--

App: 2555 Julia Allen and 4 children, Isabella, Tenn.
Rejected. Sister of #2551 and claims thru the same source. Neither applicant nor ancestors was enrolled. Does not establish fact of descent from person who was a party to the treaty of 1835-6 or '46.

App: 2556 Sarah Allen Gay, N.C.
Rejected. Sister of #2551 and claims thru the same source.

App: 2557 Vernon Cook and 1 child, Blue Ridge, Ga.
Rejected. Daughter of #2547 and claims thru the same source.

App: 2558 George W. Sizemore and 7 children, Baileytown, Ala.
Rejected. Sizemore case. See special report #417. See #21667.
App: 2559 Odey C. Sizemore, Eva, Ala.
---------- Sizemore case. See special report #417.
App: 2560 Benj. C. Sizemore, Balileytown[sic], Ala.
Rejected. Sizemore case. See special report #417. R.F.D. #4
See #21424.
App: 2561 Dollie Sizemore, Bailyetown[sic], Ala.
Rejected. Sizemore case. See special report #417. See #21424.
App: 2562 John H. Sizemore and 7 children, Holly Pond, Ala.
Rejected. Sizemore case. See special report #417. R.F.D. #1
See #21664.
App: 2563 Wade H. Sizemore and 4 children, Eva, Alabama.
Rejected. Sizemore case. See special report #417. See #21669.
App: 2564 Luther S. Sizemore and 2 children, Cullman, Ala.
Rejected. Sizemore case. See special report #417. See #21425.
App: 2565 Vanor S. Chambers, Baileytown, Ala.
Rejected. Sizemore case. See special report #417.
App: 2566 Minerva Watson and 3 children, Higdon's Store, Ga
Rejected. Grand-niece of #2398.
App: 2567 Margaret S. Willson and 2 children, Higdon's Store, Ga.
Rejected. Grand niece of #2398.
App: 2568 Coleman T. Watson, Blue Ridge, Ga.
Rejected. Cousin of #2398.
App: 2569 Rosetta Thomas and 7 children, Blue Ridge, Ga.
Rejected. Grand niece of #2398.
App: 2570 Wm. J. Postell and 6 children, Higdon's Store, Ga.
Rejected. Grand nephew of #2398.
App: 2571 Mary Postell, Higdon's Store, Ga.
Rejected. Grand niece of #2398.
App: 2572 Disey Postell, Higdon's Store, Ga.
Rejected. Niece of #2398.
App: 2573 Nancy C. Moots and 5 children, Higdon's Store, Ga.
Rejected. Grand niece of #2398.
App: 2574 Margaret J. Markins and 3 children, Higdon's Store, Ga.
Rejected. Claims thru same source as #2398.
App: 2575 Clarissa J. Mathews and 7 children, Higdon's Store, Ga.
Rejected. Grand niece of #2398.
App: 2576 D.M. Newton and 3 children, Higdon's Store, Ga.
Rejected. Grand niece of #2398.
App: 2577 Laura M. Lanning, Madola, Ga.
Rejected. Grand niece of #2398.
App: 2578 G.W.A. Lanning and 6 children, Madola, Ga.
Rejected. Grand nephew of #2398.
App: 2579 J.E.F. Lanning and 5 children, Higdon's Store, Ga.
Rejected. Grand nephew of #2398.

App: 2580 John D. Lovell, Higdon's Store, Ga.
Rejected. Grandnephew of #2398.
App: 2581 Fannie Lovell, Higdon's Stre[sic], Ga.
Rejected. Niece of #2398.
App: 2582 Wiley Long, Jr., and 7 children, Higdon's Store, Ga.
Rejected. Nephew of #2398.
App: 2583 Nevada Vaughn and 3 children, Higdon's Store, Ga.
Rejected. Grand niece of #2398.
App: 2584 Mary Wynn and 11 children, Cleveland, Ala.
Rejected. Nephew of #2398.
App: 2585 July N. Watson and 4 children, Higdon's Store, Ga.
Rejected. Grand niece of #2398.
App: 2586 David W. Long and 3 children, McCays, Tenn.
Rejected. Nephew of #2398.
App: 2587 Alfred Long, Higdon's Store, Ga.
Rejected. Son of #2398.
App: 2588 Stephen J. Long and 4 children, Shady, Fla.
Rejected. Ancestors not on rolls. It is not proven that the applicant is descended from Cherokees who were parties to treaties of 1835-36 and '46.
App: 2589 Rosey Long, Higdon's Store, Ga.
Rejected. Daughter of #2398.
App: 2590 Mary Long, Higdon's Store, Ga.
Rejected. Granddaughter of #2398.
App: 2591 C.M. Kinkaid, gdn. Higdon's Store, Ga.
for Ann Waldon and 5 children,
Rejected. Grand niece of #2398.
App: 2592 C.M. Kinkaid Gdn. Higdon's Store, Ga.
for Amanda E. Early and 5 children,
Rejected. Grand niece of #2398.
App: 2593 Mary Hill for 7 children, Chestnut Gap, Ga.
Rejected. (*Handwritten Great*) Grand nieces and nephews of #2398.
App: 2594 Thomas W. Hice and 8 children, Higdon's Store, Ga.
Rejected. Grand nephew of #2398.
App: 2595 Geo. H. Hice, Gdn. of Chas. B. and Ellen Hice, Cherry Log, Ga.
Rejected. Grand niece and nephew of #2398. See #38190.
App: 2596 Catherine M. Davis and 2 children, Higdon's Store, Ga.
Rejected. Grand niece of #2398.
App: 2597 Rufiny Goss and 4 children, Higdon's Store, Ga.
Rejected. Grand niece of #2398.
App: 2598 John R. Davenport and 2 children, Higdon's Store, Ga.
Rejected. Grand nephew of #2398.
App: 2599 Drury C. Davenport and 8 children, Higdon's Store, Ga.
Rejected. Nephew of #2398.
App: 2600 Drury C. Davenport and 4 children, Higdon's Store, Ga.
Rejected. Applicant is a grand nephew of #2600[sic] and claims through the same source.

App: 2601 David J. Davenport and 4 children, Higdon's Store, Ga.
Rejected. Grand nephew of #2398.
App: 2602 Margaret Cornett and 1 child, Higdon's Store, Ga.
Rejected. Great-grandniece of #2398.
App: 2603 Drury C. Campbell and 4 children, Chestnut Gap, Ga.
Rejected. Grand nephew of #2398.
App: 2604 Wm. Campbell and 2 children, Higdon's Store, Ga.
Rejected. Great grand nephew of #2398.
App: 2605 John H. Campbell and 4 children, Higdon's Store, Ga.
Rejected. Grand nephew of #2398.
App: 2606 Catherine Beavers, Higdon's Store, Ga.
Rejected. Niece of #2398.
App: 2607 Lizzie Barker and 1 child, Kyle, Ga.
Rejected. Great grand niece of #2398.
App: 2608 Columbus M. Beavers and 3 children, Higdon's Store, Ga.
Rejected. Grand nephew of #2398.
App: 2609 Bascom Beavers and 7 children, Higdon's Store, Ga.
Rejected. Grand nephew of #2398.
App: 2610 John Ash,
Rejected. Cousin of #2398.
App: 2611 Mary A. Tidwell Vaugh and 3 children, Cass Station, Ga.
Rejected. Sister of #2554.
App: 2612 Marion J. Tidwell and 7 children, Cartersville, Ga.
Rejected. Uncle of #2554.
App: 2613 Ida Tidwell and 5 children, Cartersville, Ga.
Rejected. Minor second cousin once removed of #2554.
App: 2614 George R. Tidwell, Cartersville, Ga.
Rejected. First cousin once removed of #2554.
App: 2615 John J. Tidwell, Cartersville, Ga.
Rejected. First Cousin of #2554.
App: 2616 J.M. Tidwell and 1 child, Cartersville, Ga.
Rejected. Niece of #2554.
App: 2617 Joseph M. Tidwell, Allatoona, Ga.
Rejected. Brother of #2554.
App: 2618 Franklin I. Tidwell and 3 children, Allatoona, Ga.
Rejected. Brother of #2554.
App: 2619 John Tidwell and 4 children, Allatoona, Ga.
Rejected. Father of #2554.
App: 2620 Joseph M. Summing, Cartersville, Ga.
Rejected. First cousin of #2554.
App: 2621 O.A. Summing and 1 child, Cartersville, Ga.
Rejected. First Cousin of #2554.
App: 2622 W.M. Summing and 3 children, Cartersville, Ga.
Rejected. First Cousin of #2554.
App: 2623 D.R. Summing, Cartersville, Ga.
Rejected. First Cousin of #2554.

App: 2624 J.W. Summing and 3 children, Cartersville, Ga.
Rejected. First cousin of #2554.
App: 2625 L.S. Summing, Cartersville, Ga.
Rejected. First cousin of #2554.
App: 2626 Caroline Parker and 1 child, Dalton, Ga.
Admitted. Sister of #205 and claims thru the same source.
App: 2627 Noah Higgins, Rome, Ga.
Admitted. 1st. cousin of #24 and claims thru the same source. Son of Rachel Goble 1914 Chapman. Grandson of #1521. Nancy Goble.
App: 2628 Nancy Ann Height and 5 children, Cartersville, Ga.
Rejected. First Cousin of #2554.
App: 2629 Fannie I. Guyton, Cartersville, Ga.
Rejected. First Cousin of #2554.
App: 2630 Jenette Dudley and 2 children, Dallas, Ga.
Rejected. Claims through John Tidwell. See #16. R.F.D. #3
App: 2631 Kate Bagwell and 8 children, Rome, Ga.
Admitted. (*Handwritten above (8) another number marked out.*) See #42493. Niece of #205 and claims through the same source. (*Handwritten One child, Leona Byrd rejected for the charge that she was married at the time of application for her was filed, and she filed no separate application.*)
App: 2632 M.I. Abernathy and 3 children, Barlow, Ga.
Rejected. First cousin of #2554.
App: 2633 John C. Delozier, Almond, N.C.
Rejected. Nephew of #664 and claims thru the same source.
App: 2634 Lillie J. DeLozier Almond, N.C.
Rejected. Niece of #664 and claims through the same source.
App: 2635 Rosanna Bishop and 2 children, Atlanta, Ga.
Rejected. Blythe case. See special Report #153.
App: 2636 Jesse E. Delozier, Almond, N.C.
Rejected. Nephew of #664 and claims thru the same source.
App: 2637 Dock F. Crow, Murphy, N.C.
Rejected. Duplicate of #8395 and claims through the same source.
App: 2638 Jos. A. Parker and 2 children, Atlanta, Ga.
Rejected. Blythe case. See special report #153.
App: 2639 Cordelia ~~Spring~~ (*Handwritten Spiney*), Springplace, Ga.
Rejected. Sister of #725 and claims thru the same source.
App: 2640 Louisa A. Scroggs, Springplace, Ga.
Rejected. Sister of #725 and claims through the same source.
App: 2641 Jos. A. Ownby, Blue Ridge, Ga.
Rejected. Son of #117 and claims through the same source.
App: 2642 Addie D. Odom and 2 children, Dahlonega, Ga. R.F.D. #3
Admitted. First cousin once removed of #98 and claims through the same source.
App: 2643 Biddie D. Odom and 1 child, Dahlonega, Ga.
Admitted. First cousin once removed of #98 and claims through the same source.

App: 2644 Luna L. Davis Dahlonega, Ga.
Admitted. First cousin once removed of #98 and claims through the same source.
App: 2645 Lena Goins (nee Paden) and 8 children, Fairland, Oklahoma.
Rejected. Claims only as widow. Supplemental application for children 2645 with #55, claiming as guardian. See #2645 with #55 for children by first husband, name Paden.
App: 2645-1/2 Bennie Paden, Riley Paden, Kittie Paden, Fairland, Oklahoma.
Admitted. and Russell Paden, second cousins to #55. Grandchildren of Alfred Miller Paden enrolled by Chap. at #1733. By Lena Goins, Gdn. Application for Ezra and Okley Goins, not allowed, as they do not connect with Paden family.
App: 2646 Maud J. Paden, Doty, Wash.
Admitted. 1st. cousin to #55. Grandfather "Alfred Miller Paden 1735 Chapman".
App: 2647 Willie R. Paden, Leavenworth, Kansas. c/o Gen. Del.
Admitted 1st. cousin to #55. Grandfather, 1735 Chap. "Alfred Miller Paden".
App: 2648 Taylor Paden, Fairland, Oklahoma.
Admitted. 1st. Cousin to #55. Grandfather, "Alfred Miller Paden", 1735 Chap.
App: 2649 Myrtle A. Kelley, William Howell Kelley Fairland, Oklahoma.
Admitted. and Mamie Delilah Kelly. (*Handwritten Grandmother enrolled in 1851, Del. 367.*)
App: 2650 Ruby V. Harlan, Daisy D., Wm. A., Bessie M., Fairland, Oklahoma.
Admitted. (*Handwritten **Admitted***). By Myrtle Harlen, Gdn.
(*Handwritten , mother and grandmother enrolled in 1851, Del. 367.*)
App: 2651 Ethel Mable Cooley, Fairland, Oklahoma.
Admitted. Niece of #543 Grandfather "James Lamar, 1709 Chapman".
App: 2652 Daniel W. Freeman, Fairland, Oklahoma.
Admitted. The mother of the applicant was enrolled by Drennen in 1851 by Drennen in #27 Del. The maternal grandmother of the applicant was enrolled in 26 Del. Also his uncles.
App: 2653 Cane Harden and 2 children, Andrews, N.C.
Admitted. Son of #687 and claims thru the same source.
App: 2654 William J. Harden and 5 children, Andrews, N.C.
Admitted. Son of #687 and claims thru the same source.
App: 2655 Andrew J. Kephart, Grandview, N.C.
Rejected. Blythe case. See special report #153.
App: 2656 Matilda South,
Rejected. Same as #1514.
App: 2657 Birdie Hutchinson and 2 children, Ash Grove, Mo.
Rejected. Claims thru Alex. Brown See special report #35.
App: 2658 Sam'l. Z.G. Anglen, Ash Grove, Mo.
Rejected. Claims thru Alex. Brown See special Report #35.
App: 2659 Hattie Taylor and 2 children, Ash Grove, Mo.
Rejected. Claims thru Alex. Brown See special Report #35.
App: 2660 Charles H. Harden and 7 children, Andrews, N.C.
Admitted. Son of #687 and claims thru the same source.

App: 2661 Margaret C. Ross and 4 children, Santa Luca, Ga.
Rejected. It does not appear that any ancestors was a party to the treaties of 1835-6 or '46, nor does it appear that any ancestor was ever enrolled. Shows no real connection with the Cherokee Indians. Misc. T. p. 1392 and 1410.

App: 2662 John A. McDonald and 4 children, Grandview, N.C.
Rejected. Blythe case. See special report #153.

App: 2663 Jessie M. Griffith and 4 children, Brighton, Mo.
Rejected. Claims thru Alex. Brown. See special Report #35.

App: 2664 Rutha Whitaker and 2 children, Andrews, N.C.
Admitted. Daughter of #687 and claims thru the same source.

App: 2665 Delia Alloway, Catoosa, Oklahoma.
Rejected. The ancestors of applicant were old settlers. Father and Mother on O.S. Roll.

App: 2666 John Armstrong and no children, Vinita, Oklahoma.
Rejected. Applicant's mother and grandmother Darky and Lizzy Falling enrolled as Old Settlers in 1851 in Del. #10. Applicants' father was a white man. See Misc. Test #2245

App: 2667 William Fields and 4 children, Fairland, Oklahoma.
Admitted. Nephew of #390. Claimant's mother enrolled by Drennen in 1851, Del. 142.

App: 2668 Ada U. Howell and Willie C. Ritter by their Guardian, M.C. Gallamose, Fairland, Oklahoma.
Admitted. 1st. cousin of #2399 and their grandfather. Thos. Wolf is on Drennen Roll #927 from Delaware Dis.

App: 2669 Felix Downing, Estella, Oklahoma.
Admitted. Applicant's father and mother enrolled under names of James Downing or Blanket and Jimmie Downing. Drennen '51. roll Saline Dis. Group #500. Misc. Test p. 3604.

App: 2670 Steve on the Hill ~~and 1 child~~, Estella, Oklahoma.
Admitted. The father of the applicant was enrolled in 526 Del. by Drennen in '51. See Misc. Test p. 3686. Applicant's minor child, John, enrolled with mother, #31190.

App: 2671 Lillie B. Deitrick and 2 children, Vinita, Oklahoma.
Admitted. The grand father of applicant on her father's side was enrolled in #607. Del. Dis. Father of applicant not born in 1851.

App: 2672 Sarah Beck, Estella, Oklahoma.
Admitted. Applicant's parents enrolled by Drennen 1851 in Del. 699.

App: 2673 Liza A. Wyly, Adair, Oklahoma.
Rejected. Applicant claims through Mother to Grandfather, Moses Crittenden. Moses Crittenden O.C. Roll S.B. 16. Mother may be O.S. S. B. 16 as Eliza, applicant not sure she was living at that time. Aunts and uncles are also enrolled S.B.O.S. #16. No claim through father's side, the Wintons. Misc. Test p. 3630.

App: 2674 Laura Hilderbrand and 6 children, Vinita, Oklahoma.
Admitted. Duplicate of #2290.

App: 2675 Homer Paden and four others, Fairland, Oklahoma.
By Lucy J. Paden, Mother.

Admitted. These are the minor children of Lucy J. Paden, who filed application #3808. Her mother was enrolled by Drennen in 1851. Tahl. #251. These children are also entitled through their father's family. See application #55.

App: 2676 Maggie Paden, Fairland, Oklahoma.
Admitted. 2nd cousin to #55. Grandfather, "Alfred Miller Paden, 1735 Chap."

App: 2677 Howard Paden, Fairland, Oklahoma.
Admitted. 2nd. Cousin to #55. Grabdfather[sic] "Alfred Miller Paden, 1735 Chap."

App: 2678 John M. Bell and 5 children, Chelsea, Oklahoma.
Admitted. The father and paternal grandfather were enrolled in Saline Dis. 480 by Drennen in 1851.

App: 2679 Minnie C. Bell, Chelsea, Oklahoma.
Admitted. The mother and maternal grandmother of the applicant are enrolled in #477, Saline District by Drennen in 1851.

App: 2680 James M. Bell, Vinita, Oklahoma.
Admitted. Uncle of #2205.

App: 2681 Nancy A. Harlin, ~~Cicero~~, Oklahoma.
Admitted. Sister of #2205. (*Handwritten above, Grove*).

App: 2682 James E. Harlin, Grove, Oklahoma.
Admitted. Uncle of #1352 and claims through the same ancestors. Applicant was enrolled in 1851 in Flint Dist. #341.

App: 2683 William Landrum, Iola, Kansas.
Admitted. Grand nephew of #918. Applicant's grandfather enrolled as Jeffrey Beck at Del. #572.

App: 2684 William Funderburk and 2 children, Tupelo, Miss.
Rejected. Nephew of Barbra A. Presley #77 and claims through the same source.

App: 2685 James Funderburk and 4 children, Tupelo, Miss.
Rejected. Nephew of Barbra A. Presley #77 and claims through the same source.

App: 2686 Hettie Weaver and 1 child, Proctor, Oklahoma.
Admitted. Claims thru father and mother enrolled as Jack and Annie Crittendon. Sister and brother enrolled as Malinda, Mary, James and Nancy. G.S. #301.

App: 2687 Tianey Bendabout, Cookson, Oklahoma.
Admitted. The father of applicant and her half brothers and sisters enrolled in Flint Dist. 640 by Drennen in 1851.

App: 2688 Lucy Halfbreed, Claremore, Oklahoma.
Admitted. Niece of #27 and claims thru the same ancestors.

App: 2689 John I. Smith and 5 children, Nina, N.C.
Admitted. First Cousin of #613 and claims thru the same source. Applicant's father enrolled by Chapman #1370. Applicant enrolled by Hester #188.

App: 2690 Thomas Payne and 1 child, Letitia, N.C.
Admitted. Applicant enrolled as Thomas Payne, C. #1353. Uncle of #1861.

App: 2691 Mary A. Owenby, et al, Afton, Oklahoma.
Admitted. By Aaron L. Ownbey, Gdn. Nieces and Nephews of #360.

App: 2692 Martha Bayles and 1 child, Tahlequah, Oklahoma.

Admitted. Claims through father, Alexander Wofford, 393 G.S. Ah-ne-wa-ki Grandmother, 391 G.S. Uncle Andrew Wofford 392 G.S.

App: 2693 Lucind Youngwolf and 2 children, Christy, Oklahoma.
Admitted. Applicant is daughter of Silas Harland. Who is the son of Lucy Fourkiller enrolled in G.S. #476. Lucy's father Fourkiller G.S. #475 and brother, Hawk. Silas Harland not living in 1851.

App: 2694 Eli Harlin, Tahlequah, Oklahoma.
Admitted. Brother of #2693 and claims thru the same source.

App: 2695 Price Cochran, Hulbert,Oklahoma.
Duplicate of #151.

App: 2696 Lotty Robins, Proctor, Oklahoma
Rejected. Mother's people were old settlers, father enrolled as O.S.S.B. #30. Grandfather was not enrolled in 1851, but came west prior to 1835. See Misc. Test p. 4220.

App: 2697 Henrietta Bean,
Same as #384.

App: 2698 Gabriel Tarepen and 1 child, Stilwell, Oklahoma.
Admitted. First Cousin of #134.

App: 2699 Nancy Gritts, Stilwell, Oklahoma.
Admitted. Applicant's father Gritts and mother Ah-ke-loh-he and sister An-na-ca enrolled G.S. #498. Applicant enrolled with them as Cah-nuh-ne-ne-ske. See application for Nancy being, Cah-nah-ne-le-ske. Misc. Test p. 3161.

App: 2700 Jesse Gettingdown, Bunch, Oklahoma.
Admitted. Cousin of #3296 and claims thru same source.

App: 2700 1/2 Simon Holmes, Wauhillau, Oklahoma.
Admitted. By Jesse Settingdown, Gdn. Applicant is a son of #13761, Grandfather enrolled as David Holmes, Ill. #176.

App: 2701 Lizzie Terrapin and 2 children, Stilwell, Oklahoma.
Admitted. Applicants parents enrolled by Drennen 1851 G.S. #535.

App: 2702 Minerva Tritthart and 4 children, Wimer, Oklahoma.
Admitted. Niece of #401

App: 2703 Mary Redinger and 2 children, Chetopa, Oklahoma.
Admitted. Niece of #390. Mother enrolled by Drennen in 1851, Del. 142.

App: 2704 Joel Bean and 5 children, Clayton, N.M.
Admitted. Uncle of #537 and claims thru the same ancestors. Applicant enrolled in 1851, Tahl. Dis. #594.

App: 2705 Lorenzo D. Davis, Jr., and 3 children, Dahlonega, Ga.
Admitted. First cousin of #98 and claims thru the same source.

App: 2706 Eugene R. Hicks, Claremore, Oklahoma.
Admitted. First cousin of #47. Claims thru the same source.

App: 2707 Jim Heaven, Bunch, Oklahoma.
Included in application of mother #1440.

App: 2708 Lucy Heaven, Bunch, Oklahoma.
Included in application of mother, #1440.

App: 2709 Steve Heaven, Bunch, Oklahoma.
Included in mother's application #1440.

App: 2710 Betsy Sanders and 4 children, Bunch, Oklahoma.
Admitted. Claims thru parents enrolled in Flint #574. Ice Beaver and also Uncle Owl. Uncle Lewis 577 Flint. Misc. Test p. 2899-2932.
App: 2711 Dave Sanders, Bunch, Oklahoma.
Admitted. Brother of #1437 and claims through the same source. Applicant enrolled by Drennen Flint Dist. #575.
App: 2712 Hy-an-E Pritchitt, Bunch, Oklahoma.
Admitted. Applicant enrolled in 1851 Flint #586. Applicant's parents Tom and Caty Pritchitt enrolled in Flint District, Group #586. Brothers and sisters #586 Flint. Time of birth in application probably a mistake.
App: 2713 Cordelia Gibbons and 5 children, Marble, N.C.
Admitted. Applicant is a sister of #1815.
App: 2714 Susan Evans, Centralia, Oklahoma.
Admitted. Applicant claims through father Ephraim Adair enrolled in Flint #399. Grand parents Calvin and Lucinda Adair enrolled in F. #399.
App: 2715 Luther M. Adair and 8 children, Centralia, Oklahoma.
Admitted. Brother of #2714 and claims thru the same source.
App: 2716 Catherine Sorrells and 5 children, Lehigh, Oklahoma.
Rejected. Applicant enrolled as a Choctaw. Her children are also enrolled with the Choctaws.
App: 2717 Rose Mongrain, Burbank, Oklahoma.
Rejected. Niece to Victoria Ware (899) and affiliated with the Osages.
App: 2718 Martha J.R. Marshal and 7 children, Temple, Texas.
Admitted. Niece of #159 and claims thru the same ancestors. R.F.D. #7
Mother of applicant enrolled by Chapman #2029.
App: 2719 Emma Nidiffer, Fairland, Oklahoma.
Admitted. Sister of #810 and claims thru the same source.
App: 2720 Dan Mitchel, Fairland, Oklahoma.
Admitted. Nephew of #2915 and claims thru the same source.
App: 2721 Jane Hughes, Melvin, Oklahoma.
Admitted. First cousin of #1079 and claims through same source.
App: 2722 George Vann, Melvin, Oklahoma.
Admitted. Uncle of #1902 and claims thru the same ancestors. Father of applicant, Arch Vann, enrolled in Skin Bayou Dis. #66.
App: 2723 George Vann,
Duplicate of #2722.
App: 2724 Ermina Craig, Proctor, Oklahoma.
Admitted. Claims through self enrolled as ~~Samuel~~ (*Handwritten above, Ermina*) Still. Half brother and sister, enrolled as Ellis, Edward Nelson and Polly Foreman. Brother enrolled as Thomas Still. All of whom were enrolled by Drennen in 1851. G.S. #G[sic]. #325.
App: 2725 Johnan Carlile and 3 children, Tahlequah, Oklahoma.
Admitted. Daughter of #2724 and claims thru same source.
App: 2726 Hiram T. Landrum, Echo, Oklahoma.
Admitted. Jesse Van Landrum and Roxie Ann Landrum. By Dino Bowman, Gdn. Nephew of #265 and claims thru the same source.

App: 2727 Robert E. Lee Carey and 6 children, Grove. Oklahoma.
Admitted. Son of #496 and claims thru the same source.
App: 2728 Savillia Brackett Dahlonega, Ga.
Admitted. Applicant claims thru father, Samuel M. Howell enrolled by Chap. #2067 Hester #2559. Grandfather Pinkney Howell enrolled Chap. #2066, Hester #2556.
App: 2729 Eudalia J. Walker and 3 children, Dahlonega, Oklahoma.
Admitted. Sister of #2728 and claims thru the same source. (Note, city is likely right but the state is likely Georgia, film shows Oklahoma.)
App: 2730 Samantha McDougal and 3 children, Marblehill, Ga.
Admitted. Sister of #2728 and claims thru the same source.
App: 2731 Sarah A. Sparks and 4 children, Dahlonega, Ga.
Admitted. Sister of #2728 and claims thru same source.
App: 2732 Mary Ann Evans and 4 children, Marble Hill, Ga.
Admitted. Sister of #2728 and claims thru the same source.
App: 2733 Leonard W. Williams and 4 children, Mark, Oklahoma.
Admitted. Uncle of #741. Applicant's mother Sarah Williams, nee Bigby enrolled by Drennen in Flint Dis. #525.
App: 2734 Sallie Manns, Welling Oklahoma.
Admitted. Applicant born in 1850; enrolled in 1851 in G.S. Dis. Group, 556. Applicant's parents Peachter and Anny enrolled by Drennen in G.S. Dis. Group #556.
App: 2735 Josie Spade and 4 children, Welling Oklahoma.
Admitted. 1/2 aunt of #2234. Father of applicant enrolled in 1851 in Flint District #238.
App: 2736. Caldona Haden, Knobnoster, Mo. Box #133.
Admitted. Niece of #1353 and claims thru the same ancestors. Mother of applicant, Edosia Clark (Weir) enrolled in 1851 in Del. Dis. #78.
App: 2737 Rebecca V. Wilson and 4 children, Phillip, Oklahoma.
Admitted. Applicant claims thru father W.J. McKee, enrolled by Chap. 1189 and grand mother Eliza McKee, enrolled by Chap. 1188 (blurred, could be 1182).
App: 2738 Bird Gritts, Jr. Tahlequah, Oklahoma.
Admitted. Duplicate of #1125.
App: 2739 Rebecca J. Conner and 1 child, Fairland, Oklahoma.
Admitted. Niece of Margaret Odell #575.
App: 2740 Annie Schaffer, Moodys, Oklahoma.
Admitted. Applicant enrolled with her mother Ceily Seabott, S.B. #29.
App: 2741 John Roach and 3 children, Hadley, Oklahoma.
Admitted. Brother of #931.
App: 2742 Anna I. Williams and 1 child, Tahlequah, Oklahoma.
Admitted. Claims thru father enrolled as McLemore Benge. Skin Bayou #165.
App: 2743 Margaret Benge, Moodys, Oklahoma.
Admitted. Sister of #2740 and claims thru the same source.
App: 2744 Susannah Henson, Melvin, Oklahoma.
Admitted. Applicant enrolled Tahl. #460, as "Susannah Henson". Sister of #607.
App: 2745 Jennie Weems, Tahlequah, Oklahoma.
Admitted. Sister of #2742 and claims through the same source.

App: 2746 Thomas Roach and 3 children, Gidion[sic],Oklahoma.
Admitted. Nephew of #278 and claims thru the same source. Applicant's mother, Nancy A. Gourd enrolled by Drennen. Tahl. Dis. #478.
App: 2747 Nettie R. Lindsey and 4 children, Sallisaw, Oklahoma.
Rejected. Applicant's mother is on the Old Settler Roll and applicant's father was a white man. Misc. Test. p. 4280.
App: 2748 Henry Dreadfulwater, Gideon, Oklahoma.
Admitted. Applicant's mother enrolled by Drennen 1851. Tahl. #30.
App: 2749 Nancy Raper, Melvin, Oklahoma.
Admtted. Applicant enrolled as Nancy Raincrow in Tah. #396. Applicant's mother Ah-lee enrolled Tah. 396 and the sister Betsy or Quaity. Father Cat Fields 250 Ill. xxxxx (*Note, x's cover word "Group"*). Grandfather and mother Raincrow and Sarah 517 Saline.
App: 2750 Nancy Raper.
Duplicate of #2749.
App: 2751 Peggy Shade, Hulbert, Oklahoma.
Admitted. Applicant was probably not born until after 1851. Father John with grandfather Bird Chopper and several aunts are enrolled in Tahl. #104.
App: 2752 Luella Crain, Moody, Oklahoma.
Admitted. Brother of #2742 and claims thru same source.
App: 2753 Sallie Stop, Peggs, Oklahoma.
Admitted. Applicant probably mistaken about being enrolled as Sa-le Tuck-See. Applicant enrolled with her mother Takee Tarpin, father Tarpin, brother Joseph and his wife Ya-ka-nee, and other brothers and sisters, S.B. #156. Misc. Test. p. 3333.
App: 2754 Ollie Taripin, Peggs, Oklahoma.
Admitted. Sister to #2753 and claims thru same source.
App: 2755 Thomas E. Beavert, Melvin, Oklahoma.
Admitted. The applicant and his mother were enrolled by Drennen in 1851 in 373 Tahlequah Dis. under the names of Charlatee Beavert and Thomas Beavert. Misc. Test #3515.
App: 2756 John L. Moore, Tulsa, Oklahoma.
Rejected. Brother of #1312.
App: 2757 John T. Tanner and 3 children, Claremore, Oklahoma.
Rejected. Cousin of #551 and claims thru the same ancestors.
App: 2758 Ross Davis and 1 child, Poreem[sic], Oklahoma.
Rejected. Claiming share of deceased wife who died Nov. 26, 1905. Minor child in this case was admitted and enrolled in Misc. Test #4217. #10,000.
App: 2759 Frank M. Morgan, Ft. Smith, Arkansas.
Admitted. Brother of #18 and claims thru the same source.
App: 2760 Caleb Birdchopper, Hulbert, Oklahoma.
Admitted. Brother to Peggy Shade (2751) and claims from the same source.
App: 2761 Octavia N. Nichols, Duluth, Ga.
Admitted. Applicant's mother enrolled by Chapman at #1844. Grandfather John Rogers also on #1835 roll. Applicant herself enrolled by Hester at #2221.
App: 2761-1/2 Sarah Beck, Estella, Oklahoma.
Admitted. Claims through father and mother enrolled as Ta-se and A-ge, also brothers Soo-wau-yah and Un-nah-ye. Del. #699. (Handwritten, *Duplicate of 2672.*)

App: 2762 Octavia N. Nichols, Duluth, Ga.
Admitted. Duplicate of #2761.
App: 2763 Octavia N. Nichols,
Duplicate of #2761.
App: 2764 Octavia N. Nichols,
Duplicate of #2761.
App: 2765 Octavia N. Nichols,
Duplicate of #2761.
App: 2766 John J. Law, Duluth, Ga.
Admitted. Duplicate of #2767.
App: 2767 John J. Law, Duluth, Ga.
Admitted. Brother of #2761 and claims thru the same source. Applicant is on Chap. Roll himself at #1846. Also enrolled by Hester at #2240.
App: 2768 John J. Law, Duluth,Ga.
Admitted. Duplicate of #2767.
App: 2767 John J. Law, Duluth,Ga.
Admitted. Duplicate of #2767.
App: 2768 John J. Law, Duluth,Ga.
Admitted. Duplicate of #2767.
App: 2769 John J. Law, Duluth,Ga.
Admitted. Duplicate of #2767.
App: 2770 John J. Law, Duluth,Ga.
Admitted. Duplicate of #2767.
App: 2771 John J. Law,
Duplicate of #2767.
App: 2772 Alva R. Bowman and 1 children, Chattanooga, Tenn.
Admitted. Mother of applicant, Mary Hildebrand" enrolled by Chap. #1537. Hester #2621. Grandfather enrolled "John W. Hildebrand" Chap. #1536. Cousin of #859, once removed. Index gives mother as "Mary Hannah".
App: 2773 Ora L. Brown and 3 children, East Chattanooga, Tenn.
Admitted. Applicant's mother enrolled in 1851 by Chapman #1537. Hester #2621 as "Mary Hildebrand". Grandfather "John W. Hildebrand" Chap. #1536.
App: 2774 James M. Hannah and 3 children, East Chattanooga, Tenn.
Admitted. Mother of applicant enrolled as Mary Hildebrand by Chap. #1537 in 1851. Cousin once removed of #859. Also acting guadian[sic] for two minors under #20196. Grandfather JOHN W. HILDEBRAND, CHAP. 1536.
App: 2775 Jack W. Hannah and 3 children, Chattanooga, Tenn.
Admitted. Mother "Mary Hildebrand enrolled "Chapman 1537 "H. 2621. Cousin once removed of #859. Grandfather John W. Hildebrand, Chap. #1536.
App: 2776 Susan J. Reed, Chattanooga, Tenn.
Admitted. Applicant's mother enrolled in 1851 by Chapman #1537. Cousin once removed of #859. (Mary Hildebrand) Also grandfather "John W. Hildebrand 1536 Chapman".
App: 2777 Dave F. Hannah and 4 children, Sherman Heights, Tenn.
Admitted. Applicant's mother "Mary Hildebrand" #1537. Chap. Cousin once removed of #859. Applicant's grandfather enrolled in 1851, "John W. Hildebrand" Chap. 1536.

App: 2778 David T. Bivins by Walter M. Bivins, his atty. Leavenworth, Kansas.
Rejected. Claimants claims thru his mother only, whose maiden name was Catherine Cheek, and mother's mother Betsey or Eliza Cheek, who appear to be on O.S. Roll Ill. 239 and 236. Ancestors do not appear on any emigrant Cherokee roll. Applicant #2778 and 79 have both been notified and failed to appear in the field for examination.
App: 2779 Walter M. Bivins, Ramona, Oklahoma.
Rejected. Applicant is a full brother of #2778.
App: 2780 Francis B. Wilson, Hally[sic] Springs, Ga.
Rejected. Neither applicant nor ancestors were enrolled. Does not establish fact of descent from any person who was a party to the treaties of 1835-6 or '46. Misc T. p. 977.
App: 2781 Mary I. Wheeler and 7 children, Woodstock, Ga.
Rejected. Sister of #2780. R.F.D. #2
App: 2782 Martha A. Reece, Woodstock, Ga.
Rejected. Claims thru Abraham Helton. See #2780.
App: 2783 Manvera A. McGinnis, Marietta, Ga.
Rejected. Aunt of #2780. Claims thru same source.
App: 2784 Bill Beamer and Rosie Beamer, Row, Oklahoma.
Admitted. Niece of John Beamer. See #4943 same group. By Nancy Beamer, Gdn. Grandmother, Lucy Downing (before marriage) G.S. #61. Misc. Test pg. 3439-2667-8.
App: 2785 Arie Linn, Row, Oklahoma.
Admitted. Sisters to minors #2785.
App: 2786 Benjamin Barnett, Flint, Oklahoma.
Admitted. First cousin of #1374. Mother of applicant enrolled in 1851 in G.S. #323.
App: 2787 John Barnett, Flint, Oklahoma.
Admitted. First Cousin of #1374. Mother of applicant enrolled in 1851 in G.S. #323.
App: 2788 Lydia Olson and 4 children, Afton, Oklahoma.
Admitted. The mother of applicant was enrolled in Flint Dis. in 1851. 299 by Drennen, as Jane Drowning Bear, or Flint #297.
App: 2789 Charles L. Foreman, Afton, Oklahoma.
Admitted. Half brother to #2788 Claims thru same mother Jane Drowning Bear, Flint #299.
App: 2790 Celie Brown, Dec'd. Vinita, Oklahoma.
Admitted. Applicant and mother enrolled by Drennen in 1851. "Wah-ne-nau-he and Celia" 151 Flint. Died June 20, 1907.
App: 2791 Clarinda S. Ray, Fairland, Oklahoma.
Admitted. Applicant's father enrolled by Drennen under the name of Thomas Munroe at #27 Disputed. Applicant's grandmother enrolled in Disputed Dis. at #25 under the name of Nancy Carrol. 1st. cousin of #2158.
App: 2792 Jim Still, Flint, Oklahoma.
Admitted. Uncle of #1374. Father of applicant enrolled in 1851 in G.S. #323.
App: 2793 George Barnett, Flint, Oklahoma.
Admitted. First cousin of #1374. Mother of applicant enrolled in 1851 in G.S. #323.

App: 2794 Lucinda Linn, (*Handwritten 2 children),* Cherokee City, Arkansas.
Admitted. Sister to #2784. Claims thru same source.
App: 2795 Lizzie Ketcher, Flint, Oklahoma.
Admitted. Aunt of #1374. Applicant enrolled in 1851 as Lizzie Still G.S. #323.
App: 2796 Laura E. Crow and 1 child, Alluwe, Oklahoma.
Admitted. Sister of #62. Claims thru same source.
App: 2797 Mary E. Cobb and 5 children, Craig, Oklahoma.
Admitted. The mother, father and sister enrolled by Drennen in 1851, 40 Canadian. Father is marked ("Not inc.").
App: 2798 Urena Copeland and 4 children, Sadie, Oklahoma.
Admitted. Applicant is a daughter of James B. Choate enrolled by Drennen in 1851 in Disp. Dis. Group #75. Applicant is a cousin of Minerva A. Springwather. #1866, whose father, Anderson Choate, was enrolled in skin bayou[sic] dis. Group. #120.
App: 2799 Samuel A. McLemore and 2 children, Murphy, N.C.
Admitted. The mother and grandmother of the applicant were enrolled by Chapman in 1851 in No. 1358 and 1857. Applicant and his parents enrolled by Hester in 1884. Nos. 1376-1379.
App: 2800 Sarah E. Robertson, Tahlequah, Oklahoma.
Admitted. Applicant's father Eli Spears enrolled in 1851 in Tahl. #234. Dawes Comission #14833. Misc. Test p. 3285.
App: 2801 Wm. F. Whitaker,
Same as #23755.
App: 2802 Thomas Ballard and 3 children, Grove, Oklahoma.
Admitted. Brother of #1820.
App: 2803 Betsie H. Boone, ~~Grant, Oklahoma.~~
(*Handwritten above,513 Dodson Ave. East Chattanooga,Tenn.*)
Admitted. Applicant's mother "Mary Hildebrand"[sic] enrolled by Chapman #1537. Grandfather "John W. Hildebrand"[sic] 1536 Chap. Cousin of #859 once removed.
App: 2804 George Pumpkinpile, Lormeta, Oklahoma.
Admitted. The applicant, his parents, brothers and sisters were enrolled in 29 Saline by Drennen in 1851.
App: 2805 Frank Pumpkinpile and 1 child, Choteau, Oklahoma.
Admitted. Applicant's father "Too-too-wah, 29 Saline". Nephew of #2804.
App: 2806 Lydia Linn and 1 child, Row, Oklahoma.
Admitted. Sister to minors #2784.
App: 2807 William Still, Flint, Oklahoma.
Admitted. Uncle of #1374. Applicant enrolled in 1851 G.S. #373.
App: 2808 Veda E. Welch and Eva A. Welch, Needmore, Oklahoma.
Admitted. By Randoph Ballard, Gdn. Parents born after 1851. Grandfather of applicants "106 Delaware". Daniel Huss. Also grandmother "Jane Huss".
App: 2809 Kate F. Howell and 3 children, Madill, Oklahoma.
Rejected. Sizemore case. See special report #417.
App: 2810 Ben Birdchopper, Locust Grove, Oklahoma.
Admitted. Grandson of #87.
App: 2811 Nellie Bridge, Locust Grove, Oklahoma.
Admitted. Grand-daughter of #87. Claims thru same source.

App: 2812 Pickens E. Willis, Dawsonville, Ga.
Duplicate of #159.

App: 2813 Pickens E. Willis, Dawsonville, Ga.
Rejected. Duplicate of #159.

App: 2814 Tyler Chuckleluck, Locust Grove, Oklahoma.
Admitted. The father of applicant and his paternal grandmother were enrolled by Drennen in 1851 in 840 Del. Dis. under the names of Un-taw-You-lah and Cho-ko-he.

App: 2815 Huckleberry Birdchopper, Locust Grove, Oklahoma.
Admitted. Grandson of #87.

App: 2816 Robin Pann, Melvin, Oklahoma.
Admitted. Nephew of #376.

App: 2817 Ross B. Smith, Nina, N. C.
Admitted. Applicant enrolled by Chapman 1851 #1369. Uncle of #613.

App: 2818 Littlebird Buckskin, Locust Grove, Oklahoma.
Admitted. Half brother of #84.

App: 2819 Deck Pickeep and 3 children, Locust Grove, Oklahoma.
Admitted. Uncle of #443 and claims thru same source.

App: 2820 Wm. L. D. Keith and 3 children, Bear, Arkansas.
Rejected. It does not appear that ancestors of applicant were a party to the treaties of 1835-6 or '46, nor that any ancestors were ever enrolled. Shows no real connection with the Eastern Cherokees. Misc. Test 2042.

App: 2821 Eva Shoup and 1 child, Star City, Arkansas.
Rejected. Daughter of 2821 and claims thru the same source.

App: 2822 George McCuen (dead) Akin, Oklahoma.
Admitted. Applicant is a nephew of #1050. Grandfather, "Geo. Blair" 641 Flint".

App: 2823 John Lucas and 1 child, Flint, Oklahoma.
Admitted. Applicant's grandfather "Stephen Hildebrand" enrolled "Tahl. 540", Neph. of #859. Bro. to Nancy Taylor, #13632.

App: 2824 Margaret Starks and 5 children, Siloam Spgs, Ark.
Admitted. First cousins of #1374. Mother of applicant enrolled in 1851 in G.S. #323.

App: 2825 Sarah Lucas and 2 children, Flint, Oklahoma.
Admitted. Aunt of #1374. Father of applicant enrolled in 1851 in G.S. #823.
(*Handwritten below 8, "5"*)

App: 2826 Andrew Polecat and 3children, Long, P.O., Oklahoma.
Admitted. The parents of applicant were enrolled by Drennen in 1851 in 534 Del. Dis. "Polecat and Sealy" Applicant probably mistaken as to date of birth (1850) or under different name.

App: 2827 Polly Steps and 3 children, Evansville, Arkansas.
Admitted. Applicant is a full blood and is of eastern[sic] Cherokee descent- as shown by her testimony. Misc. Test p. 5301 and by testimony of Saw-ney taken at Stilwell, Oklahoma., March 23, 1909. p. 3992. Also see Misc. test of half sister Aggie Vance p. 3052.

App: 2828 Lucy Bigfeather and 2 children, Maple, Oklahoma.

Admitted. Applicant's parents enrolled by Chapman 1852 No. 798 and 799. Dick Grape and Sallie Grape, parents enrolled as Too-ches-tah and Uh-wa-tih. (See letter) Misc. Test. p. 2913.

App: 2829 Sallie Vann and 2 children, Melvin, Oklahoma.
Admitted. Applicant claims thru mother Nakey 134 G.S. Grand parents OO-lee-s-tah and Aley 135 G.S. Misc. Test p. 4082. and 3328.

App: 2830 Ella L. Crocker, Stilwell, Oklahoma.
Rejected. Claims thru John Tidwell. See #16. Duplicate of #23366.

App: 2831 Lyd-da Liver and 4 children, Stilwell, Oklahoma.
Admitted. Niece of #1914 and claims thru the same source.

App: 2832 John Liver, Stilwell, Oklahoma.
Admitted. The father and grandmother of the applicant were enrolled by Drennen under the name of Ave and Darkey Flint #9. Misc. Test p. 3071.

App: 2833 James W. Bell, Wolf Creek, N.C.
Rejected. Brother of #1661.

App: 2834 Jennie Wolf, Proctor, Oklahoma.
Admitted. Mother of #1609.

App: 2835 Fannie Higgins (deceased) Claremore, Oklahoma.
Rejected. By W.D. Higgins, Husband. Fannie Higgins, died September 3rd, 1899.

App: 2835-1/2. Isabell Higgins, Paul Higgins, Porum, Oklahoma.
Admitted. (*Handwritten Admitted.*) By Mary E. Robbs,
Grand niece and grand nephew of #159 and claims thru the same ancestors. Mother of children enrolled Hester #2451. Grandmother enrolled by Chapman, 2006.

App: 2836 Rachel A. Weinberger and 3 children, Big Cabin, Okla.
Admitted. Niece of #456.

App: 2837 Daisy Perry Smart and one child, Vinita, Oklahoma.
Rejected. Applicant's father is a white man. Also her husband. (See appl. 25146. Claimant's mother, maternal grandmother and uncles and aunts enrolled in Old Settler Roll in 1851. Non. Rec. 14. See misc. Test 3673.

App: 2838 Sara P. Nelms, Vinita, Oklahoma.
Rejected. Aunt of #2837.

App: 2839 Ruth E. Galloway and 1 child, Coffeyville, Kan.
Admitted. Applicant's father enrolled by Chapman #1831 with other relatives. (Father, John Howard Rogers).

App: 2840 Annie Meggs and 1 child, Locust Grove, Okla.
Admitted. Applicant's father To-lees-kih enrolled Chap. #943, uncles Sow-win-woo-kah and Westih C. 941-942. Grandparents Joe Locust and Kul-sti-ih C. 939-940. Other uncles C. 945-946 Misc. Test. p. 3773.

App: 2841 Nannie Wolfe and 1 child, Locust Grove, Okla.
Admitted. The father and grandmother of applicant were enrolled as Old Settlers in Flint District #22. Grandfather on father's side was enrolled by Drennen in Flint Dis. #14. under the name of David Consene.

App: 2842 John Tahquett, Hulbert, Okla.
Admitted. Claimant's parents, one brother and two sisters enrolled by Chapman in 1851, C. 1124 to 28, inc. (Note: #1124 the first, (1), looks like it is crossed out.)

App: 2843 William M. Hughes, Lometa, Oklahoma.
Admitted. Applicant claims through father, John Hughes enrolled in 1851 in Saline 18. Misc. Test p. 3579.
App: 2844 Nanny G. Butler and 1 child, Muskogee, Okla.
Rejected. Applicant's father was adopted by the Creek tribe and applicant was enrolled by the Dawes Commission as a Creek. Misc. Test. p. 3041.
App: 2845 Hester O. Wood,
Duplicate of #42563.
App: 2846 Charles Reese and 2 children, Muskogee, Oklahoma.
Admitted. Claimant's father enrolled by Drennen in 1851 Can. 15 under name of Charles Reese. Claimant enrolled by Dawes Commission #16930 as a half blood. See Misc. Test 3465.
App: 2847 Theodore C. Kelley, Afton, Oklahoma.
Admitted. Claimant's maternal Grandfather enrolled by Drennen in 1851 Del. 335. See misc. test #2666. Claimant enrolled by the Dawes Commission #30450 as a quarter blood.
App: 2848 Ruth K. Downing and 4 children, Muskogee, Oklahoma.
Admitted. Applicant born since 1851. Enrolled by the Dawes Commission #5886. Mother Akey Kenah enrolled 190 S.B. Original shows Akey an orphan which accounts for her standing alone on the Roll.
App: 2849 Annie Blackwood and 3 children, Baron, Oklahoma.
Admitted. Claimant's father who has filed application #13109, enrolled by Drennen in 1851 under name of Oo-you-chus-ey. Father's father and step mother and grand-parents enrolled in Tahl. #513 and 557 respectively. Claimant's fathers mother enrolled in Flint 196 as Ta-aky.
App: 2850 Nancy Jack, Gans, Oklahoma.
Admitted. Aunt of #1214. Applicant's father is on Drennen's Roll #212. Applicant was born in 1852.
App: 2851 Sarah A. Moor and 1 child, Atlanta, Ga.
Admitted. Sister of #2761 and claims thru the same source. Applicant herself on Chapman Roll #2241.
App: 2852 Sarah A. Moore and no children, Atlanta, Ga.
Admitted. Duplicate of #2851.
App: 2853 Sarah A. Moore and 1child, Atlanta, Ga.
Admitted. Duplicate of #2851.
App: 2854 Sarah A. Moore, Atlanta, Ga.
Admitted. Duplicate of #2851.
App: 2855 Sarah A. Moore and 1child, Atlanta, Ga.
Admitted. Duplicate of #2851.
App: 2856 Sarah A. Moore and 1child, Atlanta, Ga.
Admitted. Duplicate of #2851.
App: 2857 Mary A. McDonoald[sic] and 2 children, Watova, Oklahoma.
Admitted. Claimant's father, Paternal Grandmother and aunts enrolled by Drennen in 1851 Dis. 73. See Misc. Test 3085.
App: 2858 Florence E. McSpadden and 2 children, Chelsea, Oklahoma.
Admitted. Niece of #253 and claims thru the same source. Applicant's father, Hyman Hoyt enrolled by Drennen, Disputed Dis. #41.

App: 2859 Geo. H. Johnston,
Same as #8032.

App: 2860 Annie Evans and 2 children, Kansas, Oklahoma.
Admitted. Sister of #1596 and claims thru the same ancestors.

App: 2861 Richard Hawk and 2 children, Stilwell, Oklahoma.
Admitted. Claimant's mother and maternal grandfather enrolled by Drennen in 1851, Fl. 379. See Misc. Test. 3162 for name of G.F., maternal grandfather's brothers and sisters enrolled in Flint #376. See Misc. Test 3047-3162. Maternal Grandmother enrolled in Del. 995. See Misc. Test 3047. Paternal grandfather enrolled in Flint 12. Claimant enrolled by the Dawes Commission #32770. as full blood.

App: 2862 John Hitcher, Stilwell, Oklahoma.
Admitted. Claims thru his mother Quaty and grandfather Corn silk who were enrolled in 1851 by Drennen in G.S. #445. Misc. T. p. 3307.

App: 2863 John Hooper, Christie, Oklahoma.
Admitted. Claimant's father, paternal grandfather and uncles and aunt enrolled by Drennen in 1851. Flint #664. See Misc. Test 3160.

App: 2864 Lizzie Starr and 2 children, Stilwell, Oklahoma.
Admitted. Claimant's mother, maternal grandmother and uncles enrolled by Drennen 1851 Flint #304.

App: 2865 Silk Dougherty and 4 children, Stilwell, Oklahoma.
Duplicate of #2070.

App: 2866 Eva Teller, Bunch, Oklahoma.
Admitted. Aunt of #2484 and claims thru the same source.

App: 2867 Polly Christie, Bunch, Oklahoma.
Admitted. Applicant claims Emigrant Cherokee descent thru her grand parents, Joe and Lizzie Teller enrolled by Drennen in 1851 in Flint Dis. Group #117. Daughter of #2866.

App: 2868 Nancy R. Panter and 3 children, Stilwell, Oklahoma.
Admitted. Niece of #2273. Father of applicant enrolled in 1851 in G.S. #715.

App: 2869 Sarah Coon, Stilwell, Oklahoma.
Admitted. Claimant, her parent and sister enrolled by Drennen in 1851 G.S. #455.

App: 2870 George Ross, Locust Grove, Oklahoma.
Admitted. Half brother of #99.

App: 2871 Mary J. Shoap, Welch, Oklahoma.
Admitted. Sister of #1131 and claims thru same source.

App: 2872 Lucy Shell and 6 children, Stilwell, Oklahoma.
Admitted. Sister to #2861.

App: 2873 Maggie Sixkiller, Stilwell, Oklahoma.
Admitted. Claimants grandparents on father's side and father's older brothers and sisters enrolled by Drennen in 1851. Ill. #202. Parents probably not born until after '51.

App: 2874 Daisy Harris,
Duplicate of #24057.

App: 2875 Jefferson Baldwin and 5 children, Grant, Va.
Rejected. Sizemore case. See special report #417.

App: 2876 Julia A. Baldwin, Park, Va.
Rejected. Sizemore case. See special report #417.
App: 2877 Anderson H. Neal, Aska, Ga.
Rejected. It does not appear that any ancestor was ever enrolled or that any ancestor was a party to the treaties of 1835-6 or '46. Ancestors did not live in the Cherokee domain at the time of the treaties. Shows no real connection with the Eastern Cherokees. Misc. Test p. 1438.
App: 2878 Isaac L. Garland and 7 children, Wilscot, Ga.
Rejected. Claims thru same source as #690.
App: 2879 James W. Davis and 4 children, Due, Ga.
Rejected. Claims thru same source as #690.
App: 2880 Polly C. Garland, Wilscot, Ga.
Rejected. Claims thru the same source as #690.
App: 2881 Sarah J. Neal, Aska, Ga.
Rejected. Claims thru same source as #690.
App: 2882 Geo. W. Davis, Due, Ga.
Rejected. Claims thru the same source as #699[sic]. (probably #690)
App: 2883 Anna Smith Wilscot, Ga.
Rejected Sister of 18140 and claims thru the same source.
App: 2884 Dudley Johnson, Tahlequah, Oklahoma.
Admitted. Claimant's father, Paternal grandmother, uncles and aunt enrolled by Chapman in 1851, C. 1322 to 26 inc.
App: 2885 Susanna Kirk and 6 children, Tahlequah, Oklahoma.
Admitted. Niece of #2686 and claims thru the same source.
App: 2886 Isaac Johnson, Tahlequah, Oklahoma.
Admitted. Brother of #2884.
App: 2887 Miah (or Myer) Johnson, Tahlequah, Oklahoma.
Admitted. Brother of #2884.
App: 2888 Alexander Sutton, Grove, Oklahoma.
Admitted. Claimant's father enrolled in '51 by Drennen under name of Jack Sutton, G.S. #76. Claimant's father's half brother enrolled in G.S. #77. See Misc. Test 2670.
App: 2889 Elizabeth J. Clark, Grove, Oklahoma.
Admitted. Sister of #2888.
App: 2890 Elizabeth Meadows, Buren, Ga.
Admitted. Sister of #1122. This applicant died August 13, 1908. See application of daughter #45112.
App: 2891 Martha A. Huggins and 4 children, Young Harris, Ga.
Admitted. Niece of #1122. Mother of applicant enrolled in 1851 by Chapman #2806.
App: 2892 Mary J. Meadows, ~~XXX~~Buren, Ga.
Admitted. Duplicate of #2892.
App: 2893 David T. Meadows, ~~Voyles, Ga.~~
(Handwritten above, Culbertson, N.C., R. #1 Box 51)
Admitted. Nephew of #1122. Mother of applicant enrolled in 1851 by Chap. #2086.

App: 2894 N. Isabella St. Jermain, Lac Du Flambeau, Wis.
Admitted. Claimant's father, paternal grandparents, uncle and aunt enrolled by Chapman in 185, C. 1218 to 1222 inc. Children in Supplemental rejected by reason of being affiliated with Chippewas. See letter marked "A"

App: 2895 Melissa M. Presley and 3 children, Brighton, Mo.
Rejected. Claims through Alex. Brown. See special report #35.

App: 2896 Frank J. Hardin and 4 children, Andrews, N.C.
Admitted. Son of #687 and claims through the same source.

App: 2897 Mary J. Melton and 6 children, Hayesville, N.C.
Rejected. Cousin of #126 and claims through the same ancestors. R.F.D. #1

App: 2898 Callie Sitton and 1 child, Bryson City, N.C.
Rejected. Niece of #664 and claims thru the same source.

App: 2899 Anna M. Tovey and 4 children, Hudson, Oklahoma.
Admitted. 1st. cousin of #805. Mother, Mary Langley, 1904 Chapman. Uncle, Noah Langley, 1905 Chapman. Aunt, Nancy Gobel (#1521) 1913 Chapman. Aunt, Cynthia Moton. 91 Disputed.

App: 2900 John W. Leach, Claremore, Oklahoma.
Admitted. Brother of #2899. First cousin of #805 and claims through the same source. Mother, Mary Langley 1904 Chapman. Uncle, Noah Langley, 1905.

App: 2901 Andy Hill and 5 children, Blue Ridge, Ga.
Admitted. Brother of #743 and claims thru the same source.

App: 2902 Henry Brooks and 2 children, Tishomingo, Oklahoma.
Rejected. The ancestors of applicant were not enrolled. They were born 200 miles from the Eastern Cherokee Domain. Were not parties to treaties of 1835-6 and 1846.

App: 2903 Nancy Petitt, Cookson, Oklahoma.
Admitted. Sister of #1596 and claims thru the same ancestors. Applicant is enrolled, Ill. Dis. #7

App: 2904 Bertha Tabor, Greene Forest, Ark.
Rejected. It does not appear that any ancestor was ever enrolled or that any ancestor was a party to the treaties of 1835-6 or '46. Shows no real connection with the Eastern Cherokees. Ancestors did not live in the Cherokee domain. Misc. Test. 2610 and 2611.

App: 2905 Amanda J. Raymond, Venita[sic], Okla.
Admitted. Enrolled as Amanda McCrary, Del. #25. Sister of #735. Applicant herself enrolled in Del. Dis. #25.

App: 2906 Josephine West and 3 children, Spavinaw, Okla.
Admitted. Sister of #1745, and claims thru the same ancestors.

App: 2907 Walter Smith and 6 children, Fairland, Oklahoma.
Admitted. Brother of #1745 and claims thru the same ancestors.

App: 2908 Clara A. Ward, New York City, N.Y.
Admitted. Duplicate of #979.

App: 2909 Mary E. Agnew and 1 child, Keefeton, Oklahoma.
Admitted. Claims thru self enrolled as *(Handwritten above, Mary)* Jane Vickrey. All were enrolled by Chapman in 1851. Nos. 1875 to 78 inc. Sister and brother enrolled as Josephine and Josephus Vickrey.

App: 2910 Laura Robinson and 6 children, Keefeton, Oklahoma.
Admitted. Claims thru mother enrolled as Sarah Riley. Grandmother enrolled as Susan Riley. Aunt and Uncle enrolled as Jane and Harrison Riley. All were enrolled by Drennen in 1851 in Flint District Group #613.
App: 2911 Jesse V. Wright and 2 children, Baron, Oklahoma.
Admitted. First cousin of 2692 and claims thru the same source. Applicant enrolled in G.S. 450.
App: 2912 Ella Daniels and 1 child, Westville, Oklahoma.
Admitted. Sister of #1614 and claims thru the same source. 2913.
App: 2913 N. Hatcher Berry, Kansas City, Mo.
Rejected. Applicant claims through father. The father was 1800 Grove St.
as slave. Applicants parents born in Va. and probably never lived within the Cherokee domain. It seems they were never enrolled and were not parties to the treaties of 1835-6 or '46.
App: 2914 James Baldwin and 6 children, Rugby, Va.
Rejected. Sizemore case. See special report #417.
App: 2915 Sabra E. Fields, Grove, Oklahoma.
Admitted. Applicant was enrolled by Chapman #2099 as Sabry E. Ward.
App: 2916 Dora M. Drake and 6 children, Big Cabin, Oklahoma.
Admitted. Niece of #998. Applicant's mother enrolled as "Caroline Lynch, 373 Saline.
App: 2917 Mary E. Robbs and 1 child, Porum, Oklahoma.
Admitted. Niece of #159 and claims thru the same ancestors. Applicant enrolled by Hester #2453. Mother of applicant enrolled by Chapman, #2029.
App: 2918 Editha A. Ritter, ~~Battlesville~~, Oklahoma.
Admitted. 1st. cousin of #2399 and her grandfather Thomas Wolf is on Drennen Roll #927. Del. Dis. applicant's mother born after 1851. (*Handwritten above city, Bartlesville.)*
App: 2919 Geo. W. Clark and 2 children, Vinita, Oklahoma.
Admitted. Applicant enrolled as George Clark Disputed 36. Mother enrolled as Mary Clark 36 Disputed. Brothers and sisters, James, John, Lucy and Louisa enrolled in Disputed 36.
App: 2920 Lydia Ann Clark, Vinita, Oklahoma.
Admitted. Applicant enrolled in 1851 in G.S. #677. Parents enrolled in 1851 in G.S. #677. Several brothers in 677. G.S.
App: 2921 Addelia Chatter, Dahlongea[sic], Ga.
Rejected. Ancestors not on rolls. Does not show genuine connection with Cherokee Tribe. Misc. Test p. 1510.
App: 2922 Jesse H. Chatter and 1 child, Dahlonega, Ga.
Rejected. Sister of #2921.
App: 2923 John E. S. Chatin[sic] (or Chatter) and 1 child, Dahlonega, Ga.
Rejected. (*Handwritten Rejected.*) Brother of #2921.
App: 2924 John Lowry McLenore and 2 children, Grape Creek, N.C.
Admitted. Brother to #2799.
App: 2925 Martha Starr, Sallisaw, Oklahoma.
Admitted. Sister of #316 and claims thru the same source.

App: 2926 Ellis Starr and 2 children, Sallisaw, Oklahoma.
Admitted. Applicant claims thru mother Cynthia P. Starr who is enrolled in Flint District Group #355. Sisters, Sarah J. and Mary T. are enrolled 375 F1. Grand mother Margaret Triplet, Flint #497.

App: 2927 Martha Starr,
Duplicate of #2925.

App: 2928 George Sanders, Baron, Oklahoma.
Admitted. Nephew of #1776.

App: 2929 Clara Woodall, Baron, Oklahoma.
Admitted. Half sister of 1729 and claims thru the same ancestor. Applicant was enrolled in 1851 under name of Clarinda, with her mother Nancy Catcher in G.S. #239.

App: 2930 Israel Kingfisher, Locust Grove, Okla.
Admitted. Son of #712.

App: 2931 Thomas J. Henry and 2 children, Locust Grove, Okla.
Admitted. Neither parent probably living in 1851. Grand parents on mother's side Watte and Nancy Christy enrolled 233 Saline. Misc. Test #3760

App: 2932 William H. Wood and 2 children, ~~Miggs~~, Oklahoma.
Admitted. Brother of #1131. Claims thru the same source. (*Handwritten above city, Peggs.)*

App: 2933 Charlie Christie, Locust Grove, Okla.
Admitted. Son of #2494.

App: 2934 Tillman England and 5 children, Locust Grove, Okla.
Admitted. Son of #515 and claims from the same ancestors. Application for Cora E. England, minor child, is not allowed, as said child was born after Ma~~8~~*y* 28/0~~8~~*6* (*Handwritten the (y) in May is written over an 8 and the a (6) is written below a blurred (8).*)

App: 2935 Jess Sanders, Locust Grove, Okla.
Admitted. Half nephew of #407. Son of #10469. Paternal grand parents enrolled in #322 Tahl.

App: 2936 Sallie Stealer and 3 children, Locust Grove, Okla.
Admitted. Applicant claims through her father Owl or oo-goo-koo. Enrolled in Del. Dis. #795 Group. Mother Hah-loo-ke (*H looks like a C*) and grand mother Caty enrolled in Del. Dis. Group 616. Misc. Test 3797.

App: 2937 Nellie Sake, Robbinsville, N.C.
Admitted. Applicant enrolled by Chapman 923 Misc. T. 1667.

App: 2938 Wah-leas-cie Kingfisher and 3 children, Peggs, Oklahoma.
Admitted. Claims thru mother as Ti-an-ah McCoy. Ill. Dis. #202.

App: 2939 Sarah Dreadfulwater, Locust Grove, Okla.
Admitted. Applicant claims thru father Cheh-ska-yee-hee. Enrolled with his parents James and Wee-kee Hogskin in Saline #164. Applican[sic] also claims thru mother Yo-wee-see enrolled with her parents in G.S. #136. Misc. Test P. 3767.

App: 2940 Emma Downing and 1 child, Locust Grove, Okla.
Admitted. Daughter of #515 and claims thru the same ancestors.

App; 2941 Jennie Bolin and 3 children, Locust Grove, Okla.
Admitted. Daughter of #2494.

App: 2942 Ida Henry, Locust Grove, Okla.

Admitted. Niece of Lizzie Downing (1872). Applicant's father born in 1852 and probably not enrolled. See application #1873. Misc. Test #3742.

App: 2943 John Swimmer and 1 child, Locust Grove, Oklahoma.
Admitted. This applicant's father Swimmer or Ah-dah-wos-ke Christy are enrolled by Drennen from Del. Dis. under group #847. Mis. T. 3784.

App: 2944 Lucy Downing, Locust Grove, Okla.
Admitted. Niece of #1245 and claims thru same ancestors. Father of applicant enrolled in 1851 under name of Oo-soh-tsar-ne-tah in Saline District #103.

App: 2945 George W. Bark, Locust Grove, Oklahoma.
Admitted. Applicant claims thru father OO-hul-loo-ke enrolled 327 Saline. Applicant also claims thru mother Caty Mouse enrolled with her parents Lacy and Betsy Mouse in Saline Dis. #213.

App: 2946 Reubin Mullins and 6 children, Muskogee, Okla.
Rejected. The ancestors of the applicant were never enrolled with the Eastern Cherokees. Were not parties to treaties of 1835-6 and 1846. Ancestors were born out of Eastern Cherokee domain.

App: 2947 Elizabeth Mullin, Muskogee, Oklahoma.
Rejected. The ancestors of applicant were never enrolled. They were born 100 miled[sic] from the Cherokee domain and were not parties to the treaties of 1835-6 or '46.

App: 2948 Charlotte Hummingbird and 3 children, Rose, Oklahoma.
Admitted. Applicant claims thru mother Tes-te enrolled, in Saline 135. Tee-we-tsa to 134 Saline and daughter Lydia Great-grandfather Ar-stor-lar Saline #131. Tsa-te 1/2 brother John Thompson 136 Saline. Misc. Test p. 3763-3769-3838.

App: 2949 Robin Puller, Locust Grove, Oklahoma.
Admitted. Applicant probably enrolled as Low-in-er 105 Tahlequah. Applicant's father Te-sah-skee enrolled in Tahl. #156. See application for Te-sa-skee. Misc. T. p. 3736

App: 2950 Eliza Journeycake and 3 children, Nowata, Okla.
Admitted. Claims thru mother enrolled as Catherine Benge. Skin Bayou #164.

App: 2951 George Daniels and 3 children, Locust Grove, Okla.
Admitted. Applicant claims thru mother Sarah Tinson enrolled in Tahl. #554. Sarah's brothers and sisters are enrolled in same group Tahl. #554. See application.

App: 2952 Waddie T. McCoy and 1 child, Kansas, Oklahoma.
Admitted. Brother of #2679.

App: 2953 Dick Christy, Locust Grove, Okla.
Admitted. This applicant's grandfather Arch Christy and also his father Ah-dah-wos-ke Christy are enrolled by Drennen from Del. Dis. under group #847. Misc. Test p. 3784 and 3440.

App: 2954 William Christy, Locust Grove, Okla.
Admitted. Brother of Dick Christy #2953.

App: 2955 Sallie Co~~u~~seen[sic], (*Handwritten "n" above u*) Tomathy, N.C.
Admitted. Applicant is enrolled by Chapman 1059 and by Hester 1165. Misc. Test 1669. Died about Xmas. 1907.

App: 2956 Kate Conseen and 1 child, Robbinsville, N.C.
Admitted. 1st. cousin of #730 and claims thru same source. Niece of #728. Mother and father "Quh-la-leet and Aul-cin-nih, 1058 and 1059. Chap. Grandmother of applicant Jimmie 980 Chap. Grandfather 979 Chap.

App: 2957 Os-kin-nee or Ohlee-kee-nee, Robbinsville, N.C.
Admitted. Applicant claims thru mother Ail-cih Chap. 920. Applicant's grand mother Sa-kee Chap. 919. Applicant's grand father, Cho-le-lo-ga. 918 Chap. Misc. Test p. 1665.

App: 2958 Sam Canoe, Locust Grove, Oklahoma.
Admitted. Applicant claims thru grand parents Taw-you-ne-see and Lydia enrolled in Flint, Group #23. Great grand parents Arch and Jimmy Roe enrolled in Flint #21. Parents were not born in 1851. Misc. Test. p. 3726.

App: 2959 Ellen Hughes and 2 children, Rose, Oklahoma.
Admitted. Half sister of #641. Applicant enrolled in 1851 as Ellen Smith. G.S. #15.

App: 2960 Sallie Garland, Chelsea, Oklahoma.
Admitted. Applicant herself enrolled Chap. 1156. Hester 1911. Mother, Nicy Daws, Chap. #1153. Many of mother's brothers and sisters, Ned. C. 1285. James Welch, Chapman #1276, Jonathan, Chap. #1281. Richard Chap. #1283. Others to numerous to mention.

App: 2961 Lloyd R. Dawes and 2 children, Chelsea, Oklahoma.
Admitted. Brother of #2960.

App: 2962 Elizabeth M. Garland and 1 child, Chelsea, Oklahoma.
Admitted. Sister of #2960. Enrolled in 1851 by Chapman #1154.

App: 2963 Martha A. Dawes, Chelsea, Oklahoma.
Admitted. Sister of #2960.

App: 2964 Jonathan W. Dawes and 7 children, Chelsea, Oklahoma.
Admitted. Brother of #2960.

App: 2965 Joseph M. Hart and 2 children, Rugby, Va.
Rejected. Sizemore case. See special report #417.

App: 2966 Charley Hudson and wife and 2 children, Rugby, Va.
Rejected. Sizemore case. See special report #417.

App: 2967 Sarah E. Emerson and 1 child, Rugby, Va.
Rejected. Sizemore case. See special report #417.

App: 2968 Emma Pickup and 5 children, Spavinaw, Okla.
Admitted. Applicant claims thru father Ah-le-teve-ky enrolled in Del. 1001. Uncle Moses or Wor-see and James Downing also enrolled Del. #1001.

App: 2969 Sallie Downing and 2 children, Peggs, Oklahoma.
Admitted. Sister to #2970.

App: 2970 Nellie Roach, Peggs, Oklahoma.
Admitted. The father and mother of applicant were enrolled under the names of Scah-ha-char and Uc-te-yah in 458 Tahl. Dis. by Drennen in 1851.

App: 2971 Joe Blossom and 3 children, Locust Grove, Okla.
Admitted. Brother of #78 and claims thru the same source.

App: 2972 Mary Glory and 1 child, Tahlequah, Okla.
Admitted. Applicant claims thru mother Celie. According to application 2972 Celie was living in 1851. The application of one half brother shows mother not born until after 1851, which explains her non appearance on the roll. The grand-parents To-choo-lau-eh and Chi-co-na-lah are enrolled in G.S. #194.

App: 2973 Edward A. Trent and 3 children, Valeda, Oklahoma.

Rejected. Applicant's father white (See application). Mother and grand mother Kamilla and Margaret Scott are Old Settlers. Group #26, page 67. Applicant's wife, white. (See application and supplemental. Also rejected. Misc. T. p. 2247.

App: 2974 Andrew M. Trout and 4 children, Spavinaw, Oklahoma.
Admitted. Brother of #971 and claims thru the same source.

App; 2975 Eliza Riggs, Chelsea, Oklahoma.
Admitted. Applicant claims thru father, David Su-wa-gee, enrolled as Dave-se in Del. #98. Father's parents, Tom and Chah-wah-you-cah. Su-wa-ga and sisters We-ke, Ah-noo-wa-ke, and Che-caw-na-la are all enrolled in Del. #98. Misc. Test p. 2597.

App: 2976 Charles D. Kenney and 2 children, Vinita, Oklahoma.
Admitted. Brother to Mary Yeorgain #1972 and claims thru the same source. Mother Del. #499.

App: 2977 Mary Elizabeth Kenworthy and 1 child, Woodley, Oklahoma.
Admitted. Claims thru self enrolled as Elizabeth Schrimsher. Mother enrolled as Ruthy Schrimsher. Brothers and sisters enrolled as John, Newton and Louisa Schrimsher. All were enrolled by Drennen in 1851 in Del. Dis. Group #966.

App: 2978 Lizzie Smith, Welch, Oklahoma.
Rejected. Applicant white. Claims thru husband who died Feb. 1906, but left no children.

App: 2979 Thomas Woodall and 3 children, Seneca, Missouri.
Rejected. It does not appear that the ancestors of applicant were enrolled. While his ancestors came from the old Cherokee domain it does not appear that they lived with the Eastern Cherokees or that they were parties to the treaties of 1835-6 and 1846. Ancestors are not on any of the Eastern Cherokee rolls.

App: 2980 Sabray C. Green and 1 child, Joplin, Missouri.
Rejected. Sister of #2979 and claims through the same source.

App: 2981 Thomas F. Armstrong, Valeda, Kansas.
Rejected. Brother of #2666 and rejected for the same reasons.

App: 2982 Johnson Lyman and 3 children, Vinita, Oklahoma.
Admitted. Applicant claims thru mother, Ruth Foreman, enrolled in Saline #218. Mother's brother and sister George and Emily Foreman also enrolled #218 Saline. Probably mother living with another man in 1851. Misc. Test. p. 3671.

App: 2983 Susan Deal and 1 child, Estella, Oklahoma.
Admitted. Claimant's father under name of You-nah, and father's mother, Elizabeth; grandmother, Aim-se, and his brothers and sisters enrolled by Drennen in 1851. Del. 1024. See Misc. Test. p. 4378.

App: 2984 Bettie Woodall and 1 child, Vinita, Oklahoma.
Admitted. Applicant claims thru father, James Perdue, enrolled in Disputed Dis. Group 58. An uncle, Joseph, Disputed 57. An aunt, Polly, Disputed 59.

App: 2985 Andrew Bark, Chapel, Oklahoma.
Admitted. Brother of #2945 and claims thru same source.

App: 2986 Jack Rowe, Locust Grove, Okla.
Admitted. Nephew of #10, and claims thru the same source.

App: 2987 Peggie Bluebird and 1 child, Locust Grove, Okla.
Admitted. Grandparents Arch and Jennie Row, or Roe, were enrolled by Drennen, Group 21, Flint. Her father enrolled in #22 Flint.

App: 2988 Susan Pann, Hulbert, Oklahoma.
Admitted. Applicant a full blood. Enrolled by the D.C. #16256, Jim Pann testified at Tahlequah that applicant was an emigrant. She does not appear on the Old Settler roll. She was born in Tennessee in 1834. Misc. Test. p. 3419.

App: 2989 Mose Fuling, Tahlequah, Oklahoma.
Admitted. Applicant's grandfather, Oo-too-lah-ta-nah, enrolled by Drennen in Tahl. #175.

App: 2990 Nancy J. Chastain and 5 children, Eureka, Oklahoma.
Admitted. Cousin of #671, and claims thru same source.

App: 2991 Bertha Clark and 2 children, Chelsea, Oklahoma.
Admitted. Niece of #38 and claims thru the same source.

App: 2992 Jos. R. Sanders and 1 child, Adair, Oklahoma.
Admitted. Half brother of #1205.

App: 2993 James E. Elliott and 1 child, Adair, Oklahoma.
Admitted. First cousin of #1396 and claims thru same source.

App: 2994 Jane Buckner, Wayton, Ark.
Rejected. Daughter of #415 and claims thru same source.

App: 2995 Allie E. Ferguson, Stilwell, Oklahoma.
Admitted. Applicant's mother, Vianna Raper and her grandfather Charles Raper were enrolled by Chapman #1419 and 1417 respectively.

App: 2996 Samuel L. Sanders, Melvin, Oklahoma.
Admitted. Brother of #2995 and claims thru same source.

App: 2997 Aley A. Johnson, Stilwell, Oklahoma.
Admitted. Aunt of #2995 and claims thru same source.

App: 2998 Lydia A. Coble and 5 children, Cornet, Mo.
Rejected. Claims thru Alex. Brown. See special report #35.

App: 2999 John H. McGhee and 2 children, Kinnison, Oklahoma.
Admitted. First cousin of No. (*Handwritten 1912.)*

App: 3000 Joseph Hines, Chilloco, Okla.
Rejected. Claimant's mother is a full sister of #6958 and his father is a white man. He should be rejected for the same reason as #6958.

www.ingramcontent.com/pod-product-compliance
Lightning Source LLC
Chambersburg PA
CBHW020249030426
42336CB00010B/680

9781649681447